LEARNING WITH ANIMATION

The use of animations is increasingly common in multimedia teaching and learning. Animations are assumed to increase interest and motivation, to direct attention, to illustrate procedures, and to explain how things work. Recent research shows that animations are not inherently effective. Their educational effectiveness depends on how the characteristics of animations interact with the psychological functioning of the learner.

This book presents the first comprehensive treatment of learning with educational animation. Based on research of internationally recognized experts, it aims to clarify and integrate the major themes of current research into learning with animation. In addition, it explores requirements for the principled design of learning resources that incorporate animation. Such materials can be successful only if their design reflects principles governing how learners develop understanding when they work with animations. The overarching goal of the book is, therefore, to improve the way educational animations are designed and used within a variety of learning contexts.

Richard Lowe is Professor of Learning Technologies at Curtin University in Perth, Australia. Following undergraduate studies in chemistry and education, he completed a Ph.D. in educational psychology at Murdoch University. As a result of his work in industry, education, and textbook publication, he developed an interest in factors influencing the effectiveness of explanatory graphics. From an early focus on the comprehension of static graphics, his research has extended in recent years to include investigations of the educational effectiveness of animated and interactive graphics. In addition to his research, he continues to work as a practicing instructional designer for industry and government organizations that rely on complex and dynamic graphic information displays for their operations. He is currently an Associate Editor for the international journal *Educational Research Review*.

Wolfgang Schnotz is Professor of General and Educational Psychology at the University of Koblenz-Landau in Germany, where he is the head of the Multimedia Research Group and the head of the Graduate School on Teaching Processes. His main interests are in the fields of learning from text and graphics, learning from multimedia, as well as conceptual change. Dr. Schnotz was the chief editor of the international journal *Learning and Instruction*, and a member of the Executive Committee of the European Association for Research on Learning and Instruction, and acted as the chair of the Division of Educational Psychology in the German Association of Psychology. He has given keynote addresses at numerous international conferences and has published extensively in European and international psychology journals.

Learning with Animation

Research Implications for Design

Edited by

RICHARD LOWE

Curtin Education of Technology, Australia

WOLFGANG SCHNOTZ

University of Koblenz-Landau, Germany

CAMBRIDGE UNIVERSITY PRESS
Cambridge, New York, Melbourne, Madrid, Cape Town, Singapore, São Paulo, Delhi

Cambridge University Press
32 Avenue of the Americas, New York, NY 10013-2473, USA

www.cambridge.org
Information on this title: www.cambridge.org/9780521851893

First published 2008

Printed in the United States of America

A catalog record for this publication is available from the British Library.

Library of Congress Cataloging in Publication Data

Learning with animation : research implications for design / edited by
Richard Lowe.
p. cm.
Includes bibliographical references and index.
ISBN 978-0-521-85189-3 (hardback) – ISBN 978-0-521-61739-0 (pbk.)
1. Visual education.   2. Animation (Cinematography)
I. Lowe, Richard, 1945–   II. Title.
LB1043.5.L386   2008
371.33'5–dc22   2007003604

ISBN   978-0-521-85189-3 hardback
ISBN   978-0-521-61739-0 paperback

Contents

Preface

Animations have become an increasingly prominent feature of technology-based learning environments in recent years. However, much of the animation now used for the purposes of education and training may be far less effective than is generally supposed. This is because its design is not based on an understanding of what is required for people to learn from animation. The rapid development in educational applications of animation has been driven largely by progress in information and communications technology. In this context, designers of these animations have had little research to draw on for guidance regarding educational effectiveness. As a result, their approaches to design have tended to rely on intuition rather than being based on principled guidelines derived from empirical investigation. The purpose of this book is to contribute to the development of a more principled approach to the design and development of educational animations. It brings together leading international scholars in the field to provide a first account of the present research-based understanding of how learners perceive and cognitively process animations. While charting the current landscape of research on learning with animation, it also identifies major issues that remain to be addressed by researchers.

The practical feasibility of using animation for teaching and learning depends on the availability of powerful authoring and presentation technologies. As a result, the widespread application of animations in education has a relatively short history. This is in marked contrast to the many hundreds of years over which static graphics have been used to support education and training. When asked to produce educationally effective static graphics, designers can draw on a rich heritage of expertise that has been accumulated over the centuries. However, this is not the case for animated graphics, due to their much more recent arrival on the educational scene. Current practices in the educational application of animations indicate that they are assumed to increase interest and motivation, to direct attention, to illustrate procedures, and to explain how things work. However, recent research shows that animations are not inherently effective in supporting learning. Indeed, this research indicates that under some circumstances the effects of animation on learning can be negative. The educational effectiveness of animations depends on how their characteristics interact with the psychological functioning of the learner. Contributions in this book examine various aspects related to these influences on educational effectiveness. The chapters are organized into four sections, each of which covers a major theme of current research.

Section 1, "Information Search and Processing," addresses the fundamental issues of how to extract task-relevant information from an animated presentation and deal with it appropriately. It contains chapters by Mary Hegarty and Sarah Kriz ("Effects of Knowledge and Spatial Ability on Learning from Animation"); Richard Mayer ("Research-Based Principles for Learning with Animation"); and Richard Lowe ("Learning from Animation: Where to Look, When to Look").

Section 2, "Individual Differences and Strategies," moves the focus to the capacities and approaches that influence learner success in learning from animations. The chapters in this section are by Rolf Ploetzner, Daniel Bodemar, and Sieglinde Neudert ("Successful and Less Successful Use of Dynamic Visualizations in Instructional Texts"); Wolfgang Schnotz and Thorsten Rasch ("Functions of Animation in Comprehension and Learning"), Daniel Schwartz, Kristen Blair, Gautam Biswas, Krittaya Leelawong, and Joan Davis ("Animations of Thought: Interactivity in the Teachable Agent Paradigm"), and Mireille Bétrancourt and Alain Chassot ("Making Sense of Animation: How Do Children Explore Multimedia Instruction?").

The first half of the book concludes with a commentary by John Kirby on issues raised by contributors to Sections 1 and 2.

Section 3, "Interactivity and Learning," addresses the growing opportunities provided by advances in technology for animated learning materials to include responsive and interactive capacities. Various perspectives on the utility and potential of interactivity are presented in chapters by Roxana Moreno ("Animated Pedagogical Agents: How Do They Help Students Construct Knowledge from Interactive Multimedia Games?"); Jean-Michel Boucheix ("Young Learners' Control of Technical Animations"); and Teresa Hübscher-Younger and Hari Narayanan ("Turning the Tables: Investigating Characteristics and Efficacy of Student-Authored Animations and Multimedia Representations").

Section 4, "Instructional Issues," draws together several research themes that are of direct relevance to making best use of animations to support learning. The future of educational animation is a common thread running through chapters by Barbara Tversky, Julie Heiser, Rachel Mackenzie, Sandra Lozano, and Julie Morrison ("Enriching Animations"); Yvonne Rogers ("A Comparison of How Animation Has Been Used to Support Formal, Informal and Playful Learning"); and Wolfgang Schnotz and Richard Lowe ("A Unified View of Learning from Animated and Static Graphics").

The book concludes with a commentary by Susan Goldman on issues raised by contributors to Sections 3 and 4.

Richard Lowe and Wolfgang Schnotz

SECTION ONE

INFORMATION SEARCH AND PROCESSING

Effects of Knowledge and Spatial Ability on Learning from Animation

Mary Hegarty and Sarah Kriz

INTRODUCTION

Static diagrams have been used to present scientific and technical information since the invention of the printed book (Ferguson, 1992). However, animations are a relatively recent graphic invention. With the growth of computer technology in everyday life, educational settings, and in the workplace, the ability to communicate information through animation is increasing. However, to use this technology effectively in communication, education, and training, we need to understand how and under what circumstances people learn from animations.

Initial results on the effectiveness of animations have been disappointing, suggesting that they are no more effective than static diagrams. For example, in a review of dozens of studies that compared learning from animations and static media, Tversky Morrison, and Bétrancourt (2002) found no evidence for an advantage of animations over static diagrams when the information presented in the two media was controlled. A common response to this result is to assume that the animations used in early research were poorly designed, so that the solution is to improve the design of animations. Thus, several researchers have suggested principles for the design animations, including adding interactive control, adding devices to draw the user's attention to the most important information in the animation, and adding explanatory text (Faraday & Sutcliffe, 1997a; 1997b; Mayer, 2001; Tversky et al., 2002). When based on theory and research in cognitive psychology, these are referred to as *cognitive design principles*.

This research was funded by grants N00014-96-1-0525, N00014-97-1-0601, and N00014-03-1-0119 from the Office of Naval Research.

This current emphasis on ways of improving animations implicitly assumes a *bottom-up* model of animation comprehension. According to this account, comprehension is primarily a process of encoding the information in the external display, so that improving that display necessarily improves understanding. In contrast, less attention has been given to how learning from animations is affected by learners' abilities, skills, prior knowledge, and misconceptions, that is, *top-down* influences on comprehension. In this chapter, we take an individual differences approach to examining learning from animations. Rather than assuming that there is a "best" type of information display that is equally effective for all learners, we start with the premise that individuals will bring different abilities, skills, and knowledge to the comprehension process, so that different types of information displays (animated vs. static; different types of animations) may be effective for different learners. We review a series of studies in which we examined the effects of spatial ability and prior domain knowledge on learning from animations, and derive recommendations about how to use animation effectively for different types of individuals.

Our research focuses on the use of animations to communicate how machines work. This is a good place to start looking at the effects of animation, because mechanics is essentially about movement. Understanding a machine involves developing an internal representation of the shapes and composition of the parts of the system, and how they are connected and arranged in space, that is, the *configuration* of the machine. But more critically, it includes knowledge of how the components move and affect each other's motions, that is, the *behavior* of the machine. Central to this is knowledge of the causal chain or chains of events in the machine's behavior. It includes both *kinematic* understanding of how the different machine components move in space and affect each other's movements, and *dynamic* understanding of the forces that bring about these movements. Finally, it involves understanding the *function* of the machine, that is, what it is designed to do, and how the configuration and behavior achieve this function This knowledge comprises an individual's *internal representation* or mental model of a machine (Chi, de Leeuw, Chiu, & LaVancher, 1994; Hegarty & Just, 1993; Narayanan & Hegarty, 1998).

Any display (e.g., diagram, animation, or text) that depicts or describes a machine is an *external representation* of the machine, that is, a representation that exists in the world rather than in the mind. Different types of external representations vary in how much information they represent about the machine, in how explicitly that information is represented, and in the type of mapping between the external representation and its referent (cf. Palmer,

1978). For example, a static diagram such as the one in Figure 1.1 can explicitly represent the configuration of the machine. This diagram is isomorphic to the machine that it represents, in the sense that the shapes of the parts correspond to the shapes of components of the machine, and the spatial relations between the parts correspond to the spatial relations between machine components. In contrast to a static diagram, an animation can explicitly represent both the configuration *and* kinematics of the machine. That is, in an animation, the movements of parts of the animated diagram are isomorphic to the movement of parts of the actual machine. Because force is not a visible entity, neither static nor animated diagrams can represent dynamics in a way that is isomorphic to reality. However, both static and animated diagrams can be accompanied by linguistic descriptions, which are more abstract in that they do not resemble the entities that they represent, and their comprehension depends on knowledge of conventions, such as the meaning of words. Linguistic descriptions have more expressive power than diagrams (Oestermeier & Hesse, 2000), so they may be better able to describe abstract ideas, such as the non-visible forces underlying the kinematics of a machine. Non-visible entities, like force, can also be represented by arrows, which are also conventional symbols.

Narayanan and Hegarty (1998) proposed a model of the process of understanding a machine from static diagrams and text. According to this model, people construct a mental model of a machine by first decomposing it into simpler components, retrieving relevant background knowledge about these components, and mentally encoding the relations (spatial and semantic) between components to construct a static mental model of the configuration of the machine parts. They then transform this static mental model to a kinematic/dynamic model, which represents how the components move and constrain each other's motion when the machine is in operation. This process, which we term mental animation, is accomplished by determining the causal chain of events in the system and inferring the motion of machine components sequentially, in order of the causal chain, using either spatial visualization processes or rule-based reasoning (Hegarty, 1992; Narayanan, Suwa, & Motoda, 1994).

This model can be seen as an extension of constructivist theories of text processing (e.g., Chi et al., 1994; Graesser, Singer, & Trabasso, 1994; Kintsch, 1988) and is related to a more general model of multimedia comprehension proposed by Schnotz (2002). These theories view comprehension as an interplay between top-down and bottom-up process in which the learner encodes the new information in a text and integrates it with his or her prior knowledge of the domain. In addition to text comprehension skills, our model proposes that comprehension is dependent on spatial abilities and skills for integrating information in text and graphics, and encoding and inferring information from graphic displays (Hegarty & Sims, 1994). The model therefore predicts that what one understands from text and graphics is dependent on one's prior domain knowledge and spatial abilities, in addition to the information presented in the display.

In this chapter, we examine learning from animations in the context of this comprehension model. We first review theory and research concerning the effects of spatial ability and domain knowledge on perception, comprehension, and learning from diagrams and animated displays. We then review some of our recent research on comprehension of animations alone, focusing on whether and how spatial ability and domain knowledge affect their comprehension. Next, we consider our recent research on comprehension of multimedia displays that include both diagrams (static and animated) and text, again focusing on the effects of spatial ability and knowledge. Finally, we make recommendations about how to best use animations in instruction about machines for individuals with different knowledge and ability levels.

REVIEW OF PRIOR LITERATURE

Effects of Spatial ability

In this section, we review theory and prior research regarding the effects of spatial ability on comprehension of animations. Although there are several subcomponents of spatial ability (see Hegarty & Waller, 2005; Lohman, 1988; McGee, 1979) in this review, we will focus on spatial visualization ability. Tests of this ability involve imagining a series of spatial transformations of an object (such as the folding and unfolding of pieces of paper) or the mental transformations of complex three-dimensional figures (for example mental rotation of 3D objects). Cognitive analysis of performance on tests of spatial ability has suggested that individual differences in performance on these tests reflect differences in speed of processing spatial information (Salthouse, 1996), spatial working memory capacity (Shah & Miyake, 1996; Miyake et al., 2001), and strategies for processing spatial information (Lohman, 1988; Just & Carpenter, 1985). More generally, spatial visualization ability has been characterized as the ability to construct and maintain high-quality internal spatial representations (spatial images) and to accurately transform these representations (Hegarty & Waller, 2005).

Animations and static diagrams can be thought of as external visualizations (external visual-spatial representations) and spatial ability can be thought of as internal visualization ability. Thus, effects of spatial ability on learning from animations can be framed in terms of in terms of the interplay between perception of external visualizations and internal visualization processes (Hegarty, 2004a). This is most evident in considering the comprehension processes involved in understanding kinematic and dynamic processes from animated versus static diagrams. Because an animation of a machine shows how it moves, the process of constructing an internal model from an animation depends on *perception* of motion. In contrast, constructing a mental model of a machine from static diagrams depends on *inference* of motion, which at least sometimes is a spatial visualization process (Hegarty, 2004b).

How might we expect spatial ability to influence learning from animations and other external visualizations? In the psychometric literature, spatial ability has been found to be highly correlated with mechanical ability (Bennett, 1969), which is not surprising given that an accurate mental mode of a mechanical systems must include a representation of spatial properties such as shape of components, configuration, and movement. Thus, even without instruction, people with high spatial ability are better able to understand mechanical processes. In any study that involves comprehension of mechanical systems, we might therefore expect a main effect of spatial ability on comprehension outcomes, and many studies of learning from text, diagrams, and animations have shown this effect (e.g., Hegarty & Just, 1993; Mayer, 2001).

A more interesting question concerns possible aptitude-treatment interactions (cf. Chronbach & Snow, 1977) between spatial abilities and the format of instruction. One possibility is that an external visualization such as an animation can compensate for lack of internal spatial visualization ability. More specifically, viewing an animation on a computer may compensate for lack of mental animation ability. If this were true, an animation could act as a cognitive "prosthetic" for those with low spatial abilities and we predict an aptitude treatment interaction such that low-spatial individuals would learn relatively more from animations than high-spatial individuals (who presumably don't need to view external animations because they can mentally animate).

A second possibility is that spatial visualization ability may be a requirement for accurate perception and comprehension of external visualizations such as animations. For example, because spatial visualization partially reflects speed of processing (Salthouse, 1996), it might affect speed of encoding spatial information from an animation, such that if the animation is played a relatively fast speed, only high-spatial individuals will be able to keep up with the pace. Furthermore spatial visualization ability is related to greater spatial working memory capacity (Shah & Miyake, 1995; Miyake et al., 2001) which may be necessary to internally maintain spatial information presented at different stages of an animation so that it can be integrated and related in memory.

Thus, perception and comprehension of an animation may depend on the same spatial abilities as mental animation. If this is the case, we expect an interaction such that animations are more effective for high-spatial individuals than low-spatial individuals.

A third possibility, is that external animations augment internal visualizations, that is, provide information or insights that are additional to those that can be provided by internal visualizations. For example, an external visualization might show a more complex process than can be internally visualized within the limited capacity of visual-spatial working memory. In this case, we might expect animations to be effective in communicating about dynamic processes for both high- and low-spatial individuals.

Finally, it is possible that external animations may impede comprehension for both high- and low-spatial individuals. Previous research on mental animation has suggested that people conceptualize the movement of a mechanical system as a causal series of events, such that the motion of each component in a mechanical system affects the motion of the next component in the causal chain (Hegarty, 1992; Hegarty & Sims, 1994). In contrast, a realistic animation shows all components moving continuously. Therefore, comprehension may be impaired by a mismatch between internal and external representations (Tversky et al., 2002).

Previous research on mechanical comprehension does not uniformly support any one of these possibilities. On the one hand, research in naïve physics suggests that under some circumstances, people's judgments of mechanical events are more accurate if they view an animated rather than a static diagram. For example, McCloskey, Caramazza, and Green (1980) found that many people incorrectly predict that a ball emerging from a curved tube will continue to move in a curved trajectory (in fact it moves in a straight path). This can be interpreted as a failure to correctly mentally animate the movement of the ball. Kaiser, Proffitt, and Anderson (1985) later showed that if people with this misconception are shown different animations of a ball emerging from a curved tube, some showing an incorrect curved path and one showing the correct straight path, they are able to choose the animation that shows the correct path. Thus, people have superior performance when they see an animation than when they see a static view and imagine the motion. Kaiser et al. (1985) did not measure spatial ability in this research, so it is unclear whether these animations augmented cognition for all individuals, or were more effective for people with low or high spatial ability.

On the other hand, some studies suggest that spatial ability may enhance one's ability to perceive or comprehend an animation. For example, Isaak and Just (1995) studied ability to judge the trajectory of a point on a rolling ball, which involves both translation and rotation. In this situation, people are subject to an illusion called the curtate cycloid illusion, which can be explained by a model in which they temporarily fail to process the translation component of motion at a critical point in the rolling motion. Isaak and Just found that people with high spatial visualization ability were less subject to the illusion than people with low spatial visualization ability. They proposed that spatial working memory, necessary for generating internal visualizations, was also necessary to simultaneously process the rotation and translation components of motion in perception of the external display, to accurately understand how the ball rolled.

Learning from external visualizations may also depend on spatial abilities. Mayer and Sims (1994) examined the role of spatial ability in learning from animations that explain how mechanical and biological systems work. They considered two alternative hypotheses. The first hypothesis was that viewing an animation would compensate for low spatial ability. The second hypothesis was that spatial ability would be a necessary prerequisite for learning from an animation. The results were consistent with the second hypothesis – high-spatial individuals learned more from the animations than low-spatial individuals. A later experiment indicated that this was only true if the animation was well designed, such that the commentary and graphics were presented simultaneously. With poorly designed animations in which these were presented sequentially, high spatials learned no more than low-spatial participants (Mayer, 2001).

Finally, in the field of medical education, Garg, Norman, Spero, and Maheshwari (1999) found that viewing three-dimensional rotations of carpal bone configurations impaired spatial understanding of the anatomy for low-spatial students whereas it improved understanding for high spatials. In a later experiment, they found that giving the user control of the animation eliminated this effect, so that both high- and low-spatial students learned from the animation. It appears, therefore, that spatial visualization ability may be a necessary prerequisite for learning from some external animations, but that the size of this effect depends on the design of the animation.

Effects of Prior Knowledge

In this section, we review theory and prior research regarding the effects of knowledge on comprehension of animations. Chi (2000) has identified four types of prior knowledge that learners may possess: domain-specific knowledge, domain-relevant knowledge, misconceptions, and domain-general world knowledge. With respect to domain-general world knowledge,

Vosniadou (2002) has proposed that over the course of a lifetime, one's perceptual experiences become organized into an explanatory framework, often referred to as naïve physics understanding, which often includes misconceptions, for example the belief that physical objects are solid and stable. Everyday interactions with machines may also affect our naïve physics understanding. In discussing effects of prior knowledge on learning, therefore, it is important to distinguish between domain-specific prior knowledge and domain-general world knowledge, and not simply "high" or "low" levels of prior knowledge. For example, knowledge acquired from physics classes may have different effects on learning than knowledge acquired from practical experience interacting with machines.

How might knowledge affect learning from animations? On the one hand, we might expect animations to be relatively more effective for low-knowledge individuals. Inference of motion from static diagrams can depend on knowledge as well as spatial visualization abilities (Naryanan & Hegarty, 1998; Hegarty 2004b; Schwartz & Black, 1996). Animations may be relatively more effective for those with low prior knowledge, because animations show the motion in a mechanical system explicitly, and do not rely on the learner's ability to infer motion from static diagrams. Again, we can conceptualize this as a tradeoff between perception of an external representation and internal inference processes.

However, there are also several reasons to expect that comprehension of animations may be enhanced by prior domain knowledge. Constructivist theories of comprehension (e.g., Chi et al., 1994; Graesser et al., 1994; Kintsch, 1988; Schnotz, 2002) assume that learning involves the integration of new information into existing knowledge structures. The result of this integration process depends not only on how the new information is presented, but also on the quantity, specificity, and accuracy of the existing knowledge. In studies of verbal comprehension, students with low domain knowledge have trouble interpreting events in terms of the larger goal structure of the discourse, so that they remember fewer macrostructural propositions or main ideas (Chiesi, Spilich, & Voss, 1979; Hambrick & Engle, 2002). It seems reasonable to assume that prior knowledge may have similar effects to learning from animations.

Prior domain knowledge may also help a learner recognize what he or she does not understand when acquiring new information. Miyake (1986) has proposed that developing a mental model of a mechanical system is often an iterative process of understanding, in which learners move back and forth between states of understanding and misunderstanding as they gain deeper understanding of how the system works. In this process, revising a mental model can only occur when a conflict between the external representation and the internal representation is perceived (Chi, 2000). A learner with a high level of prior domain knowledge should be better able to assess these "gaps" in their internal models or conflicts between internal and external representations. In contrast, low domain knowledge learners may be overconfident in judging their understanding of mechanical phenomena, as proposed by Rozenblit and Keil (2002). Because of this overconfidence, "novice scientists" may not perceive any gaps or inconsistencies between their internal models and external animations.

Relying on everyday knowledge may cause a learner to develop an erroneous mental model from an animation. That is, if a learner's prior knowledge includes misconceptions, the movements displayed in the animation may not be interpreted to construct accurate dynamic or functional models. For example, relying on domain general knowledge has been shown to lead learners to attribute "everyday" causality to complex systems such as meteorology, when this is not appropriate in the domain (Lowe, 1999).

Knowledge may also affect how a learner directs her visual attention while viewing a visual display such as an animation. Whereas students with high domain-specific knowledge should attend to and integrate visual information on the basis of their pre-existing schemas, learners with domain-general knowledge may misdirect their visual attention to features of the display that are highly salient but not relevant. In fact, Lowe's (1994; 1999; 2003) studies in the domain of meteorology indicate that novices attend to perceptually salient rather than thematically relevant aspects of the displays. In other words, their processing of the animations tended to be bottom-up and data-driven.

Several researchers have proposed cognitive design principles that specifically address some of the problems that low-knowledge individuals may encounter in learning from animations. One possible remedy for attentional problems is to augment the visual display with cues, such as highlighting, to help direct novices' attention to relevant areas of the display. Additional visual features such as arrows can point attention to specific parts or events of the process (Faraday & Sutcliffe, 1997a, 1997b). Arrows can also appear in multiple places at the same time, suggesting a causal relationship between the parts that they signal. These additional features may aid low domain knowledge viewers by pointing out parts and processes that, due to lack of domain-specific knowledge, would not have been deemed as important.

Learners' attention can also be directed by language, that is, an accompanying text or commentary. For example, Hegarty and Just (1993) monitored students' eye fixations while they read text accompanied by diagrams describing how pulley systems work. We examined where people switched between reading the text and viewing the diagram in the course of comprehension, and what they looked at in the diagram each time they switched. People tended to switch from reading the text to viewing the diagram at the end of a clause of text, and when they switched to the diagram, they looked at the parts of the diagram that depicted the objects they had just read about in the text. Thus, the eye fixations indicated that the text was directing processing of the diagram.

Language can be also used to communicate information that is not easily conveyed in a diagram. Because language has a linear structure, it is particularly important for communicating sequential information, such as the causal chain of events in a mechanical system. A verbal text or commentary can also provide information that is not easily communicated in static or animated diagrams, for example information about non-visible entities such as forces. Thus, people learn more about mechanical systems when diagrams and animations are accompanied by verbal instruction. Research by Mayer and his colleagues (Mayer, 2001) shows that low-knowledge individuals, in particular, benefit from the addition of text to illustrations. Their studies compared students learning about physical systems either through diagrams alone or through a combination of diagrams and text. Whereas high-knowledge learners were somewhat successful in understanding the systems from the diagrams alone, low-knowledge learners scored higher on retention tests when they received both text and diagrams.

Recent studies have suggested, however, that aids such as language that are intended to help low domain knowledge learners can be detrimental to learners with a high degree of domain-specific knowledge. For example, in some situations low-domain knowledge learners benefit from the integration of linguistic descriptions and visual materials, but the same materials are ineffective for high-domain learners. This phenomenon, called the Expertise Reversal Effect (Kalyuga, Ayers, Chandler, and Sweller, 2003) might generalize to animations, suggesting that animations and text designed for learners at one level of domain knowledge may not be suitable for learners possessing a different level of knowledge.

Summary

In summary, in this literature review we have conceptualized learning from animated versus static displays as a tradeoff between perception of external events shown in an animation versus inference of these events from static diagrams, a process that can depend on spatial visualization and prior knowledge. We have seen that it is difficult to make a priori predictions about whether animations will be more effective for certain learners than others. Although viewing an animation might compensate for inability to infer motion, previous research suggests that the same spatial abilities and knowledge that are necessary for inferring motion from static displays may also enhance perception and comprehension of external animations. Finally, what is learned from an animation may depend on how it is designed, and design features such as interactivity, signaling, and adding text to an animation may also influence their relative effectiveness for different individuals.

OVERVIEW OF OUR EXPERIMENTS ON LEARNING FROM ANIMATION

In the remainder of this chapter, we review the results of eight experiments conducted over the last few years in which we examined the effects of spatial ability, physics knowledge, and practical experience with machines on learning about how a machine works. Each study discussed in the following section examined comprehension of the same mechanical device, a flushing cistern, which is a device most commonly used to flush toilets. Figure 1.1 shows a diagram of the flushing cistern and a description of how it works. In some cases, students were presented with one or more static diagrams, and in other cases they were presented with variations of an animation depicting the flushing cistern in motion. In some experimental conditions they learned from diagrams (static or animated) alone and in some cases the diagrams were accompanied by the verbal description in Figure 1.1.

In all but one experiment, comprehension was measured by asking participants to describe, step by step, what happens when the cistern flushes and the measure of comprehension was the number of correct steps in the causal chain that they described. In some experiments, we also examined participants' ability to answer troubleshooting questions, (i.e., diagnose breakdown scenarios) on the basis of what they learned from the graphics. In all experiments, the Paper Folding Test (Ekstrom, French, Harman, & Derman, 1976) was used as a measure of spatial visualization ability. We also collected information on two types of prior knowledge. First, as a measure of theoretical knowledge we asked participants to state how many physics or engineering classes they had taken in the past. Second, as a measure of practical knowledge, we asked them about their prior experiences fixing various household mechanisms, bicycles, and cars. In all experiments, we classified participants as high or low spatial on the basis of a median split on performance on the paper folding text and as high or low in practical experience on the basis of a median split on that measure. We classified participants as having theoretical knowledge if they

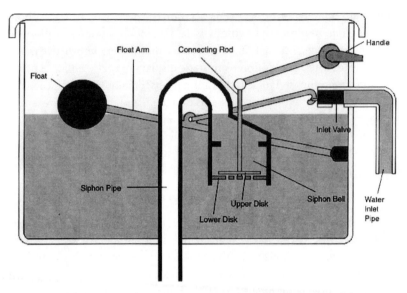

When the handle is pressed down, the connecting rod is pulled up, causing the lower disk to rise and press against the upper disk, pushing it up. Water is forced to the top of the siphon pipe and down into the toilet bowl. Once the handle is released, the two disks start to drop again and separate from each other. Because the lower disk has holes, water from the tank can pass through the holes in the lower disk and around the edges of the upper disk. This allows the water to continue to flow through the siphon pipe. When the water is so low that the air enters the siphon bell, this breaks the suction in the siphon pipe and water stops flowing through the pipe.

As the water in the tank empties, the float drops toward the bottom of the tank. As the float drops, the float arm also drops pulling out the inlet valve. When the inlet valve is pulled out, it uncovers a hole in the inlet pipe, allowing water to enter the tank. This makes the water level in the tank rise. The float and float arm rise with the water level. When the water level, float and float arm are high enough, the inlet valve is pushed back into its original position, stopping the incoming water.

FIGURE 1.1. Diagram and text describing how a flushing cistern works.

had taken at least one physics or engineering class and as lacking theoretical knowledge if they had never taken such a class.

LEARNING FROM ANIMATIONS ALONE

In this section, we review studies of the effects of spatial ability and prior knowledge on understanding the flushing cistern from diagrams or animations alone (i.e., without verbal instruction). In most of the research comparing animated and static graphics to date, the animations have been accompanied by verbal commentaries so that in fact they are studies of multimedia comprehension, rather than comprehension of animation per se. When we examine comprehension of animations that are accompanied by texts, it is not possible to tell whether comprehension outcomes result from viewing the animations, reading the text, or both. Thus if our goal is a scientific account of how animations are understood, it is important to experimentally isolate the cognitive processes and comprehension outcomes that result from exposure to animated graphics alone, without the influence of verbal comprehension. This scientific account, in turn, can be the basis of a set of principles for the design of multimedia presentations (cf. Narayanan & Hegarty, 1998, 2002), for example by specifying when and how animations should be augmented by text.

Animations versus Static Diagrams

In one study (Experiment 3, Hegarty, Kriz, & Cate, 2003) we compared learning from an animation versus static diagrams. Students at the University of California, Santa Barbara studied either a single static diagram of the flushing cistern, a series of three static diagrams showing the configuration of machine components in different key stages of the flushing cistern in operation, or an animation of the flushing cistern in motion. Twenty participants were assigned to each condition based on their paper folding test scores to ensure that all groups had even numbers of high- and low-spatial participants.

As reviewed earlier, it might be argued that low-ability learners should benefit from an animation compared to a single static diagram or a series of static diagrams. When presented with static diagrams people have to mentally animate how the system works, whereas when viewing an animation they merely have to perceive how the system works. Mental animation depends on prior knowledge of mechanics as well as spatial ability (Hegarty, 2004b), so that low-knowledge learners may also be at a disadvantage when they have to infer motion from a static diagram. On the other hand, spatial ability may also enhance perception of animations and prior knowledge may help direct attention to the most relevant parts of an animation.

The main effect of instruction (static or animated) revealed that learners viewing the animation did not learn more than those who viewed the three phase diagrams, although these two groups had superior performance compared to the group who learned from a single static diagram (Hegarty et al., 2003). But were the animations more or less effective for individuals differing in spatial ability and prior knowledge? Table 1.1 lists the effects of individual differences on learning across the eight experiments reviewed in this paper. The results of this experiment (Experiment 3, Hegarty et al., 2003) show that neither spatial ability nor prior theoretical training had an effect on learning,

TABLE 1.1. *Effects of Individual Differences on Comprehension in the Eight Experiments Discussed in This Chapter. Interactions Examined were Between the Individual Differences Measures and the Format of Instruction (i.e., Static vs. Animated Diagrams).*

	Spatial Ability		Physics Knowledge		Practical Experience	
	Main Effect	Interaction	Main Effect	Interaction	Main Effect	Interaction
Graphics Only						
Hegarty et al. (2003). Experiment 3	No	No	No	No	Yes (recall)	No
Interactivity Exp.	No	No	No	No	No	No
Signaling Exp.	No	No	No	No	No	No
Kriz & Hegarty (2004).	Yes (recall)	–	Yes (recall)	–	Yes	–
Graphics + Verbal						
Hegarty et al. (2003). Experiment 1	Yes (recall and troubleshooting)	No	Yes (troubleshooting)	No	No	No
Hegarty et al. (2003). Experiment 2	Yes (recall and troubleshooting)	No	No	No	No	No
Hegarty et al. (1999). Exp 1	Not Measured	Not Measured	No	No	Yes (motion questions)	No
Narayanan & Hegarty (2002).	Yes (recall and troubleshooting)	No	No	No	No	No

but individuals with more practical mechanical experience reported more steps in the recall task than did low experience learners. No significant interactions between the format of instruction and either spatial ability, theoretical knowledge, or practical experience were found. Thus, there was no evidence that a particular format of instruction was more or less effective for people with different abilities and skills.

Effects of Interactivity

In a separate series of experiments, we evaluated whether specific design features of an animation provided learning benefits to participants with low spatial ability or low knowledge. Unlike the previously reported study, we selected students who had not taken college-level physics or engineering classes to ensure these students were low in theoretical knowledge.

In the first experiment in this series, we tested whether participant-control (i.e., interactivity) provided benefit to the low-knowledge learners. Forty participants (20 in each condition) viewed either a participant-controlled animation or a computer-controlled animation. The participant-controlled animation allowed learners to pause, advance the animation at their own pace, and move forwards or backwards in the series of frames. With this control, participants could match the speed of the animation to the speed of their comprehension processes, pause to integrate the information they had just encoded, and review parts of the animation that they did not initially understand, so we predicted that this animation would be more effective than one that plays continuously at a constant rate. This difference may be essential for low-knowledge learners who are less able to process an animation that plays at a fast pace (cf. Isaak & Just, 1995). It was predicted that learners with low spatial ability would benefit from a participant-controlled animation because they could match the speed of the external animation to the speed of their perception and comprehension processes.

The results indicated that the learners using the participant-controlled animation performed no better than the learners who viewed the computer-controlled animation. Furthermore, spatial ability, prior theoretical knowledge (high school physics) and practical experience did not have an effect on the recall. As Table 1.1 indicates, there were no main effects of the individual differences measures on learning. Contrary to our predictions, participant-controlled animations did not provide additional benefits to low-knowledge or low-spatial learners.

Effects of Signaling

A second experiment evaluated whether visual signaling affected the amount of information low-knowledge learners extracted from an animation. The participant-controlled animation used in the previously described experiment was manipulated so that arrows signaling the movements of critical components of the flushing cistern appeared throughout the animation. The appearance of these arrows was designed to guide individuals along the causal chain of events in the system and to point out important steps in the process that happened very quickly or were not visually salient. This animation was presented to 20 undergraduate participants. The same animation, without the arrows, was presented to a second group of 20 participants. Again, we hypothesized that the low knowledge learners would benefit more from the animation that contained signaling devices because the arrows cue the important physical processes that occur in the system. Furthermore, the arrows appear in a causally related order, so they may help organize the animation into a more coherent set of causal steps. This was predicted to benefit the low-knowledge learners, more than high-knowledge learners.

There were no significant differences between participants who saw the animation with signaling and participants who saw the animation without signaling. As Table 1.1 shows, spatial ability, prior theoretical knowledge (having taken High School physics), and prior practical experience did not produce any main effects in learning. Furthermore, no interactions between individual differences and design of the animation were found. These results, taken together with the results of the interactivity experiment suggest that these two cognitive design principles did not provide a benefit to low-knowledge or low-spatial-ability learners.

Verifying that Advanced Features of Animations were Used

It is possible that the participants were not utilizing the enhanced features of the animations, and the null effects found in the animation design experiments were due to this lack of utilization. For example, previous studies have shown that participants do not necessarily use the additional interactivity afforded by computer learning environments (Hegarty, Narayanan, & Freitas, 1999; Spoehr, 1994). We conducted a follow-up study to explore whether participants actually used the enhanced features of the animations. In this study we monitored participants' eye-fixations while they interacted with animations varying whether the animations included attentional cues (arrows) as described above. To measure interactivity, we examined how often participants paused and moved backwards in the animations. To examine the effects of the attentional cues, we assessed whether participants were more likely to look at the areas highlighted by the signaling devices. The data indicated that learners did utilize the interactivity and cueing provided to them in the animations. However null effects in this and the experiments described above suggest that interactivity and cueing do not seem to provide an additional benefit to low-ability or low-knowledge learners. It is possible that added benefits of interactive animations depend on particular patterns of interaction, that is, on *how* people use the interactive animations. Preliminary measures of how much people used the controls were not related to performance, but examining different patterns of interactivity is an important goal for future research.

Effects of Domain Knowledge on Mental Model Revision from Animations

Although the experiments on comprehension of animations showed few effects of prior knowledge, one might argue that the differences in domain knowledge between participants were not great in these studies. In particular, most of the participants classified as having physics knowledge had taken just one physics class. To better test the effects of prior knowledge on learning from animation, we conducted another study in which we compared the comprehension of 10 individuals with high theoretical domain knowledge (engineering graduate students) to nine individuals with low theoretical domain knowledge (graduate students in humanities and social sciences). The high domain knowledge individuals had taken at least five years of physics-related courses.

In this experiment we also examined the effects of prior knowledge on revision of mental models. As mentioned previously, high domain knowledge learners are at an advantage in determining the gaps in their internal models. Because they possess more prior information about the topic at hand, they are more likely to perceive incongruities between their internal models and external representations. However, this advantage may only be seen if they are allowed multiple viewings of the animation. With a single viewing of an animation a learner may just construct an initial mental model. Identifying inconsistencies between internal and external models must be done after an internal model is built. Because most studies allow just one learning session from an animation, empirical data addressing the effect of prior knowledge on the iterative process of learning (cf. Miyake, 1986) are scarce in animation research.

Participants first viewed the learning materials and then answered the written comprehension questions (for details of the methodology, see Kriz & Hegarty, 2004). Because we were testing the effect of domain knowledge and not the effect of a specific design feature on learning, we allowed the participants to view the visual materials used in all our previous experiments. Thus, they viewed a static diagram of the flushing cistern, the series of phase diagrams, the animation with arrows, the animation without arrows, and the non-interactive animation. After they had answered all the written questions, the participants were asked to view the visual materials again. The participant-controlled animation without arrows was displayed and participants were asked to orally report to the researcher the sequence of events in a single flush of the cistern. This part of the experiment was videotaped for later analysis.

Domain knowledge affected how many steps in the causal chain participants reported in their written responses. Specifically, the physics experts tended to report more events in their description of the causal chain of events. Similarly, learners who had reported fixing more than five household mechanical or electronic devices reported more events than learners who had fewer practical experiences. A main effect of spatial ability was also found. We interpret these results to suggest that levels of prior knowledge, obtained from practical experience and formal classroom instruction, can affect how well learners can extract information from non-verbal, visual displays. However, we interpret the significant effect of spatial ability with caution. We did not obtain significant main effects of spatial ability in our other non-verbal animation studies, suggesting that the significant main effect found here may be confounded with the other factors measured. The high spatial students were generally the engineers, who also had high theoretical knowledge and more practical experience than the low spatial students.

In evaluating the iterative process of learning, we found that the high knowledge individuals were more likely to identify problematic areas of their models and revise them into correct representations. As Figure 1.1 describes, the flushing cistern stops allowing water out of the tank when the water level is so low that air enters the siphon bell and the suction in the siphon bell is broken. However, a common misconception is that the disks "seal" together and stop the water from exiting the tank. We evaluated the frequency with which the two groups of learners reported this misconception. In their initial written descriptions of the causal chain, five engineering students and five humanities students reported the misconception, whereas only two engineering students and one humanities student reported the correct process.[1] However, after the students saw the animation again and reported the steps of the causal chain while viewing the animation, seven of the 10 engineering students accurately reported that the air enters and breaks the siphoning process and only two engineering students reported the misconception. On the other hand, six of the humanities students reported the misconception in their final oral reports, and none reported the correct explanation.

The evaluation of the iterative process of learning about machines through animations suggests that high-knowledge individuals benefit from multiple exposures. These findings indicate that the high-knowledge participants were able to identify incorrect aspects of their models and revise them into physically correct descriptions, although they were not given additional information during the second viewing. Apparently, the low domain knowledge learners did not have the available information to identify inconsistencies between their mental models and the external representation. Thus, domain knowledge seems to play a role in not only the initial extraction of information, but also in the iterative learning process that comes from multiple viewings of an animation.

In summary, there was no evidence in this set of experiments that animations are more effective than static diagrams for a particular group of individuals, or that specific design features of animations (user control and signaling) enhance their effectiveness when individuals are given just one learning experience. However, when individuals were given multiple learning experiences with animations, prior knowledge enhanced their ability to detect inconsistencies between their mental models and the external representation, and revise their mental models accordingly.

LEARNING FROM ANIMATIONS ACCOMPANIED BY VERBAL INSTRUCTION

In this section, we review studies of the effects of spatial ability and prior knowledge on understanding machines from animations accompanied by text. There are many ways in which a text can enhance what is learned from an animation. First, a verbal description provides information in a verbal code, in addition to the visual-spatial code provided by static or animated diagrams. Second, verbal instruction can direct processing of diagrams as

---

[1]   The rest of the participants did not state how this process ended, thus their mental models cannot be evaluated.

described above (Hegarty & Just, 1993). Third, because language has a linear structure, verbal instruction can be important for communicating sequential information, such as the causal chain of events in a mechanical system. Finally, a verbal text or commentary can provide information that is not easily communicated in static or animated diagrams, for example information about non-visible entities such as forces. It is not surprising, therefore, that several studies have shown that people learn more from diagrammatic representations if they are accompanied by verbal instruction (e.g., Hegarty & Just, 1993; Mayer, 2001), but this is not our focus here. In contrast, our purpose in this section is to review how spatial ability, prior theoretical knowledge and prior practical experience affect learning from animations accompanied by verbal instruction.

Animations Accompanied by Text

We first review two experiments in which people learned from static or animated diagrams accompanied by verbal instruction (Hegarty et al., 2003, Experiments 1 and 2). In the first experiment in this series we examined the effects of (1) predicting how the system works on the basis of viewing diagrams of the machine in different stages of its operation, and (2) viewing an animation of the system that was accompanied by an auditory commentary (a narration of the verbal description in Figure 1.1). There were four groups in the experiment, a control group that neither predicted nor learned from the animation, a group that learned from the animation and commentary but did not predict, a group that predicted how the machine works on the basis of viewing the three phase diagrams but did not see the animation and commentary, and a group that first predicted how the machines works from the three phase diagrams and then learned from the animation and commentary. The results indicated that both predicting how the machine works and studying the animation and commentary had positive effects on learning (see Hegarty et al., 2003). Examination of the effects of individual differences (summarized in Table 1.1) revealed that in all conditions, high-spatial individuals outperformed low-spatial individuals on the comprehension measures. Individuals who had taken a course in physics also had better performance on the troubleshooting problems than those without formal training in physics. However there were no interactions of the type of instruction with either spatial ability or prior knowledge.

In the second experiment in this series (Hegarty et al., 2003, Experiment 2) we varied whether participants received static or animated diagrams of the mechanical system as well as the effects of first predicting how the machine works. There were again four groups of participants in the experiment; one group learned from an animation and commentary, a second group first predicted how the system would work and then learned from an animation and commentary, a third group learned from a static diagram accompanied by a text containing the same words as the commentary (presented in Figure 1.1), and a fourth group first predicted how the system worked and then learned from the static diagram and text. As before there was a positive effect of first predicting how the machine would move, but we found no differences in comprehension outcomes between those who learned from static versus animated instruction. Analysis of individual differences (summarized in Table 1.1) indicated a main effect of spatial ability on the comprehension outcomes, but no effects of prior knowledge and no significant interactions between the format of instruction (static or animated) and either spatial ability or knowledge.

Hypermedia Manuals

Finally we review two studies in which people learned how the flushing cistern works from "hypermedia computer manuals" (Hegarty, Quilici, Narayanan, Holmquist, & Moreno, 1999; Narayanan & Hegarty, 2002). These computer manuals were designed on the basis of the cognitive model of multimedia comprehension, proposed by Narayanan and Hegarty described earlier, and embodied several design principles derived from that model. They were made up of different subsections, such as a section introducing individuals to the components of a flushing cistern, a section focusing on how they are connected, a section explaining the physical principle underlying the operation of a siphon and finally a section showing an animation accompanied by a commentary describing how the machine works. Participants were free to review any section of the manual at any time during the study period.

An experiment with an early version of the manual (Hegarty et al., 1999) compared learning from the online manual, a printed version of the complete manual containing the same verbal instruction but static rather than animated diagrams, and an abbreviated printed version containing only the sections describing the subsystems, the siphon principle and how the parts of the system move when it is operation (essentially the text and diagram shown in Figure 1.1). The measures of comprehension included a series of "motion" questions asking students to predict how different parts of the system move (e.g., "Imagine the handle is being pushed down, what is happening to the float?) and a series of troubleshooting questions.

There were no effects of type of instruction on the learning outcomes. As summarized in Table 1.1, examination of individual differences indicated that participants with more practical experience with machines were better able to answer the comprehension questions. There was no main effect of theoretical knowledge and no interaction of knowledge with type of instruction. Spatial ability was not measured in this experiment.

On the basis of this experiment, we redesigned the hypermedia manual, so that it contained only the content included in the abbreviated printed version in the experiment just described (because the additional information had no effect on comprehension outcomes). In a later experiment (Narayanan & Hegarty, 2002) we compared learning from this manual to learning from a static printed version of the same manual. In this experiment we also compared the effectiveness of our hypermedia manual to that of award-winning commercially available materials from "The Way Thing Work" books and CD-Roms (Macaulay, 1988, 1998). Thus there were four groups; one learned from our hypermedia computer manual including animations, a second learned from a static printed version of the same material, a third learned from an animation of the flushing cistern, from "The Way Things Work" CD-Rom (Macaulay, 1998) and a fourth group learned from the static text and diagram description of how a machine works in the book "The Way things Work" (Macaulay, 1988).

Comprehension outcomes (recall and troubleshooting) indicated that people learned more from our materials, which were based on cognitive design principles than from the commercially available materials. However, there was no difference between comprehension of the static and animated versions of our manuals. Examination of individual differences revealed a main effect of spatial ability on the comprehension outcomes, but no main effect of theoretical or practical prior knowledge, and no interactions of any of the individual differences measures with the type of instruction.

In summary, in all studies of learning from text and diagrams in which we measured spatial ability, this ability had a main effect on comprehension outcomes. In these studies there were few effects of theoretical and practical knowledge on comprehension outcomes. As in the case of learning from animations alone, there was again no evidence for interactions of format of instruction (static or animated) with any of the individual differences measures.

CONCLUSIONS AND PRACTICAL IMPLICATIONS

In conclusion, in this chapter, we started with the premise that individuals will bring different abilities, skills, and knowledge to the process of understanding an animation, so that different types of information displays (animated vs.

static; different types of animations) may be effective for different learners. We reviewed eight studies in which we examined comprehension of a relatively complex mechanical system (a flushing cistern) from a variety of media including static and animated diagrams presented alone (without accompanying verbal instruction) and multimedia instruction in which these types of diagrams were accompanied by verbal instruction. Examination of the results summarized in Table 1.1 reveals several patterns. With respect to spatial ability, there is a consistent pattern such that when information is learned from diagrams (static or animated) alone, spatial ability has no effect on comprehension, but when learning is from diagrams accompanied by verbal instruction, there is always an effect of spatial ability. This result suggests that spatial ability may be more related to comprehension of verbal information, or to integration of verbal and diagrammatic material, than it is to perception and comprehension of diagrams or animations. For example, spatial ability may be particularly important in constructing an internal spatial mental model from a verbal description, and relating that internal model to an external spatial representation (i.e., a diagram or animation).

In general we found few effects of prior knowledge on comprehension of either diagrams alone, diagrams accompanied by text, or hypermedia manuals. In interpreting this result, it is important to realize that in most of our experiments, almost all of the participants were novices and the differences in knowledge or expertise between participants were not great. In the one experiment in which we selected groups with large differences in prior knowledge (engineering graduate students versus humanities and social science graduate students, Kriz & Hegarty, 2004) we observed large effects of knowledge on comprehension outcomes.

Perhaps the most striking result of this review is that in 20 comparisons across eight experiments, there was no evidence for any interactions between ability or knowledge and the type of instruction that learners received (aptitude-treatment interactions). Thus although there is intuitive appeal to the idea that different media may be more or less effective for different learners, there is no evidence in any these studies that animations or static diagrams are more or less effective for individuals with different abilities or knowledge, or that different types of animations are more or less effective for different individuals.

Practical Implications

There are several practical implications that we can derive from these results. First, as found in previous research, there is no empirical basis for the idea that people learn more from animations than from static diagrams, at least in the mechanical domain considered here. A novel result of this review is that there is also no evidence that a particular subgroup of individuals, such as, low-spatial individuals or low-knowledge individuals learn more from animations than from static diagrams. The practical implication is that the additional cost of producing animations compared to printed diagrams may not be justified.

A second result is that there are limitations in how much individuals can learn from diagrams (animated or static). Our research on learning from diagrams alone suggests that most low-knowledge learners are not able to extract important information about "invisible" processes such as pressure or force. Thus, we suggest that language be used to supplement animations with high-level physical information that is not readily perceptible in the visual medium.

Third, the studies reviewed here suggest that a single exposure to any form of instruction may not lead to optimal comprehension outcomes. Although most animation studies evaluate a participant's single interaction with animated materials, our research suggests that giving students multiple learning experiences can illuminate how they build and revise mental models (Hegarty & Kriz, 2004). Furthermore, results from Experiment 2 of Hegarty et al. (2003) illustrate how prediction can provide a complimentary exercise to learning from animations. Predicting how a machine works from a series of key frames before seeing an animation of the machine in motion forces a learner to create a mental model of the process. While the learner views the animation, rather than constructing a mental model from the information, he can compare his previously created model to the external model shown in the animation. Presentation of the key frames may also cue crucial steps in the process, such that learners pay more attention to these steps when they view the animation.

In conclusion, we have viewed learning from animations and static diagrams as a process of constructing an internal representation (mental model) from external representations. This involves a complex interplay between top-down and bottom-up processes, including perception, encoding and inference processes. Our research suggests that optimizing learning from animations is not merely a matter of improving the external display. Although we have emphasized the importance of considering aptitude-treatment interactions, we have also found that optimizing learning from animations is not a matter of matching different types of displays to different types of learners. Our experiments suggest that animations can be useful and important tools for teaching, but they seem to be most effective when they are treated as a component of a larger learning situation, so more attention should be given to designing the larger learning context in which animations are used.

References

Bennett, C. K. (1969). *Bennett mechanical comprehension test.* San Antonio: The Psychological Corporation.

Chronbach, L., & Snow, R. E. (1977). *Aptitudes and instructional methods. A handbook for research on interactions.* New York: Irvington.

Chi, M. T. H. (2000). Self-explaining expository texts: The dual process of generating inferences and repairing mental models. In R. Glaser (Ed.), *Advances in Instructional Psychology: Vol 5. Educational Design and Cognitive Science* (pp. 161–238). Mahwah, NJ: Lawrence Erlbaum Associates.

Chi, M. T. H., de Leeuw, N., Chiu, M., & LaVancher, C. (1994). Eliciting self-explanations improves learning. *Cognitive Science, 18,* 439–478.

Chiesi, H., Spilich, G., & Voss, J. (1979). Acquisition of domain-related information in relation to high and low domain knowledge. *Journal of Verbal Learning and Verbal Behavior, 18,* 257–273.

Ekstrom, R. B., French, J. W., Harman, H. H., & Derman, D. (1976). *Kit of Factor Referenced Cognitive Tests.* Princeton, NJ: Educational Testing Service.

Faraday P., & Sutcliffe, A. (1997a). An empirical study of attending and comprehending multimedia presentations. *Proceedings of ACM Multimedia 96 Conference,* 265–275.

Faraday, P., & Sutcliffe, A. (1997b). Designing effective multimedia presentations. *Proceedings of ACM conference on human factors in computing systems (CHI '97),* 272–278.

Ferguson, E. S. (1992). *Engineering and the mind's eye.* Cambridge, MA: MIT Press.

Garg, A. X., Norman, G. R., Spero, L., & Maheshwari, P. (1999). Do virtual computer models hinder anatomy learning. *Academic Medicine, 74,* 87–89.

Graesser, A. C., Singer, M., & Trabasso, T. (1994). Constructing inferences during narrative text comprehension. *Psychological Review, 101,* 371–395.

Hambrick, D. Z., & Engle, R. W. (2002). Effects of domain knowledge, working memory capacity, and age on cognitive performance: An investigation of the knowledge-is-power hypothesis. *Cognitive Psychology, 44,* 339–387.

Hegarty, M. (1992). Mental animation: Inferring motion from static diagrams of mechanical systems. *Journal of Experimental Psychology: Learning, Memory and Cognition, 18,* 1084–1102.

Hegarty, M. (2004a). Diagrams in the mind and in the world: Relations between internal and external visualizations. In A. Blackwell, K. Mariott & A. Shimojima (Eds.). *Diagrammatic representation and inference. Lecture notes in artificial intelligence 2980.* Berlin: Springer.

Hegarty, M. (2004b). Mechanical reasoning as mental simulation. *TRENDS in Cognitive Sciences, 8,* 280–285.

Hegarty, M., Kriz, S., & Cate, C. (2003). The roles of mental animations and external animations in understanding mechanical systems. *Cognition and Instruction, 21,* 325–360.

Hegarty, M., & Just, M. A. (1993). Constructing mental models of machines from text and diagrams. *Journal of Memory and Language, 32*, 717–742.

Hegarty, M., Narayanan, N. H., & Freitas, P. (2002). Understanding machines from multimedia and hypermedia presentations. In Otero, A. C. Graesser & J. Leon (Eds.). *The Psychology of Science Text Comprehension.* Mahwah, NJ: Lawrence Erlbaum Associates.

Hegarty, M., Quillici, J., Narayanan, N. H., Holmquist, S., & Moreno, R. (1999). Multimedia instruction: Lessons from evaluation of a theory-based design. *Journal of Educational Multimedia and Hypermedia, 8*, 119–150.

Hegarty, M., & Sims, V. K. (1994). Individual differences in mental animation during mechanical reasoning. *Memory & Cognition, 22*, 411–430.

Hegarty, M., & Steinhoff, K. (1997). Use of diagrams as external memory in a mechanical reasoning task. *Learning and Individual Differences, 9*, 19–42.

Hegarty, M., & Waller. D. (2005). Individual differences in spatial abilities. In P. Shah & A. Miyake (Eds.). *Handbook of higher-level spatial cognition* (pp. 121–169). New York: Cambridge University Press.

Isaak, M. I., & Just, M. A. (1995). Constraints on the processing of rolling motion: The curtate cycloid illusion. *Journal of Experimental Psychology: Human Perception and Performance, 21*, 1391–1408.

Just, M. A., & Carpenter, P. A. (1985). Cognitive coordinate systems: Accounts of mental rotation and individual differences in spatial ability. *Psychological Review, 92*, 137–172.

Kaiser, M. K., Proffitt, D. R., & Anderson, K. (1985). Judgments of natural and anomalous trajectories in the presence and absence of motion. *Journal of Experimental Psychology: Learning, Memory, & Cognition, 11*, 795–803.

Kalyuga, S., Ayres, P. Chandler, P., & Sweller, J. (2003). The expertise reversal effect. *Educational Psychologist, 38*, 23–31.

Kintsch, W. (1988). The role of knowledge in discourse comprehension: A construction integration model. *Psychological Review, 95*, 163–182.

Kriz, S., & Hegarty, M. (2004). Constructing and revising mental models of a mechanical system: The role of domain knowledge in understanding external visualizations. In K. Forbus, D. Gentner, & T. Regier (Eds.), *Proceedings of the 26th Annual Conference of the Cognitive Science Society.* Mahwah, NJ: Lawrence Erlbaum Associates.

Lohman, D. F. (1988). Spatial abilities as traits, processes, and knowledge. In R. J. Sternberg (Ed.), *Advances in the psychology of human intelligence* (pp. 181–248). Hillsdale, NJ: Lawrence Erlbaum Associates.

Lowe, R. (1994). Selectivity in diagrams: Reading beyond the lines. *Educational Psychology, 14*(4), 467–491.

Lowe, R. (1999). Extracting information from an animation during complex visual learning. *European Journal of Psychology of Education, 14*(2), 225–244.

Lowe, R. (2003). Animation and learning: Selective processing of information in dynamic graphics. *Learning & Instruction, 13*, 157–176.

Macaulay, D. (1988). *The way things work.* Boston: Houghton Mifflin Company.

Macaulay, D. (1998). *The new way things work.* CD-ROM. New York: DK Interactive Learning.

Mayer, R. E. (2001). *Multimedia learning.* New York: Cambridge University Press.

Mayer, R. E. & Sims, V. K. (1994). For whom is a picture worth a thousand words? Extensions of a dual-coding theory of multimedia learning. *Journal of Educational Psychology, 86*, 389–401.

McCloskey, M. Caramazza, A., & Green, B. (1980). Curvilinear motion in the absence of external forces: Naïve beliefs about the motion of objects. *Science, 210*, 1139–1141.

McGee, M. G. (1979). Human spatial abilities: Psychometric studies and environmental, genetic, hormonal, and neurological influences. *Psychological Bulletin, 86*, 889–918.

Miyake, A., Rettinger, D. A., Friedman, N. P., Shah, P., & Hegarty, M. (2001). Visuospatial working memory, executive functioning and spatial abilities. How are they related? *Journal of Experimental Psychology: General, 130*, 621–640.

Miyake, N. (1986). Constructive interaction and the iterative process of understanding. *Cognitive Science, 10*, 151–177.

Narayanan, N. H. & Hegarty, M. (1998). On designing comprehensible hypermedia manuals. *International Journal of Human-Computer Studies, 48*, 267–301.

Narayanan, N. H. & Hegarty, M. (2002). Multimedia design for communication of dynamic information. *International Journal of Human-Computer Studies, 57*, 279–315.

Narayanan, N. H., Suwa, M., & Motoda, H. (1994). A study of diagrammatic reasoning from verbal and gestural data. *Proceedings of the 16th Annual Conference of the Cognitive Science Society* (pp. 652–657). Mahwah, NJ: Lawrence Erlbaum Associates.

Oestermeier, U. & Hesse, F. W. (2000). Verbal and visual causal arguments. *Cognition, 75*, 65–104.

Palmer, S. E. (1978). Fundamental aspects of cognitive representation. In E. E. Rosch & B. B. Lloyd (Eds.), *Cognition and categorization* (pp. 259–303). Mahwah, NJ: Lawrence Erlbaum Associates.

Rozenblit, L. & Keil, F. (2002). The misunderstood limits of folk science: An illusion of explanatory depth. *Cognitive Science, 26*, 521–562.

Salthouse, T. A. (1996). The processing-speed theory of adult age differences in cognition. *Psychological Review, 103*, 403–428.

Schnotz, W. (2002). Towards an integrated view of learning from text and visual displays. *Educational Psychology Review, 14*, 101–120.

Schwartz, D. L. and Black, J. B. (1996). Shuttling between depictive models and abstract rules: Induction and fall-back. *Cognitive Science, 20*, 457–497.

Shah, P. & Miyake, A. (1996). The separability of working memory resources for spatial thinking and language processing: An individual differences approach. *Journal of Experimental Psychology: General, 125*, 4–27.

Spoehr, K. T. (1994). Enhancing the acquisition of conceptual structures through hypermedia. In K. McGilly (Ed.), *Classroom lessons: Integrating cognitive theory and practice*, Cambridge, MA: MIT Press.

Tversky, B., Morrison, J. B., & Bétrancourt, M. (2002). Animation: Can it facilitate? *International Journal of Human-Computer Studies, 57*, 247–262.

Vosniadou, S. (2002). On the nature of naive physics. In M. Limon & L. Mason (Eds.), *Reconsidering conceptual change: Issues in theory and practice* (pp. 61–76). Berlin: Springer.

2

Research-Based Principles for Learning with Animation

Richard E. Mayer

Animation has potential for helping students understand scientific and mathematical material. For example, consider the explanation of how a bicycle tire pump works that is given in Table 2.1. Our research (Mayer & Anderson, 1991, 1992) shows that students who merely listened to material containing this explanation remembered about half of the material when they are asked, "Please write down an explanation of how a bicycle tire pump works," and had difficulty in applying what was presented to solving new problems such as, "Suppose you push down and pull up the handle of a pump several times but no air comes out. What could have gone wrong?"

Next, consider the narrated animation depicted in Figure 2.1. The figure shows frames from the animation and the words that were spoken by the narrator. Note that these words are identical to those shown in Table 2.1. Our research (Mayer & Anderson, 1991, 1992) shows that adding a simple animation such as this one results in large increases in problem-solving transfer performance, indicating a large increase in the learner's understanding of the presented explanation. We refer to this result as a *multimedia effect* – people learn better from animation and narration than from narration alone. In our studies the effect size, based on three comparisons, was well above 1 based on Cohen's d, indicating a large effect. Similarly, in a recent review of research, Fletcher and Tobias (2005) concluded that there is strong and consistent support for the multimedia principle.

Although animation can be effective in promoting student understanding of scientific and mathematical material, all animations are not equally effective. Learning with animation poses serious challenges to the human information processing system. Recent reviews have concluded that animation is not always superior to static diagrams in promoting learning, and in some cases may even

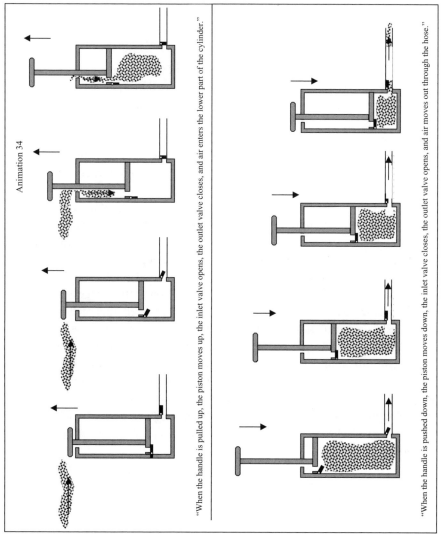

Animation 34

"When the handle is pulled up, the piston moves up, the inlet valve opens, the outlet valve closes, and air enters the lower part of the cylinder."

"When the handle is pushed down, the piston moves down, the inlet valve closes, the outlet valve opens, and air moves out through the hose."

FIGURE 2.1. Selected frames from an animation on how pumps work.

31

TABLE 2.1. *Script for Narration on How a Pump Works*

When the handle is pulled up, the piston moves up, the inlet valve
opens, the outlet valve closes and air enters the lower part of the
cylinder. When the handle is pushed down, the piston moves down,
the inlet valve closes, the outlet valve opens, and air moves out
through the hose.

be less effective (Bétrancourt, 2005; Hegarty, 2004; Tversky Bauer-Morrison &
Bétrancourt, 2002). Designing instruction with animation is particularly challenging when cognitive load issues are considered because (a) typically animation is presented at a pace determined by the instructor, (b) typically the
images are transitory, and (c) typically animation does not highlight the key
frames in the sequence. The premise of this chapter is that instructional animations are most effective in promoting meaningful learning when they are
designed in ways that are consistent with how people learn.

My argument is based on the distinction between technology-centered
and learner-centered approaches to educational technology (Mayer, 2001).
Some designers, in their zeal for implementing the latest technology, take a
technology-centered approach to educational technology. For example, they
may begin with cutting-edge advances in computer-based graphics, and apply
them to instructional programs. Their goal is to deliver cutting-edge technology to learners. My concern with the technology centered approach is that
it can result in instructional scenarios that are not sensitive to how people
learn. In contrast, other designers take a learner-centered approach, in which
they begin with an understanding of how people learn, and attempt to infuse
technology as an aid to human learning. For example, they use graphics in
ways that do not overload the learner's cognitive system. Their goal is to adapt
technology to the way people learn, so that technology can be used as a learning tool. In this chapter, I take a learner-centered approach to educational
technology.

In recent years, there has been increasing research activity aimed at improving student learning through graphics in general (Schnotz & Lowe, 2003) and
animation in particular (Anglin, Vaez, & Cunningham, 2004; Ploetzner &
Lowe, 2003). However, in a recent review, Hegarty (2004) has noted the need
for theory-based research that accounts for how people process multimedia
lessons in their cognitive systems during learning. In this chapter, I examine 10 predictions of the cognitive theory of multimedia learning concerning
how people learn from multimedia lessons. In the next section, I describe the
cognitive theory of multimedia learning and spell out 10 predictions that are

TABLE 2.2. *Three Elements in a Cognitive Theory of Multimedia Learning*

Dual channels	Learners possess separate channels for processing auditory/verbal material and visual/pictorial material.
Limited capacity	Each channel can process a limited amount of material at one time.
Generative processing	Meaningful learning occurs when learners engage in appropriate cognitive processing, such as selecting relevant words and pictures for further processing, organizing selected words into a verbal model and organizing selected images into a pictorial model, and integrating verbal and pictorial models with each other and with prior knowledge.

relevant to the instructional design of multimedia lessons. In the subsequent sections, I review research testing each of these predictions, resulting in 10 research-based principles for learning with animation.

Cognitive Theory of Multimedia Learning

What are the features of the human information processing system that are most relevant to learning with animation? Understanding the role of the learner's cognitive processing during learning is particularly important for animation-based instruction because animation can easily overload the learner's information processing system. In building a cognitive theory of multimedia learning, I draw on three major ideas from cognitive science theories of learning: dual-channels (Baddeley, 1986, 1999; Paivio, 1986), limited capacity (Baddeley, 1986, 1999; Chandler & Sweller, 1991; Sweller, 1999, 2005), and generative processing (Grabowski, 2004; Mayer, 1996, 2003; Wittrock, 1989). First, the dual-channels idea is that humans possess two channels for processing information – a visual/pictorial channel for processing pictures and an auditory/verbal channel for processing words. Second, the limited capacity idea is that each channel has a limited capacity for processing information. Third, the generative processing idea is that deep understanding occurs when learners engage in appropriate cognitive processing such as selecting relevant information, organizing the selected information, and integrating the selected information with prior knowledge and other representations. These ideas are summarized in Table 2.2.

Figure 2.2 presents a cognitive model of multimedia learning which consists of three memory stores – sensory memory, working memory, and long-term memory – and five cognitive processes – selecting words, selecting images,

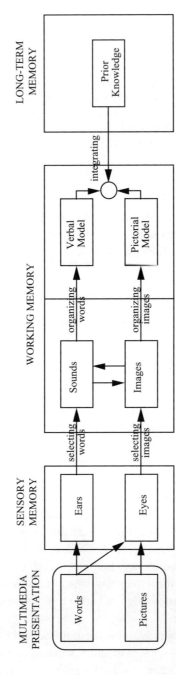

FIGURE 2.2. Cognitive theory of multimedia learning.

organizing words, organizing images, and integrating. Animations and printed words from the outside world impinge on the eyes and enter through the visual channel whereas narration impinges on the ears and enters through the auditory channel. The result is a brief sensory image in sensory memory – sound images (or sounds) for spoken words and visual images (or images) for animations and printed text. The first cognitive process is *selecting* relevant material for further processing: If the learner pays attention to some of the sounds in sensory memory they are transferred to working memory for further processing (i.e., indicated by the *selecting words* arrow), and if the learner pays attention to some of the images in sensory memory, they are transferred to working memory for further processing (i.e., indicated by the *selecting images* arrow). Some of the incoming printed words may be converted into sounds in working memory, as indicated by the arrow from images to sounds; some of the incoming sounds, may be converted into images in working memory, as indicated by the arrow from sounds to images. The second cognitive process is *organizing* the selected material into coherent representations: The learner mentally organizes the words into a verbal model (as indicated by the *organizing words* arrow), and the learner mentally organizes the images into a pictorial model (as indicated by the *organizing images* arrow). Finally, the third process is integrating the verbal and pictorial models with each other and with prior knowledge (as indicated by the *integrating* arrow).

When learners do not adequately select the appropriate words and images, the learning outcome is no learning. This outcome is indicated by poor performance on retention and transfer tests. When learners adequately select words and images, but do not engage in large amounts of organizing and integrating, the learning outcome is rote learning. This outcome is indicated by good performance on retention tests but poor performance on transfer tests. When learners adequately engage in selecting, organizing, and integrating – that is, all five processes indicated in Figure 2.2 – the learning outcome is meaningful learning. This outcome is indicated by good performance on both retention and transfer tests. These three types of learning outcomes are summarized in Table 2.3. In the research reported in this chapter, I focus only on transfer test performance because I am mainly interested in how to promote meaningful learning.

In any learning situation the learner has a limited amount of cognitive capacity that must be allocated among three competing demands (Mayer, 2005; Paas, Renkl, & Sweller, 2003; Sweller, 1999, 2005): extraneous processing, which involves cognitive processing that is not related to the instructional objective (such as viewing entertaining video clips that are interspersed in a lesson); essential processing, which involves basic cognitive processing of

TABLE 2.3. *Three Types of Learning Outcomes*

Type	Cognitive Processes During Learning	Retention Test Performance	Transfer Test Performance
No learning	None	Poor	Poor
Rote learning	Selecting	Good	Poor
Meaningful learning	Selecting, organizing, and integrating	Good	Good

material that is relevant to the lesson's objective (such as selecting words and images and the initial stages of organizing words and images); and generative processing, which involves deep processing of material that is relevant to the lesson's objective (such as extended amounts of organizing words and images, and integrating). These three types of processing demands are summarized in Table 2.4. Sweller (1999, 2005; Pass, Renkl, & Sweller, 2003) uses the term *intrinsic load* to refer to essential processing and *germane load* to refer to generative processing. Learning with animation can be particularly challenging when the material is difficult, when it is presented at a rapid pace, and when the learner is not familiar with the material. Table 2.5 lists three types of learning challenges and how to overcome them: reducing extraneous processing, managing essential processing, and fostering generative processing. These three challenges are examined in the next three sections of the chapter.

PRINCIPLES FOR REDUCING EXTRANEOUS PROCESSING

Extraneous overload occurs when the learner must allocate so much cognitive capacity to processing that is extraneous to the goal of instruction that the learner does not have enough remaining capacity to deeply process the essential material in the lesson. The need for extraneous processing can be caused by having extraneous material in the lesson or by poor layout of the

TABLE 2.4. *Three Processing Demands on Cognitive Capacity*

Type of Processing	Definition	Cognitive Processes
Extraneous processing	Cognitive processing that is not related to the objective of the lesson.	None
Essential processing	Initial cognitive processing that is relevant to the objective of the lesson.	Selecting & some organizing
Generative processing	Deep cognitive processing that is relevant to the objective of the lesson.	Organizing & integrating

TABLE 2.5. *Ten Ways to Overcome Challenges to Learning with Animation*

Reducing Extraneous Overload

Coherence principle: People learn better when extraneous animation or narration elements are excluded rather than included.

Signaling principle: People learn better when cues are added that highlight the organization of the animation or narration.

Redundancy principle: People learn better from animation and narration than from animation, narration, and on-screen text.

Spatial contiguity principle: People learn better when corresponding elements of the animation and on-screen text are presented near rather than far from each other on the screen.

Temporal contiguity principle: People learn better when corresponding animation and narration are presented simultaneously rather than successively.

Managing Essential Overload

Segmenting principle: People learn better when a narrated animation is presented in learner-paced segments than as a continuous unit.

Pre-training principle: People learn better from a narrated animation when they have had training in the names and characteristics of the main concepts.

Modality principle: People learn better from animation and narration than from animation and on-screen text.

Fostering Generative Processing

Personalization principle: People learn better when narration is in conversational style rather than formal style.

Voice principle: People learn better when the narration is spoken in a standard-accented human voice than a machine voice or accented human voice.

---

lesson. Animations can have extraneous images that are not related to the theme of the lesson, can be accompanied by sounds that are distracting, or can be accompanied by narrations that contain extraneous information. In this section, I review five principles aimed at reducing extraneous overload in learning with animation: the coherence principle, the signaling principle, the redundancy principle, the spatial contiguity principle, and the temporal continuity principle.

Coherence Principle

A major design flaw in teaching with animation occurs when too much extraneous material is presented. For example, in an effort to spice up a narrated animation, a designer might be tempted to add interesting video slips, background sounds, instrumental music tracks, or additional facts. However, according to the cognitive theory of multimedia learning and cognitive load theory, when learners allocate their limited cognitive capacity to

TABLE 2.6. *Experimental Tests of Ten Ways to Overcome Challenges to Learning with Animation*

Principle	Median Effect Size	Number of Tests
Reducing Extraneous Processing		
Coherence principle	0.58	4 of 4
Signaling principle	0.70	1 of 1
Redundancy principle	0.69	6 of 6
Spatial contiguity principle	0.82	1 of 1
Temporal contiguity principle	1.31	8 of 8
Managing Essential Processing		
Segmenting principle	0.98	3 of 3
Pre-training principle	0.85	5 of 5
Modality principle	1.03	16 of 16
Fostering Generative Processing		
Personalization principle	1.08	8 of 8
Voice principle	0.79	4 of 4

processing the extraneous material they have insufficient capacity left over to engage in deep processing of the essential material in the lesson. Mayer (2003, 2005) refers to this situation as *extraneous overload*: the requirements of essential processing (i.e., cognitive processing of the essential material in the lesson) and extraneous processing (i.e., cognitive processing of the extraneous material in the lesson) exceed the learner's cognitive capacity. The coherence principle is that people learn better when extraneous material is excluded rather than included. As shown in the top row of Table 2.6, this principle has been tested and confirmed in 4 of 4 experiments involving animation of lightning, brakes, and ocean waves (Mayer, Heiser, & Lonn, 2001, Expt. 3; Mayer & Jackson, 2005, Expt. 2; Moreno & Mayer, 2000a, Expt. 1 & Expt. 2), yielding a median effect size of 0.58. In each test, students learned more deeply – as indicated by superior performance on a problem-solving transfer test – with a concise narrated animation rather than one that was spiced up with short interspersed video clips, background sounds, instrumental music, or additional facts. These results provide support for an important design recommendation for reducing extraneous overload based on the coherence principle: Eliminate extraneous material from narrated animations.

Signaling Principle

In some cases it might not be feasible or desirable to eliminate all extraneous material from a narrated animation. In these cases, an alternative method for reducing extraneous cognitive load is to provide cues for the learner concerning what to attend to and how to organize it. Signals (such as using deeper intonation for key ideas and pointer words such as "first . . . second . . . third") can help the learner allocate cognitive processing to essential material rather than extraneous material. Mautone and Mayer (2001) refer to this idea as the signaling principle: People learn better when cues are added that highlight the organization of narrated animation. As shown in the second row of Table 2.6, this principle has been tested and confirmed in 1 experiment involving an animation depicting how airplanes achieve lift (Mautone & Mayer, 2001, Expt. 3), yielding an effect size of 0.70. In particular, students learned more deeply from a narrated animation in which the narrator signaled the three main steps in the process and emphasized the main ideas through intonation. This result provides support for an important design recommendation for reducing extraneous overload based on the signaling principle: Provide cues for how to process the lesson, such as pointer words such as, "first . . . second . . . third" and verbal intonation emphasis on the key ideas.

Redundancy Principle

In an effort to accommodate the learning styles of all learners, instructional designers might be tempted to add concurrent on-screen text to a narrated animation. According to this view, auditory learners can listen to the narration whereas as visual learners can the read the words for themselves. The problem with this approach is that the added on-screen text can create another form of extraneous overload in which learners waste their precious cognitive capacity on decoding both verbal streams and in trying to reconcile them. Instead, it would be more efficient to process the animation in the visual/pictorial channel and the words as narration in the auditory/verbal channel. We refer to this idea as the redundancy principle: People learn better from animation and narration than from animation, narration, and on-screen text. As shown in the third row of Table 2.6, this principle has been upheld in 6 of 6 tests involving animations of lightning and an environmental science game (Craig, Gholson, & Driscoll, 2002, Expt. 2; Mayer, Heiser, & Lonn, 2001, Expts. 1 and 2; Moreno & Mayer, 2002a, Expts. 2a & 2b; Moreno & Mayer, 2002b, Expt. 2b), yielding a median effect size of 0.69. In each case, people performed better on tests of problem-solving transfer after viewing a narrated animation rather than a narrated animation with concurrent on-screen text. The design implications of the redundancy principle are clear: Avoid presenting identical steams of printed and spoken words concurrently with corresponding animation.

Spatial Contiguity Principle

Another way to create extraneous overload is to use a confusing layout that forces the learner to engage in extraneous processing. For example, extraneous processing is required when a learner views an animation that has on-screen text printed along the bottom of the screen. In this case, the learner must allocate precious processing capacity to visual scanning – that is, reading words at the bottom of the screen and searching in the animation for what they refer to. When the learner must use processing capacity for this kind of extraneous processing, less capacity is available for essential processing – that is, making sense of the essential material in the lesson. One way to reduce extraneous processing is to place printed words next to the portion of the animation they describe. For example, when the text says, "The negative particles fall to the bottom of the cloud" this sentence can be placed next to the bottom of the cloud in the animation (rather than at the bottom of the screen). The spatial contiguity principle is that people learn better when corresponding elements of the narration and on-screen text are presented near rather than far from each other on the screen. As shown in the fourth line of Table 2.6, this principle was supported in an experiment by Moreno and Mayer (1999, Expt. 1) involving an animation on lightning, yielding an effect size of 0.82. The design implications of the spatial contiguity principle are straightforward: Place printed words near corresponding parts of the animation to reduce visual scanning.

Temporal Contiguity Principle

Even when a multimedia lesson consists of spoken words and animation, poor layout can create extraneous overload. For example, consider a situation in which a learner first listens to an explanation of how something works and then views an animation depicting the explanation, or vice versa. You might assume that this form of presentation (which we call sequential presentation) would result in better learning that presenting the animation and narration concurrently (which we call simultaneous presentation) because the learner gets two separate exposures to the explanation. However, based on the cognitive theory of multimedia learning and cognitive load theory, sequential presentation of animation and narration creates a form of extraneous overload because the learner must allocate limited cognitive capacity to mentally holding the words in working memory (which we call representational holding) until the animation is presented, or vice versa. If the learner must use a lot of cognitive capacity for representational holding, then less capacity is available to engage in deep processing of the essential material. The temporal contiguity principle is that people learn better when corresponding animation and narration are presented simultaneously rather than successively. As shown in the fifth row of Table 2.6, in 8 of 8 experimental tests involving animations of pumps, brakes, lightning, and the human respiratory system (Mayer & Anderson, 1991, Expts. 1 & 2a; Mayer & Anderson, 1992, Expts. 1 & 2; Mayer & Sims, Expts. 1 and 2; Mayer, Moreno, Boire, & Vagge, 1999, Expts. 1 & 2), simultaneous presentation of animation and narration resulted in better transfer test performance than did successive presentation, yielding a median effect size of 1.31. Thus, an important implication for instructional design is to present corresponding narration and animation at the same time to minimize the need to hold representations in working memory.

PRINCIPLES FOR MANAGING ESSENTIAL PROCESSING

The foregoing section focused on situations in which learners may have difficulty in learning with animation because the lesson requires too much extraneous processing. In this section, I focus on situations in which learners may have difficulty in learning with animation because the to-be-learned material is intrinsically complex, thereby requiring too much essential processing. Essential overload occurs when the amount of essential processing (i.e., cognitive processing needed to understand the essential material in the lesson) exceeds the learner's cognitive capacity. For example, when a narrated animation about how an electric motor works is presented at a fast pace, the learner might not be able to keep up with the presentation. Lessons involving animation can be particularly problematic because they typically provide information at a fast pace that is not under the learner's control. In this section, I explore three principles aimed at managing essential overload: the segmenting principle, the pre-training principle, and the modality principle.

Segmenting Principle

Suppose someone is given a narrated animation that explains the working of a complex system (such as an electric motor) at a fast pace not under the learner's control. Even though the narrated animation follows all of the principles for reducing extraneous load described in the previous section, learners still might not be able to keep up with the lesson. These learners – particularly, those with little prior knowledge – might experience essential overload, in which the amount of processing required to make sense of the essential material in the lesson exceeds their cognitive capacity. One way to manage essential overload is to break the narrated animation into meaningful segments, and allow the learner to control the onset of each one. For example, a lesson on how a lightning storm develops could be broken into 16 segments, each describing one major event. After a segment is presented, the learner can get the next segment by clicking on the continue button. In this way, the learner can fully process one segment before moving on to the next. The segmenting principle is that people learn better when a narrated animation is presented in learner-paced segments rather than as a continuous unit. As shown in the third row of Table 2.6, in 3 of 3 experimental comparisons involving animations of lightning and electric motors (Mayer & Chandler, 2001, Expt. 2; Mayer, Dow, & Mayer, Expts. 2a & 2b), people performed better on transfer tests when the animation was segments whose pacing was controlled by the learner than when the presentation was a continuous unit, yielding a median effect size of 0.98. In designing narrated animation, an important design implication is to allow the learner to control the time between bite-size segments of the presentation. Further research is needed to disentangle the independent contributions of segmenting and learner control.

Pre-training Principle

Another way to manage essential overload is to make sure that the learner knows the names and characteristics of the main components depicted in the narrated animation. In viewing the narrated animation, learners must engage in two demanding learning tasks: building component models (i.e., knowledge of the possible states of the component) and building a causal model (i.e., knowledge of how a change in the state of one component causes a change in the state of another component). For example, in viewing a narrated animation about how hydraulic brakes work in a car, the learner must build component models of the brake pedal (which can be up or down), piston in the master cylinder (which can be forward or back), fluid in the brake line (which can be compressed or not), smaller pistons in the wheel cylinders (which can be forward or back), brake shoes (which can be extended or not), and brake drum (which can be pressed against or not). In addition, the learner must build a cause-and-effect chain (e.g., pressing on the pedal causes a piston to move forward in the master cylinder, which causes the brake fluid to compress, which causes the smaller pistons to move forward, and so on). If the learner already knows the names and possible states of the components (such as that the master cylinder can move forward or back), then the learner can devote more cognitive resources to processing the steps in the causal chain.

The pre-training principle is that people learn better from a narrated animation when they have had training in the names and characteristics of the main concepts. As shown in the seventh row in Table 2.6, in 5 of 5 experiments involving animations explaining brakes, pumps, and a geology simulation game (Mayer, Mathais, & Wetzell, 2002, Expts. 1, 2, & 3; Mayer, Mautone,

& Prothero, 2002, Expts. 2 & 3), students who received pre-training learned more deeply with scientific animation than did students who had not received pre-training, yielding a median effect size of 0.85. This result is consistent with the expertise reversal effect (Kalyuga, 2005) in which support in multimedia learning is more beneficial for learners with low experience than for learners with high experience. Overall, research on the pre-training principle suggests providing low-experience learners with pre-training in the names and characteristics of the components they are about to see a narrated animation.

Modality Principle

Finally, consider a multimedia lesson consisting of animation and concurrent on-screen text concerning a complex system presented at a fast pace. In this situation, the learner's visual channel may become overloaded by essential processing demands – that is, the learner's eyes must pay attention to the essential material in the animation and to the essential material in the printed text at the same time. One way to manage essential overload in this situation is to off-load some of the essential processing from the visual channel to the auditory channel by presenting the words in spoken form. In this way, the visual channel can be used for processing the animation and the auditory channel can be used for processing the words. The modality principle is that people learn better from animation and narration than from animation and on-screen text. As shown in the eighth line of Table 2.6, in 16 of 16 experimental tests involving animations of brakes, lightning, electric motors, an aircraft simulation game, and an environmental science game (Mayer & Moreno, 1998, Expts. 1 & 2; Moreno & Mayer, 1999, Expts. 1 & 2; O'Neil et al., 2000, Expt. 1; Moreno et al., 2001, Expts. 4a, 4b, 5a, & 5b; Craig, Gholson, & Driscoll, 2002, Expt. 2; Moreno & Mayer, 2002b, Expts. 1a, 1b, 1c, 2a, & 2b; Mayer, Dow, & Mayer, 2003, Expt. 1), students performed better on transfer tests after learning from animation and narration than from animation and on-screen text, yielding a median effect size of 1.03. The modality principle has received the most research support of all the principles described in this chapter. An important instructional implication is to present words as narration rather than as on-screen text when they accompany an animation.

PRINCIPLES FOR FOSTERING GENERATIVE PROCESSING

Generative processing consists of selecting relevant portions of the animation and narration, mentally organizing the material into pictorial and verbal mental models, and integrating the models with each other and with prior knowledge. Generative processes lead to deep understanding, as reflected in transfer test performance. One way to foster generative processing is to build a sense of social partnership between the learner and the computer-based instructional program. If a student feels that the narrator in the instructional lesson is a social partner who is engaging in conversation, then the rules of social conversation come into play (Reeves & Nass, 1996). That is, the student will try hard to make sense of the narrator's message – including the use of generative processing. Animations are particularly problematic because on the surface they do not appear to be social. In this section, I consider two principles for fostering social partnership with narrated animation – using conversational style rather than formal style (personalization principle), and using a human voice rather than a machine voice (voice principle).

Personalization Principle

In a narrated animation explaining how the human respiratory system works, the narration script includes the following words (Mayer, Fennell, Farmer, & Campbell, 2004): "During inhaling the diaphragm moves down creating more space for the lungs, air enters through the nose or mouth, moves down through the throat and bronchial tubes to tiny air sacs in the lungs. . . . " This style of talking is somewhat formal because it is based on third-person constructions. In contrast, the narration script can be converted to conversational style by replacing "the" with "your" in 12 locations such as the following: "During inhaling your diaphragm moves down creating more space for your lungs, air enters through your nose or mouth, moves down through your throat and bronchial tubes to tiny air sacs in your lungs. . . . "

The personalization principle is that people learn better when narration is in conversational style rather than formal style. As shown in the ninth line of Table 2.6, in 8 of 8 studies involving animations explaining the human respiratory system, lightning, and an environmental science game (Moreno & Mayer, 2000b, Expts. 1, 3, & 5; Moreno & Mayer, 2004, Expts. 1a & 1b; Mayer, Fennell, Farmer, & Campbell, 2004, Expts. 1, 2, & 3), students scored higher on tests of problem solving transfer after receiving an animated narration in conversational style than in formal style, yielding a median effect size of 1.08. An important instructional design implication is to present narration in conversational style, that is, using first- and second-person constructions.

Voice Principle

Another way to promote a sense of social conversation in the learner concerns the voice of the narrator. When the narrator's voice is machine simulated (or has a heavy accent), learners might be less likely to accept the lesson as a social conversation. When the narrator's voice comes from a human with a standard accent, learners might be more likely to accept the lesson as a social conversation. The voice principle is that people learn better when the narration is spoken in a standard-accented human voice than in a machine voice or a foreign-accented human voice. As shown in the bottom line of Table 2.6, in 4 of 4 experimental test involving animations on lightning and mathematics word problems (Mayer, Sobko, & Mautone, 2003, Expts. 1 & 2; Atkinson, Mayer, & Merrill, 2005, Expts. 1 & 2), students scored higher on problem-solving transfer tests when they had learned with narrated animation that had a standard-accented human voice than a machine voice or a foreign-accented human voice. The median effect size was 0.79. This result suggests a straightforward design principle: Use a standard-accented human voice in narrations.

SUMMARY

Towards a Cognitive Theory of Multimedia Learning from Animation

Overall, the 10 principles reviewed in this chapter help to shape a cognitive theory of multimedia learning that focuses specifically on animation (Mayer, 2001, 2005). Each principle is based on an experimental test of a prediction of the theory concerning how to reduce extraneous processing, manage essential processing, or promote generative processing. Sweller (1999, 2005; Paas, Renkl, & Sweller, 2003) refers to these as extraneous load, intrinsic load, and germane load, respectively. By testing theoretical predictions, research on the design of multimedia messages contributes to cognitive theory, such as the cognitive theory of multimedia learning described in the introduction.

Towards Evidence-Based Practice

There are numerous books on how to design multimedia instruction involving animation, but most are based on the wisdom of the author rather than empirical evidence or cognitive theory. The major theme of this chapter is that there is a growing research base capable of supporting evidence-based practice – that is, evidence-based practice involves basing instructional design decisions on empirical research and research-based theory rather than on the opinions of experts. The 10 research-based principles described in this chapter provide a modest starting point for the evolution of evidence-based practice in multimedia design.

Limitations and Future Directions

The research reviewed in this chapter can be criticized on the grounds that it generally involved short lessons, that the context of learning was generally in non-school settings, and that the outcome of learning was generally evaluated with immediate tests. Further research is needed that investigates whether the 10 principles described in this chapter apply in more authentic learning situations – that is, with longer lessons, in educational settings, and on delayed tests. In addition, further research is needed to determine the conditions under which animation is an effective instructional device, including the characteristics of the learner, material, and presentation features. In particular, Hegarty (2004) has shown that the next phase of research on learning with animation should move beyond asking whether animation is effective to asking how people learn with animation.

References

Anglin, G. J., Vaez, H., & Cunningham, K. L. (2004). Visual representations and learning: The role of static and animated graphics. In D. H. Jonassen (Ed.), *Handbook of research on educational communications and technology* (2nd ed; pp. 865–916). Mahwah, NJ: Lawrence Erlbaum Associates.

Atkinson, R. K., Mayer, R. E., & Merrill, M. M. (2005). Fostering social agency in multimedia learning: Examining the impact of an animated agent's voice. *Contemporary Educational Psychology, 30*, 117–139.

Baddeley, A. D. (1986). *Working memory.* Oxford, England: Oxford University Press.

Baddeley, A. D. (1999). *Human memory.* Boston: Allyn & Bacon.

Bétrancourt, M. (2005). The animation and interactivity principles in multimedia learning. In R. E. Mayer (Ed.), *Cambridge handbook of multimedia learning* (pp. 287–296). New York: Cambridge University Press.

Chandler, P., & Sweller, J. (1991). Cognitive load theory and the format of instruction. *Cognition and Instruction, 8*, 293–332.

Craig, S. D., Gholson, B., & Driscoll, D. M. (2002). Animated pedagogical agent in multimedia educational environments: Effects of agent properties, picture features, and redundancy. *Journal of Educational Psychology, 94*, 428–434.

Fletcher, D. & Tobias, S. (2005). The multimedia principle in multimedia learning. In R. E. Mayer (Ed.), *Cambridge handbook of multimedia learning* (pp. 117–134). New York: Cambridge University Press.

Grabowski, B. (2004). Generative learning contributions to the design of instruction and learning. In D. H. Jonassen (Ed.), *Handbook of research on educational communications and technology* (2nd ed; pp. 719–744). Mahwah, NJ: Lawrence Erlbaum Associates.

Hegarty, M. (2003). Dynamic visualizations and learning: Getting to the difficult questions. *Learning and Instruction, 14*, 343–342.

Kalyuga, S. (2005). Prior knowledge principle in multimedia learning. In R. E. Mayer (Ed.), *Cambridge handbook of multimedia learning* (pp. 325–338). New York: Cambridge University Press.

Mautone, P. D., & Mayer, R. E. (2001). Signaling as a cognitive guide in multimedia learning. *Journal of Educational Psychology, 93*, 377–389.

Mayer, R. E. (1996). Learning strategies for making sense out of expository text: The SOI model for guiding three cognitive processes in knowledge construction. *Educational Psychology Review, 8*, 357–371.

Mayer, R. E. (2001). *Multimedia learning.* New York: Cambridge University Press.

Mayer, R. E. (2003). *Learning and instruction.* Upper Saddle River, NJ: Merrill Prentice Hall.

Mayer, R. E. (2005). A cognitive theory of multimedia learning. In R. E. Mayer (Ed.), *Cambridge handbook of multimedia learning.* New York: Cambridge University Press.

Mayer, R. E., & Anderson, R. B. (1991). Animations need narrations: An experimental test of a dual-coding hypothesis. *Journal of Educational Psychology, 83*, 484–490.

Mayer, R. E., & Anderson, R. B. (1992). The instructive animation: Helping students build connections between words and pictures in multimedia learning. *Journal of Educational Psychology, 84*, 444–452.

Mayer, R. E., & Chandler, P. (2001). When learning is just a click away: Does simple user interaction foster deeper understanding of multimedia messages? *Journal of Educational Psychology, 93*, 390–397.

Mayer, R. E., Dow, G., & Mayer, S. (2003). Multimedia learning in an interactive self-explaining environment: What works in the design of agent-based microworlds? *Journal of Educational Psychology, 95*, 806–813.

Mayer, R. E., Fennell, S., Farmer, L., & Campbell, J. (2004). A personalization effect in multimedia learning: Students learn better when words are in conversational style rather than formal style. *Journal of Educational Psychology, 96*, 389–395.

Mayer, R. E., Heiser, H., & Lonn, S. (2001). Cognitive constraints on multimedia learning: When presenting more material results in less understanding. *Journal of Educational Psychology, 93*, 187–198.

Mayer, R. E., & Jackson, J. (2005). The case for coherence in scientific explanations: Quantitative details can hurt qualitative understanding. *Journal of Experimental Psychology: Applied, 11*, 13–18.

Mayer, R. E., Mathias, A., & Wetzell, K. (2002). Fostering understanding of multimedia messages through pre-training: Evidence for a two-stage theory of mental model construction. *Journal of Experimental Psychology: Applied, 8*, 147–154.

Mayer, R. E., Mautone, P., & Prothero, W. (2002). Pictorial aids for learning by doing in a multimedia geology simulation game. *Journal of Educational Psychology, 94*, 171–185.

Mayer, R. E., & Moreno, R. (1998). A split-attention effect in multimedia learning: Evidence for dual processing systems in working memory. *Journal of Educational Psychology, 90*, 312–320.

Mayer, R. E., Moreno, R., Boire, M., & Vagge, S. (1999). Maximizing constructivist learning from multimedia communications by minimizing cognitive load. *Journal of Educational Psychology, 91*, 638–643.

Mayer, R. E., & Sims, V. K. (1994). For whom is a picture worth a thousand words? Extensions of a dual-coding theory of multimedia learning? *Journal of Educational Psychology, 86*, 389–401.

Mayer, R. E., Sobko, K., & Mautone, P. D. (2003). Social cues in multimedia learning: Role of speaker's voice. *Journal of Educational Psychology, 95*, 419–425.

Moreno, R., & Mayer, R. E. (1999). Cognitive principles of multimedia learning: The role of modality and contiguity. *Journal of Educational Psychology, 91*, 358–368.

Moreno, R., & Mayer, R. E. (2000a). A coherence effect in multimedia learning: The case for minimizing irrelevant sounds in the design of multimedia messages. *Journal of Educational Psychology, 92*, 117–125.

Moreno, R., & Mayer, R. E. (2000b). Engaging students in active learning: The case for personalized multimedia messages. *Journal of Educational Psychology, 92*, 724–733.

Moreno, R., & Mayer, R. E. (2002a). Verbal redundancy in multimedia learning: When reading helps listening. *Journal of Educational Psychology, 94*, 156–163.

Moreno, R., & Mayer, R. E. (2002b). Learning science in virtual reality multimedia environments: Role of methods and media. *Journal of Educational Psychology, 94*, 598–610.

Moreno, R., & Mayer, R. E. (2004). Personalized messages that promote science learning in virtual environments. *Journal of Educational Psychology, 96*, 165–173.

Moreno, R., Mayer, R. E., Spires, H. A., & Lester, J. C. (2001). The case for social agency in computer-based teaching: Do students learn more deeply when they interact with animated pedagogical agents? *Cognition and Instruction, 19*, 177–213.

O'Neil, H. F., Mayer, R. E., Herl, H. E., Niemi, C., Olin, K., & Thurman, R. A. (2000). Instructional strategies for virtual aviation training environments. In H. F. O'Neil & D. H. Andrews (Eds.), *Aircrew training and assessment* (pp. 105–130). Mahwah, NJ: Lawrence Erlbaum Associates.

Paas, F., Renkl, A., & Sweller, J. (2003). Cognitive load theory and instructional design: Recent developments. *Educational Psychologist, 38*, 1–4.

Paivio, A. (1986). *Mental representations: A dual coding approach.* New York: Oxford University Press.

Ploetzner, R., & Lowe, R. (2003). Dynamic visualizations and learning. *Learning and Instruction, 14*, 235–240.

Reeves, B., & Nass, C. (1996). *The media equation.* New York: Cambridge University Press.

Schnotz, W. & Lowe, R. K. (2003). External and internal representations in multimedia learning. *Learning and Instruction, 13*, 117–123.

Sweller, J. (1999) *Instructional design in technical areas.* Camberwell, Australia: ACER Press.

Sweller, J. (2005). Implications of cognitive load theory for multimedia learning. In R. E. Mayer (Ed.), *Cambridge handbook of multimedia learning.* New York: Cambridge University Press.

Tversky, B., Bauer-Morrison, J., & Bétrancourt, M. (2002) Animation: Can it facilitate? *International Journal of Human-Computer Studies, 57*, 247–262.

Wittrock, M. C. (1989). Generative processes of comprehension. *Educational Psychologist, 24*, 345–376.

3

Learning from Animation

Where to Look, When to Look

Richard Lowe

INTRODUCTION

Despite the increasing popularity of animations among producers of technology-based learning materials, a growing body of research evidence suggests that they are not necessarily superior to static depictions (Schnotz, Böckheler, & Grzondziel, 1999; Bétrancourt & Tversky, 2000). In some cases, potential educational benefits from animation's capacity to depict dynamics explicitly (saving learners having to infer dynamics from static representations) could be outweighed by the perceptual and cognitive processing costs of comprehending animated presentations. These costs are likely to be particularly high for animations depicting complex content with a high degree of dynamic realism (see Kaiser, Proffitt, & Whelan, 1990). Under these circumstances, learners may fail to deal with the material adequately because the animation presents its content in a manner that is not well matched to their processing capacities. User-controllable animations appear to address this potential mismatch by allowing individual learners to adjust the way information is presented to suit their particular needs. Control over presentation rate, direction, and continuity seems to offer learners opportunities for dealing with animation's processing challenges. However, despite some encouraging findings (e.g., Gonzales, 1996), the extent to which learners take advantage of these opportunities remains uncertain. Although educator enthusiasm for the potential of user-controllable animation to facilitate learning has led to its rapid adoption, research into how learners actually make use of the available control is lacking. This chapter reports an investigation of learners' interrogations of a user-controllable animation as they undertook a prediction task requiring application of the animation's content.

COMPREHENDING DYNAMICS

A major uncertainty facing developers of multimedia learning materials has been a lack of principled guidance on how the various elements of such materials should be designed in order to facilitate comprehension. This problem is particularly acute in the case of their pictorial elements due to our limited current understanding of the interaction between these external representations and learners' internal representations (Scaife & Rogers, 1996). We also lack a full understanding of how these representations interact with text representations (Schnotz, 2002; Schnotz & Lowe, 2003). It is important to make a clear distinction between pictorial materials themselves and the mental models that learners construct from them. These external and internal representations differ considerably in terms of their level of abstraction, thematic emphasis, and elaboration on the basis of prior knowledge (Schnotz, 2001). The challenges posed in designing educational graphics are compounded when they are required to explain subject matter that is intrinsically dynamic in nature. Narayanan and Hegarty (1998) have developed a five-stage processing model for guiding multimedia design that addresses the issue of dealing with dynamic subject matter. They suggest that people comprehend an external representation of a dynamic system on the basis of a mental model constructed to internally represent its component parts and their relations. The running (mental animation) of this internal model from its initial condition using prior knowledge and spatial visualization processes allows subsequent states of the system to be determined. The quality of predictions made as a result depends on how effectively the mental model used to derive them represents the referent situation. In turn, the utility of this model depends on how successfully the individual viewer carries out various processes involved in mental model construction.

In the first instance, the viewer must extract and internalize those aspects of the external representation that are necessary for constructing an appropriate mental model. According to Narayanan and Hegarty's model, in the case of a graphic representation this requires the portrayal of the system as a whole to be decomposed into constituent entities that correspond to meaningful elements of the domain. Visual properties such as shape, size, and arrangement influence this decomposition in a bottom-up fashion whereas the viewer's goals and prior knowledge about the depicted content exert top-down influence. In all but the simplest of systems, there is embedding of graphic entities within a series of hierarchical levels so that appropriate decomposition may be challenging, especially if these levels are not clearly cued and the viewer lacks relevant prior knowledge. Once the depiction has been correctly decomposed, its constituent entities must be related to one another in an appropriate fashion, either by virtue of their direct connections and contact, or by way of more abstract forms of linkage. Narayanan and Hegarty (2002) have shown with both 'high-tech' and 'low-tech' learning materials that effective explanations of dynamic systems can be designed on the basis of their model.

These authors have also proposed a range of possible comprehension problems associated with animations (c.f. Lowe, 1999). They have particular concerns with the early stages of processing involving the decomposition and relation-building referred to above. The essence of their argument is that certain of animation's distinctive characteristics may make it a far-from-ideal context within which to carry out this preliminary analysis and synthesis. One possibility considered by Narayanan and Hegarty for reducing comprehension problems is that such preliminaries be tackled before viewers are actually presented with the animation itself. Alternatively, the work of Faraday and Sutcliffe (1997) indicates that approaches such as visual highlighting can be effective *within* animations in helping viewers distinguish the various display components. Yet again, the dynamic changes that graphic entities undergo during the course of an animation may themselves act as cues about how the display could be decomposed and how its components could be related to each other. However, with domain novices, this decomposition and relation formation may be carried out inappropriately on the basis of perceptual influences, such as a dynamic field-ground effect (Lowe, 2003), rather on the basis of thematic relevance.

ANIMATION AND PROCESSING

Narayanan and Hegarty suggest that some aspects of the way animations present dynamic information are poorly matched to viewers' processing characteristics and abilities. Three potential sources of such problems they identify relate to how change is depicted:

(i) Concurrency: if the changes are depicted in a behaviorally realistic, concurrent manner that conflicts with the limited, serial way in which people are thought to perform mental animations,

(ii) Speed: if the changes are depicted at a speed that is inconsistent with the capacity of a viewer to perceive and cognitively process task-relevant information,

(iii) Complexity: if the changes involved in a complex system are depicted just as they occur so that the viewer is confused by the myriad of components altering at once.

To ameliorate such mismatch problems, full user-control could be provided over animations; individuals would then have the opportunity to 'tailor' their viewing experience. Being able to replay sections of the animation as well as being able to vary the speed, continuity and direction of play would appear to offer considerable potential advantages over a 'pre-determined' delivery regime. Indeed, Narayanan and Hegarty speculate that such control may ultimately help less informed or less able users to build up an appropriate dynamic mental model in memory. However, an important proviso in educational contexts is that learners who were given such user-control would in fact employ it in effective ways. In order to yield accurate and comprehensive information of high task relevance, this would require a learner's interrogation of the animation to be analytical, thorough, and well targeted.

There seems to be an expectation among many developers of educational materials that the interactivity available with user-controllable animations will lead to learners engaging in a deeper form of processing (c.f. Palmier & Elkerton, 1993). Unfortunately, this expectation may not always be realized in practice. There is evidence to suggest that learners who are novices in a depicted domain may be poorly equipped to carry out effective interrogation of such animations, particularly if the depiction is complex. In previous studies of learners' interrogation of a user-controllable weather map animation, Lowe (2003, 2004) found that novices in the domain of meteorology were unlikely to extract certain higher level relational information necessary for building coherent mental models of meteorological dynamics. Rather, their interrogations appeared to result in a fragmentary understanding of weather map behavior in which the changes in individual meteorological features were largely unconnected with those of their surrounding context. Although there were indications in this research that some deficiencies may have been a result of insufficient interrogation, problems with the specific nature of the interrogations themselves were also implicated.

For user-controllable animations to be effective, learner interrogation needs to target those aspects that are of most relevance to the current learning task. In some ways, this is analogous to the interrogation requirements for learning from static depictions where learners must be able to locate and identify relevant aspects as they explore the picture space. Even with static pictures, this type of strategic exploration may be difficult for those who are domain novices because they lack the specific background knowledge to guide them to relevant material (Winn, 1993). However, these problems are compounded with user-controllable animations because in addition to this search of the *picture* space, learners must also be able to search productively through the *temporal* 'space' constituting the animated sequence. Further, the fugitive nature of the information presented in animations means that there must be far greater reliance on memory when comparisons are required between temporally separated aspects of the content. Animation's transience imposes particular challenges with respect to analytical processes such as those required to decompose the display into appropriate parts prior to mental model construction. When the demands of dealing with highly complex dynamic information are added, it is not entirely surprising that learners had only limited success with the user-controllable weather map animation used in the studies referred to above.

THE STUDY

The present investigation focused on the process by which learners interrogated the user-controllable weather map animation employed in previous studies. As before, their task was to draw a prediction of the meteorological markings expected to appear 24 hours later than those provided on a static Australian summer weather map. In order to draw a prediction of what that original weather map's markings will look like 24 hours afterwards, it could be assumed learners would mentally animate the markings to their new configuration.

Because the participants had no special knowledge of meteorology, any mental model activity they engaged in would have to be based largely upon (a) the original static map and (b) information they extracted from the user-controllable weather map animation. This animated sequence shows a very typical example of how weather maps change during summer. Although this example sequence incorporates information that is highly applicable to the prediction task, it comes from an earlier year than the original and so contains neither that map nor any of its successors. Accordingly, the information that participants would need to extract from the animation in order to build a satisfactory dynamic mental model should be generic rather than specific in nature. Successful performance of the prediction task therefore requires them to determine from the animation the characteristic behaviors of summer weather map markings in general and apply those generalizations to the original's specifics.

The weather map animation used in this study is a potential source of several types of problems identified by Narayanan and Hegarty as likely to prejudice the participants' ultimate building of a satisfactory dynamic mental model. First, it is highly complex in that many components exhibiting a diverse range of changes are presented together throughout the sequence. Second, despite its lack of realism with respect to appearance (i.e., a highly abstract and diagrammatic portrayal of weather phenomena), it presents the *behavior* of meteorological systems in a highly realistic way (i.e., concurrently). Third, there is no provision made for helping learners to carry out the stages of analysis and synthesis that Narayanan and Hegarty suggest are necessary preconditions for building an effective mental model.

The overall aim of this investigation was to explore the potential of user control of itself to ameliorate the processing disadvantages likely to be associated with using animation to learn about a complex dynamic system. It focused upon three main questions:

- To what extent do learners take advantage of an animation's user-control facility?
- What approaches do learners take when interrogating a user-controllable animation?
- How consistent are these approaches with the requirements for building an accurate and comprehensive mental model of a dynamic system?

PROCEDURE

Participants

The 10 randomly selected undergraduate teacher education students who participated in this study had no specialized knowledge of meteorology. Their limited experience of weather maps was typically derived from sources such as high school geography lessons, the newspaper, and television weather reports.

Materials

The computer-based animation consisted of 28 frames depicting the sequence of changes that occurred in an Australian summer weather map across a seven-day period. Control via the mouse allowed the animation to be interrogated in a highly flexible manner. In addition to varying the speed and play direction, participants could pause the animation on any frame or move through it frame by frame in a stepwise fashion. The animation also provided ongoing visual information about the user's current location within the 28 frame sequence and the passage of time (6 hourly intervals).

Two A-4 sized sheets displaying an outline map of the Australian continent were also provided. One of these (the 'Original') also contained the meteorological markings of a typical summer weather map (but not one of those comprising the animated sequence) and was positioned close to the computer screen. The other sheet (the 'Blank') was blank except for the outline map and was fixed to a glass-topped table surmounting a video camera that recorded

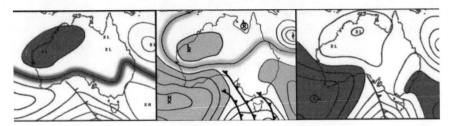

FIGURE 3.1. Early (LHS) and late (RHS) frames from animation compared with markings on original map (middle). Shaded areas indicate features having close correspondence.

the participant's drawing actions. A second video camera recorded the overall situation including the computer screen, two maps, and participant. Camera and animation video streams were combined in real time then recorded to hard disc.

Due to the nature of the task facing subjects in this study, the degree of correspondence between the original map and information contained in the animation is an important consideration. Because of the cyclic nature of weather phenomena, the initial and final portions of the animated sequence both contain frames showing markings that bear quite a close superficial resemblance to those present in the original map. However, neither of these portions corresponds fully with the entire set of original markings. Rather, as shown in Figure 3.1, a different subset of features resembling those in the original is present in each portion. For example, the initial portion of the animation shows an entering High in the south-west and Heat Low in the north-west that both have characteristics somewhat similar to features in the original. However, the gradient shown in this part of the animation between these two features is weaker (fewer isobars) and its retreating south eastern High is very different in location, size, and shape from its counterpart in the original. The correspondence with these features of the original is much closer in the final portion of the animation.

In contrast, there are no comparable obvious similarities between the original and the animation's middle frames. However, the middle portion does contain potentially useful information about such things as the broader scale behavioral characteristics of features, particularly their generic, cyclical patterns of change. It shows the growth then decay of a cyclone and how the changes in markings that occur are always tightly coordinated across the entire map surface. It also contains more specific snippets of useful information, such as a fleeting and somewhat inconspicuous example of a *group* of Cold Fronts moving across the map in concert. This particular episode is relevant to the task faced by subjects in this study because the original map shows a group of three Fronts whereas the instances of frontal movement in the initial and final portions of the animation show only single Fronts.

Method

Participants undertook the investigation task individually. It consisted of a learning phase followed by a test phase. Before being shown the investigation materials, participants were informed that their task was to learn how Australian weather maps change over time so that they could later complete a weather map prediction test. They were told that in this test phase, they would be given a weather map showing the meteorological markings on a particular day (the original) and required to draw on a blank map the pattern of markings they would expect to be present 24 hours later than the original. A learning phase completed beforehand would prepare them for this test. In this preparatory stage, they would carry out the same activity as in the test but with a 'practice' original map that was different from the test original. However, on this practice occasion only, they would have the aid of a weather map animation. It was stressed that because the animation would not be available in the later test phase, participants should use it as effectively as possible with the practice prediction for learning how weather maps change over time. Participants were asked to think aloud as they carried out the learning task and to use gesture to specify any aspects they were referring to during those verbalizations. They were then shown the animation and its controls were demonstrated. After briefly practicing to become fluent in operation of the animation's controls, they then carried out the learning phase of the task. Upon completion of their practice prediction, the animation was removed and the learning phase maps replaced with those for the test phase. Participants then drew their predictions for the new original map.

Data Analysis

This chapter focuses on a subset of data obtained from video recordings of the first phase of the investigation, in particular how each participant explored the animated sequence. Interrogation plots of animation frame visits versus time were analyzed with respect to the direction, scope, and speed of exploration. Each plot was divided into (a) sweeps during which the participant was actively scanning through the animation and (b) pauses during which a single static frame remained in view for more than three seconds. This pause criterion allowed for a lag in participants manipulating the animation's controls in order to change direction. Scanning actions were classified as either forward or reverse sweeps with a new sweep being counted either at a (sustained) change in direction or after a pause. The scope of each sweep was the difference between the starting and ending frame numbers. Four categories of sweep scope were used to summarize individual interrogation episodes; short (7 or fewer frames), medium (8 to 14 frames), long (15 to 21 frames), and extensive (22 or more frames). Sweep speeds were calculated in frames per second and classified as fast (greater than 6 fps), moderate (between 4 and 6 fps), slow (between 2 and 4 fps), and step (less than 2 fps). The threshold set for stepping was determined both by rating of participants' segments by three independent observers and from the lower limit recommended by professional animators to produce an illusion of continuous change. The fast, moderate, and slow speed categories are relative and specific to the context of this study (because animators generally recommended considerably higher frame rates in order to maximize the smoothness and realism). The extent to which sections of the animation were replayed by participants was assessed by determining the number of times they made repeated forward sweeps covering four or more frames. This lower limit was set because smaller sweeps were almost always of very short duration and the result of adjusting the termination points of the sweep.

Results

Overall Approach

Subjects used the animation's controls in a range of ways to interrogate the weather map sequence. The main pattern of exploration consisted of alternating forward and reverse sweeps through the animation that varied in scope and speed. Typically, subjects undertook an extended period of interrogation before starting to draw their predictions of the future weather map pattern. This drawing activity occurred as a series of episodes carried out while the animation was paused, with successive episodes being punctuated by further periods of interrogation. Other pauses in which there was no drawing activity were also distributed across the task period. During these non-drawing pauses, subjects often gestured within and between the original weather map and the animation frame currently displayed on the computer screen, making analytical and comparative comments about the meteorological features shown on the original and animation maps.

Figures 3.2 gives graphical representations of two contrasting interrogation protocols. These examples have similar durations and were chosen to illustrate the considerable variety found in the way subjects employed the animation's user-control facility. Example 'a' begins with a very gradual scan though the whole sequence of 28 frames and a quick return to the start. This is followed (after a brief pause) by another full to-and-fro sweep made far more briskly. After a further short pause, there is a third excursion to the last frame where

Example 'a'

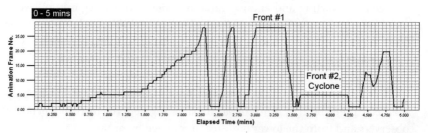

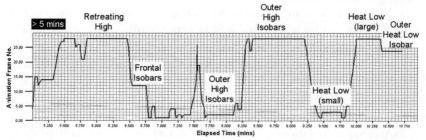

Example 'b'

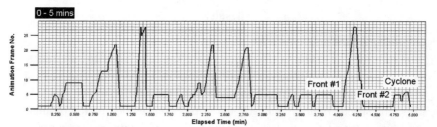

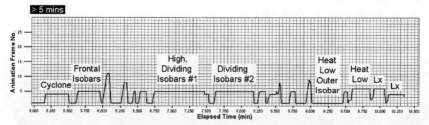

FIGURE 3.2. Two contrasting interrogation protocols showing different subject approaches to exploration of animation.

the animation remains paused for just under half a minute during which the first feature was drawn (Front #1 in this case). The pattern of interrogation that follows then becomes more variable in the scope of each sweep (number of frames covered), the duration of visits to frames, and the temporal region of the animation being explored. This latter section contains both drawing and non-drawing pauses. Moving on to example 'b', a most noticeable difference is the continual preoccupation with just a few frames that are located in the initial portion of the animation. This becomes even more pronounced in the second half of the interrogation. Although two brisk sweeps are made that span all frames from 1 to 28, the final portion of the animation remains relatively neglected compared with example 'a.' This second example also exhibits a more fragmented ('staccato') appearance overall, with many successive to-and-fro sweeps being made over much the same group of frames.

The total time that individual subjects spent working with the animation ranged from 6.94 to 31.98 minutes ($M = 13.93$, $SD = 7.23$). Of this total, subjects spent from 1.18 to 15.89 minutes in active interrogation ($M = 4.56$, $SD = 4.21$) with the animation being paused on a single frame for the remainder of the time. Of this remainder, 1.40 to 10.60 minutes were non-drawing pauses during which there no markings were added to the blank map ($M = 4.67$, $SD = 3.13$) and 2.90 to 7.20 minutes were drawing pauses ($M = 4.71$, $SD = 1.46$) during which one or more markings were produced. It should be noted that the drawing activity itself rarely occupied the entire drawing pause period. Figure 3.3 shows the considerable variation between subjects in how they allocated time while working with the animation. Subjects also varied considerably in how intensively they interrogated the animation during this period. A broad indication of interrogation intensity is given by the overall rate at which each subject visited individual animation frames. Subjects' frame visit rates ranged from 14.8 to 50.4 frames visits per minute ($M = 31.81$, $SD = 11.70$).

Distribution of Visits to Frames
Analysis of the number of visits made to each of the animation's frames revealed differences between subjects in how they distributed their interrogation across the 28 frame sequence. The ratio of the 14 most-frequently visited frames to the 14 least-frequently visited was used as a broad index of how evenly the interrogation was spread across the frame sequence (higher numbers indicating more asymmetrical visit distributions). This ratio ranged from 1.47 to 7.40 ($M = 3.24$, $SD = 1.89$).

The interrogations carried out by individual subjects fell into four main types of distribution pattern, as shown by the illustrative examples in

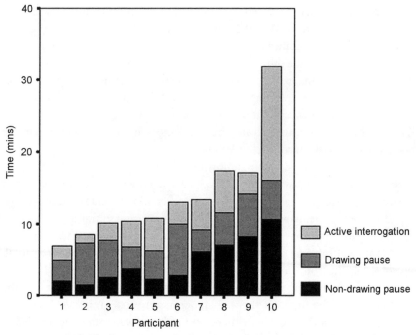

FIGURE 3.3. Individual participants' allocations of time while working with user-controllable animation to draw weather map prediction.

Figure 3.4. The two most common of these (4 subjects each) were (1) a highly asymmetrical pattern in which visits were concentrated around the initial frames of the sequence (as in Figure 3.4a) and (2) a bimodal pattern with visits concentrated at both ends of the sequence (as in Figure 3.4c). For one subject there was an asymmetrical pattern favoring the final frames of the sequence (Figure 3.4b) while the remaining subject distributed interrogation in a more symmetrical manner, spreading visits such that the initial, middle, and final portions of the sequence received similar attention (Figure 3.4d). In summary, apart from this last case, subjects tended to neglect the middle section of the animation while concentrating most of their interrogation activity on one or both of its ends.

Scope of Interrogation

Subjects overall tended to make much more use of small-scale scans comprising just a few frames, than of larger sweeps extending across most or all of the animation sequence. Short scans (66%) exceeded all other scan categories combined. This general trend is summarized in Figure 3.5 and is clearly

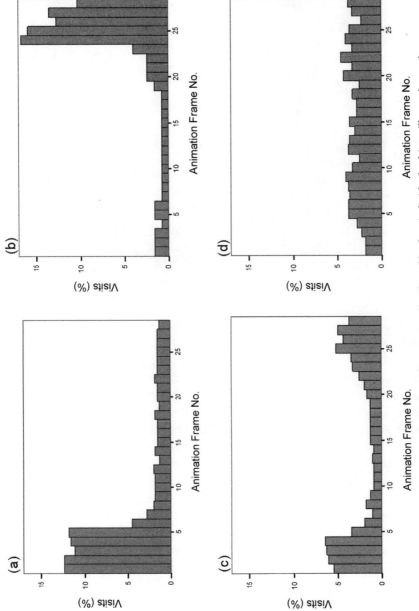

FIGURE 3.4. Examples of how visits to animation frames were distributed by four individual subjects illustrating main patterns of exploration focus: (a) initial (b) final (c) initial+final (d) spread.

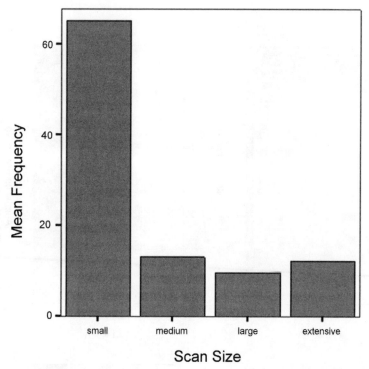

Scan Size

FIGURE 3.5. Frequency with which subjects used scans of different sizes during interrogation of animation.

illustrated in example 'b' of Figure 3.2 where much of the protocol is composed of sweeps encompassing several frames only. The limited scope of these scans approximates the number of frames involved in the passage of a 24-hour period within the animation. There tended to be a concentration of longer scans in the early part of protocols. Video records of subjects' comments suggest that these comprehensive sweeps were being used to 'survey' the animation in order to locate frames showing markings resembling those on the original map. There was little evidence in these records of subjects tracking the behavior of markings across the duration of the animation. Longer scans were thus used more as part of a temporal search process than as a means of establishing the characteristic dynamic changes associated with particular meteorological features over an extended time scale.

Interrogation Speed

Figure 3.6 shows that subjects' interrogations overall were dominated by stepwise and to a lesser extent slow playing of the animation. Nearly half of the interrogation activity across the subject group was carried out step by step,

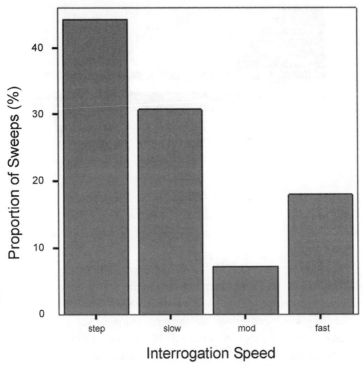

FIGURE 3.6. Overall proportions of different interrogation speeds used when exploring animation.

that is, below the speed required to give the illusion of continuous change. In effect, subjects were slowing the animation to the point where they were looking through a series of separate static frames one by one. These stepwise episodes were predominantly in the forward direction. It should be noted that this result excludes the drawing and non-drawing pauses mentioned above. Although nearly 20% of the sweeps fell into the fast category, most of these were made in the reverse direction and often involved a rapid return of the animation to its beginning. Comparisons using the Wilcoxon Signed Ranks test showed that for most subjects (7 out of 10), there was a significant tendency for the reverse arms of to-and-fro sweeps to be played faster than their partner forward arms. Quite often, these reverse sweeps were made very rapidly indeed with the frames flashing past as little more than a blur.

Replay of Animation Sections
Replays were defined as instances where at least 2 forward sweeps were made through the same section of the animation. The number of different sections replayed per subject ranged from 0 to 13 ($M = 3.7$, $SD = 3.9$). Major trends in

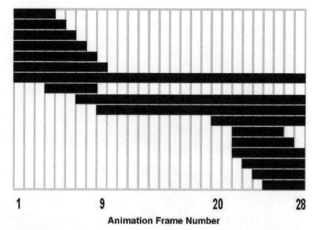

Animation Frame Number

FIGURE 3.7. Shaded frames indicate those sections of the animation that were replayed by at least one subject.

how subjects replayed frames are revealed by splitting the animation sequence into three approximately equal sections. Figure 3.7 shows that much of the replay activity was localized within the first 'third' of the sequence (frames 1–9) where 58% of the replays occurred. All but one of the subjects replayed at least one group of frames lying within this first section. The total number of sweeps per participant confined within that section ranged from 0 to 23 sweeps ($M = 9.6$, $SD = 9.2$.). Figure 3.2b above exemplifies the way many subjects repeatedly returned to replay this early section of the animation while partly or wholly neglecting other sections. The final third of the animation contained 21% of replays whereas no replays were located entirely within its central section. The remaining 21% of replays were long sweeps, mostly through all 28 animation frames.

Discussion

Although all subjects took advantage of the user control facility to some extent, they exploited the range of opportunities it offered in a quite limited fashion. For some subjects, it was clear that the total time spent working with this complex material was simply too short to deal with it adequately. Then there is the question of how subjects spent that time. Apart from the great differences between subjects in how intensely they interrogated the animation, there were important within-subject aspects to consider. Both static and dynamic episodes occurred in subjects' exploration of the animation. However, when the extended static periods (i.e., pauses) and stepwise interrogation are considered together, they account for by far the greater proportion of time spent on the task. In other words, when given the choice, these learners opted to study the animation's information largely in the form of static rather than dynamic pictures. Although some use was made of rapid sweeps through the animation, these tended to be in the reverse rather than the forward direction. Often, the only function they seemed to serve was to return the learner quickly to a particular region of interest within the animation. Upon arrival at such a region, interrogation was most likely to revert to a stepwise approach. The limited usage and restricted purpose of larger sweeps reduced subjects' opportunities for gathering information about important broad scale aspects of weather map change. A predominance of short, slow scans meant that the potential for extended rapid sweeps to reveal higher order temporal structures remained largely unrealized. Further, there was very little evidence that subjects took advantage of the reverse play facility's potential as a powerful additional tool for close analysis of weather map changes.

The approaches learners adopted during their interrogations are consistent with attempts to deal with a mismatch between (1) how this animation presented its information and (2) the learners' own processing capacities. Much of their interrogation appeared to be directed towards making the animation more tractable as a source of information for performing the prediction task. The results suggest that subjects focused upon only one or two features of the weather map at a time and hence restricted themselves to dealing with spatially localized changes that occurred over a 24-hour period. Subjects' verbal and gestural cross-references suggest a major emphasis on locating frames in the animation that showed close superficial correspondence with discrete aspects of the meteorological pattern given in the original map. This is reflected in subjects' asymmetrical interrogation patterns. Most subjects concentrated either on the initial portion or divided the majority of their visits between the initial and final portions. It seems that whereas the former group circumscribed their interrogation somewhat once they discovered useful-looking material in the initial portion, the latter group went on to detect a fresh meteorological cycle containing task-relevant information in the animation's final portion. The comparative neglect of the animation's middle portion by both groups may indicate that subjects were generally unable to appreciate the task relevance of the relational information it contained.

Once subjects found material obviously similar to that in the original, their typical approach was to advance the animation through a 24-hour period in a stepwise fashion to see how it changed. In the latter part of protocols, this was usually followed by drawing of the targeted feature's predicted form and position onto the blank map. This 'piece-by-piece' strategy provided subjects with a mechanical yet systematic way to assemble a prediction. It had the virtue of tackling the very types of problems that Narayanan and Hegarty have identified as possible impediments to processes that are prerequisites for mental model building. Advancing the animation step by step across just a few frames should have helped subjects to deal with its concurrent presentation of complex information. The tendency to favor static rather than dynamic images while working through the animation provides a situation that could support the type of visuospatial analysis required for decomposition of individual frames and appreciation of the more immediate spatial relationships between their component entities. However, this is done at the expense of the higher levels of analysis required to capture broader meteorological patterning, particularly with respect to temporal structure. It might be expected that such patterning would be revealed by repeated playing of sections of the animation, something suggested by Narayanan and Hegarty as a potential benefit of user control. However, by concentrating both their exploration and replays on the ends of the animation while neglecting its middle section, the subjects in this study were looking in the wrong place. It is likely that their lack of background knowledge in the depicted domain led to subjects' search being dominated by the seductive effects of perceptual salience rather than by thematic relevance.

Although the user control facility allowed subjects to customize their learning experiences, their customizations were not always consistent with the requirements for building accurate and comprehensive mental models of weather map dynamics. In general, subjects' limited exploitation of the available interrogation options resulted in insufficient analysis of the animation. As a consequence, there was only partial decomposition of the animated subject matter into its main elements. The piecemeal interrogation was largely focused on discrete meteorological features (Primary features such as Highs, Cyclones, Fronts, and Lows) while neglecting perceptually less-obvious higher order Secondary features (Troughs, ridges, cols) that contribute an organizing function and are essential for cohesion. The absence of these higher order organizing constraints produces inaccuracies in the details of individual Primary features. The accuracy of both the static and dynamic characteristics of these entities is compromised as a result. A mental model constructed on the basis of such faulty and incomplete information would be of limited value for processes such as prediction and inference.

Conclusion

The animation used in this study presents changes concurrently and with no allowance made in its design for the inherent complexity of the subject matter.

Both of these characteristics are identified by Narayanan and Hegarty as likely sources of processing problems. Providing user control does appear to result in learners interrogating animation in ways that attempt to deal with such problems. In this sense, the study provides support for Narayanan and Hegarty's suggestion that user control may be able to ameliorate processing problems associated with animation's distinctive characteristics. However, the findings indicate that for the particular task used here, such amelioration is only partial. It is acknowledged that to some extent, this may be an artefact of the specific materials and procedures used. For example, Schwan and Riempp (2004) found user control of video-based instruction to be effective for relatively straightforward learning tasks of low visual complexity (i.e., knot-tying).

Considering the highly dynamic nature of the content being depicted in this presentation, participants' extensive use of the step facility to isolate individual frames and view them one by one appears to conflict with the intention of providing animated representations. However, this behavior can perhaps be accounted for in terms of the need for extensive analytical work to be carried out in the stages that precede the building of a mental model. This result has resonances with findings about the limited scope and serial nature of the processing involved in mental animation (Hegarty, 1992; Hegarty & Sims, 1994). Taken together with the present findings about subjects' tendency to limit the scope of their scans, it is possible that the animation's controls were being used to coordinate the processes occurring with external and internal representations. It is notable that for much of the interrogation, this meant that subjects were essentially converting an external dynamic representation into a quasi-static form. When given the opportunity, learners took advantage of user control to tailor the presentation in ways that in large part minimize rather than maximize its dynamic character. This direct evidence from learner interrogation further challenges the widespread faith in the superiority of animations over static depictions as a way of portraying dynamic content.

Findings from this study raise questions about the effectiveness of providing animations with user control. They indicate that simply immersing learners in a complex set of dynamic information, even if it does include user control, will not necessarily equip them for building effective dynamic mental models. User control may help to make complex animations more *tractable* but this can be quite different from making the information they contain more *available* to domain novices. In order for the potential of user-controllable animations to be fulfilled, these learners may require additional support within the animation or as a supplement that helps them to take better advantage of the opportunities offered.

References

Bétrancourt, M. & Tversky, B. (2000). Effect of computer animation on users' performance: a review. *Le travail Humain, 63*, 311–330.

Gonzales, C. (1996). Does animation in user interfaces improve decision making? *Proceedings of the International Conference in Computer Human Interaction CHI '96* (pp. 27–34). New York: ACM Press.

Hegarty, M. (1992). Mental animation: Inferring motion from static diagrams of mechanical systems. *Journal of Experimental Psychology: Learning, Memory and Cognition, 18(5)* 1084–1102.

Hegarty, M. & Sims, V. K. (1994). Individual differences in mental animation during mechanical reasoning. *Memory & Cognition, 22*, 411–430.

Kaiser, M. K., Proffitt, D. R., & Whelan, S. (1990). Understanding wheel dynamics. *Cognitive Psychology, 22*, 342–373.

Lowe, R. K. (1999). Extracting information from an animation during complex visual learning. *European Journal of Psychology of Education, 14*, 225–244.

Lowe, R. K. (2003). Animation and learning: Selective processing of information in dynamic graphics. *Learning and Instruction, 13*, 157–176.

Lowe, R. K. (2004). Interrogation of a dynamic visualization during learning. *Learning and Instruction, 14*, 257–274.

Mayer, R. E., & Moreno, R. (2002). Animation as an aid to multimedia learning. *Educational Psychology Review, 14*, 87–99.

Narayanan, N. H. & Hegarty, M. (1998). On designing comprehensible interactive hypermedia manuals. *International Journal of Human-Computer Studies, 48*, 267–301.

Narayanan, N. H. & Hegarty, M. (2002). Multimedia design for communication of dynamic information. *International Journal of Human-Computer Studies, 57*, 279–315.

Palmer, S. & Elkerton, J. (1993). Animated demonstrations for learning procedural computer-based tasks. *Human-Computer Interaction, 8*, 193–216.

Scaife, M., & Rogers, Y. (1996). External cognition: How do graphical representations work? *International Journal of Human-Computer Studies, 45*, 185–213.

Schnotz, W. (2001). Sign systems, technologies, and the acquisition of knowledge. In J.-F. Rouet, J. J. Levonen, & A. Biardeau (Eds.), *Multimedia learning: Cognitive and instructional issues* (pp. 9–29). London: Pergamon.

Schnotz, W. (2002). Towards an integrated view of learning from text and visual displays. *Educational Psychology Review, 14*, 101–120.

Schnotz, W., Böckheler, J., & Grzondziel, H. (1999). Individual and co-operative learning with interactive animated pictures. *European Journal of Psychology of Education, 14*, 245–265.

Schnotz, W. & Lowe, R. K. (2003). External and internal representations in multimedia learning. *Learning and Instruction, 13*, 117–123.

Schwan, S. & Riempp, R. (2004). The cognitive benefits of interactive videos: learning to tie nautical knots. *Learning and Instruction, 14*, 293–305.

Winn, W. D. (1993). An account of how readers search for information in diagrams. *Contemporary Educational Psychology, 18*, 162–185.

SECTION TWO

INDIVIDUAL DIFFERENCES AND STRATEGIES

4

Successful and Less Successful Use of Dynamic Visualizations in Instructional Texts

Rolf Ploetzner, Daniel Bodemer, and Sieglinde Neudert

DYNAMIC VISUALIZATIONS: POTENTIAL FOR LEARNING AND
OBSERVED LEARNING DIFFICULTIES

Computerized learning environments commonly comprise different sources of information such as texts and static and dynamic visualizations, frequently combined with the possibility of modifying them interactively. In this context, visualizations are frequently employed in such a way that they complement the information presented in texts, resulting in a more complete representation of a learning domain. For instance, static and dynamic visualizations may visually explicate spatial and temporal concepts and relations that simply cannot be explicated by texts due to the fundamental differences in the underlying representational systems (cf. Stenning, 1998; Stenning & Oberlander, 1995). Therefore, whenever a learning domain is described by means of spatial and temporal concepts and relations, the presentation of static and dynamic visualizations in instructional texts has the potential to improve learning.

During the last 10 years, however, psychological and educational research has collected extensive evidence that the presentation of static and dynamic visualizations in computerized learning environments might not only not improve learning but even impede learning. Due to their spatial and temporal features, static and dynamic visualizations do not only offer various opportunities for learning but also place specific processing demands on learners. For instance, learners have to process large amounts of information displayed in different regions of the visualization and thus have to simultaneously direct their attention to different sections of the visualization. In addition, as in

The research reported in this paper was supported by the state of Baden-Wuerttemberg within the Virtual University in the Upper Rhine Valley (VIROR, www.viror.de) and by the Deutsche Forschungsgemeinschaft under contract PL 224/7-1. We thank Prof. Dr. Dieter Heuer from the University of Wuerzburg for providing us with the learning environment PAKMA.

dynamic visualizations the displayed information changes over time, it can only be viewed for a limited amount of time (e.g., Lowe, 1999, 2004).

Very often, these processing demands seem to overburden the learners resulting in only little learning. Furthermore, the explication of dynamic processes may even prevent learners from performing cognitive processes relevant to learning (e.g., Schnotz, Böckheler, Grzondziel, Gärtner, & Wächter, 1998). In order to cope with these demands, learners frequently seem to make use of a strategy that limits their processing to certain components of a dynamic visualization. Very often, however, these components are not the most relevant, but the perceptually most compelling ones of the visualization (e.g., Lowe, 1999, 2004).

Learners also frequently seem to not be able to systematically relate the information presented in texts and the information presented in visualizations to each other (e.g., Ainsworth, Bibby, & Wood, 1998, 2002). As a consequence, these learners fail to integrate the different sources of information into coherent mental representations, resulting in fragmentary and disjointed knowledge structures. During problem solving, for example, these learners might switch back and forth between different mental representations of a posed problem, without being able to determine which representation contributes in which ways to the problem's solution (e.g., Anzai, 1991).

The presentation of interactive visualizations in instructional texts frequently aims at inducing constructive learning processes (e.g., Schnotz, 2002; Schnotz & Bannert, 2003). For example, in simulation environments for discovery learning, learners are encouraged to infer an underlying domain model by changing the values of variables and by observing the consequences of these changes in the shown representations (e.g., de Jong & van Joolingen, 1998). However, many learners do not interact with the representations in a structured and goal-oriented way and fail to formulate, test, and evaluate hypotheses systematically.

THE DESIGN OF EXTERNAL REPRESENTATIONS AND THE DESIGN OF LEARNING STRATEGIES: TWO COMPLEMENTARY APPROACHES?

In current research on learning with external representations such as dynamic visualizations the focus is clearly on the design of external representations. For instance, current theories on learning with multiple external representations, such as John Sweller's cognitive load theory (e.g., Sweller, van Marriënboer, & Paas, 1998) and Richard Mayer's theory on multimedia learning (e.g., Mayer,

2001), comprise various assumptions about how learners process information in their memory. Nevertheless, the main focus of these theories is on how to design external representations in which texts, static and dynamic graphics as well as audio is combined in such a way that learners can process them with as little effort as possible (e.g., Chandler & Sweller, 1991; Clark & Mayer, 2003).

A growing body of research, however, indicates that learning success does not only depend on the design of the external representations but also on the strategies the learners apply to the external representations (e.g., Lowe, 2003, 2004; Schnotz et al., 1998; Yeo et al., 2004). It might well be that the learners' external and internal activities that are actually applied to external representations predict learning success even better than the design of external representations does. However, we know only little about how learners could systematically be supported in applying appropriate external and internal activities when learning from dynamic visualizations.

One example in which the design of external representations has been successfully complemented with the design of learning strategies is learning from text. Numerous principles have been identified of how texts are to be designed in order to guide, ease and support students' learning from texts (e.g., Gropper, 1991; Jonassen, 1985). These principles address issues of content as well as issues of structure and layout of texts. However, nobody assumes that texts designed according to these principles ensure students' success in learning from these texts. Instead, from the elementary level to the university level, students are taught reading and learning strategies, which take into account the specific characteristics of texts. These strategies involve internal learning activities such as previewing and formulating questions (e.g., Thomas & Robinson, 1972) as well as external learning activities such as highlighting phrases, taking notes and making drawings (e.g., Leutner & Leopold, 2003). In so doing, after many years of education, students have acquired and exercised a number of internal and external strategies that help them to systematically approach especially complex and difficult texts.

A second example is learning from hypertext. One frequently observed difficulty in learning from hypertext is conceptual disorientation (e.g., Foltz, 1996; Gerdes, 1997). Conceptually disoriented students are no longer able to relate the information provided in one text node to the information provided in other text nodes nor are they able to appreciate what the information provided in a text node contributes to the overall theme of the hypertext. Ploetzner and Härder (2001) were able to demonstrate that students' difficulties in constructing a coherent mental model from hypertext can be significantly reduced when provided with a learning strategy that takes into account the specific characteristics of hypertext.

What makes us assume that students do not need to learn how to learn from dynamic and interactive visualizations? In order to better understand what makes students succeed or fail during learning with dynamic and interactive visualizations in instructional texts, we conducted an empirical study. Two main questions were addressed. First, how much time do students spend on processing dynamic and interactive visualizations in instructional texts during learning and problem-solving? Do less successful learners process visualizations less intensively than successful learners? For instance, Schnotz, Picard, and Hron (1993) investigated learning with text and static visualizations in the domain of geography. They found that less successful learners referred less frequently to the visualizations than successful learners. Second, if students make use of dynamic and interactive visualizations in instructional texts, how do they take advantage of them during learning and problem solving? Do students make use of the visualizations in order to verify their own ideas, to better understand the information provided in the instructional texts, or merely to find solutions to posed problems?

EMPIRICAL STUDY METHOD

Design

Two groups of students were investigated. One group was made up of psychology students in the third semester and the other group was made up of physics students in the first semester. Both groups took advantage of two different computerized learning environments, one about statistics and one about mechanics. With respect to each learning domain, the students processed a pre-test, the textual and graphical learning materials, a set of problems, and a post-test. The psychology students started to work with the learning environment on statistics and – within one week – proceeded to work with the learning environment on mechanics. The physics students dealt with the two learning environments the other way round.

Participants

Overall, nine psychology students in the first semester (eight females and one male) and eight physics students in the third semester (three females and five males) participated in the study. They were paid for their participation.

The data of one psychology student were excluded from the analysis due to technical problems with the recording of data.

Materials and Procedure

With respect to each learning domain, the learning procedure comprised five phases. Phase 2 was only realized once the students had worked on the first learning domain.

Phase 1: Pre-Test
In the first phase, students took a pre-test which was made up of four different types of questions: (1) questions which required the students to transform one textual representation into another textual representation, (2) questions which asked the students to transform a textual representation into a graphical representation, (3) questions which required the students to transform a graphical representation into a textual representation, and (4) questions which asked the students to transform one graphical representation into another graphical representation. Figure 4.1 shows an example of each type of question in the domain of mechanics. The pre-test included two questions of each type.

Phase 2: Exercising to Verbalize One's Own Thoughts
Because students were asked to verbalize their thoughts during problem solving (cf. Chi, 1997; Ericsson & Simon, 1980), in the second phase they first watched a video demonstrating the verbalizations of a person solving a puzzle on the computer. Thereafter, the students exercised thinking aloud while solving a variation of the same puzzle on the computer.

Phase 3: Studying the Instructional Materials
In the third phase, the students had 30 minutes to study the instructional materials on a computer. In both learning domains, the instructional materials consisted of a hypertext and various dynamic and interactive visualizations. In the learning domain of statistics, the instructional materials addressed the principle of least squares in the one-way analysis of variance. The visualizations were taken from the interactive learning environment VISUALSTAT[1] (Ploetzner, Bodemer, & Feuerlein, 2001). Figure 4.2 shows an example of a visualization in VISUALSTAT. In the upper section, examples of pre-defined data sets can interactively be selected on the left-hand side. The selected data sets are displayed in the table on the right-hand side. Alternatively, new data

---

[1]   www.psychologie.uni-freiburg.de/visualstat/

Target representation

Source representation	Textual	Graphical
Textual	A car moves along a straight road for 30 seconds at constant velocity of 20 m/s and then for 48 seconds at 12 m/s. Finally, it moves back at the velocity of -14 m/s to the starting point. How long does it take the car to return?	A hedgehog and a rabbit run a race. The hedgehog runs at constant velocity for 1 minute. The rabbit moves differently. The first 20 seconds it runs at a constant velocity which is higher than the hedgehog's velocity. Then it rests for 20 seconds. After this break, it runs at the same velocity for another 20 seconds. Draw a velocity-time graph of the hedgehog's and the rabbit's motions!
Graphical	The diagram shows a velocity-time graph of a car. What total distance did the car cover? 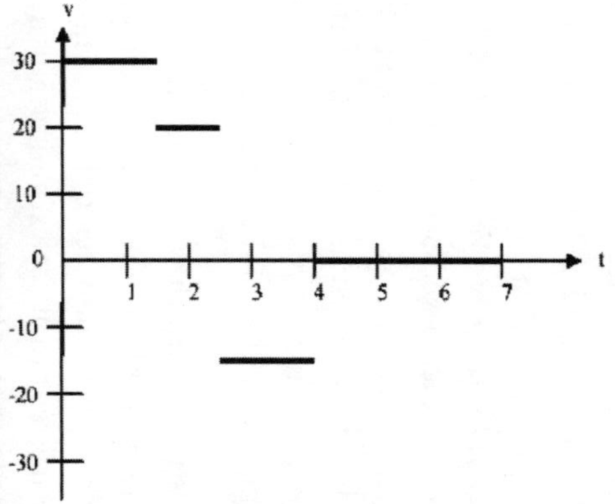	The diagram shows a velocity-time graph. Draw the corresponding position-time graph. Distinguish four time intervals! 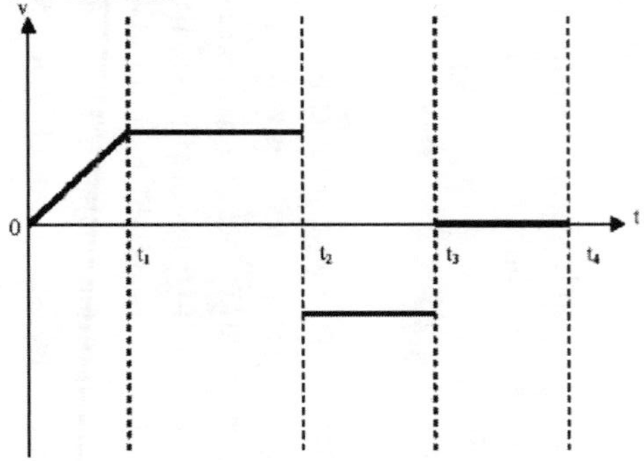

FIGURE 4.1. Examples of pre-test questions in the learning domain of mechanics.

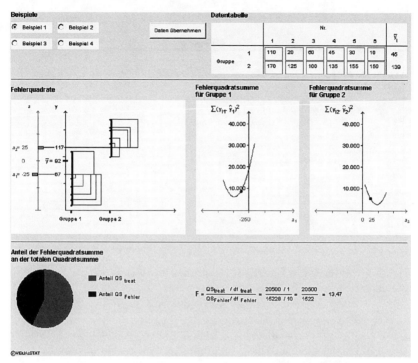

FIGURE 4.2. A dynamic and interactive visualization in statistics addressing the principle of least squares.

sets can interactively be entered into the table by the students. In the middle section, the squared errors in the data are displayed on the left-hand side and the sums of squared errors in the data are displayed on the right-hand side. The estimators a_1 and a_2 on the left-hand side can interactively be changed by the students resulting in different squared errors and sums of squared errors. In the lower section, the sum of squared errors is visually put into relation to the overall sum of squares and the F-value is displayed.

In the learning domain of mechanics, the instructional materials addressed motion in one dimension. The visualizations were taken from the interactive learning environment PAKMA[2] (Blaschke & Heuer, 2000). Figure 4.3 shows an example of a visualization in PAKMA. In the upper section, various buttons allow for initializing a simulation, starting, stopping, and rewinding a simulation run as well as stepping through a simulation run. In the middle section, different parameters relevant to the simulation can interactively be changed.

[2] didaktik.physik.uni-wuerzburg.de

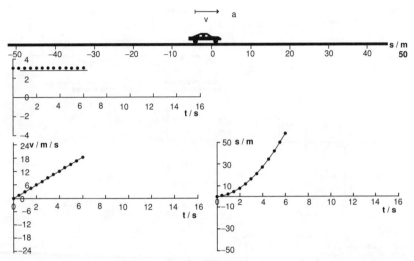

FIGURE 4.3. A dynamic and interactive visualization in mechanics addressing motion in one dimension.

In the example displayed in Figure 4.3, students may change the car's acceleration a and initial speed v_0. Three line graphs are dynamically displayed during the simulation: (1) a time-acceleration graph (middle section, left-hand side), (2) a time-speed graph (lower section, left-hand side), and (3) a time-distance graph (lower section, right-hand side).

Phase 4: Problem-Solving

In the fourth phase, the students had to solve four problems. The first and third problem addressed transformations within textual representations as well as transformations from textual to graphical representations. The second and fourth problem addressed transformations from graphical to textual representations as well as transformations within graphical representations. Each problem was processed in four stages. In the first stage, students were asked to solve the problem as far as possible on the basis of what they had previously learned and without making use of instructional materials. In the second stage, students could take advantage of the instructional materials in order to complete their solution attempts. During the first two stages, the students' verbalizations of their thoughts about their problem-solving attempts as well as their use of the instructional materials were recorded on the computer. In the third stage, students were given feedback on the basis of a complete and correct problem solution. In the fourth stage, students were given the

TABLE 4.1. *Relative Average Solution Frequencies (M) and Standard Deviations (SD) in the Pre- and Post-Test for all Types of Questions in the Learning Domain of Statistics*

Field of Study		Textual-Textual		Textual-Graphical		Graphical-Textual		Graphical-Graphical		Overall	
		Pre	Post	Pre	Post	Pre	Post	Pre	Post	Pre	Post
Physics	M	.50	.53	.00	.64	.17	.65	.00	.57	.17	.60
	SD	.00	.27	.00	.27	.15	.22	.00	.33	.04	.23
Psychology	M	.54	.65	.11	.55	.36	.72	.06	.49	.27	.60
	SD	.13	.19	.22	.16	.18	.16	.11	.30	.08	.15
Overall	M	.52	.60	.06	.59	.27	.69	.03	.53	.22	.60
	SD	.09	.23	.17	.22	.19	.19	.08	.31	.08	.18

opportunity to make use of the instructional materials in order to clarify remaining questions.

Phase 5: Post-Test

Finally, students took a post-test which was made up of the same four types of questions as the pre-test. The post-test included four questions of each type.

RESULTS

Overall Achievement in the Pre- and Post-Test

Whereas Tables 4.1 and 4.2 show the descriptive and inferential statistics in the learning domain of statistics, Tables 4.3 and 4.4 show the descriptive and inferential statistics in the learning domain of mechanics. Figure 4.4 visualizes the relative average solution frequencies in the pre- and post-test across all types of questions in both learning domains.

Surprisingly, after two semesters of statistics, on average the psychology students did not perform significantly better than the physics students in statistics (cf. Field of study in Table 4.2). Obviously, the principle of least squares, which is one of the most important principles in inferential statistics, is difficult to understand even after two semesters of statistics. Nevertheless, across all types of questions, the performances of the psychology students as well as of the physics students increased significantly from the pre- to the post-test in statistics (cf. Learning gain in Table 4.2).

Conversely, in the learning domain of mechanics, on average the physics students exhibited a ceiling effect (cf. Field of study Physics in Table 4.3 and

TABLE 4.2. *The Results of Multivariate (Wilks-Lambda) and Univariate Two-Way Analyses of Variance in the Learning Domain of Statistics*

Source of Variation	Dependent Variable	df	F
Between subjects			
Field of study	Across all types of questions	4, 12	1.28
	textual-textual	1, 15	2.27
	textual-graphical	1, 15	.03
	graphical-textual	1, 15	4.35
	graphical-graphical	1, 15	.02
Within subjects			
Learning gain	Across all types of questions	4, 12	21.41^{**}
	textual-textual	1, 15	1.21
	textual-graphical	1, 15	63.79^{**}
	graphical-textual	1, 15	47.66^{**}
	graphical-graphical	1, 15	49.33^{**}
Learning gain x field of study	Across all types of questions	4, 12	.98
	textual-textual	1, 15	.38
	textual-graphical	1, 15	2.17
	graphical-textual	1, 15	.91
	graphical-graphical	1, 15	.86

Note: $^{*}p < .05, ^{**}p < .01.$

Field of study in Table 4.4). In this case, the various kinematic and dynamic laws that underlie motion in one dimension turned out to be well understood by physics students in the first semester. The psychology students' performance in mechanics increased significantly from the pre- to the post-test across all types of questions (cf. Learning gain in Table 4.4).

TABLE 4.3. *Relative Average Solution Frequencies (M) and Standard Deviations (SD) in the Pre- and Post-Test for all Types of Questions in the Learning Domain of Mechanics*

Field of Study		Textual-Textual		Textual-Graphical		Graphical-Textual		Graphical-Graphical		Overall	
		Pre	Post	Pre	Post	Pre	Post	Pre	Post	Pre	Post
Physics	M	.98	.96	.88	.84	.88	.80	.91	.92	.91	.88
	SD	.04	.09	.08	.14	.23	.12	.17	.11	.09	.08
Psychology	M	.56	.78	.67	.69	.04	.57	.36	.61	.41	.66
	SD	.21	.21	.23	.14	.13	.18	.42	.31	.21	.17
Overall	M	.76	.86	.77	.76	.43	.68	.62	.76	.64	.30
	SD	.27	.04	.20	.16	.46	.19	.42	.28	.77	.17

TABLE 4.4. *The Results of Multivariate (Wilks-Lambda) and Univariate Two-Way Analyses of Variance in the Learning Domain of Mechanics*

Source of Variance	Dependent Variable	df	F
Between subjects			
Field of study	Across all types of questions	4, 12	22.83**
	textual-textual	1, 15	23.17**
	textual-graphical	1, 15	7.89*
	graphical-textual	1, 15	58.46**
	graphical-graphical	1, 15	11.03**
Within subjects			
Learning gain	Across all types of questions	4, 12	7.00**
	textual-textual	1, 15	5.26**
	textual-graphical	1, 15	.05
	graphical-textual	1, 15	26.58**
	graphical-graphical	1, 15	6.13*
Learning gain x field of study	Across all types of questions	4, 12	13.14**
	textual-textual	1, 15	8.04*
	textual-graphical	1, 15	.45
	graphical-textual	1, 15	48.26**
	graphical-graphical	1, 15	4.78*

Note: ** $p < .05$, ** $p < .01$.

In the pre-test the students' performance was best with respect to questions that addressed transformations within textual representations (cf. the different columns in Table 4.1 and Table 4.3). However, with respect to these questions, the students exhibited the smallest learning gains. Inversely, in the pre-test the students' performance was worst with respect to questions that addressed graphical representations (cf. the different columns in Table 4.1 and Table 4.3). However, with respect to these questions, the students achieved significant learning gains. These observations are especially clear with respect to the learning domain of statistics as shown in Figure 4.4.

These observations possibly indicate that the students are more used to interpreting and constructing textual representations than to interpreting and constructing abstract graphical representations. Nevertheless, by taking advantage of the instructional materials during learning and problem solving, the students learned to interpret and construct graphical representations successfully. However, it could be that some students learned much more successfully to make use of graphical representations than others.

The question of what distinguishes successful learners from less successful learners forms the focus of the further analyses. However, because the physics

Application domain statistics

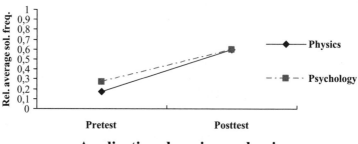

Application domain mechanics

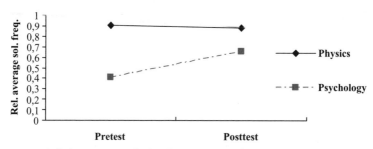

FIGURE 4.4. Relative average solution frequencies in the pre- and post-test across all types of questions in the learning domain of (a) statistics and (b) mechanics.

students exhibited a ceiling effect in the learning domain of mechanics, we restrict the further analyses to the learning domain of statistics.

Differences in Achievement in the Pre- and Post-Test Between Successful and Less Successful Learners

On the basis of their learning gains in the learning domain of statistics, we selected the two most successful psychology students as well as the two most successful physics students. Correspondingly, we selected the two least successful psychology students as well as the two least successful physics students. Table 4.5 shows the relative average solution frequencies and standard deviations in the pre- and post-test for the four students with the most and the four students with the least learning gains. Figure 4.6 visualizes the relative average solution frequencies in the pre- and post-test.

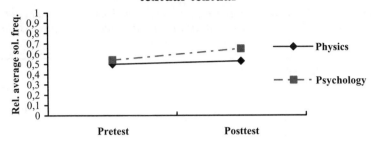

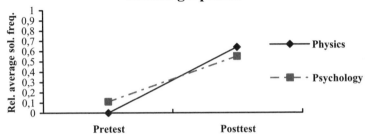

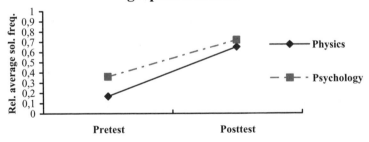

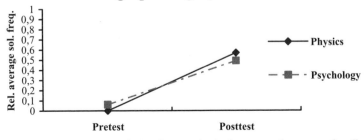

FIGURE 4.5. Relative average solution frequencies in the pre- and post-test for all types of questions in the learning domain of statistics.

TABLE 4.5. *Relative Average Solution Frequencies (M) and Standard Deviations (SD) in the Pre- and Post-Test for the Students with the Most and Least Learning Gains in the Learning Domain of Statistics*

Learning Success		Textual-Textual		Textual-Graphical		Graphical-Textual		Graphical-Graphical		Overall	
		Pre	Post	Pre	Post	Pre	Post	Pre	Post	Pre	Post
High	M	.50	.73	.00	.79	.13	.88	.06	.89	.17	.82
	SD	0	.32	0	.22	.25	.21	.13	.11	.09	.15
Low	M	.59	.41	.13	.31	.28	.58	.00	.33	.25	.41
	SD	.19	.06	.25	.05	.12	.06	0	.12	.06	.01

The successful learners exhibited more learning gains not only with respect to single types of questions but consistently with respect to all types of questions. Except for the questions that addressed transformations within textual representations, the less successful learners also improved moderately from the pre- to the post-test.

Again, in the pre-test the students' performance was best with respect to questions that addressed transformations within textual representations. However, with respect to these questions, the less successful learners' performance even declined and the successful learners' performance rose only slightly. Inversely, the students' performance in the pre-test was worst with respect to questions that addressed graphical representations. However, with respect to these questions, the students achieved notable learning gains. These observations may again indicate that the less successful as well as the successful learners are more used to interpreting and constructing textual representations than to interpreting and constructing abstract graphical representations.

TABLE 4.6. *Average Processing Times (M) in Minutes and Standard Deviations (SD) for the Different Phases of the Learning Procedure*

Learning Success		Studying Instructional Materials: Text	Studying Instructional Materials: Visualizations	Problem-Solving: Without Materials	Problem-Solving: Using Text	Problem-Solving: Using Visualizations
High	M	21:37	07:56	35:00	14:47	20:33
	SD	03:28	02:25	12:43	10:57	11:03
Low	M	20:36	09:13	27:00	21:12	36:46
	SD	03:42	04:32	11:21	17:02	11:54

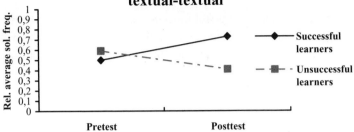

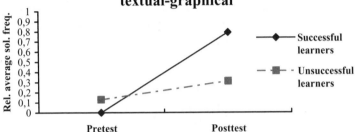

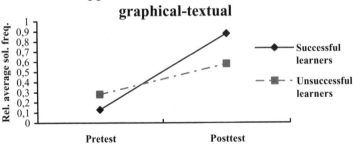

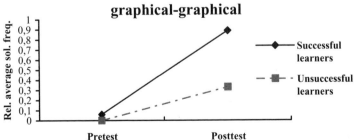

FIGURE 4.6. Relative average solution frequencies in the pre- and post-test for the students with the most and least learning gains in the learning domain of statistics.

Nevertheless, the less successful learners may have processed the instructional materials differently from the successful learners. It could be, for example, that less successful learners spent less time on processing the visualizations than successful learners (cf. Schnotz et al., 1993) or it could be that less successful learners spent as much time on processing the visualizations as successful learners but made use of them in a different way.

Differences in Processing the Instructional Materials Between Successful and Less Successful Learners

Table 4.6 shows the average processing times for the different phases of the learning procedure. Because the time for processing the instructional materials was limited to 30 minutes, on average the less successful learners as well as the successful learners took equal advantage of the time provided. Furthermore, while studying the instructional materials (cf. Phase 3), less successful learners as well as successful learners spent about two thirds of the time on studying the learning text and one third on studying the visualizations.

The first important difference between less successful learners and successful learners is that during the first stage of problem solving, the less successful learners spent 23% less time on trying to solve the problems on their own without making use of the instructional materials than the successful learners. Whereas the less successful learners processed only 63% of the various (sub-) problems, the successful learners processed 89% of the (sub-) problems.

The second important difference between less successful learners and successful learners is that during the second stage of problem solving, the less successful learners spent 45% more time on making use of the instructional text and 80% more time on making use of the visualizations than the successful learners. Furthermore, after the less successful learners took advantage of the instructional materials during problem solving, they solved 63% of the different (sub-) problems correctly. The successful learners, in contrast, solved 88% of the different (sub-) problems correctly.

It could well be that the use of visualizations did not facilitate but impede learning. If this was the case, the students who spent more time on processing the visualizations are probably the students who exhibited smaller learning gains. An informal analysis of the verbal protocols and action protocols taken during problem-solving, however, revealed that the less successful learners and the successful learners adopted completely different strategies during learning.

It appears that the less successful learners adopted the following strategy: As soon as they faced difficulties during problem solving they went back to the instructional materials. When making use of the interactive and dynamic visualizations, they attempted, more or less by trial and error, to interactively set up visual configurations that were as close as possible to the visual configurations given in the problem descriptions. Apparently, the less successful learners hoped that they would be able to read something out of the visual configurations that would provide the solutions to the problems.

The successful learners, in contrast, seem to have adopted a completely different strategy. In a first step, they attempted to solve a problem as far as possible. As they knew that they could go back to the instructional materials later on, they sometimes even proposed solutions while being aware that they were not necessarily correct. In a second step, they took advantage of the instructional texts and visualizations in order to evaluate their solution attempts, modify and complete their solution attempts, and clarify questions that were raised during problem solving.

DISCUSSION

Obviously, in the learning and problem-solving setting described in this chapter, less successful learners did not spend less time on processing the dynamic visualizations than the successful learners did. In contrast, less successful learners spent a considerably larger amount of time making use of the visualizations than the successful learners did. In this respect, the observations made in this study differ from the observations made by Schnotz et al. (1993) who investigated learning with texts and static visualizations. The less successful learners as well as the successful learners were probably aware of the fact that the information included in the visualizations was important to their problem-solving success.

However, while processing the different problems, the less successful learners adopted a strategy that was completely different from the strategy adopted by the successful learners. The observations made in this study indicate that the less successful learners were not willing to invest the same amount of mental effort (cf. Salomon, 1983) during problem solving as the successful learners. Whereas the successful learners made use of the dynamic visualizations in a very structured and goal-oriented way, the less successful learners employed them with only little understanding of what the visualizations represent. It appears that with respect to the successful learners the interaction with the dynamic visualizations was a method for learning. In contrast, with respect to the less successful learners the interaction with the dynamic visualizations was something like a weak problem-solving method.

Recently, similar observations have been made by Yeo, Loss, Zadnik, Harrison, and Treagust (2004). They investigated how students interact with and learn from multimedia presentations in physics. Yeo et al. (2004) also found that very often students interact superficially with multimedia presentations. They noticed that many students fell " . . . into a pattern of action/response which seemed almost automatic, carried out as if to complete a task rather than to learn from it" (Yeo et al., 2004, p. 1354).

Various prominent theories on learning with multiple external representations, such as John Sweller's cognitive load theory (e.g., Sweller, van Marriënboer, & Paas, 1998) and Richard Mayer's theory on multimedia learning (e.g., Mayer, 2001), focus on how to design external representations in such a way that learners can process them with as little effort as possible (e.g., Chandler & Sweller, 1991; Clark & Mayer, 2003). A growing body of research, however, indicates that the design of external representations is only one side of the coin. The other side of the coin consists of the external and internal learning activities, which the learners actually apply to the external representations (e.g., Lowe, 2003, 2004; Schnotz et al., 1998; Yeo et al., 2004). For instance, in order to improve the less successful learners' use of dynamic visualizations during learning and problem solving, these learners possibly need to learn how to identify and analyze the relevant components of dynamic visualizations. Less successful learners might also need to learn how to relate the information presented in dynamic visualizations to other sources of information such as instructional texts.

Bodemer, Ploetzner, Feuerlein, and Spada (2004) encouraged learners to systematically and interactively integrate different representations in the external environment. Learners were provided with spatially separated pictorial and symbolic representations on the screen and were asked to relate components of familiar representations to components of unfamiliar representations by drag and drop. This external process corresponds to the mental process of structure mapping as described by Gentner (1983; Gentner & Markman, 1997) and Schnotz and Bannert (2003). Whereas the (inter-) active relation of different external representations is intended to directly support coherence formation, the simultaneous construction of an integrated format is supposed to gradually reduce unnecessary cognitive load (e.g., Chandler & Sweller, 1991, 1992). Bodemer et al. (2004) were able to demonstrate that – compared to the presentation of information in a pre-integrated or in a split-source format – learning outcomes can be improved significantly when learners actively integrate static information before interacting with dynamic visualizations (cf. also Bodemer, Ploetzner, Bruchmüller, & Häcker, 2005).

During the last 10 years, psychological and educational research has identified various problems learners face when learning with dynamic and interactive visualizations. We now need to not only develop guidelines for the external design of dynamic visualizations but also for learning strategies made up of external as well as internal activities that we can teach to learners and that help them to successfully process the information presented in dynamic and interactive visualizations.

References

Ainsworth, S., Bibby, P. A., & Wood, D. J. (1998). Analysing the costs and benefits of multi-representational learning environments. In M. W. van Someren, P. Reimann, H. P. A. Boshuizen & T. de Jong (Eds.), *Learning with multiple representations* (pp. 120–134). Amsterdam: Pergamon Press.

Ainsworth, S., Bibby, P. A., & Wood, D. J. (2002). Examining the effects of different multiple representational systems in learning primary mathematics. *The Journal of the Learning Sciences, 11*(1), 25–61.

Anzai, Y. (1991). Learning and use of representations for physics expertise. In K. A. Ericsson & J. Smith (Eds.), Toward a general theory of expertise – Prospects and limits (pp. 64–92). New York: Cambridge University Press.

Blaschke, K. & Heuer, D. (2000). Dynamik-Lernen mit multimedial-experimentell unterstütztem Werkstatt-Unterricht [Learning dynamics in multimedia projects]. *Physik in der Schule, 38*(2), 1–6.

Bodemer, D., Ploetzner, R., Bruchmüller, K., & Häcker, S. (2005). Supporting learning with interactive multimedia through active integration of representations. *Instructional Science, 33*, 73–95.

Bodemer, D., Ploetzner, R., Feuerlein, I., & Spada, H. (2004). The active integration of information during learning with dynamic and interactive visualisations. *Learning and Instruction, 14*(3), 325–341.

Chandler, P. & Sweller, J. (1991). Cognitive load theory and the format of instruction. *Cognition and Instruction, 8*(4), 293–332.

Chandler, P. & Sweller, J. (1992). The split-attention effect as a factor in the design of instruction. *British Journal of Educational Psychology, 62*, 233–246.

Chi, M. T. H. (1997). Quantifying qualitative analyses of verbal data: A practical guide. *Journal of the Learning Sciences, 6*(3), 271–315.

Clark, R. C. & Mayer, R. E. (2003). E-Learning and the science of instruction. San Francisco, CA: Pfeiffer.

de Jong, T. & van Joolingen, W. R. (1998). Scientific discovery learning with computer simulations of conceptual domains. *Review of Educational Research, 68*(2), 179–201.

Ericsson, K. A. & Simon, H. A. (1980). Verbal reports as data. *Psychological Review, 87*(3), 215–251.

Foltz, P. W. (1996). Comprehension, coherence, and strategies in hypertext and linear text. In J.-F. Rouet, J. J. Levonen, A. Dillon & R. J. Spiro (Eds.), *Hypertext and cognition* (pp. 109–136). Mahwah, NJ: Lawrence Erlbaum Associates.

Gentner, D. (1983). Structure-mapping: A theoretical framework for analogy. *Cognitive Science, 7*, 155–170.

Gentner, D. & Markman, A. B. (1997). Structure mapping in analogy and similarity. *American Psychologist, 52*(1), 45–56.

Gerdes, H. (1997). *Lernen mit Text und Hypertext [Learning with text and hypertext]*. Lengerich: Pabst Verlag.

Gropper, G. L. (1991). *Text displays – Analysis and systematic design*. Englewood Cliffs, NJ: Educational Technology Publications.

Jonassen, D. H. (Ed.). (1985). *The technology of text – Principles for structuring, designing, and displaying Text*. Englewood Cliffs, NJ: Educational Technology Publications.

Leutner, D. & Leopold, C. (2003). Selbstreguliertes Lernen als Selbstregulation von Lernstrategien – Ein Trainingsexperiment mit Berufstätigen zum Lernen aus Sachtexten [Self-regulated learning as self-regulation of learning strategies – A training experiment on learning from texts]. *Unterrichtswissenschaft, 31*(1), 38–56.

Lowe, R. K. (1999). Extracting information from an animation during complex visual learning. *European Journal of Psychology of Education, 14*(2), 225–244.

Lowe, R. K. (2003). Animation and learning: Selective processing of information in dynamic graphics. *Learning and Instruction, 13*(2), 157–176.

Lowe, R. K. (2004). Interrogation of a dynamic visualisation during learning. *Learning and Instruction, 14*(3), 257–274.

Mayer, R. E. (2001). *Multimedia learning*. New York: Cambridge University Press.

Ploetzner, R., Bodemer, D., & Feuerlein, I. (2001). Facilitating the mental integration of multiple sources of information in multimedia learning environments. In C. Montgomerie & J. Viteli (Eds.), Proceedings of the World Conference on Educational Multimedia, Hypermedia & Telecommunications (pp. 1501–1506). Norfolk, VA: Association for the Advancement of Computing in Education.

Ploetzner, R. & Härder, J. (2001). Unterstützung der Verarbeitung externer Repräsentationen am Beispiel des Lernens mit Hypertexten [Supporting the processing of external representations – Learning from hypertexts]. *Unterrichtswissenschaft, 29*(4), 367–384.

Salomon, G. (1983). The differential investment of mental effort in learning from different sources. *Educational Psychologist, 18*(1), 42–50.

Schnotz, W. (2002). Towards an integrated view of learning from text and visual displays. *Educational Psychology Review, 14*(1), 101–120.

Schnotz, W. & Bannert, M. (2003). Construction and interference in learning from multiple representations. *Learning and Instruction, 13*(2), 141–156.

Schnotz, W., Böckheler, J., Grzondziel, H., Gärtner, I., & Wächter, M. (1998). Individuelles und kooperatives Lernen mit interaktiven animierten Bildern [Individual and cooperative learning with interactive animated pictures]. *Zeitschrift für Pädagogische Psychologie, 12*(2/3), 135–145.

Schnotz, W., Picard, E., & Hron, A. (1993). How do successful and unsuccessful learners use text and graphics? *Learning and Instruction, 3*, 181–199.

Stenning, K. (1998). Representation and conceptualisation in educational communication. In M. W. van Someren, P. Reimann, H. P. A. Boshuizen & T. de Jong (Eds.), *Learning with multiple representations* (pp. 320–333). Amsterdam: Pergamon Press.

Stenning, K. & Oberlander, J. (1995). A cognitive theory of graphical and linguistic reasoning: Logic and implementation. *Cognitive Science, 19*(97–140).

Sweller, J., van Merriënboer, J. J. G., & Paas, F. G. W. C. (1998). Cognitive architecture and instructional design. *Educational Psychology Review, 10*(3), 251–296.

Thomas, E. L. & Robinson, H. A. (1972). Improving reading in every class: A source-book for teachers. Boston, MA: Allyn & Bacon.

Yeo, S., Loss, R., Zadnik, M., Harrison, A., & Treagust, D. (2004). What do students really learn from interactive multimedia? A physics case study. *American Journal of Physics, 72*(10), 1351–1358.

5

Functions of Animations in Comprehension and Learning

Wolfgang Schnotz and Thorsten Rasch

INTRODUCTION

Animations are frequently used in today's multimedia learning environment. Animated displays of information are assumed to be more attractive and inherently instructionally superior to static displays. Although any visual element displayed on a computer screen can be animated, the most frequent use of animation deals with animated pictures. Animated pictures can be used to support 3D perception by showing an object from varying perspectives. They can also direct the observer's attention to important (or unimportant) aspects of a display, convey procedural knowledge (e.g., in software training), demonstrate the dynamics of subject matter, and allow exploratory learning through manipulating a displayed object. Furthermore, animations can have a supplantation effect (Salomon, 1994) by which they help learners to perform a cognitive process that they could not otherwise perform without this external support. Despite the widespread belief in the instructional power of animation, the chapters of this book demonstrate that animation is not always beneficial for learning and that animated pictures can have different functions under different conditions.

In this chapter, we will analyze different functions of animation in comprehension and learning from the perspective of cognitive load theory. First, we will briefly describe the role of working memory in learning from animation. We will show that different kinds of animations can impose different kinds of cognitive load on the learner's working memory. Second, we will argue that animation can have two basic functions in supporting comprehension and learning, depending on the learner's level of expertise in the corresponding knowledge domain: an enabling function and a facilitating function. Third, we will compare static and animated pictures on the basis of an empirical study that focused on these different functions of static and animated displays. Fourth we will extend this analysis by a further study that analyzed these effects more closely for different kinds of animations. Based on the results of these studies, we will fifth relate the concept of cognitive load within the framework of Vygotski's zone of proximal development. Sixth, we will reconsider the cognitive load of animation within this framework, and finally draw some theoretical and practical conclusions on learning from animations.

COGNITIVE LOAD IN LEARNING FROM ANIMATION

A basic assumption underlying recent models of multimedia learning is that human cognitive architecture includes different subsystems: various sensory registers, a working memory and a long-term memory (cf. Atkinson & Shiffrin, 1971; Baddeley, 1986; Mayer, 2001, 2005; Mayer & Moreno, 1998; Schnotz, 2005; Schnotz & Bannert, 2003). According to these models, information from the environment enters the cognitive system via sensory organs (e.g., the ear, the eye etc.) and is briefly stored in a sensory register (e.g., the auditory register, the visual register, etc.). Information is then transmitted through different sensory channels from the sensory registers to working memory, where it is further processed together with information from long-term memory (i.e., prior knowledge) to construct different kinds of mental representations such as propositional representations and mental models. The processes of constructing these mental representations in working memory are referred to as comprehension. When comprehension and other kinds of cognitive processing lead to changes in long-term memory, these changes are referred to as learning. A bottleneck in processing information from the environment is the human working memory due to its limited capacity of information storage and processing (Baddeley, 1986, 2000). All kinds of information processing impose, if the information originates from the outside world, a cognitive load on working memory. Because working memory capacity is limited, this cognitive load has to be adapted to the available capacity (Chandler & Sweller, 1991; Sweller, 1999; Sweller & Chandler, 1994). According to Sweller, van Merriënboer, and Paas (1998), different kinds of cognitive load can be distinguished: intrinsic load, extraneous load, and germane load.

The *intrinsic load* is determined by the complexity of the instructional content or the task to be performed relative to the degree of expertise of the learner. The complexity of the instructional content or task is a function of the element interactivity. Any interactions between elements to be held in working memory require working memory capacity. Intrinsic cognitive load therefore corresponds to the number of related elements to be held and coordinated simultaneously in working memory. With a specific learning task in a specific learning situation, the intrinsic load cannot be manipulated.

In contrast, the *extraneous load* is determined by the instructional format rather than the nature of the content. More specifically, it is generated by an inappropriate instructional format; by the way the information is structured and presented to the learner. Extraneous load reflects the effort to process poorly designed instruction. When load can be reduced without changing the task, then the load is extrinsic. Accordingly, instructional design should aim to decrease extraneous cognitive load.

The *germane load* reflects the effort of detecting relevant regularities and of forming appropriate schemata during the process of learning. Individuals can and should be encouraged to engage in cognitive processing that facilitates schema construction and increases the learners' level of expertise. Appropriate instructional design should therefore direct the learner's resources to processes that are germane to the task of constructing schemata. In contrast to extraneous load, germane load should not be reduced, but rather increased provided that the total cognitive load stays within the limits of working memory capacity (Paas & van Merriënboer, 1994).

ENABLING FUNCTIONS AND FACILITATING FUNCTIONS OF ANIMATIONS IN LEARNING

We assume that animations can have different functions regarding the cognitive load on working memory: an enabling function and a facilitating function. The enabling function means that due to a reduction of cognitive load, processes become possible which otherwise would have remained impossible. The facilitating function means that due to a reduction of cognitive load, processes that were already possible but only with a great deal of mental effort, become possible with less effort. Both the enabling function (impossible processes become possible) of multimedia and the facilitating function (possible difficult processes become easier) of multimedia result from a reduction of cognitive load (cf. Mayer, 2001; Sweller & Chandler, 1994; Sweller, van Merriënboer, & Paas, 1998).

For example, when students learn about time phenomena related to the earth's rotation, animated pictures like those in Figures 5.1 and 5.2 can be useful. In these figures, the earth is depicted as a sphere viewed from the North Pole that rotates in a space where different locations are associated with different time states. The picture shown in Figure 5.1 can be manipulated by the learner to define specific times of day for specific cities. After clicking on the OK button, the earth moves into the corresponding time state. This type

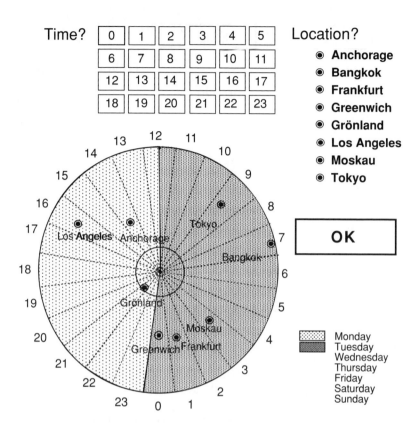

FIGURE 5.1. Example of a manipulation picture that can be used to explore the depicted subject matter. Earth time zones are shown as seen from the North Pole. Learners can select different times of the day for different cities and turn the earth to the corresponding position.

of picture will be termed a manipulation picture. Because a manipulation picture enables learners to investigate many different time states (something that would not be possible on the basis of a static picture), such a picture is assumed to have an enabling function.

The picture shown in Figure 5.2 can be used to simulate the earth's rotation. The learner can choose different ways in which a traveler can circumnavigate the earth (symbolized by a black dot moving in Western or Eastern direction with different speeds depending on the learner's choice). After pressing the SIMULATION button, the earth starts rotating and the traveler's dot starts moving on the rotating earth. This type of picture will be termed a simulation picture. It is likely to be much easier for a student to observe the rotation of the earth and the movement of an object in a simulation picture than to

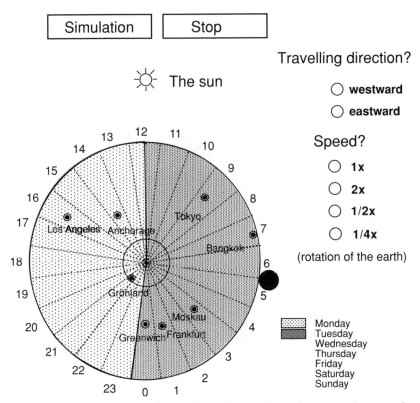

FIGURE 5.2. Example of a simulation picture that can be used as external support for mental simulations. Earth time zones are shown as seen from the North Pole. Learners can select among different kinds of circumnavigations of a traveller (symbolized by a black dot) around the world and observe the earth's rotation plus the circumnavigation.

perform the corresponding mental simulations on his/her own with only a static picture (Forbus, Nielsen, & Faltings, 1991; Lowe, 1999, 2003, 2004; Sims & Hegarty, 1997). If so, such a picture is assumed to have a facilitation function.

STATIC VERSUS ANIMATED PICTURES

In a study on learning from animation from a cognitive perspective, we compared learning from animated (manipulation and simulation) pictures and learning from static pictures (Schnotz & Rasch, 2005). The rationale for this study was as follows. If animated pictures *enable* the learner to perform additional cognitive processing, the learner's total amount of processing should increase. As additional processing needs additional time, the enabling function of animations should lead to an increase of learning time compared to the corresponding static pictures. The enabling function is expected to be more pronounced when individuals have high learning prerequisites (high cognitive ability and high prior knowledge) because these learners will be able to use the possibilities of animations more extensively than individuals with low learning prerequisites (cf. Kirby, 1993; Lanca & Kirby, 1995). If animated pictures *facilitate* cognitive processing, the learner needs less effort with animated pictures than with static ones, because the animation reduces cognitive load to a degree that is easier to cope with. Thus, if the facilitating function of animations applies, learners will invest less learning time for animated pictures than for corresponding static pictures. The facilitating function is expected to be more pronounced when learners have low prerequisites because these individuals need more external support than learners with high prerequisites.

If animated pictures enable individuals with high learning prerequisites to do additional cognitive processing, these learners will spend more time observing animated pictures than static pictures. If animated pictures facilitate processing for individuals with low learning prerequisites, these learners will spend less time observing animated pictures than static pictures. Following this line of reasoning, one can assume an interaction between learning prerequisites (high/low) and type of pictures (animated/static) on learning time.

Forty university students participated in the study and were tested for their prior knowledge about the topic and for their intelligence. Both variables were combined into a joint variable of learning prerequisites. Then, the students received a hypertext about time and date differences on the earth presented with static pictures or with animated pictures. After the learning phase, the participants completed a comprehension test, which consisted of 12 items referring to time differences between different places on the earth (e.g., *What is the time in Anchorage, if it is Thursday 9 o'clock p.m. in Tokyo?*) and 12 items which referred to time phenomena related to circumnavigations of the world (e.g., *Why did Magellan's companions think, upon their arrival after sailing around the world, that it was Wednesday when it was actually already Thursday?*).

The results of this study are presented in Figure 5.3a–c: Figure 5.3a shows the picture observation times for participants with either low or high prerequisites when learning from static or from animated pictures. An ANOVA indicated a significant interaction *Picture Type x Learning Prerequisites* ($F(1,36) = 3.171, p = .042$). Students with high learning prerequisites spent more time for animated pictures than for static pictures. However, students with low learning

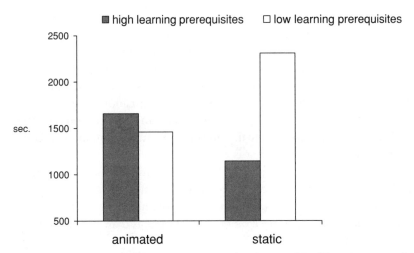

FIGURE 5.3a. Average picture observation times of students with high learning prerequisites and students with low learning prerequisites during learning from animated pictures and learning from static pictures.

prerequisites spent less time for animated pictures than for static pictures. Thus, the results supported the assumption that the enabling function of animations applies to students with higher learning prerequisites, whereas the facilitating function applies to students with lower learning prerequisites.

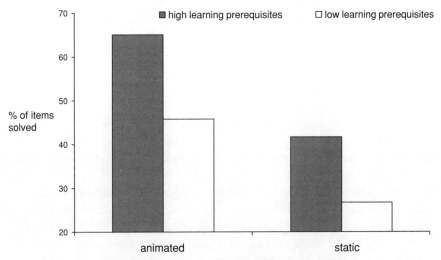

FIGURE 5.3b. Average performance of students with high learning prerequisites and students with low learning prerequisites in answering time difference questions after learning from animated pictures and after learning from static pictures.

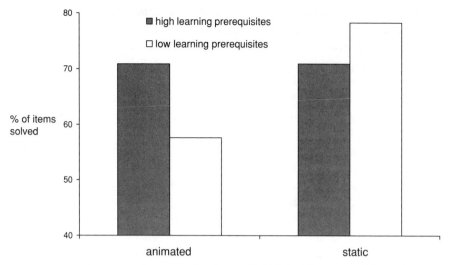

FIGURE 5.3C. Average performance of students with high learning prerequisites and students with low learning prerequisites in answering circumnavigation questions after learning from animated pictures and after learning from static pictures.

Figure 5.3b shows how well the participants answered the time-difference questions. An ANOVA revealed a highly significant effect of picture type ($F(1,36) = 8.553$, $p = .003$), but no interaction effect. Students with animated pictures outperformed students with static pictures in answering time difference questions. Figure 5.3c shows the students' performance with the circumnavigation questions. This pattern of results was totally different from the previous pattern with neither a significant main effect nor a significant interaction effect. However, students with low learning prerequisites answered circumnavigation questions significantly better after learning with static pictures than after animated ones ($t(13.5) = 2.380$, $p = .033$). Animated pictures did not have positive effects on answering these questions, but were harmful when students had lower learning prerequisites.

To summarize, for individuals with high prerequisites, animations seemed to have an enabling rather than a facilitating function. For individuals with low learning prerequisites, animations seem to have a facilitating rather than an enabling function. Findings concerning the answering of time-difference questions supported the assumption that animations result in better learning due to their enabling or facilitating function. However, findings concerning answering circumnavigation questions did not support this assumption. Learners with high learning prerequisites did not profit from the animations, and learners with low learning prerequisites surprisingly performed even better with static pictures than with animated ones.

In order to understand this unexpected divergence between time-difference and circumnavigation scores, it is helpful to analyze the cognitive processes required by the corresponding test items more closely. Answering time difference items requires knowledge about time coordinates of various cities around the world and the time differences between them. Manipulation pictures such as shown in Figure 5.1 can be used to display many different time states, which should be a good basis for extracting information about time differences. Thus, the superior performance of the animation group in answering time difference questions may be a result of the enabling function of the animation.

Answering circumnavigation questions requires mental simulations. Simulation pictures such as displayed in Figure 5.2 provide external support for such simulations. Possibly, this function is beneficial for learning if the individual lacks the abilities to perform a mental simulation on his/her own (Salomon, 1994; Sweller & Chandler, 1994). One explanation for the results obtained in this study is that facilitation can also have a negative effect on learning. If individuals are perfectly capable of performing such mental simulations by themselves, external support can lead to a decrease in productive processing. Accordingly, students invest less cognitive effort in learning from animation than when learning from static pictures. From the perspective of cognitive load theory, animation can unnecessarily reduce cognitive load associated with deeper meaningful cognitive processing. Most students obviously had sufficient skills for mental simulations without external support, but students with lower cognitive prerequisites were apt to accept unneeded external support.

Animations appear capable of having different effects for different tasks. Because the manipulation pictures seem to allow a more elaborated analysis of time differences, their enabling function results in better performance with time difference questions. Simulation pictures, on the contrary, seem to make mental simulations easier, but this facilitating function may be harmful for learning. In this case, animation has an inhibiting effect on learning due to an inappropriate reduction of cognitive load.

EFFECTS OF DIFFERENT KINDS OF ANIMATIONS

In a second study, we analyzed the effects of different kinds of animations (cf. Schnotz & Rasch, 2005). Based on our previous investigation, we assumed that the primary effect of manipulation pictures would be an enabling function (especially important for time-difference questions), in contrast, simulation pictures would primarily have a facilitating function (especially important for circumnavigation questions). Although the manipulation pictures used in study 2 were the same as those in study 1, the simulation pictures of study 2 were somewhat different. In study 1 we had used only one kind of simulation pictures but in study 2, we used two kinds. Simulation pictures that were the same as in the first study showed the earth's rotation as a continuous movement once the learner had clicked on the SIMULATION-button (see Figure 5.2). We will now call these pictures 'continuous simulation pictures.' The other kind of simulation pictures allowed only a stepwise, incremental simulation of the earth rotation by substituting a STEPWISE-button for the SIMULATION-button. Every click on the STEPWISE-button caused an incremental (counter-clockwise) rotation of the earth's picture by 3 degrees. The learner could rotate the earth by repeated clicking on the STEPWISE button. Without any click, the picture remained static. We will call these 'stepwise simulation pictures.'

As in the first study, we expected manipulation pictures to have primarily an enabling function. Because they allow a more elaborated analysis of time differences, they should therefore result in better performance with time difference questions. Accordingly, we expected students with manipulation pictures to perform better on time difference questions than students with either continuous simulation pictures or stepwise simulation pictures. Based on the results of the first study, we expected continuous simulation pictures to have primarily a facilitating function, however, with a negative effect on learning due to an inappropriate reduction of cognitive load. We therefore expected lower performance from students with continuous simulation pictures on circumnavigation questions than from students with manipulation pictures.

With regard to the stepwise simulation pictures, we had less specific expectations. These pictures combined features of a static picture with features of a continuous simulation picture: When the learner did not click on the STEPWISE-button, the picture was static. When the learner clicked on the button, the picture became animated and displayed some limited rotation of the earth according to the amount of the learner's activity. The stepwise simulation pictures therefore showed a less explicit depiction of the earth's rotation than the continuous simulation pictures. Consequently, the stepwise simulation pictures should provide less facilitation and more possibilities for learners to engage in their own, self-directed mental simulation than would continuous simulation pictures. Further, the learners could control the display of stepwise simulation pictures. If they wished to analyze a specific configuration more closely, they could stop clicking and investigate the present state for as long as they liked. This opportunity was not available for the continuous simulation pictures due to their fluent nature. In other words, the stepwise simulation pictures provided less facilitation, but provided a better basis for a conceptual analysis of the earth's rotation. They also allowed learners to

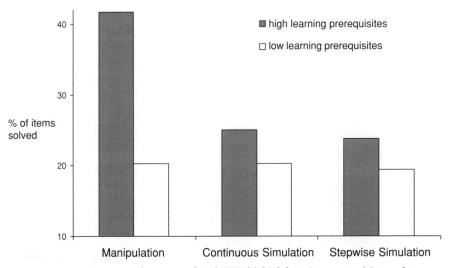

FIGURE 5.4a. Average performance of students with high learning prerequisites and students with low learning prerequisites in answering time difference questions after learning from manipulation pictures, after learning from continuous simulation pictures and after learning from stepwise simulation pictures.

adapt the speed of information presentation to their current working memory conditions thus preventing cognitive overload. Accordingly, we expected more advantages and less disadvantages from stepwise simulation pictures than from continuous simulation pictures

In addition to these general benefits, we expected on the one hand the enabling function to be more pronounced when individuals have high learning prerequisites (high cognitive ability and high prior knowledge) than when individuals have low learning prerequisites. On the other hand, we expected the facilitating function to be more pronounced when learners have low prerequisites because these individuals are more likely to be reliant on external support than learners with high prerequisites.

Thirty-nine university students participated in the study. The learning material and the test material were the same as in the previous study except that a first group received a text including only manipulation pictures, a second group received a text including only continuous simulation pictures, and a third group received a text including only stepwise simulation pictures. The remainder of the procedure was the same as in the previous study.

The results of this study are presented in Figure 5.4a–b. Figure 5.4a displays how the participants answered time-difference questions. An ANOVA showed only a significant effect of learning prerequisites ($F(1,33) = 5.714$; $p = .023$),

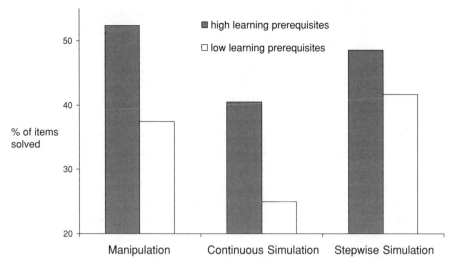

FIGURE 5.4b. Average performance of students with high learning prerequisites and students with low learning prerequisites in answering circumnavigation questions after learning from manipulation pictures, after learning from continuous simulation pictures and after learning from stepwise simulation pictures.

whereas the animation type and the interaction between animation type and learning prerequisites were not significant. However, as expected, students with high learning prerequisites performed significantly better after learning with manipulation pictures than after learning with continuous simulation pictures ($t(16) = 2.069$; $p = .028$). Students with manipulation pictures also performed better than students with stepwise simulation pictures ($t(16) = 2.300$; $p = .018$). In contrast, when students had low learning prerequisites, no such differences were found. The findings support the assumption that manipulation pictures have an enabling function, which is helpful for answering time difference questions, and that the enabling function plays an important role when individuals have high rather than low learning prerequisites.

Figure 5.4b displays how the participants answered circumnavigation questions. An ANOVA revealed a significant effect of animation type ($F(2,33) = 3.577$; $p = .039$) and of learning prerequisites ($F(1,33) = 8.221$; $p = .007$), but no significant interaction effect. However, as we had expected, students with low learning prerequisites had lower performance in answering circumnavigation questions after learning from continuous simulation pictures than after learning from manipulation pictures ($t(16) = 1.982$; $p = .033$). Furthermore, students with low learning prerequisites had lower performance after learning from continuous simulation pictures than after learning from stepwise simulation pictures ($t(16) = 2.742$; $p = .007$). When students had high learning prerequisites, no significant differences could be found. Thus, the findings support the assumption, that continuous simulation pictures have a facilitating function especially for students with low learning prerequisites, and that this function affects answering of circumnavigation questions. However, this function turned out again to be harmful for these learners, because the external support had made processing unnecessarily easy.

These negative effects of the facilitating function disappeared, however, when stepwise simulation pictures were used instead of continuous simulation pictures. Stepwise simulation pictures both allowed more learner control with a minimum of cognitive effort and provided a better basis for a conceptual analysis of the subject matter than was possible with continuous simulation pictures due to their fluent nature. In other words, the stepwise simulation pictures provided less facilitation and more possibilities for the learners to engage in self-directed cognitive processing. This result is similar to the finding of Mayer and Chandler (2001), who showed that a simple control over an animation (that stopped automatically after few seconds and required the user to click on a button to resume playing) resulted in significantly better learning. This form of user control allowed more self-directed exploratory cognitive activities with less time constraints without essential cost for handling the device (cf. Lowe, 2004).

To summarize, our results indicate that the different kinds of animations can have different functions in teaching and learning. Whereas the manipulation pictures seem to have primarily an enabling function, the continuous simulation pictures seem to have primarily a facilitating function. Manipulation pictures seem to be primarily beneficial for answering time-difference questions. Learners can use such pictures to generate various time states of the earth in order to extract information about time differences and this was obviously helpful for answering time-difference questions. This function seems to be especially pronounced when students have higher learning prerequisites because these learners have sufficient resources available to use these possibilities. Continuous simulation pictures seem to affect primarily the answering of circumnavigation questions. They have a facilitating function insofar as they allow the following of an external simulation process that makes the corresponding mental simulation much less demanding. Under specific conditions, this function might be beneficial for learning, namely when individuals would not be able to perform the required mental simulation without external support (cf. Mayer, 1997, 2001; Salomon, 1994; Schnotz, Boeckheler, & Grzondziel, 1999; Tversky, Morrison, & Bétrancourt, 2002). However, for learners who are able to perform the mental simulation on their own, the external support offered by a continuous simulation picture could prevent them from performing learning-relevant cognitive processes by themselves. In this case, the facilitating function is beneficial for processing, but not for learning. Stepwise simulation pictures provide less of this facilitating function. They allow somewhat more learner control and more possibilities for self-directed cognitive processing with a deeper conceptual analysis of the subject matter than continuous simulation pictures. Less facilitation seems to be more beneficial for learning in this case.

One might argue that the continuous simulation pictures increased extraneous load. At first sight, it seems they did. Learners were able to perform the mental simulations on their own. Thus, the simulation pictures provided process information, which was in fact no longer required by the learner and therefore redundant. Providing redundant information is generally considered to increase extraneous cognitive load because the learner has to process unneeded information. Redundancy can result in an expertise reversal effect when individuals with higher learning prerequisites perform better without, rather than with, additional information (Kalyuga, Chandler, & Sweller, 1998, 2000). However, this pattern does not fit the results of the experiments presented above because the negative effects of animation were found primarily when students had low learning prerequisites rather than high learning prerequisites. Therefore it seems that the negative facilitating effect is something different from the expertise reversal effect.

THE ZONE OF PROXIMAL DEVELOPMENT FROM A COGNITIVE LOAD PERSPECTIVE

We argued earlier that animations can reduce cognitive load for learners and that this can have an enabling function or a facilitating function. The enabling effect means that processes become possible that otherwise would have remained impossible. The facilitating effect means that processes that are already possible, but that still require high mental effort, become possible with less effort. The following discussion presents a closer analysis of the enabling effect and the facilitating effect. For the sake of simplicity, the analysis will assume that there is no extraneous load.

Intrinsic load is determined by the intellectual complexity of the task to be performed relative to the degree of expertise of the learner. Figure 5.5 shows the relation between different levels of learners' expertise, learners' performance on a specific task X and the intrinsic load imposed by this task on working memory. The upper part of the figure shows how the learner's expertise (represented on the abscissa of the figure) determines the likelihood

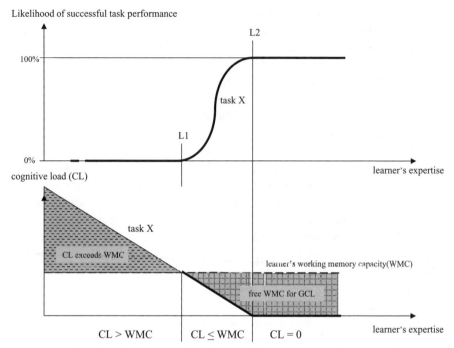

FIGURE 5.5. Task performance (top) and cognitive load (bottom) of a hypothetical task X for learners with different levels of expertise.

of the learner's successful performance (represented on the ordinate of the figure) on task X. Within the region of low expertise on the left, the likelihood of successful performance remains at 0% up to the expertise level L1. Between the expertise level L1 and the expertise level L2, the likelihood of successful performance increases from 0% to 100%. Beyond the expertise level L2, the likelihood of successful performance remains at 100%. In other words, if the learner's expertise level is below L1, the task is too difficult for the learner. If the learner's expertise level becomes higher than L1, the task becomes more and more tractable for the learner. At the expertise level L2 and beyond, the task is so easy that performance is likely to be perfect.

The lower part of Figure 5.5 shows how the intrinsic cognitive load associated with task X varies with the learner's level of expertise. Up to L1, the cognitive load (CL) associated with performance of task X exceeds the learner's working memory capacity (WMC). The learner is therefore unable to perform the task successfully. Between L1 and L2, the cognitive load of the task is lower than the learner's working memory capacity. Therefore, the learner is able to perform the task, and there is free capacity of working memory left that can be used for germane cognitive load activities (GCL). At L2, the cognitive load of task X drops down to essentially zero, because task performance becomes automated and does not need working memory capacity any more. The available working memory capacity can therefore in principle be used for other activities.

Tasks can be performed without help or with help. If appropriate help is available, students can perform better on a task than without such help. The increase of performance as a result of instructional help is the core of the zone of proximal development (ZPD). The zone of proximal development has been defined by Vygotski (1963) as the range between a lower limit and an upper limit of task difficulty. The lower limit of the ZPD is defined as the most difficult task the learner can perform successfully without help. The upper limit of the ZPD is defined as the most difficult task that the learner can perform successfully with optimal help. The lower limit task is of course easier than the upper limit task.

Figure 5.6 displays the ZPD concept in a cognitive load framework. The ZPD is represented by the shaded area between the two tasks mentioned before, the easier task performed without help and the more difficult task performed with help. The left-hand curve shows the performance characteristics of the easier task, which is the most difficult task an individual at learning state L3 can perform successfully without help. The right-hand curve shows the performance characteristics of the most difficult task that the individual can perform successfully only with optimal help.

In order to effectively promote learning, instruction should include learning tasks within the limits of the particular individual's ZPD. If the task difficulty is higher than the ZPD, the learner's cognitive capacity is overwhelmed, because the cognitive load exceeds the learner's working memory capacity. If the task difficulty is lower than the ZPD, the learner would be sub-challenged and a great deal of the available cognitive capacities remain unused for the learning process.

RECONSIDERATION OF COGNITIVE LOAD IN LEARNING FROM ANIMATION

Within the framework of cognitive load and the zone of proximal development, we can now describe the effects of animation on learners' working memory more precisely. In the studies mentioned above, manipulation pictures provided learners with the possibility of exploring a high number of

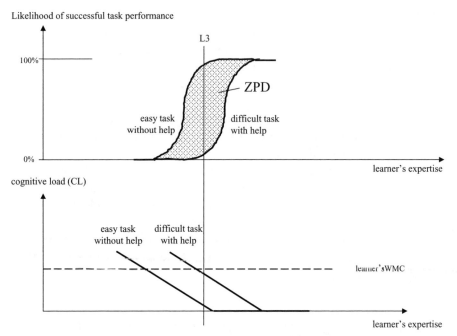

FIGURE 5.6. Task performance (top) and cognitive load (bottom) of an easy task which can be solved by a learner at expertise level L3 without help as well as task performance (top) and cognitive load (bottom) of a difficult task which can be solved by learner at expertise level L3 only with help. The range of difficulty between the two tasks is known as the zone of proximal development (ZPD).

different time states on the earth. The assumed effects of manipulation pictures compared to static pictures in terms of cognitive load theory are visualized in Figure 5.7. Accordingly, generating a high number of different time states only on the basis of a static picture is too difficult for learners at expertise level L3, the average expertise level of participants in these studies. Under this condition, only very few time states (if any) can be generated beyond the states explicitly provided in the static pictures. Most learners in the studies described above were probably unable to generate the required additional time states in their mind due to their limited available processing capacity.

The use of manipulation pictures changed the situation dramatically. Learners using these pictures were now able to click on a few buttons in order to generate many different time states and explore them systematically. This possibility was not available with static pictures. In other words, the manipulation pictures shifted the task of generating multiple time states from a too high level of difficulty down to a lower level of difficulty within the students' zone

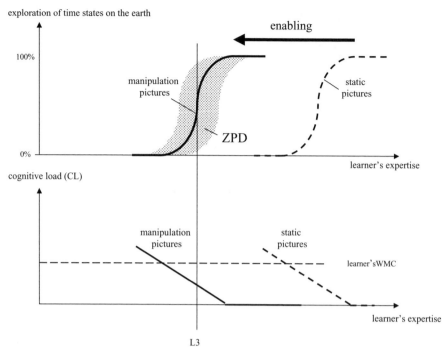

FIGURE 5.7. Illustration of the enabling function of manipulation pictures. Whereas an exploration of different times states on the earth with static pictures is beyond the zone of proximal development ZPD of a learner at expertise level L3, the use of manipulation pictures shifts the task difficulty into the learner's ZPD.

of proximal development. In this way, the students were enabled to perform a task that they could not perform on the basis of static pictures. Accordingly, the manipulation pictures had an enabling function for the learners.

The function of the continuous simulation pictures used in our studies was different from that of the manipulation pictures. The continuous simulation pictures demonstrated the earth's rotation around its axis and, thus, facilitated the corresponding mental simulations compared to static pictures. The assumed effect of continuous simulation pictures compared to static pictures in terms of cognitive load theory is visualized in Figure 5.8. Accordingly, learners at expertise level L3 (which is again the assumed average expertise level in the studies) were able to perform a mental simulation of the earth's rotation even on the basis of a static picture. In this case, a mental simulation based on a static picture was within the learners' zone of the proximal development.

Continuous simulation pictures reduced the difficulty of the mental simulation. Because learners were able to click on a few buttons in order to see a

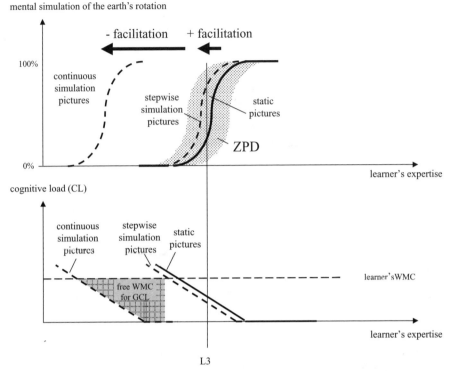

FIGURE 5.8. Illustration of facilitating functions of simulation pictures. For a learner at expertise level L3, performing a mental simulation of the earth's rotation on the basis of static pictures is within his/her zone of proximal development (ZPD). A minor facilitation through stepwise simulation pictures can have a beneficial effect on learning to perform this mental simulation (+ facilitation). However, continuous simulation pictures make the process of mental simulation too easy, because the learner can follow the animation in a passive mode. In this case, the use of simulation pictures shifts the task difficulty out of the learner's ZPD (– facilitation).

picture of the earth rotating around its axis, they were not required to infer the movement of the earth by themselves. Instead, they could perform the mental simulation just by watching the animated picture, by passively following the perceived rotation of the earth. Accordingly, the continuous simulation pictures used in the studies had a facilitating function for the learners, because the mental simulation became much easier. However, this facilitation turned out to have a negative effect on learning. As Figure 5.8 illustrates, the continuous simulation pictures shifted the task of mental simulation, which was within the learners' zone of proximal development with static pictures, down to the area of a too low task difficulty outside the students' zone of proximal development. In other words: The continuous simulation pictures had a facilitating function, but they made the mental simulation too easy by providing unneeded support for the learners.

The findings indicate that the stepwise simulation pictures were far better adapted to our learners' individual prerequisites. They provided a modest level of help for the mental simulation process by displaying minor rotation steps, but still left enough room for self-directed elaborated cognitive processing. We therefore assume that the stepwise simulation pictures provided an appropriate degree of facilitation while nevertheless maintaining the task difficulty within the learners' zone of proximal development and which is indicated in Figure 5.8 as a positive facilitating effect. However, if a facilitation shifts the task difficulty out of the learner's zone of proximal development, the facilitation is likely to have negative effects on learning.

CONCLUSIONS

Animated pictures provide additional information that seems capable of having different functions with respect to learning. On the one hand, animations can enlarge the set of possible cognitive processes and, thus, allow the learner to perform more processing than s/he would be able to perform with static pictures. This is the enabling function of animations. On the other hand, animations can trigger dynamic cognitive schemata that make specific cognitive processes easier. This is the facilitating function of animations.

Different kinds of animated pictures seem to fulfil different functions for learning. Animations can be used to generate and display a large number of static pictures and show different states or show a subject matter from different perspectives. Such animations seem to have primarily an enabling function. They enable a learner to perform more cognitive processing than s/he would be able to do with static pictures. On the contrary, animations allowing the display of dynamic processes seem to have primarily a facilitating function. These animations can provide external support for corresponding mental simulations and, thus, make these mental processes easier to perform. Individuals with high learning prerequisites seem to benefit primarily from the enabling function, whereas individuals with low learning prerequisites seem to be affected primarily by the facilitating function of animations.

Both the enabling function and the facilitating function of animation can be considered as providing a reduction of cognitive load (Sweller, van Merriënboer, & Paas, 1998). The facilitating function of animations can be helpful for learners with very low learning prerequisites who would not be able to perform the corresponding mental simulations on their own. However, the facilitating function of animations may also be harmful, when learners who would be already able to perform the mental simulations on their own nevertheless make use of the available, but unneeded external support. Animation can keep learners from doing relevant cognitive processing not only due to increased task difficulty, but also due to an inappropriate facilitation of the task. In this latter case, the animation reduces cognitive load by unintentionally shifting the intrinsic load of the task out of the learner's zone of proximal development. Thus, the use of animation in multimedia learning environments seems to be beneficial only under some circumstances, whereas it can have negative effects under other circumstances. Adequate use of animation will only be possible on the basis of a sufficient understanding of the interplay between animated displays and the functioning of the learner's perceptual and cognitive system.

References

Atkinson, C. & Shiffrin, R. M. (1971). The control of short-term memory. *Scientific American, 225*, 82–90.

Baddeley, A. (2000). The episodic buffer: A new component of working memory? *Trends in Cognitive Science, 4*, 417–423.

Baddeley, A. (1986). *Working memory*. Oxford, U.K.: Oxford University Press.

Chandler, P. & Sweller, J. (1991). Cognitive load theory and the format of instruction. *Cognition and Instruction, 8*, 293–332.

Forbus, K. D., Nielsen, P., & Faltings, B. (1991). Qualitative spatial reasoning: The Clock project. *Artificial Intelligence, 51*, 417–471.

Kalyuga, S., Chandler, P., & Sweller, J. (1998). Levels of expertise and instructional design. *Human Factors, 40*, 1–17.

Kalyuga, S., Chandler, P., & Sweller, J. (2000). Incorporating learner experience into the design of multimedia instruction. *Journal of Educational Psychology, 92*, 126–136.

Kirby, J. R., Moore, P. J., & Schofield, N. J. (1988). Verbal and visual learning styles. *Contemporary Educational Psychology, 13*, 169–184.

Lanca, M. & Kirby, J. R. (1995). The benefits of verbal and spatial tasks in contour map learning. *Cartographic Perspectives, 21*, 3–15.

Lowe, R. K. (1999). Extracting information from an animation during complex visual learning. *European Journal of Psychology of Education, 14*, 225–244.

Lowe, R. K. (2003). Animation and learning: Selective processing of information in dynamic graphics. *Learning and Instruction, 13*, 157–176.

Lowe, R. K. (2004). Interrogation of a dynamic visualisation during learning. *Special Issue on Learning with Dynamic Visualisations, Learning and Instruction, 14*(3), 257–274.

Mayer, R. E. (1997). Multimedia Learning: Are we asking the right questions? *Educational Psychologist, 32*, 1–19.

Mayer, R. E. (2001). *Multimedia learning*. New York: Cambridge University Press.

Mayer, R. E. (Ed.) (2005). *Cambridge Handbook of Multimedia Learning*. Cambridge: Cambridge University Press.

Mayer, R. E. & Chandler, P. (2001). When learning is just a click away. *Journal of Educational Psychology, 93*, 390–397.

Mayer, R. E. & Moreno, R. (1998). A split-attention effect in multimedia learning: Evidence for dual processing systems in working memory. *Journal of Educational Psychology, 90*, 312–320.

Paas, F. & van Merriënboer, J. G. (1994). Instructional control of cognitive load in the training of complex cognitive tasks. *Educational Psychology Review, 6*, 357–371.

Salomon, G. (1994). *Interaction of media, cognition, and learning.* Hillsdale, NJ: Lawrence Erlbaum Associates.

Schnotz, W. (2005). An integrated model of text and picture comprehension. In R. E. Mayer (Ed.), *Cambridge Handbook of Multimedia Learning* (pp. 49–69). Cambridge: Cambridge University Press.

Schnotz, W. & Bannert, M. (2003). Construction and interference in learning from multiple representations. *Learning and Instruction, 13*, 141–156.

Schnotz, W. & Rasch, T. (2005). Enabling, facilitating, and inhibiting effects of animations in multimedia learning: Why reduction of cognitive load can have negative results on learning. *Educational Technology Research and Development, 53*, 47–58.

Schnotz, W., Böckheler, J., & Grzondziel, H. (1999). Individual and co-operative learning with interactive animated pictures. *European Journal of Psychology of Education, 14*, 245–265.

Sims, V. K. & Hegarty, M. (1997). Mental animation in the visuospatial sketchpad: Evidence from dual-tasks studies. *Memory & Cognition, 25*, 321–332.

Sweller, J. (1999). *Instructional design in technical areas.* Camberwell, Australia: ACER Press.

Sweller, J. & Chandler, P. (1994). Why some material is difficult to learn. *Cognition and Instruction, 12*, 185–223.

Sweller, J., van Merriënboer, J. G., & Paas, F. (1998). Cognitive architecture and instructional design. *Educational Psychological Review, 10*, 251–296.

Tversky, B., Morrison, J. B., & Bétrancourt, M. (2002). Animation: Does it facilitate? *International Journal of Human-Computer Studies, 57*, 247–262.

Vygotski, L. S. (1963). Learning and mental development at school age (J. Simon, Trans.). In B. Simon & J. Simon (Eds.), *Educational psychology in the U.S.S.R.* (pp. 21–34). London: Routledge & Kegan Paul.

6

Animations of Thought

Interactivity in the Teachable Agent Paradigm

Daniel L. Schwartz, Kristen P. Blair, Gautam Biswas,
Krittaya Leelawong, and Joan Davis

INTRODUCTION

Animations are a versatile media for displaying changes over time. They can show cellular processes, a billion years of continental drift, the assembly of a desk, and even the invisible shifting of political tides. Most animations depict changes to a situation, such as a desk being assembled. In this chapter, we describe a series of software environments, called Teachable Agents (TAs) that use animations in another way. Rather than displaying a situation, the TAs animate the thoughts an individual might use to reason about that situation. For example, using the same well-structured representations as experts, TAs can visually model how to reason through the causal chains of an ecosystem. This is worthwhile, because the goal of learning is often to emulate an expert's reasoning processes, and animations of thought make that reasoning visible. For novices, learning to reason with an expert's knowledge organization is as important as learning the bare facts themselves.

We build TA systems to capitalize on the adage that an effective way to learn something is to teach it. For instance, many graduate students state that they never really understood statistics until they had to teach it. Students teach their TA by constructing a visible knowledge organization. For example, with the TA called "Betty," students can create a concept map that teaches Betty about a river eco-system. Betty then solves problems based on what she was taught. Given a question about a river eco-system, for example, Betty can visually trace her reasoning through the concept map. This constitutes the animation

Additional contributors to this work include Nancy Vye and John Bransford. Justine Cassell provided invaluable advice. This material is based upon work supported by the National Science Foundation under Grants REC-0231946, REC-0231771. Any opinions, findings, and conclusions or recommendations expressed in this material are those of the authors and do not necessarily reflect the views of the National Science Foundation.

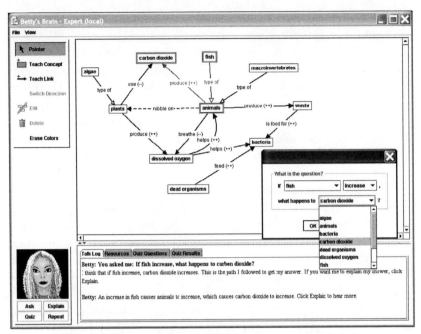

FIGURE 6.1. The Teachable Agent Formerly Known as Betty's Brain.

of thought, and depending on the conclusion that the agent reaches, students can revise their TA's knowledge and their own.

TAs introduce two differences from traditional uses of animation. One difference is that TAs animate expert processes of reasoning about a situation, rather than the situation itself. A second difference is that students help build the animation rather than just watch. TA environments are highly interactive. Students share their ideas with the agents by teaching them. At the same time, the TAs use artificial intelligence techniques to solve problems independently – though still based on what they have been taught. This creates an environment of shared ideas and shared initiative between the student and the agent. The thesis of this chapter is that the shared ideas and initiative of the TA animations help create an interactive "sweet spot" that optimizes motivation and learning. In the second and third sections we develop the framework of this thesis, and in the fourth and fifth sections we provide relevant evidence. First, however, we take a quick detour to provide a concrete example of a Teachable Agent.

A QUICK TOUR OF A TEACHABLE AGENT

Figure 6.1 shows an example of the TA named Betty's Brain, or Betty for short (for instances of other agents, see <aaalab.stanford.edu>). Students teach Betty by creating a visual network of nodes and links comprised of qualitative causal relations (i.e., increase, decrease, depends-on, is-a, and has-a semantics). Students use a point-and-click graphics editor to create the nodes (e.g., algae, oxygen) and links (e.g., produce). Students use pull-down menus to specify the qualitative relation implied by the link (e.g., algae *increase* oxygen). The directed graph and the qualitative semantics provide a well-structured representation that is common among experts discussing causal propagation, plus it enables the students to build the thoughts that are animated when Betty reasons.

Once taught, Betty can answer questions. Students can ask Betty a question using a floating panel that appears when students click on the "Ask" button. Students can ask questions like "If <fish> <increase> what happens to <carbon dioxide>?" Betty answers the question using the map, which represents her knowledge organization. This constitutes the animation of thought – she successively highlights nodes and links as she reasons through the network. Changes in color indicate whether she is inferring an increase or decrease for each node while she progresses through the map. The animation is relatively impoverished, but the simple dynamic changes to the directed graph make it easy for students to follow the agent reasoning. Unlike many animations, where students need to penetrate the surface motion of the animation to learn the underlying principles (for discussion, see Lowe 1999, 2004), Betty makes the critical relations explicit and available for inspection.

To answer questions, Betty uses a simple reasoning engine that adopts generic graph traversal algorithms (e.g., depth and breadth first search) coupled with qualitative inference schemes that can reason through causal and hierarchical chains (Biswas et al., 2005). Betty always reasons "logically," even if the premises she has been taught are incorrect. This helps students learn to emulate Betty's reasoning methods, while also helping students identify gaps in knowledge when Betty reaches a wrong conclusion based on the information they provided.

Figure 6.1 shows the results of a graphical animation and a text-based response that Betty offers for the question, *"If fish increase, what happens to carbon dioxide?"* Betty inferred that fish are a type of animal. She then reasoned that animals produce carbon dioxide, so an increase in fish will increase the amount of carbon dioxide. Betty can reason forward through much more intricate chains of causes, and she can also reason backward to diagnose what might cause an increase or decrease for a given entity in the map. Students can also ask Betty to explain her answer. Through a multi-step animation, Betty decomposes her chains of reasoning as she provides answers in a sequence of steps. Betty can also unfold her inference through spoken dialog and a text window. Betty's responses help students reflect on the implications of the ideas they taught.

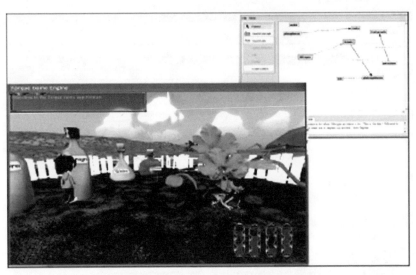

FIGURE 6.2. Betty in a guided-discovery videogame application. The window in the corner shows Betty reasoning about a challenge in the game world.

Betty does not learn automatically by using machine learning algorithms. Instead, students must explicitly teach Betty, and this teaching helps students structure their own knowledge. One benefit of the TA paradigm is that it capitalizes on the well-defined teaching schema that includes instruction, assessment, and remediation. This pre-existing schema can help organize otherwise complex student interactions with the computer (cf. Schnotz, Boeckheler, & Grzondziel, 1999), much as people's well-defined schemas for spatial organization inspired the desktop metaphor for computer operating systems. With the TA metaphor, students bring to bear a host of prior ideas about teaching that help them engage the computer in complex learning interactions. The Betty "kernel" shown in Figure 6.1 provides basic functionality in a modular, agent architecture (Viswanath, Adebiyi, Biswas, & Leelawong, 2004). This permits us to integrate her into more complex applications and environments. We do not envision Betty as the only means of instruction. Rather, Betty helps novices abstract and reflect upon important knowledge structures relevant to understanding a domain. We provide three quick examples of how Betty can integrate with other environments.

The first example is a guided-discovery video game called *Pumpkin World* (Blair & Schwartz, 2004; Hartman & Blair, 2005). Figure 6.2 provides a sample screen shot. Betty takes the form of an embodied agent in a virtual world. Students teach Betty to grow giant pumpkins (so villagers have a place to live). There are other agents with whom Betty interacts (e.g., a store owner, a passer-by), and she can directly affect her world (e.g., she adds nitrogen, if

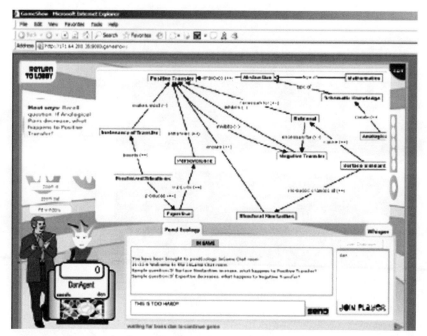

FIGURE 6.3. A customized agent performs in an on-line game show with other students and agents.

she infers the pumpkins need it). Students learn about plant growth through various simulations in the videogame, and they formalize their understanding by teaching Betty so she can take productive actions.

Our second example is an online game show designed to change homework practices. In the Triple-A Game Show, developed with Paula Wellings, a student teaches an agent and customizes its looks. The student and agent then participate in an on-line game show with other students and their agents (Figure 6.3). Students can log on from home or from school. The game host asks the agents to answer questions and explain their reasoning. The application also includes a chat environment so students can discuss and cheer (or jeer) an agent's performance. Students can also teach their agent a portion of a domain and then "jigsaw" with other agents by merging concept maps to create a Team Betty (Sears & Schwartz, 2004).

As a final example of how TAs can be extended, we developed a front-of-the-class assessment environment that can be projected on a large screen. In Figure 6.4, each panel shows an agent map created by a student. The classroom teacher can ask a question of all the agents simultaneously. A hidden expert map determines the correct answer and compares it to each agent's answer. The

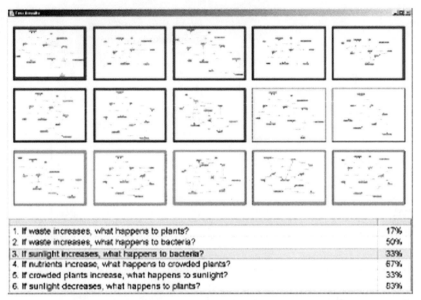

1. If waste increases, what happens to plants?	17%
2. If waste increases, what happens to bacteria?	50%
3. If sunlight increases, what happens to bacteria?	33%
4. If nutrients increase, what happens to crowded plants?	67%
5. If crowded plants increase, what happens to sunlight?	33%
6. If sunlight decreases, what happens to plants?	83%

FIGURE 6.4. Front of class quiz system for showing agents perform.

results are tabulated and indicated by color coding (red = incorrect; green = correct; yellow = correct for wrong reason). The classroom teacher can zoom in to show why an agent gave the answer it did, and then compare it to another map. If we shed the TA metaphor, one way to think of this system is that students are creating executable models, and then the models get tested. So, rather than the student answering a small subset of questions, the student needs to create a model that can answer any legitimate question in the domain. In a formal study in college classrooms, we found that the front-of-the-class system significantly helped students learn complex relations compared to just seeing the performance of their own agent.

A FRAMEWORK FOR ACHIEVING A LEARNING SWEET SPOT IN INTERACTIVITY

Our thesis is that there is an interactive "sweet spot" for learning that applies to TAs and beyond. TAs operate under a social model of interactive learning rather a physical one. Often, discussions of interactivity tacitly borrow from models of physical interaction, where people probe a stable environment to help induce its underlying rules or causes. These models lead designers to focus on the contingency of the system; for example, is timely feedback more useful than delayed feedback (Mathon & Koedinger, 2003)? Social interactivity

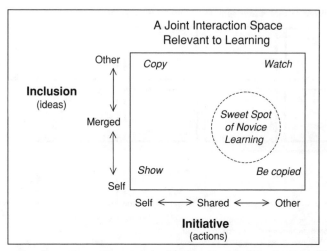

FIGURE 6.5. Two dimensions of interactivity relevant to novice learning. Each dimension captures the degree to which the self and another person or technology engages the interaction. The examples in each corner represent non-interactive experiences from the perspective of the learner.

presents a different root metaphor that supports a host of new interactive possibilities (e.g., Moreno, Mayer, Spires, & Lester, 2001). For example, Deutsch (1973) describes the minimal criteria for cooperative interactions, "A cooperative process is characterized by open and honest communication of relevant information among participants. Each is interested in informing, and being informed by, the other" (p. 29). One does not think of a physical environment as having interests or communicative intents, but with a social model of interaction it is possible.

We propose that there is a sweet spot of social interaction that generates both high motivation and high learning. The defining quality of the sweet spot is that participants can produce, share, and see their ideas reflected, transformed, and acted upon by another person (or agent). Elsewhere, we review the motivational basis of the sweet spot, which we termed *productive agency* (Schwartz, 1999). For example, the most satisfying academic conversations occur when people acknowledge and give credit to one another's ideas, and then build on them in a way that new ideas emerge. The least satisfying interactions occur when the participants do not listen to each other, or one has no agency to produce or share ideas at all.

For learning, there are two key dimensions to sweet spot social interactions: initiative of action and inclusion of ideas. Figure 6.5 presents a qualitative portrayal of the two dimensions. The circle in the center reflects our proposal that optimal novice learning occurs when initiative is shared and ideas are merged among participants.

The vertical dimension of interaction – inclusion – captures the degree to which participants incorporate and merge their ideas with one another. People often adopt one another's words and gestures (Bernieri & Rosenthal, 1991; Brennan, 1996). This can draw them closer together (Bailenson & Yee, 2005), and the opportunity to see how people modify one's idea can be highly informative. Steiner (1972) reviewed the literature on small group interactions and found that tasks that permit the cumulative building of ideas improve group performance. Moreover, when participants merge their ideas, they can co-create ideas that neither would have developed alone (Schwartz, 1995). The second dimension of interactivity – initiative – captures the degree to which each participant can guide the interaction and take independent action. Cassell (2004) demonstrated a story-telling system where young children and an embodied conversational agent took turns creating a narrative, and this improved the children's linguistic skills. Permitting other people to take the initiative offers alternatives to one's own inertia. It also generates "projective" feedback by revealing the variations another person applies to one's ideas. Coaches, for example, may learn a great deal by watching their players take the initiative to adjust a play during a game. In contrast, when an interaction is characterized by an imbalance of initiative there is less learning. Barron (2004) found that small groups that blocked the initiative of one of its members often failed to capitalize on the correct ideas that the individual provided, and therefore, the group members did not perform or learn very well.

Inclusion and initiative are especially important for early learning. Experts who have well-structured knowledge and a wealth of prior experiences can learn by quietly watching or listening. Novices do not have equal knowledge, and they may need more interactive opportunities. An example of an infant-mother dialog can further clarify the sweet spot:

SON: Ball.
MOTHER: You want me to get the ball?
MOTHER: That is an apple.
SON: Apple?

The child initiates the exchange and includes an idea (ball) into the joint space. In turn, the mother builds upon the child's ideas, so the child can both recognize his original idea and what is new in what the mother says (apple).

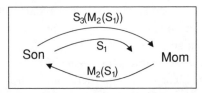

FIGURE 6.6. A schematic notation of the mother-child interaction. Arc S_1: The son initiates the exchange and includes an idea into the joint space. Arc $M_2(S_1)$: The mother incorporates the child's intent and takes the initiative to turn the conversation into an object naming lesson. She introduces her name for the object. Arc $S_3(M_2(S_1))$: The child picks up the mother's meaning and tentatively renames the object.

The mother's initiative is relevant to the child's own, and this helps the child see the implications of his initiative (e.g., If you want an object, then you have to give it the right name.) The recursive structure of the exchange, shown in Figure 6.6, makes new information from the mother more comprehensible to the child and leads to better learning. Tomasello and Farrar (1986), for example, demonstrated that infants learn object names more effectively if the mother labels an object the child is handling compared to a situation where the mother labels an object she is handling.

Teaching involves interactions that can create a sweet spot (for reviews, see Biswas et al., 2001, 2005; Renkl, 1995). Learning through peer-tutoring (Cohen, Kulik, & Kulik, 1982) and reciprocal teaching (Palincsar & Brown, 1984) can be highly effective. Teachers naturally have the initiative and include their ideas into the interaction. At the same time, good teachers reflect on how students build on those ideas and how students take the conversation in new and unexpected directions. This can help teachers to see new implications and connections, to seek out new sources of examples and evidence, and to abstract out more fundamental structures in their own knowledge. Teachers may find that they need to rethink how they describe a domain, and this can result in a search for more effective explanatory structures.

Of course, not all teachers and students find the sweet spot. Teachers may be overly didactic, and as a consequence, they will not learn much in the act of teaching. Students may also fail to contribute to the interaction. Moreover, if inexperienced children are asked to teach, they may not have sufficient skills to keep teaching interactions in the sweet spot. This is one reason why TAs can be valuable. TAs help to avoid a potential problem of peer-teaching, where students are put at risk if the child-teacher, or the child-pupil, are not very good. Moreover, TAs make their knowledge visible in their animations, which helps children overcome the problem that they may not be able to infer what their pupil has in mind.

PUTTING THE SWEET SPOT INTO TECHNOLOGY

Interactive technologies and their animations can optimize the two dimensions of interactivity to varying degrees. Simply watching an animation would be low on student initiative and ideas. Though students must take some initiative to watch and interpret the animation, they cannot substantively alter the course of the interaction, and their primary task is to extract information from the animation rather than contribute to it. For novices, it is not clear that passively viewing an animation yields superior learning compared to studying a well-crafted still image (Tversky, Morrison, & Bétrancourt, 2002). Enabling novices to slow down or replay segments of an animation improves the balance of initiative and should help (Lowe, 2004), but the animation still does not include the students' ideas.

Intelligent computer tutors are another important interactive technology for learning (e.g., Koedinger & Anderson, 1998). The student and the system share the initiative, because the student has some latitude in how to solve problems, and the system has the latitude to redirect the student and introduce problems. However, the computer tutor does not merge ideas with the student. The explicit goal of the program is to entrain the student into its way of thinking. Computer chess programs and other learning games are similar in that they share initiative with the player. However, whereas a tutor program explicitly enforces its ideas, a chess program explicitly hides its ideas. A novice, who cannot infer the chess program's underlying strategy, may learn less than if there were a shared representation of the program's strategy.

In designing TAs, our goal is to foster the sweet spot. We believe this goal is implicit in other learning systems that use agents that are neither completely ignorant nor all-knowing (e.g., Learning Companions, Chan, 1995; People-power, Dillenbourg & Self, 1992). TAs are explicitly designed to support the merging of ideas. Students provide the facts of the matter, and the TA provides conventional knowledge structures and reasoning mechanisms in the form of dynamic visual representations. For example, students introduce concepts to Betty, but they use Betty's directed graph structure to organize those concepts. Betty then animates how she reasons with their shared representation. Our assumption is that this visible merging and animation of student ideas and agent reasoning helps students adopt the TA's knowledge structures to organize and reason with their own concepts. The two studies in the following section test this assumption.

The TAs also have provisions for shared initiative. Each TA has the ability to take independent actions based on how it has been taught. For example,

Betty can answer questions. This permits students to reflect on Betty's reasoning, and we suppose this helps them learn more deeply. It is also possible to enhance a TA's initiative beyond answering questions, and the two studies in the Empirical Studies on the Dimension of Initiative section examine the value of enhanced shared initiative.

EMPIRICAL STUDIES ON THE DIMENSION OF INCLUSION

To examine the first dimension of the "sweet spot," two studies explored whether merging ideas and representations with Betty, plus watching her animate "expert" reasoning processes, leads students to adopt her knowledge organization. Both studies used the basic Betty kernel to teach about biological systems. Biological systems are well suited to Betty's qualitative causal reasoning.

Study 1: Adopting the Structure of the Agent's Thoughts

The first study examined whether learners incorporate Betty's knowledge structure into their own. The study complements research on the positive benefits of concept mapping (e.g., Kinchin & Hay, 2000; Novak, 1996). However, Betty differs from most concept-mapping activities, because she enforces semantic relations that students might otherwise violate in paper and pencil activities. For example, students often use concept map links to indicate a vague notion of "related to," whereas Betty requires students to use semantics that enable her to reason about causality (e.g., increase, decrease). Plus, Betty shows the implications of those relationships by answering questions, something concept maps, by themselves, cannot do.

Sixteen undergraduates read a four-page passage on metabolism. Half of the students were assigned to the Summary condition. They wrote a summary of cell metabolism. They were told to write about things like the relation between ATP resynthesis and lactic acid. Students in the Betty condition taught Betty about cell metabolism. They were shown how to teach and query Betty using the ATP – lactic acid example. We videotaped the sessions and asked the participants to think aloud. All Betty students worked to the cutoff point of 40 minutes. The Summary students averaged 32 minutes of work.

During the session, the Betty students were much more attentive to issues of causality than the Summary students. Every Betty student, but only one Summary student, recognized that they had been thinking in terms of correlations rather than causation. For example, one Betty student realized that he did not know whether mitochondria increase ATP resynthesis or vice versa.

Three-fourths of the Betty students considered the size of a causal effect, whereas none of the Summary students considered amounts of change. For example, one Betty student taught Betty that (a) oxygen increases ATP resynthesis, and (b) lactic acid inhibits resynthesis. This student wondered whether oxygen and lactic acid cancelled each other out.

As a simple posttest, we removed all the materials and gave students a paper with five metabolism terms (e.g., mitochondria, lactic acid, etc.). For each term, students had to "list relations to other entities and processes in cellular metabolism." Students in the Summary condition tended to assert single relations; for example, "mitochondria increase ATP resynthesis." Students in the Betty condition tended to assert chains of two or more relations; for example, "mitochondria with glycogen or free fatty acid increase ATP resynthesis." On average, the Betty students produced 3.75 chains of two or more relations, compared to 1.0 for the Summary students ($p < .05$). It is possible that the Summary students also learned about complex causal pathways, and they simply did not think it was important to include them in their lists. Even so, we can reiterate that the Betty students incorporated Betty's way of thinking and took that incorporation as an important task demand.

In summary, Betty influenced the students' knowledge. The Betty students became aware that they had not sufficiently differentiated between causation and correlation when reading the passage. Teaching Betty also influenced how students structured their own knowledge. When asked to list relations, the Betty students tended to list complex causal pathways as compared to the Summary students. These results make sense because developing chains of causal relations is exactly what Betty illustrates and requires. The results demonstrate that merging ideas with Betty can shape students' domain knowledge.

Study 2: The Benefit of Animated Thought

The first study demonstrated that students adopt Betty's representations, but it did not isolate the value of animating Betty's thoughts. In the study, we compared teaching Betty to writing a summary. Maybe simply asking students to draw a concept map would work as well as teaching Betty. Therefore, we conducted a second study to see if Betty's animations make a difference for whether students' incorporate her reasoning structures.

Twenty-five 5th-grade students taught Betty about river ecosystems across three one-hour sessions. Students had online resources to help them learn the relevant content needed to teach Betty (see Biswas et al., 2004). In the Animation condition ($n = 13$), students could ask Betty questions and activate her animations. In the No Animation condition ($n = 12$) students simply made

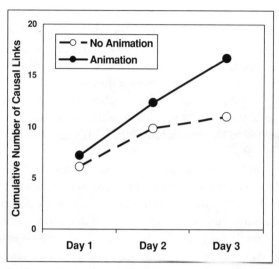

FIGURE 6.7. Students who see Betty animate her reasoning add more causal links.

Betty's map without ever asking questions and seeing the map animate. Thus, both conditions used Betty's formalism, but only the students in the animate condition saw how Betty incorporated their ideas into her reasoning.

Figure 6.7 shows that students in the Animation condition generated maps that accumulated more causal links; $F(1, 23) = 4.24$, $MSe = 15.7$, $p > .05$. This makes sense because Betty animates causal chains in her reasoning. Evidently, animations of thought make a difference. This is a useful finding, because Tversky, Morrison, and Bétrancourt (2002) found that static diagrams can be as effective as animations. However, their work did not examine the interactive potential of animations, which in the current study, were more useful than static drawings. Merging ideas into an animation can help students learn to think with the structures that drive that animation.

EMPIRICAL STUDIES ON THE DIMENSION OF INITIATIVE

The previous studies examined the joint inclusion of ideas. The first examined the effect of mergining Betty's knowledge structures with the student's teaching. The second looked at the benefits of animating these merged ideas to solve problems These studies used the basic Betty kernel, which is relatively low on initiative. This version of Betty only reacts and responds to the student when asked to do so. For novices, this relatively simple initiative can appear to yield choice-filled behavior in the TA, because the performance setting provides complexity (Simon, 1996). Even so, the TA cannot initiate actions on its own. In the next two examples, we capitalize more fully on the TA metaphor for enhancing shared initiative. The studies also raise the standard for demonstrating that students learn. In the previous studies, we largely inferred what students learned based on the maps they created or the reasoning they applied while creating the maps. In the following studies, we measure student learning once they have left the original environment of teaching.

Study 3: Shared Initiative to Promote Metacognition

In exit interviews from our previous Betty studies, the students often emphasized that they would have liked Betty to take more initiative and exhibit characteristics of a good student during the teaching phase. One student, for instance, wanted Betty to "react to what she was being taught and ask questions on her own." Our assumption is that people learn more by teaching when their pupils can introduce their own issues. Tutors, for example, gain a deeper understanding when they answer tutee questions, explain materials, and uncover misconceptions (Chi et al., 2001; Graesser, Person, & Magliano, 1995; Uretsi, 2000).

For children, an agent that initiates a discussion about its learning can be especially valuable, because children have fewer metacognitive skills for managing learning with interactive media (Hegarty, 2004). If an agent can take the initiative to model how it monitors its own thinking, this may help students learn to perform this type of metacognition (Lin & Lehman, 1999; Palinscar & Brown, 1984). Shimoda, White, and Frederiksen (2002), for example, developed metacognitive coaches that students can modify to give hints for managing their scientific investigations, and Baylor (2002) found that agents can improve pre-service teachers' meta-cognitive awareness.

To address these issues, we gave Betty's initiative over how she is being taught, and we put her into a larger performance environment (Biswas et al., 2005). Under specific conditions, Betty spontaneously offers a meta-cognitive strategy or concern. For example, as students build Betty's map, she occasionally starts animating her map to draw inferences. She then remarks (right or wrong) that the answer she is deriving does not seem to make sense. These spontaneous prompts help students reflect on what they are teaching, and hopefully like a good teacher, check on their tutee's learning progress (and their own). Table 6.1 provides some examples of the actions Betty initiates and under what conditions.

The meta-cognitive Betty environment comes with a number of other assets, including online resources for learning content, quiz sets, and a mentor agent named, Mr. Davis. Mr. Davis helps to complete the teaching narrative, because he administers and grades Betty's quizzes. Mr. Davis also provides meta-cognitive tips when students ask for help. Mr. Davis does not give factual

TABLE 6.1. *Examples of Betty Taking Initiative*

Student Action	State of System	Samples of Betty's Dialog
Tell Betty to take a quiz	Student has not asked Betty a question since the last quiz.	"I still do not feel prepared to take a quiz. I don't understand enough about the causal relationships in the river. Please ask me some causal questions to see if I understand. Mr. Davis can help you learn more about being a good teacher."
Tell Betty to take a quiz	Betty's answers have changed since the last quiz	"What you have taught me has changed my thinking. I had some questions right on the quiz, but now I think I would answer them wrong."
Add a link	First causal link in the session	"Hey! Let me see if I understand this." (Betty reasons with link, and explains her reasoning)
Add a link	First causal path with two or more links	"OK. I think I know how this works." (Betty reasons with path, and explains her reasoning)

answers, but rather, he suggests strategies. As instances, he can suggest which of the online resources is helpful for a particular concept; how to be a good teacher (e.g., "test Betty and examine her answers closely"); and, how to be a good learner (e.g., "set goals").

To evaluate the benefits of shared-initiative, 54 5th-grade students worked for five 45-minute sessions on river ecosystem concepts. The study included three conditions. In the Shared-Initiative Teaching condition, students worked with the enhanced Betty system. Students taught Betty so she could pass a test to become a member of a school science club. Betty sometimes took initiative in the interactions, and Mr. Davis provided metacognitive tips to the student. In the Basic Teaching condition, students also prepared Betty for the club test, but Betty was similar to the prior studies where she simply took a quiz and answered student questions when asked. She did not take inititiative in the interactions, and Mr. Davis did not provide tips on teaching and learning. Instead, he provided feedback to Betty on each quiz question. Finally, in the Being-Taught condition, there was no cover story of teaching an agent, and Betty was not present in this environment. The students simply had to construct a concept map. Mr. Davis told the students to construct concept maps to demonstrate their learning. They were told to examine the quiz

TABLE 6.2. *Quality of Student Maps when Learning about Nitrogen Cycle at Transfer*

Student Maps Included:	Shared-Initiative M (SD)	Teaching M (SD)	Being Taught M (SD)
Expert Concepts	6.1 [a] (0.6)	5.2 (0.5)	4.1 (0.6)
Expert Causal Links	1.1 [ab] (0.3)	0.1 (0.3)	0.2 (0.3)

Notes: [a] Significantly greater than Being Taught; [b] Significantly greater than Teaching.

questions as a guide for what to learn. Students could ask Mr. Davis if their concept map was correct for a given quiz question. Mr. Davis would tell the student the correct answer and provide directive feedback for how to correct the map. Thus, the Being-Taught condition replicated standard computer-based instruction, where the computer has the initiative to teach and test the student.

After students completed the five sessions, they drew their maps from memory. The maps from the three conditions looked about the same. This result was not a surprise, because the students had worked for a long time developing their maps in each condition. This was not where we expected to find the difference between the conditions.

Our hypothesis was that the Shared-Initiative condition would show its benefits later. We thought the meta-cognitive emphasis would prepare students to learn about a new, related topic. Because the Shared-Initiative students interacted with Betty's metacognitive strategies, we thought they might incorporate those strategies when learning new content.

A month after the instructional intervention, students had two new sessions on the land-based nitrogen cycle. Students had not been taught about the nitrogen cycle, so they would have to learn from resources. Students from all three conditions completed this "learning at transfer" task (Bransford & Schwartz, 1999) in the same environment, so any differences would be due to what had happened a month before. They all used a modified Being-Taught environment. Mr. Davis simply told the students whether their map was right or wrong when they asked a question or took a quiz.

Table 6.2 shows that students from the Shared-Initiative condition learned significantly more about the nitrogen cycle as reflected in their concept maps. Their performances were still relatively low, but learning about the nitrogen cycle on their own in two sessions is a difficult task for 5th-graders.

The log files help explain the advantage of the Shared Initiative students on the learning posttest. Across the five river ecosystem sessions, the Shared Initiative students increasingly asked Betty to answer questions about chains of causes. By the fifth session, theses students had asked three times as many causal questions as the Being Taught condition. During the learning posttest on the nitrogen cycle, the Shared Initiative students asked twice as many causal questions as the Being Taught condition, even though Betty was no longer mixed initiative. In other words, sharing the initiative does not reduce the students' overall initiative, but rather it increases it. Meta-cognitive Betty led the students to increase their initiative to ask her questions, and this carried over, so that the students exhibited more learning initiative a month later when they had to do it on their own. They learned to use Betty's visualization as a way to monitor the coherence of their own understanding.

Study 4: The Importance of Independent Performance

For the final study, we present a tighter experimental comparison to futher isolate the value of agent initiative. In this case, the agent does not initiate interactions with the student, but instead, it interacts independently in another context after it has been taught. The description of the study takes some extra prose, but we think it is worthwhile. The study demonstrates that when learners solve problems themselves and construct representations, they do *not* learn as well as when they construct the exact same representations (to teach) and then see the agent perform based on those representations. In other words, "watching" within the sweet spot can be more effective than doing it oneself outside the sweet spot.

To motivate this finding, consider dissertation defenses in Sweden. The doctoral candidate does not answer questions directly. Rather, there is an advocate who answers questions based on what the candidate wrote in the thesis. The advocate's ability to defend the thesis depends on the candidate, but the advocate has the initiative to decide what to say. We assume this situation leads to much more careful thinking and writing by the candidate. When people teach somebody else who has to perform, they cannot count on their "situational smarts" to generate answers on the fly or sidestep challenges as they arise. They need to formalize their knowledge in a clear and unambiguous way. Moreover, by seeing how their students perform, for example, as the students answer questions from an outsider, teachers receive projective feedback, and this provides an opportunity for additional reflection (plus a sense of responsibility).

Moby: A Hypothetico-Deductive TA

To explain how we implemented the experimental contrast, we need to take a second detour to describe the TA named Moby. Moby helps students learn

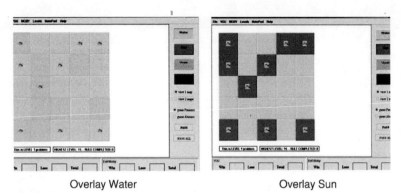

Overlay Water   Overlay Sun

FIGURE 6.8. Two examples of a student revealing a factor to induce the conditions that cause an outcome.

science through a hypothetico-deductive process. Scientific reasoning is notoriously problematic (e.g., Kuhn, 1995), so we decided to see if the TA paradigm could help students learn about deduction and induction.

With Moby, students construct visual representations of empirical hypotheses, and Moby makes predictions based on these representations. This is consistent with our emphasis on making thinking visible. Thus, Moby should be characterized as a hypothesis visualization tool rather than a data visualization tool (e.g., Gordin & Pea, 1995).

Moby resides in a game environment. Students need to complete rounds so they can progress to the next level of difficulty. Each round has four phases: Induce → Predict → Teach → Observe. Each round begins with Induce. Students receive a grid with a target outcome appearing in various cells. For example, the appearance of flowers is the target outcome in Figure 6.8. There are four factors that might be responsible for the outcome. Students click through the various factors to see where they appear in the grid. In the left panel of Figure 6.8, a student has revealed a factor (water) that is not responsible for the outcome (flowers). In the right panel, the student has revealed the correct factor (sun). The underlying rule for the grid in Figure 6.8 is, "Sun is necessary and sufficient for a flower to appear." A rule, however, can be much more complicated; for example, "Fire or shade is sufficient but not necessary for the absence of a flower." To help students find multi-factor rules, they can reveal the locations of two factors at a time.

After students believe they have induced the rule for a given round, they move to the Predict phase. In the Predict phase, they play against another agent named Joe. The game generates a new grid (based on the same rule). The grid, however, does not show the outcomes (e.g., flowers). Students need to predict which cells have the target outcome based on their hypothesis. To

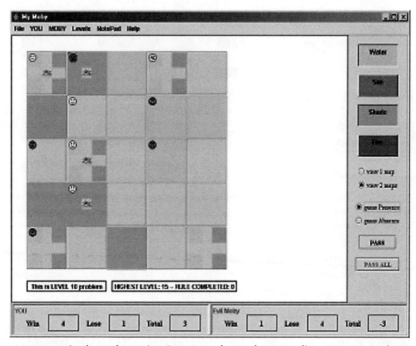

FIGURE 6.9. Students play against Joe to see who can better predict outcomes. Students overlay factors to guide their predictions. In this example, the student hypothesizes that Water and Shade are involved and reveals the location of both.

do this, they reveal where the relevant factors appear on the grid. Wherever they see the factor or factor combinations that they believe cause the outcome, they can click on that cell to see if the outcome is present. If they are correct, a smiling face appears. If they are wrong, a frowning face appears. A scoreboard keeps a tally. After the student takes a turn, Joe takes a turn, then the student, and so on, until all the outcomes have been found. Figure 6.9 shows a student and Joe in mid-game. Joe has the wrong rule, and most of his predictions are incorrect. The student has revealed two factors to guide her predictions, but she has the wrong rule as well. Based on the student's performance playing the prediction game against Joe, she can return to the Induce phase to refine her rule or move on to the Teach phase.

In the Teach phase, the students' visual understanding of a hypothesis gets merged with Moby's formal representations. Figure 6.10 shows there are two representations that students use to teach Moby. In the top of the figure, the students merge their visual rule into Moby's propositional representation. Using pull down menus, students choose factor(s), their combination, and the qualifier that governs their relation to the outcome (Necessary, Sufficient, and

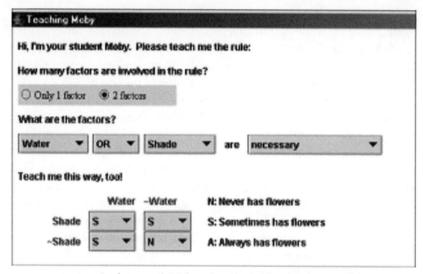

FIGURE 6.10. Students teach Moby using propositional and matrix formats.

Necessary and Sufficient). In the bottom of the figure, the students teach using a matrix representation. After choosing the factor(s), the students fill the cells with (A)lways, (S)ometimes, and (N)ever, indicating when flowers appear in these cells. If students are inconsistent between the two representations, Moby says he is confused and asks them to try again.

After students teach Moby, they move to the Observe phase. They watch Moby play the prediction game against Joe. This constitutes the major initiative and independent performance of the TA. Moby's animation consists of choosing factors and making predictions based on the rule he was taught. If Moby consistently loses to Joe, students need to re-teach, and if necessary, return to the Induce phase to develop a new hypothesis. If Moby wins twice in a row, students get to move to the next round and a more complex rule.

Isolating the Significance of Agent Initiative

Moby permitted a unique test that parceled out the value of the TA's capacity for solving problems on its own from other aspects of the TA's (e.g., visual representation). Ninety-four high school students were assigned to four conditions. In the Control condition, students never used the software and simply took a posttest. In the other three conditions, students played the game for about 90 minutes progressing through the rounds of increasing difficulty. In the Teach condition, students completed the full cycle described above. They merged their ideas into the formal representations, and they saw Moby take the initiative to play against Joe. In the Represent condition, students completed the Induce and Predict phases. When they beat Joe twice in a row, they filled in the representations from the Teach phase. However, they did *not* complete the representations in the context of teaching, and there was no independent initiative of the agent for them to observe. They were simply expressing the rule they had learned, and then they moved to the next level. Thus, these students were merging their knowledge into a formal representation, but they were not sharing initiative. Finally, in the Explain condition, students also completed the Induce and Predict phases. After beating Joe twice in a row, a text window asked them to explain the rule they had used, and they progressed to the next level. They did not see the formal representations and simply had to find a way to express the rule in words. Thus, these students neither merged their knowledge into a formal representation nor did they see any agent initiative.

If the initiative of the agent to perform independently is a valuable aspect of animations of thought, then we should expect the students in the Teach condition to do the best on the posttest, even though students in the Represent and Explain conditions had to induce, use, and formulate rules too. The students in all three software conditions reached the same game level in the same amount of time, so we can be sure there is not a time on task or relative exposure confound.

A few days after using the system, students took an 18 question posttest that included three classes of questions. Induce questions asked students to infer a rule given a combination of factors and outcomes. Imply questions provided a rule, and students had to deduce the implications. Translate questions asked students to convert between tabular and verbal expressions of a rule.

Figure 6.11 shows the posttest performance. The Teach condition produced significantly better performance across all three types of measures compared to each of the other conditions, $F(3, 90) = 4.9$, $MSe = .04$, $p < .01$. None of the other three conditions were significantly different from one another, despite the apparent descriptive differences.

The fact that the Teach students did better than the students who played and passed similar levels, but without teaching, is an important result. It shows that seeing a TA perform with feedback is more valuable than just working on problems by oneself and receiving feedback. Moreover, it showed that agent initiative is important for cashing in the value of merged representations. Students in the Represent condition merged their ideas with the same representations as the Teach students did. Even so, the Represent students did not reap the benefits of this merging. The Express students, who never saw these

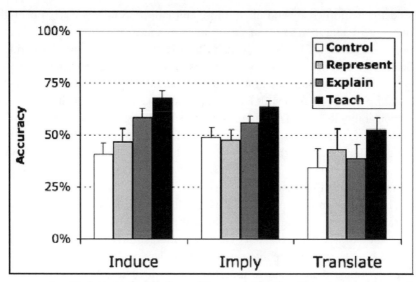

FIGURE 6.11. Students in the Teach condition were significantly more accurate on all question types compared to each of the other conditions.

representations, did about the same as the Represent students. This fits our story that the sweet spot of interactive learning occurs when there is both the merged inclusion of ideas and a shared initiative in action.

More broadly, these results suggest one possible learning benefit from programming simulations in general, and not just TAs. Simulations require a full specification of one's knowledge. The "run" of the simulation then provides independent performance and feedback that is not prone to subtle, situation-specific reasoning that can yield successful results but for the wrong reasons. To our knowledge, there has not been a direct test that compares the benefit of a simulation versus an otherwise equivalent activity of solving problems and formalizing one's knowledge, so the current results may have some value beyond the specific demonstration of the value of TAs.

CONCLUSIONS

Learning brute empirical facts is important, but for novices, learning to think with the expert's organization of those facts is equally important. Making thinking visible through animations can help. We assume that learning from an "animation of thought" can be enhanced by making the animation interactive. So, rather than having students only watch animations that demonstrate canonical forms of reasoning, we implemented the Teachable Agents where students help to create and query those animations. Students teach a computer agent, and then see the agent animate its thinking based on how it has been taught. Our TAs are particularly thin in human-like appearance and behavior, but it never ceases to surprise us how readily children (and adults) are willing to adopt and are motivated by the fiction of teaching another person (cf. Reeves & Nass, 1996). For example, we have found that children take responsibility for their TA's interests. Children willingly study more to revise their agents so they can pass a test they failed, something students are not always willing to do for themselves (Biswas et al., 2001). However, even if they do not buy into the fiction, they can still draw upon the well-known teaching schema to guide their learning interactions.

The TAs rely on a schema of social interaction, and, therefore, we developed a framework for guiding decisions about the design of TA interactions. We argued that there is a sweet spot of learning interactions that is characterized by (a) how much participants include and reflect one another's ideas, and (b) how much there is shared initiative for taking actions. In four studies, we examined whether interactive animations that targeted a sweet spot led to superior learning.

By design, TAs support a merging of ideas in an interactive context. Students provide domain specific content, whereas the agent provides canonical knowledge representations and reasoning. Each agent is designed to model a specific form of reasoning, and each agent implements a specific reasoning algorithm and associated representation. TAs are not as complete or powerful as general-purpose programming languages. Although this limits a TA's expressiveness, it also helps novices quickly engage a model of reasoning that is suited to initial domain learning (cf. Smith, Cypher, & Spohrer, 1997). The first study showed that students adopted the representation of Betty, a qualitative reasoning agent. The second study showed that, given a chance to see Betty reason, students incorporated her causal reasoning structures compared to students who simply built a static causal map. Animations of thought in an interactive context help students learn.

TAs afford different levels of shared initiative depending on the particular implementation. The basic architecture of a TA always includes the capacity for (a) being taught so the student has initiative, and (b) acting upon what it has been taught so the TA also has initiative. This bit of shared initiative is helpful. (Students who saw Betty answer questions used more causal reasoning than those who did not). Nevertheless, it is possible to enhance the shared-initiative to improve learning even more. So, in the third study, we compared three levels of shared initiative: Being Taught (lowest), Teaching (middle), and

Shared-Initiative with a meta-cognitive Betty (highest). The systems looked equally effective in the short run, but when we tested the students after a month, the Shared-Initiative students showed the greatest readiness to learn. The posttest in this study is of particular note. A goal of most conceptual instruction is to prepare students to learn in the future (Bransford & Schwartz, 1999). Except for the narrowest of training, no amount of schooling can provide students all they need to know, and they will need to learn. Therefore, it is important to use assessments of students' preparation for future learning, lest we miss the true value of an instructional approach. For example, had we not examined the students' abilities to learn new content, the value of sharing initiative with a metacognitive agent would have been missed.

In the final study using a hypothetico-deductive agent, we found strong evidence for the added-value of an agent that can initiate actions. Students who saw their agent perform did better on a posttest of hypothetico-deductive reasoning compared to students who otherwise completed the exact same activities of inducing, testing, and formalizing rules. Notably, the opportunity to merge ideas with the formal structures provided by the agent did not benefit students if they did not also get to see the implications of those rules played out in the behavior of an agent. The sweet spot of interaction requires both the merged inclusion of ideas *and* the sharing of initiative.

In conclusion, much of the research on animation has focused on animations that portray continuous changes to a referent domain. This application of animation has naturally led to comparisons between media that indicate changes over time; for example, videos versus animations, slow versus fast animations, static drawings versus animations, and texts versus (or with) animations. In this chapter, we took a turn that led us to a different set of questions. We created agents that students teach and that animate their thinking. This generated new issues for guiding design and research. In particular, it led us to explore the hypothesis that students learn better from animations when the learner and animation share ideas and initiative. We believe this sweet spot hypothesis extends to interactions without agents and animations. For example, Okita and Schwartz (2006) found that people learn more by watching their student answer examiner questions (poorly and without feedback) compared to studying those same questions themselves. The emerging empirical results have been promising, but of course, there are many studies and design possibilities that we have not explored. Hopefully, our initial work can suggest some fertile new directions for exploring how animations can improve learning when they become interactive animations of thought.

References

Bailenson, J., & Yee, N. (2005). Digital Chameleons: Automatic assimilation of nonverbal gestures in immersive virtual environments. *Psychological Science, 16*, 814–819.

Barron, B. J. (2004). When smart groups fail. *Journal of the Learning Sciences, 12*, 307–359.

Baylor, A. L. (2002). Expanding preservice teachers' metacognitive awareness of instructional planning through pedagogical agents. *Educational Technology Research & Design, 50*(2), 5–22.

Bernieri, F. & Rosenthal, R. (1991). Interpersonal coordination: Behavior matching and interactional synchrony. In R. S. Feldman & B. Rime (Eds.), *Fundamentals of nonverbal behavior* (pp. 401–432). Cambridge, UK: Cambridge University Press.

Biswas, G., Leelawong, K., Belynne, K., Viswanath, K., Vye, N. J., Schwartz, D. L., & Davis, J. (2004). Incorporating Self Regulated Learning Techniques into Learning by Teaching Environments. *26th Annual Meeting of the Cognitive Science Society.* Chicago, Illinois, pp. 120–125.

Biswas, G., Schwartz, D. L., Bransford, J. D., & Teachable Agent Group at Vanderbilt. (2001). Technology support for complex problem solving: From SAD Environments to AI. In K. Forbus & P. Feltovich (Eds.), *Smart machines in education* (pp. 71–98). Menlo Park, CA: AAAI/MIT Press.

Biswas, G., Schwartz, D. L., Leelawong, K., Vye, N., & Teachable Agent Group at Vanderbilt (2005). Learning by teaching: A new paradigm for educational software. *Applied Artificial Intelligence, 19*(3), 363–392.

Blair, K. P. and Schwartz, D. L. (2004) Milo and J-Mole: Computers as constructivist teachable agents. In Y. Kafai et al. (Eds.) *Embracing Diversity in the Learning Sciences: The proceedings of the Sixth International Conference of the Learning Sciences* (p. 588). Mahwah, NJ: Lawrence Erlbaum Associates.

Bodemer, D., Ploetzner, R., Feuerlein, I., & Spada, H. (2004) The active integration of information during learning with dynamic and interactive visualizations. *Learning and Instruction 14*(3), 325–341

Bransford, J. D. & Schwartz, D. L. (1999). Rethinking transfer: A simple proposal with multiple implications. In A. Iran-Nejad & P. D. Pearson (Eds.), *Review of Research in Education, 24*, 61–101. Washington, DC: American Educational Research Association.

Brennan, S. E. (1966). Lexical entrainment in spontaneous dialog. *Proceedings, 1996 International Symposium on Spoken Dialogue*, 41–44.

Cassell, J. (2004). Towards a model of technology and literacy development: Story listening systems. *Journal of Applied Developmental Psychology, 25*, 75–105.

Chan, T.-W. (1995). Social learning systems: an overview. In Collis, B., Davies, G. (eds.), *Innovative adult learning with innovative technologies.* IFIP Transactions A-61, North-Holland, 101–122.

Chi, M. T. H., Siler, S. A., Jeong, H., Yamauchi, T., & Hausmann, R. G. (2001). Learning from human tutoring. *Cognitive Science, 25*, 471–533.

Cohen, P. A., Kulik, J. A., & Kulik, C.-L. C. (1982). Educational outcomes of peer tutoring: A meta-analysis of findings. *American Educational Research Journal, 19*, 237–248.

Deutsch, M. (1973). *The resolution of conflict: Constructive and deductive processes.* New Haven, CT: Yale University Press.

Dillenbourg, P. & Self, J. (1992). People Power: a human-computer collaborative learning system. In Gauthier, G. & McCalla, G. (eds.), *Intelligent Tutoring Systems*. Lecture Notes in Computer Science 608, Springer Verlag, 651–660.

Gordin, D. N., & Pea, R. D. (1995). Prospects for scientific visualization as an educational technology. *Journal of the Learning Sciences, 4*, 249–280.

Graesser, A. C., Person, N., & Magliano, J. (1995). Collaborative dialog patterns in naturalistic one-on-one tutoring. *Applied Cognitive Psychologist, 1995*, 9, 359–387.

Hartman, K. & Blair, K. P. (2005). The unless switch: adding conditional logic to concept mapping for middle school students. *CHI '05 Extended Abstracts on Human Factors in Computing Systems* (pp. 1439–1442). New York: ACM Press.

Hegarty, M. (2004). Dynamic visualizations and learning: getting to the difficult questions. *Learning and Instruction, 14*, 343–351.

Kafai, Y. & Harel, I. (1999). Learning through design and teaching: Exploring social and collaborative aspects of constructionism. In I. Harel & S. Papert (Eds.), *Constructionism*. Norwood, NJ: Ablex.

Kinchin, I. M. and Hay, D. B. (2000). How a qualitative approach to concept map analysis can be used to aid learning by illustrating patterns of conceptual development. *Educational Research, 42*(1), 43–57.

Koedinger, K. R. & Anderson, J. R. (1998). Illustrating principled design: The early evolution of a cognitive tutor for algebra symbolization. *Interactive Learning Environments, 5*, 161–180.

Kuhn, D. (1995). Scientific thinking and knowledge acquisition. *Monographs of the Society for Research in Child Development, 60*(4), 152–157.

Lin, X. D. & Lehman, J. (1999). Supporting learning of variable control in a computer based biology environment: effects of prompting college students to reflect on their own thinking. *Journal of Research In Science Teaching, 36*, 837–858.

Lowe, R. (1999). Extraction information from an animation during complex visual learning. *European Journal of Psychology in Education, 6*(2), 225–244.

Lowe, R. (2004). Interrogation of a dynamic visualization during learning. *Learning and Instruction, 14*, 257–274.

Mathon, S. & Koedinger, K. R. (2003). Recasting the debate: Benefits of tutoring error detection and correction skills. In U. Hoppe, F. Verdejo, & J. Kay (Eds.), *Artificial Intelligence in Education: Shaping the Future of Learning through Intelligent Technologies, Proceedings of AI-ED 2003* (Vol 97, pp. 13–18). Amsterdam: IOS Press.

Moreno, R., Mayer, R. E., Spires, H. A., & Lester, J. C. (2001). The case for social agency in computer-based teaching. Do students learn more deeply when they interact with animated pedagogical agents? *Cognition and Instruction, 19*(2), 177–213.

Novak, J. D. (1996). Concept mapping as a tool for improving science teaching and learning. In D. F. Treagust, R. Duit, and B. J. Fraser, (Eds.) *Improving Teaching and Learning in Science and Mathematics* (pp. 32–43). London: Teachers College Press.

Okita, S. Y. & Schwartz, D. L. (2006). When observation beats doing: Learning by Teaching, *Proceedings of the 7th International Conference of the Learning Sciences* (ICLS) (Vol. 1, pp. 509–515). New Jersey: Lawrence Erlbaum Associates.

Palincsar, A. S. & Brown, A. L. (1984). Reciprocal teaching of comprehension-fostering and comprehension monitoring activities. *Cognition and Instruction, 1*, 117–175.

Reeves, B. & Nass, C. (1966). *The Media Equation: How people treat computers, televisions and new media like real people and places.* Cambridge, UK: Cambridge University Press.

Renkl, A. (1995). Learning for later teaching: An exploration of mediational links between teaching expectancy and learning results. *Learning and Instruction, 5*, 21–36.

Schwartz, D. L. (1995). The emergence of abstraction in dyad problem solving. *Journal of the Learning Sciences, 4*, 321–354.

Schwartz, D. L. (1999). The productive agency that drives collaborative learning. In P. Dillenbourg (Ed.), *Collaborative learning: Cognitive and computational approaches* (pp. 197–218). New York: Elsevier Science.

Sears, D. & Schwartz, D. L. (April, 2004). *Risks and Rewards of Jigsawing Teachable Agents.* Paper presentation at AERA. San Diego.

Shimoda, T. A., White, B., & Frederisken, J. (2002). Student goal orientation in learning inquiry skills with modifiable software advisors. *Science Education, 86*, 244–263.

Schnotz, W., Boeckheler, J., & Grzondziel, H. (1999). Individual and co-operative learning with interactive animated pictures. *European Journal of Psychology in Education, 14*(2), 245–265.

Simon, H. A. (1996). *Sciences of the Artificial, 3rd Edition.* Cambridge, MA: MIT Press.

Smith, D. C., Cypher, A., & Spohrer, J. (1997). Programming agents without a programming language. In J. M. Bradshaw (Ed.) *Software Agents* (pp. 165–190). Menlo Park, CA: AAAI/MIT Press.

Steiner, I. (1972). *Group process and productivity.* New York: Academic Press.

Tomasello, M. & Farrar, M. J. (1986). Joint attention and early language. *Child Development, 57*, 1454–1463.

Tversky, B., Morrison, J. B., & Bétrancourt, M. (2002). Animation: Can it facilitate? *International Journal of Human-Computer Studies, 57*, 247–262.

Viswanath, K., Adebiyi, B., Biswas, G., & Leelawong, K. (2004). A Multi-Agent Architecture Implementation of Learning by Teaching Systems. *4th IEEE Intl. Conference on Advanced Learning Technologies* (pp. 61–65), Joensuu, Finland.

Uretsi, J. A. R. (2000). Should I teach my computer peer? Some issues in teaching a learning companion. In G. Gauthier, C. Frasson, & K. VanLehn (Eds.). *Intelligent Tutoring Systems* (pp. 103–112). Berlin: Springer-Verlag.

7

Making Sense of Animation

How Do Children Explore Multimedia Instruction?

Mireille Bétrancourt and Alain Chassot

INTRODUCTION

With the increasing sophistication of computer technologies and decreasing production costs, multimedia documents offering highly animated and inter-active graphics are becoming ubiquitous in instructional materials. However, research on how learners process such multimedia information in order to construct a mental model of the learning material has emerged only in the last decade. From an applied perspective, a key issue is whether multimedia documents are actually beneficial to learning when compared with more tra-ditional materials. It is therefore important to identify the conditions under which educational benefit is more likely to occur. From a more fundamental research perspective, many issues still remain to be thoroughly investigated. These include questions about how people process multimedia documents and what this processing may tell us about cognitive processes involved in constructing mental models.

In this chapter we focus on instructional multimedia documents that include animated graphics or animation. An instructional multimedia doc-ument can be defined as a *"presentation involving words and pictures that is intended to foster learning."* (Mayer, 2001, p. 3). More generally, words refer not only to verbal information in natural language, but also to symbolic infor-mation that can accompany graphics, such as formulae in mathematics or chemistry. For the purposes of this chapter, animation is defined as "[...] any application which generates a series of frames, so that each frame appears as an alteration of the previous one, and where the sequence of frames is determined either by the designer or the user" (Bétrancourt and Tversky, 2000, p. 313). This definition encompasses not only computer-controlled ani-mation, but also interactive animation in which the user can control the pace or the events occurring in the presentation. In this chapter, we will use the expression "animated instruction" to instructional multimedia material that includes both verbal or symbolic information and animated pictorial information. We also define learning as the construction of a "runnable mental model" (Mayer, 1989) of the to-be-learned content.

It is generally believed that animation is effective for conveying dynamic information, and consequently should improve learners' understanding of concepts involving change over time. However, research has failed to find systematic benefits from using animation to foster conceptual understanding. As with other areas of research into multimedia learning, it is vital to pose the right type of question. In this case, the relevant question is not "*does* animation promote learning?" but rather "*when* and *why* is animation likely to promote learning?" In order to understand the conditions under which animation may be beneficial to learning, further investigation is needed of how humans construct mental models from animated graphics. In the last decade or so, research has developed powerful experimental paradigms that have led to both cognitive theories of multimedia learning (Mayer, 2001; Schnotz & Bannert, 2003) and guidelines for designers (Moreno & Mayer, 1999; Narayanan & Hegarty, 2002). However, the experimental settings employed have usually involved university students studying materials "out of context." Although this approach may be fine for investigating specific factors such as presentation and interface format, it is not suitable for capturing the behavior of actual learners in real settings. The research reported in this chapter addresses the question of how young learners in school settings study multimedia documents that include animated graphics supported by verbal commentaries. Such research is needed to provide guidelines for the design of effective multimedia instructional materials that can fully exploit the educational potential of animation. Children were chosen as participants for this investigation not only because they are a particularly relevant population of learners, but also because animation is claimed to be particularly attractive and motivating to young students. The primary purposes were to characterize the exploration behaviors that young students spontaneously exhibit when faced with animated instruction and to elicit their views on the respective roles of verbal and animated information in the instruction. A secondary purpose was to investigate whether the prospect of subsequent assessment affected students' exploration behavior and subjective reactions.

INSTRUCTIONAL USES OF ANIMATED GRAPHICS

How Visualization Helps Understanding

In the last two decades, a large body of research in cognitive psychology has investigated whether the widespread enthusiasm for the use of graphics in instructional material can be supported by empirical evidence as to their actual effectiveness in promoting learning. Most of the research in this area compared text alone with text and pictures in terms of subjects' performance on retention and inference tests. The findings largely support the claim that graphics benefit learning, with most studies indicating that graphics improved memory for the illustrated information and comprehension of the situation described in the text (Denis, 1984; Levie & Lentz, 1982; Levin, Anglin, & Carney, 1987). More recently, studies have investigated the conditions under which graphics are beneficial to memorization and comprehension (Mayer & Gallini, 1990; Scaife & Rogers, 1996; Schnotz & Kulhavy, 1994).

Various reasons have been advanced to explain the beneficial effects of graphics. Some of these reasons are associated with the affective role that graphics can fulfill. For example, graphics may be aesthetically appealing, humorous, attention-attracting, or motivating. (Levie & Lentz, 1982; Peek, 1987). However, animations may also confer benefits by fulfilling a cognitive role. According to dual-coding theory, by conveying information in both verbal and pictorial codes, a double track is provided for the processing, encoding, and retrieval of this information (Kulhavy, Brandon, & Caterino, 1985; Paivio, 1986). Graphics also provide a means to use space for representing elements and their relations, be they inherently or metaphorically spatial in nature, thus taking advantage of the power of spatial reasoning and inference in human cognitive system (Larkin & Simon, 1987; Tversky, 1995, 2001). Graphics may indeed be "worth a thousand words" when one needs to describe situations that are inherently spatial and multidimensional, such as faces, maps, knots, and the like. Finally, the proponents of mental model theory assert that, ultimately, readers form a mental representation which is structurally analogical to the situation described. From such mental models, new information can be inferred, missing information completed, and contradictions resolved (Johnson-Laird, 1983). Providing an analogical visualization through a graphic is considered to facilitate mental model construction (Mayer, 1989). Schnotz and Bannert (2003) have provided an elaborated account of mental model formation in terms of how verbal-symbolic information and depictive information are conjointly and interactively processed. Graphics could also help to facilitate mental model construction by offering an external representation that supports an internal representation, thus partially offloading information from working memory and increasing available processing capacities.

Using Animation to Convey Dynamic Information: When Does It Work?

The characteristic that distinguishes animations from other graphics is their direct visualization of changes that occur over time. Animation is used extensively in multimedia instructional materials where it may also be designed to allow interaction. Because animations visualize temporal change, they seem particularly well suited to conveying information that is inherently dynamic, such as biological processes, mechanical systems, and physical phenomena. However, many research studies have failed to find benefits of animation over static graphics, even when the subject matter involves change over time. Morrison and Tversky (2001) compared animated graphics, static graphics, and text alone for teaching the permissible paths of people or vehicles. Graphics produced better performance than text alone, but animated diagrams provided no benefits compared to (single) static diagrams. Rieber and Hannafin (1988) and Rieber (1989) found no facilitation for animation in teaching Newton's laws of motion to elementary school students. Using multimedia instructional materials designed according to guidelines and principles derived from a cognitive process model of multimedia comprehension, Hegarty and Narayanan (2002) found no difference in learning outcomes between those who viewed animation and those who viewed static graphics. A conclusion that can be drawn from such studies is that animation is not the only type of graphic that can lead to "runnable mental model" (Mayer, 1989) of the subject matter.

Tversky, Bétrancourt, and Morrison (2002) examined studies in which animation was found to be beneficial to learning and concluded that in those studies, animation conveyed information that static graphics did not. For example, Thompson and Riding (1990) used an animation to explain the Pythagorean theorem to junior high school students that incorporated rotation and translation to depict equivalence in length and area. They found that students studying the animation outperformed students studying a static graphic or a series of graphics depicting important steps. In such cases, animation is assumed to be beneficial to learning because it conveys additional information that is crucial to the process of constructing a satisfactory mental model of the subject matter. This crucial information conveyed by the animation concerns fine-grained microsteps that cannot be inferred by learners who are novices in the depicted domain (Tversky et al., 2002).

Animation can be generated by computer, recorded on video from a real scene, or be formed from a mixture of real and computer-generated features. Whereas the technology should not, in itself, change the way animation is cognitively processed, the kind of information that is conveyed from the temporal nature of animation is critical to learning. Lowe (2004) distinguished three kinds of information:

- *Transformation*, that involves form changes in graphic depicted items (shape, color, and texture);

- *Translation*, that involves the movement of whole items relative to the reference frame or relative to each other.
- *Transition*, that involves the partial or complete appearance/disappearance of items, due to temporal evolution (change in the viewpoint, or having elements added or removed).

Using animation when none of these three kinds of information is required to understand the subject matter is probably inadvisable. Inappropriate use of animation may not merely fail to provide benefits, it may even be harmful to learning (Bétrancourt, in press; Rieber, 1990; Rieber & Kini, 1991).

One of the main concerns for practitioners is how animation can be put to best educational use. Some of these possible uses are (Bétrancourt, in press):

- *Supporting the visualization*: animation can be used to visualize dynamic phenomena that are not easily perceptible (space and time scale), impossible to realize in practice (too dangerous or too expensive), or not inherently visual (representation of abstract concepts such as forces).
- *Inducing a 'cognitive conflict'*: Animation can be used to visualize phenomena that are not spontaneously conceived in the correct fashion. Research has revealed that in physics, naïve conceptions often dominate over the scientific conceptions even amongst advanced students (Kaiser, Proffitt, Whelan, & Hecht, 1992). In such cases, using correct and incorrect animations of the phenomenon could help learners to make their conceptions explicit.
- *Enabling learners to explore a phenomenon*: Animation can be used to provide a suitable interactive learning experience that encourages learners to generate hypotheses and test them by manipulating the depiction's parameters. In this case the animation becomes a simulation that is used in a discovery-learning approach (Schnotz, Böckheler, & Grzondziel, 1999; Hegarty, Quilici, Narayanan, Holmquist, & Moreno, 1999).

Instructional Uses of Animation With Children

Much of the more recent research into learning with animation has been carried out via laboratory experiments involving university students. In contrast, there have been relatively few experimental studies investigating the effect of animated visuals with primary or secondary school students. However, there is a large body of earlier educational research into the effect of audiovisual materials, such as television, in the classroom and some of this deals with visual information that was both animated and accompanied by narration. Because of the hypothesized developmental differences between visual and auditory encoding process and representation modes (Kail & Hagen,

1977), it was suspected that visual presentation would distract young children from the verbal (auditory) information. However, the findings with regard to text memorization and comprehension were mixed. Gibbons, Anderson, Smith, Field, and Fischer (1986) found that preschool children (4-year-olds) remembered actions better when they were conveyed visually than when they were described by a narrator, but the difference disappeared in older children (7-year-olds). Younger children also produced more elaborations with the visual presentation than with the audio alone and remembered dialogue better. It was hypothesized that the visual representation would supplement and complement developing verbal abilities, thus facilitating construction of a mental model of the referent situation. Moreover, children as young as 4 years showed unexpectedly good comprehension of cinematic montage conveying implied actions, character perspective, spatial relationships, and simultaneity of action (Smith, Anderson, & Fisher, 1985). Such audiovisual research provided evidence that young children have the abilities to process animated visual information effectively and derive complex information from it.

With regard to computer animation, Rieber and colleagues (Rieber 1989; 1990; 1991 a, b; Rieber and Hannafin, 1988) designed computer-based lesson to teach Newton's laws of motion to elementary school students. In some studies, a positive effect of animation was found (Rieber 1990, 1991 a, b) but in others, animation was not superior to static graphics (Rieber and Hannafin, 1988; Rieber, 1989). As was found to be the case for adults (Hegarty et al., 1999), the effects obtained were related to the instructional approach used rather than to the effect of using dynamic or static visuals (Rieber, 1990). However, animation was found to positively influence continuing motivation (Rieber, 1991 a). In a free choice situation, children studying animated instruction were more inclined to return to the instruction than children studying static graphics or text instruction. Because all three instructional materials in Rieber's study were displayed on a computer, this result cannot be explained by the attractiveness of the computer tool.

As indicated earlier, the key issue is not whether animation is beneficial to learning but rather *when and why* animated instruction may be effective. Addressing this issue requires further investigation of the cognitive processing of interactive, dynamic visualizations.

Online Processing of Animation

To date, few studies have investigated the on-line processing of educational resources that feature animated graphics. One reason that researchers have tended not to tackle this area is that there are methodological impediments because online cognitive processes are not accessible through standard measures or simple observation. Both online and offline approaches to the collection of process data have been proposed. Online methods involve the recording of indicators such as interrogation behavior, whereas offline methods include approaches such as collecting learners' retrospective accounts of the processing activity they engaged in during task performance. Lowe (2003, 2004) analyzed meteorological novices' approaches to extracting information from a weather map animation showing how meteorological features change over time. Participants first studied animated weather maps and then predicted the future pattern of meteorological markings on a blank map without the aid of animation. After completing the prediction task, learners 'replayed' a demonstration of how they interrogated the animation while at the same time explaining the actions they had taken. Attention tended to be devoted to meteorological features in the animation with high perceptual salience, to the neglect of thematically relevant features with comparatively low perceptual salience. Similar processing biases in novices' extraction of relevant information have been identified for static graphics (Zhang, 1997). Using records of interrogation activity and participants' commentaries on the replay of their performance, Lowe (2004) further analyzed the strategies used by students in processing the animation. He distinguished four *spatial* strategies (exclusive, inclusive, intra-regional, interregional) according to the area explored and the extent of the spatial relationships involved. In addition, four classes of *temporal* strategies were considered (confined, distributed, abstractive, integrative) according to the time period explored and the extent of the temporal relationships involved. The meteorological novices who participated in that study tended to use low-level strategies focused upon specific locations and specific periods while neglecting more inclusive dimensions.

In traditional primary and secondary education, the emphasis tends to be on verbal material as the main vehicle for presenting to-be-learned information, whereas depictive information is too often merely used for attracting and motivating students. A study by Holliday (1976) confronted this issue by designing an instructional situation in mathematics in which the graphics conveyed the critical information. He found that children studying the graphics alone outperformed those studying these graphics in association with text. Holliday concluded that children in school situations in which text and graphics are presented together tend to 'underprocess' the graphic information, because they think that the most critical information is conveyed by the text. In contrast, Kalyuga, Chandler, and Sweller (2000) found that providing a combination of verbal and pictorial material improved learning performances for novices trade apprentices compared with pictorial information only. However, as learners became more experienced, the pictorial material alone was more beneficial than the verbal-pictorial combination. According to the authors, providing verbal explanation for learners who no longer needed it induced a redundancy effect that resulted in cognitive overload. Although these findings do not conflict with the positive general multimedia effect found in numerous studies, they do provide evidence that "more can be less" when learners possess sufficient prerequisites to take advantage of a single representational format. Under such circumstances, processing of unnecessary verbal information may prejudice processing of the pictorial information.

It has also been suggested that insufficient processing of pictorial information may have a negative effect on learning from animated graphics, a phenomenon described by Lowe (2004) as 'underwhelming.' Such an effect could come about if an animation induces an *illusion* of understanding, due to its visualization of the whole chain of events, but does not result in comprehension of the functional and causal relationships involved. Comprehension of an animated presentation may also be compromised if learners lack the conceptual and strategic skills required to extract relevant information. Despite the optimistic claims of some semiologists (e.g., Vandendorpe, 1999), it is doubtful whether today's 'Multimedia Age' children have developed skills and, attitudes with respect to graphic information that are radically different from those of their predecessors.

RESEARCH QUESTIONS

A fundamental determinant of the potential of animation to positively affect multimedia learning is the learner's capacity to process the animated information successfully (Lowe, 2004). Previous studies by Lowe (2003, 2004) found that novice learners tend to apply ineffective strategies when interrogating complex, interactive animation. However, the research also provided evidence that adults' exploratory behaviors were systematic rather than random with a number of distinctive (yet inappropriate) search patterns being exhibited. If adults fail to adopt appropriate strategies when interrogating animations, the question arises as to how successful children are likely to be in a similar situation Given that children are one of the main targets for educational animation, this is an important but neglected educational issue.

The present research investigated how children aged 12 to 13 years navigated a multimedia learning environment that offered both text and animations. In this study, information in these two representational formats was displayed separately and organized in a weak linear structure. The following questions were addressed:

i. Do young learners invoke systematic strategies when studying the available information or do their strategies reflect opportunistic navigation? What is the nature of the strategies used?
ii. Do these learners favor text or animated information?
iii. What views do the learners report regarding their exploration of the multimedia material and the specificity of each representational format?

These issues were investigated using an experimental study in which participants (7th grade students) were asked to study a multimedia document explaining the retrograde motion of the planet Mars as seen from the Earth. Two conditions were compared. Participants in the *assessment* condition were told that at the end of the study period, they would be tested on what they had learnt. For those in the *no-assessment* condition, there was no mention of a subsequent test. We assumed that the prospect of an assessment would affect the previously mentioned questions in the following way:

i. The students in the *assessment* condition would be expected to use a more systematic strategy for studying the material and more often go back to pieces of information already explored.
ii. Students in the *assessment* condition would be expected to pay more attention to text than to animation because in primary and secondary education, formal assessments traditionally give more emphasis to verbal than to depictive information.

The approach used in this study investigated strategies from a broad rather than an in-depth perspective focusing on few participants (contrast with Lowe, 2004). All actions that students took while working with the instructional material were automatically recorded on an individual basis. Participants were not asked to provide retrospective commentaries on their behavior but instead at certain points, the students were asked to nominate a reason for their actions from alternatives provided in a multiple choice questionnaire. Our objective was to identify a broad range of strategies that children use, irrespective of individual and contextual factors, and so a large number of varied participants was involved. Further, because our focus was upon strategies, the effect of animation on learning outcomes was not investigated. Indeed, investigation of learning outcomes would imply careful attention in designing the instructional material to promote conceptual understanding (e.g., Narayanan & Hegarty, 2002), design of a control condition, and control on previous learning in the domain.

METHOD

Participants and Design

A total of 218 seventh grade students (12 to 13 years old) participated in their usual classrooms through a web-based program to which their teachers had been introduced by the experimenter. Because the participants regularly used computers at school, they were accustomed to all the required basic interface operations. Teachers volunteered to have their classes participate in the experiment and were given written instruction to be read to the participants. In cases of technical faults or other problems with the procedure, data from the participants concerned were not taken into account. The experimental design involved one between-subjects factor with two levels (*assessment* vs. *no-assessment*) with 130 participants in the *assessment* condition and 88 in the *no-assessment* condition.

Material

The material was developed using Macromedia Flash program for the client side, and php mySQL database languages for the server side. Once launched, the presentation ran automatically without intervention from the teacher or experimenter. Presentation was the same in both conditions and consisted of an identification screen, a multiple-choice questionnaire, then the instructional material. After the instructional material, participants completed the same multiple-choice questionnaire a second time. The identification screen asked the participant for some identification data (first name, school, name of the teacher) and while the protocols were subsequently de-identified, students were asked for their names in order to provide credibility for the assessment condition. The multiple-choice questionnaire consisted of six questions about astronomic facts presented in the instructional material, one question about the relative value of text and images in instruction, and four text and picture questions on relative motion. The instructional material explained the apparent retrograde motion of Mars. It opened with a navigation panel (see Figure 7.1) displaying the 16 phases of the instruction, each phase consisting of a short animation (5 seconds on average) and a short text piece (one to three sentences). The animated segments either depicted the relative position and motion of the planets in the solar system, or presented changes in viewpoint from an earth to a solar system perspective. They were logically sequenced so that the explanation in each segment directly followed from the content in its predecessor. However, students could use the navigation panel to choose which part of the instruction they wanted to study and so work through the

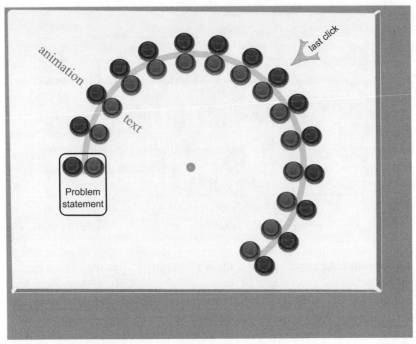

FIGURE 7.1. The navigation panel displayed for exploring the instructional material. Each of the 15 phases consisted of one piece of text and one piece of animation. In-picture captions: Problem statement (in the framed box), animation (above the curved line), text (below the curved line), and last click with the arrow, indicating the final piece of information visited.

segments in any order they wished. The semi-circular shape of the navigation panel was chosen with the intention of breaking up the implicit linear order of a straight line. No fixed study time was set for each piece of text, and animation pieces could be run as many times as desired. Whenever a text was chosen, a 'metacognitive regulation box' opened that asked why the participant was choosing either to proceed or to remain at the same step (see Appendix to this chapter). No indication was given that a piece of information had already been studied, apart from a "last click" indication signaling the final piece of information was being visited (to avoid disorientation).

Procedure

Prior to commencement, the teachers verified that participants were unfamiliar with the retrograde motion of Mars. Students participated individually in their normal computer classroom, the size of which varied depending on facilities at the school. Participants were randomly assigned to one of the

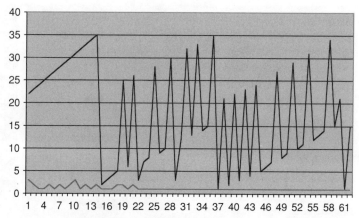

FIGURE 7.2. Example graphical representation of a student's navigation pattern.

two experimental conditions and the written instructions read aloud by the teacher before the experiment. In the *assessment* condition, students were told that they were to study an instructional document on the retrograde motion of Mars in order to prepare for a subsequent test. In the *no-assessment* condition, students were given the same general instructions but were not told they would be tested afterwards. However, participants in both conditions answered the same post-test questionnaire at the end of the experiment. After answering the pre-test questionnaire, a transition message appeared: "Thank you. Now you are going to enter the navigation panel. Here you can study text or animation for each step of the explanation." The students in both conditions studied the instructional material for a total of 20 minutes. Finally, they completed the post-test questionnaire at their own pace.

Data Analysis

Patterns of participants' navigation through the instructional material were first analyzed on an individual basis by graphing the pieces of information visited against time (actually, the student's clicks ordered by time). Figure 7.2 shows an example navigation pattern.

The y-axis represents the identifying number of the information piece (1 to 15 for text, 16 to 35 for animation) whereas the x-axis shows the click numbers ordered by time. In the example, the student clicked 61 times, first looking only at the animation pieces (click 1 to 14), then shifting to a systematic strategy where both the text and animation pieces were studied for each step. Strategies were identified and characterized according to: (a) the way the student partitioned exploration between the two representational formats (e.g., one after the other, all pieces in one representational format and then all in the other one, etc.) and (b) the regularity with which the student worked through the logical sequence of pieces (e.g., either in the suggested order or in reverse).

RESULTS

Type of Exploration Strategies

The first question addressed in this investigation was whether children invoked systematic strategies in studying such material or not. Systematic strategies are evidence of a goal-directed behavior from which underlying cognitive processes and metacognitive regulation can be hypothesized. From the graphical representation of exploration patterns, 51 categories were initially distinguished which were then conceptualized in terms of in five broad types of strategy. Table 7.1 provides a short description and an example of each strategy type.

About one fifth of the observed patterns did not correspond to any of these main strategy types. These students adopted an apparently aimless approach, or seemed to switch between strategies more than once.

Frequencies of Each Type of Strategy

As well as identifying the main strategy types used by participants, it is also important to know the relative frequency with which each strategy was used and whether the prospect of an assessment had an effect on strategy choice. Table 7.2 summarizes the percentages of participants using each strategy.

The most frequent strategy was *Systematic alternation* between the two representational formats in which the students followed the exploration order suggested by the display and paid attention to both sources of information for each step. The students tended to study the animation before the text (62% vs. 38% of the patterns in this category). *Successive study* was the second most common strategy and involved all pieces in one representational format being explored before exploration was shifted to the other format. Because this would appear to work against the making of making relations between the corresponding verbal and animated pieces of information, this is a somewhat surprising finding. The third strategy, *One representational format only*, is also rather unexpected because half of the provided information is ignored. However this strategy included 16.5% of the patterns, which represented about

TABLE 7.1. *Exploration Strategies Identified in the Protocols: Description and Examples of Pattern*

Name of the Strategy	Description	Example
Systematic alternation	Systematic alternation between the text and the animated information. In the example, the student started by viewing the animation before reading the text.	
Successive study	Successive study of the two representational formats. In the example, the student first explored all animated pieces and then studied all text pieces.	
One representational format only	Only one representational format was explored while the other was ignored. In the example, the student explored only the animated information	
Weak alternation	The students explored text and animation pieces alternately, but in a less systematic way than in the systematic alternation strategy.	
Strategy shift	The student shifted from a one representational format strategy to systematic alternation strategy. In the example, the students explored all animated pieces and then shifted to alternation at the end of the explanation.	

TABLE 7.2. *Percentage (Number in Parentheses) of Exploration Patterns Falling into Each Category*

Strategies	Assessment	No Assessment	Total
Systematic alternation	36.9% (48)	22.7% (20)	31.2% (68)
animation then text	23.1% (30)	14% (12)	19.3% (42)
text then animation	13.8% (18)	9% (8)	11.9% (26)
Successive study	20% (26)	25% (22)	22% (48)
animation first	14.6% (19)	18.2% (16)	16% (35)
text first	5.4% (7)	68.2% (6)	6% (13)
One representational format	16.1% (21)	17% (15)	16.5% (36)
Animation only	14.6% (19)	17% (15)	15.6% (34)
Text only	1.5% (2)	0	0.9% (2)
Strategy shift	5.4% (7)	0	3.2% (7)
Weak alternation	4.6% (6)	7.9% (7)	6% (13)
Anim. – text	4.6% (6)	6.8% (6)	5.5% (12)
Text – anim	0	1.1% (1)	0.4% (1)
Undetermined	16.9% (22)	27.3% (24)	21.1% (46)
Total	*100% (130)*	*100% (88)*	*100% (218)*

one student in six. Most patterns in this category involved the study of the animation only. In very few cases (1.5%, corresponding to only 2 of the 218 students) the students studied text information only. *Weak alternation* and *strategy shift* strategies were uncommon (respectively 6.4% and 3.2%). In most cases (5 out of 7 patterns), once students had shifted to alternation, they studied the text before the graphical information.

The second issue was whether the adoption of a particular strategy was affected by the prospect of receiving and assessment. A Chi-square computed on the number of protocols falling into each of the six main categories (the five strategies plus the undetermined category) revealed a significant difference in the distribution of patterns as a function of the condition ($\chi^2_{(5)} = 12.6$, $p < .05$). Because we expected that students in the *assessment* condition would explore the material in a more systematic way, the two conditions were compared with regard to the number of students using an identifiable strategy against the number of students whose strategy was not identified (undetermined category). The Chi-square revealed a marginally significant difference ($\chi^2 = 3.37$, $p = .066$). However, when we excluded from the identifiable strategies the "weak alternation" category, which is the least systematic and the most questionable, we found a significant difference between the two conditions ($\chi^2 = 4.98$, $p < .05$). Moreover, instances of shifting from one representational format to alternation appeared only in the *assessment* condition.

Because some patterns did not seem to follow the exploration order suggested by the navigation panel display, subsequent analysis was performed in order to determine the extent to which the students followed the display's regular left-to-right progression. Irregular patterns were produced by 11.9% of the participants (corresponding to 26 patterns). The most frequent of these was a progressive exploration followed by a regressive exploration (12 patterns), consistent with working around the border of the navigation panel's circular shape. In the previous analysis, all such patterns were placed into the *successive study* category. The students studied all pieces in one representational format in the progressive order then the other representational format in the regressive order. It is unclear whether those students appreciated that the pieces of information in each side of the navigation panel were related together (see the display in Figure 7.1). The reverse order exploration (regressive then progressive) was observed only twice (0.9% of the observations). Four students (1.8% of the patterns) explored the material in the reverse order, which meant going from right to left, ignoring the starting indication that was located on the left. Finally, 8 patterns (3.7% of the patterns) did not follow any regular progression, all being categorized in the undetermined strategy. No appreciable differences in the order of exploration were found between the *assessment* and *no-assessment* conditions.

Integration of Text and Pictorial Information

The second main question was whether the students favored text or pictorial information and to what extent the prospect of an assessment affected this behavior. First, the percentages of the total number of information segments studied by each student that were either text segments or animation segments was computed on an individual basis. Table 7.3 compares these percentages across the two conditions.

Contrary to our expectations, these results show a tendency to favor the animated information in both conditions with no tendency to study more text information in the *assessment* condition. Further, there was no difference between the conditions in the time spent studying the text information.

Finally, we computed the percentage of participants who tackled the text information before the graphic information when studying each step on the first time, irrespective of the strategy they invoked. Again, we found very similar proportions across condition (44% in the assessment condition and 45% in the no assessment condition). In other words, a slight majority of students chose to study the animated information first, but no effect of condition was observed.

TABLE 7.3. *Percent Pieces of Text and Animated Information Studied and Mean Number (and Standard Deviation) of Clicks Averaged Across Subjects in the Two Conditions*

	Conditions	
	Assessment	No Assessment
Animation% total	54%	54%
Mean number	17.8	17.1
SD	4.2	3.8
Text	46%	46%
Mean number	15.3	14.5
SD	**9.6**	**7.3**
Overall mean number of clicks	33.1	31.7
SD	13.5	9.6

METACOGNITIVE QUESTIONS

Two short questionnaires were administered before and after the study phase in order to assess students' attitudes toward verbal and pictorial information. When asked before studying the material which representational format (text or pictures) they thought explained the best, 50% subjects nominated pictures as more effective than text, whereas only 3% favored the text. The remaining 47% of participants considered that the text and pictures explained equally well. After studying the material, the number of students favoring the text increased to 10%.

Reflexive questions in the series of so-called 'metacognitive boxes' presented to the students while they navigated the instructional material were intended to give insights into the motivations underlying their navigation. Because the students gave an unequal number of answers, the observed differences could not be tested for statistical significance. At their first click on the navigation panel, students were asked whether they had any idea about how they were going to proceed. Thirteen percent of the students said they had very precise idea and 19% a general idea, whereas 68% responded that they did not know yet. No difference between conditions was observed.

During navigation through the instructional material, a box popped up asking why the student chose to study a piece of information concerning a step other than the step just studied, or why the choice was made to remain on the same step, whichever was the case. When choosing to explore another step, 67.6% of the answers in the *assessment* condition and 60.2% in the *no-assessment* condition were that they 'had a good understanding of the step just studied and wanted to proceed with the instruction.' Of the remainder, 13.5%

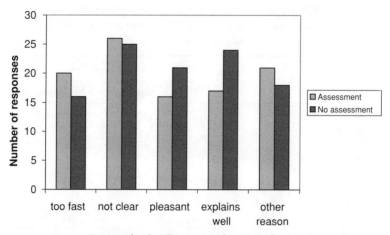

FIGURE 7.3. Reasons for deciding to run the piece of animation again.

of students answered that they were just curious (17% *no-assessment* and 10% *assessment*).

The pattern of answers regarding the reasons for choosing to study the other piece of information (text or animation accordingly) in the same step was more differentiated: 53.4% of the students reported that they understood well but sought confirmation; 24.2% of the students reported that they were not sure of their understanding and needed complementary information; and 12.8% of the students reported that they were just curious (10.2% chose none of the aforementioned reasons). No difference between the two conditions was observed.

Finally, when the students chose to run a piece of animation more than once, a question asked why they decided to do so. The box did not appear if the student visited a different piece of information before running the animation another time. The results are presented in Figure 7.3.

The most frequent reason for studying an animation segment again was that the students found it unclear. Students in the *assessment* condition mentioned that the animation was too fast more often than students in the *no-assessment* condition. Students in the *no-assessment* condition more often chose reasons related to the "positive" motivations (pleasant and explanative) than students in the assessment condition.

No data could be collected on the reasons why students decided to reread a piece of text information because the text information remained on the screen until the student decided to close it.

DISCUSSION

Young students were provided with animated instruction explaining the apparent retrograde motion of Mars as seen from Earth. The instructional material contained 15 steps, each consisting of a piece of animation and a piece of text that could not been studied simultaneously. Navigational access to the pieces of information was displayed in a semi-circular shape with buttons for choosing text or animation segments arranged along its borders. Two conditions were compared: In the *assessment* condition, students were told that there would receive an assessment test afterwards, whereas in the *no-assessment* condition, the test was not announced.

The first question concerned whether children invoked systematic strategies to explore the animated instruction. Approximately 80% of the students invoked a systematic strategy, which is higher than may have been expected for students this age given the lack of specific instruction about the regularity and unusual shape of the navigation panel. Five strategies were identified with respect to how students explored the mutually referring information in the two representational formats. The most frequently used strategy was a systematic alternation between the text and the corresponding animated information. Only one third of the students chose to explore pieces of information in both representational formats consecutively for each step. One student in five adopted a strategy that involved studying all steps in one representational format only and then all steps in the other. Although learning performances were not evaluated here, this successive strategy could be considered as likely to be comparatively ineffective because, according to the 'contiguity principle' (Moreno & Mayer, 1999) or 'integration principle' (Chandler & Sweller, 1991), the mutually referring text and animated information should be treated as closely as possible to each other in space and time. Unexpectedly, we found a significant number of students (16.5%) ignored one of the representational formats, typically the text information. In contrast to the investigations by Holliday (1976) or Kalyuga et al. (2000), verbal and pictorial information in the present study were not redundant for novices in the domain. Apart from the basic arrangement of planets that students might already have known before the experiment, animation and text were complementary, each representational format being critical to comprehension of the other in most of the steps. With regard to temporal exploration of the material, most students adopted a regular progression through the instruction, following the order suggested by the starting indication and the circular shape. This comprehensive approach differs from that found by Lowe (2004) because we did not observe any 'confined strategies' in which the focus was limited to only particular aspects of the available information. However the display in Lowe's study was a continuous animation, not a set of discrete pieces. Nevertheless, like Lowe, we found evidence of inappropriate exploration with half the students using a *successive study* strategy consisting of a progressive order followed by a regressive order. This approach was completely counter to the fact that the text and visual information were highly complementary and so intended to be processed together.

The second question concerned whether children favored one or other of the representational formats (text or animation). The results gave some support for Vanderdope's (1999) assumption that children are attracted by visual representational formats. In two thirds of the alternation strategy patterns, the animation was studied before the corresponding text information. This attraction to animation may not be detrimental because there is evidence that studying the visual before the verbal is better than the opposite (Baggett, 1984). Apart from two students, all of the 15% who studied one representational format only chose animation and ignored text information. Moreover, students overall studied in average slightly more animation than text information (54% vs. 46%). These results are consistent with previous studies on both computer animation (Rieber, 1991a) and audiovisual material (Smith, Anderson, & Fisher, 1985), indicating that children can be strongly attracted by animation, even in a school situation.

Our third question concerned children's views on learning from verbal and pictorial information. When asked which representational format offered the best explanation, they predominantly chose pictures over text, which is consistent with the assumption of an attraction for visual material. Students tended to justify their exploration behavior in terms of achieving increased understanding, and very rarely in terms of pleasure or curiosity.

Finally, we expected that the prospect of a subsequent assessment would encourage systematic exploration and a preference for verbal information. We found a significant effect of the condition on the type of strategy adopted by the students. Students who expected a test more often chose to follow a systematic strategy (*systematic alternation, successive study, one representational format*, or *strategy shift*) than did students in the *no-assessment* condition. Moreover, we observed the *strategy shift* category only in the assessment condition which may indicate students realized midway that they had to consider both sources of information in order to fully understand the explanation. Contrary to our expectations, we found that students in the *assessment* conditions neither paid more attention to text information, nor explored more pieces of information. The reasons given by students concerning their choice of information did not provide evidence of a clear contrast in the motivations underlying the students' behavior in the two groups. Differences were observed regarding the reasons for choosing to run an animation again, with the students in the *assessment* condition tending to report an understanding-based motivation whereas those in the no assessment condition tended to report a pleasure-based motivation. It is possible that the students did not consider the assessment as very important because it was not being given by their own teacher.

The types of exploration behavior found in this study were probably affected by the particular format of the instructional material. First, the strict separation of text and animated information for each step may have led students to assume that one representational format was sufficient for understanding the explanation. Second, the unusual circular shape of the navigation panel may have created an impression of circularity, thus inducing what was called irregular exploration (progressive order in one representational format than regressive order for the other). Further, this exploration order, which from a perceptual perspective could be considered as tracing around the navigation panel's border, may have been adopted to avoid disorientation in a quite complex instructional display. Finally, the metacognitive boxes may have provoked metacognitive regulation processes, that led to more frequent systematic strategies than would otherwise have been the case.

In conclusion, the results of this experiment showed that despite their young age, most of these students adopted a systematic strategy when exploring the multimedia document. However, less than one third of the students adopted what would be considered as an 'effective' strategy (as defined by multimedia learning research). Most of the students did not use strategies that would allow complementary text and graphic information to be processed conjointly and progressively, a requirement for fully understanding the explanation. Fifteen percent of the students chose to ignore the text information completely, although this proportion was slightly lower for those who expected a subsequent assessment test. Given the explanative and computational power of visualization (Larkin & Simon, 1987; Tversky, 1995, 2001), children's attraction towards visualization is potentially beneficial for learning, provided that appropriate guidance is given in the instructional material. In particular, the material should indicate clearly that verbal and pictorial information are both necessary to fully understand the explanation and so should be processed conjointly. In practical design terms, this means that the verbal information (preferably auditory than written) should be provided in a way that it cannot be avoided or overlooked. If the instructional material provides a navigation panel, the spatial layout should clearly indicate the order in which the pieces of information need to be studied, regardless of aesthetic or artistic issues. Finally, further research is needed to investigate the role of metacognitive prompts that could engage children to reflect upon their exploration strategies.

APPENDIX

Question asked in the 'metacognitive regulation boxes' (translated from French).

1. You are at the beginning of your exploration and
   a. You have a precise idea of the order in which you are going to explore the pieces of information
   b. You know roughly in which order you are going to explore the material
   c. You do not know exactly, you will see.
2. You decided to run this animation again because
   a. It was too fast
   b. It was not clear
   c. You find it pleasant
   d. You find that it explains well
   e. Other reason
3. You decided to remain on this step because
   a. You think you understood well and you wish to find a confirmation
   b. You are not sure you understood well and you want to find complementary information
   c. You are just curious, there's no particular reason
   d. None of the three propositions
4. You decide to explore another step because
   a. You think you understood this step well and you want to proceed
   b. You are not sure you understood this step well and you hope that the new step will provide complementary explanations.
   c. You are not sure you understood this step but you think that it is not necessary to understand.
   d. You are just curious, there's no particular reason
   e. None of the propositions above.

References

Baggett, P. (1984). Role of temporal overlap of visual and auditory material in forming dual media associations, *Journal of Educational Psychology, 76*, 408–417.

Bétrancourt, M. (2005). The animation and interactivity principles in multimedia learning. In R. E. Mayer (Ed.), *The Cambridge Handbook of Multimedia Learning* (pp. 287–296). New York: Cambridge University Press.

Bétrancourt, M. & Tversky, B. (2000). Effect of computer animation on users' performance: a review. *Le travail Humain, 63*(4), 311–330.

Chandler, P. & Sweller, J. (1991). Cognitive load theory and the format of instruction. *Cognition and Instruction, 8,* 293–332.

Deci, E. L. & Ryan, R. M. (1985). *Intrinsic motivation and self-determination in human behavior.* New York: Plenum Press.

Denis, M. (1984). Imagery and prose: a critical review of research on adults and children. *Text, 4,* 381–401.

Gibbons, J., Anderson, D. R., Smith, R., Field, D. E., & Fischer, C. (1986). Young children's recall and reconstruction of audio and audio-visual narratives, *Child development, 57,* 1014–1023.

Hegarty, M., Quilici, J., Narayanan, N. H., Holmquist, S. & Moreno, R. (1999). Designing multimedia manuals that explain how machines work: Lessons from evaluation of a theory based design. *Journal of Educational Multimedia and Hypermedia, 8,* 119–150.

Holliday, W. G. (1976). Teaching verbal chains using flow diagrams and texts. *Audio– Visual Communication Review, 24,* 63–78.

Johnson–Laird, P. N. (1983). *Mental Models: Toward a cognitive science of language, inference and consciousness.* Cambridge: Cambridge University Press.

Kail, H. & Hagen, J. (Eds.). (1977). *Perspectives on the development of memory and cognition.* Hillsdale, NJ:Lawrences Erlbaum Associates.

Kaiser, M. K., Proffitt, D. R., Whelan, S. M., & Hecht, H. (1992). Influence of animation on dynamical judgments. *Journal of Experimental Psychology: Human Perception and Performance, 18,* 669–690.

Kalyuga, S., Chandler, P., & Sweller, J. (2000). Incorporating learner experience into the design of multimedia instruction. *Journal of Educational Psychology, 92,* 126–136.

Kulhavy, R. W., Brandon, L. J., & Caterino, L. C. (1985) Conjoint retention of maps and related discourse, *Contemporary Educational Psychology, 10,* 28–37.

Larkin, J. H. & Simon, H. A. (1987). Why a diagram is (sometimes) worth ten thousand words. *Cognitive Science, 11,* 65–99.

Levie, W. H. & Lentz, R. (1982). Effects of text illustration: a review of research. *Educational Communication and Technology Journal, 30,* 195–232.

Levin, J. R., Anglin G. J., & Carney, R. N. (1987). On empirically validating functions of pictures in prose, in D. M. Willows & H. A. Houghton (Eds.), *The Psychology of Illustration: I. Basic Research* (pp. 116–135). New York: Springer.

Lowe, R. K. (2003). Animation and learning: selective processing of information in dynamic graphics. *Learning and Instruction, 13,* 247–262.

Lowe, R. K. (2004). Interrogation of a dynamic visualization during learning. *Learning and Instruction, 14,* 257–274.

Mayer, R. E. (1989). Models for understanding. *Review of Educational Research, 59*(1), 43–64.

Mayer, R. E. (2001). Multimedia learning. New York: Cambridge University Press.

Mayer, R. E. & Gallini, J. K. (1990). When is an illustration worth ten thousand words? *Journal of Educational Psychology, 82,* 715–726.

Morrison, J. B. & Tversky, B. (2001). The (in)effectiveness of animation in instruction. In J. Jacko & A. Sears, Eds. *Extended Abstracts of the ACM Conference on Human Factors in Computing Systems* (pp. 377–378). Seattle: ACM.

Moreno, R. & Mayer, R. E. (1999). Cognitive principles of multimedia learning: the role of modality and contiguity. *Journal of Educational Psychology, 91,* 358–368.

Narayanan, N. H. & Hegarty, M. (2002). Multimedia design for communication of dynamic information. International *Journal of Human–Computer Studies, 57,* 279–315.

Paivio, A. (1986). *Mental representations: a dual coding approach.* New York: Oxford University Press.

Peek, J. (1987). The role of illustration in processing and remembering illustrated text. in D. M. Willows & H. A. Houghton (Eds.), *The Psychology of Illustration: I. Basic Research* (pp. 115–151). New York: Springer.

Rieber, L. P. (1989). The effects of computer animated elaboration strategies and practice on factual and application learning in an elementary science lesson. *Journal of Educational Computing Research, 5,* 431–444.

Rieber, L. P. & Kini, A. S. (1991). Theoretical foundations of instructional Applications of computer-generated animated visuals. *Journal of computer-based Instruction, 18,* 83–88.

Rieber, L. P. (1990). Using computer animated graphics in science instruction with children. *Journal of Educational Psychology, 82,* 135–140.

Rieber, L. P. (1991a). Animation, incidental learning, and continuing motivation. *Journal of Educational Psychology, 83,* 318–328.

Rieber, L. P. (1991b). Effects of visual grouping strategies of computer–animated presentations on selective attention in science. *Educational Technology, Research, and Development, 39,* 5–15.

Scaife, M. & Rogers, Y (1996). External cognition: how do graphical representations work? *International Journal of Human–Computer Studies, 45,* 185–213.

Schnotz, W. & Bannert, M. (2003). Construction and interference in learning from multiple representations. *Learning and Instruction, 13,* 141–156.

Schnotz, W., Böckheler, J., & Grzondziel, H. (1999). Individual and co-operative learning with interactive animated pictures. *European Journal of Psychology of Education, 14,* 245–265.

Schnotz, W. & Kulhavy, R. W. (1994). *Comprehension of Graphics.* Amsterdam: Elsevier.

Smith, R., Anderson, D., & Fischer, C. (1985). Young children comprehension of montage. *Child development, 56,* 962–971.

Thompson, S. V. & Riding, R. J. (1990). The effect of animated diagrams on the understanding of a mathematical demonstration in 11 – to 14–year–old pupils. *British Journal of Educational Psychology, 60,* 93–98.

Tversky, B. (1995). Cognitive origins of conventions. In F. T. Marchese (Ed.), *Understanding Images,* pp. 29–53. New York: Springer-Verlag.

Tversky, B. (2001). Spatial schemas in depictions. In M. Gattis (Ed.), *Spatial Schemas and Abstract Thought* (pp. 79–111). Cambridge: MIT Press.

Tversky, B., Morrison, J. B., & Bétrancourt, M. (2002). Animation: can it facilitate? *International Journal of Human-Computer Studies, 57,* 247–262.

Vandendorpe, C. (1999). *Du papyrus à l'hypertexte: essai sur les mutations du texte et de la lecture,* Paris: Editions La Découverte.

Zhang, J. (1997). The nature of external representations in problem solving. *Cognitive Science, 21,* 179–217.

8

Mental Representations, Cognitive Strategies, and Individual Differences in Learning with Animation: Commentary on Sections One and Two

John R. Kirby

My earliest memories of "learning with animation" come from an introductory Chemistry course that I took as a first-year university student, many years ago. There were too many thousands of students in the course for us to all fit into one lecture theatre, and it would have been too tedious, or expensive, or both, to have us taught in separate groups of even 500. My university decided to innovate with the educational technology of the time, film. The lectures were filmed in a studio, and then played to us (in groups of 800). Two features of these lectures stand out (I confess I remember none of the chemistry). First, every once in a while, the professor teaching the course would hold up a model of an atom or molecule, and attempt to count the electrons (or other bits) that stuck out. He was fine when there were small numbers of these sticking-out bits, but when there were more than about 10, he either lost count, couldn't find enough, or found too many. When this happened, he would become flustered and start again, to howls of merriment from his audience. (The films were not edited, or if they were, not in a way that flattered the lecturer.) Without an in-class professor to glare at us and threaten retribution, the howls would continue and increase long after the event, interfering with any learning that might have otherwise occurred. Not a banner day for educational technology.

The second feature was more successful. The instructors were concerned, I imagine, that students might not show up on time, or might take too long to "settle down" in the absence of a flesh-and-blood professor in the room to admonish offenders. Their solution was to show, at the beginning of each class, a few minutes of an old movie from the *Flash Gordon* series (e.g., *Peril from Planet Mongo*). (I've since acquired the complete set on videocassette, the only residue from the Chemistry course. They are terrible films, with particularly appalling special effects.) The tactic worked: we showed up on time, and were instantly quiet when the film began. The disruptions only began as the chemistry content intruded.

I'm optimistic that the course and the educational technology used in it have improved substantially over the last 40 years! Because part of my responsibility is to comment on individual differences, I should add that at least one of my classmates in introductory Chemistry went on to do a Ph.D. in a related field (though I doubt that even he would say that he did so *because of* the instruction he received in that course).

The lessons I draw from that experience, and from a few others over the years, are (a) no matter how good (or bad) the technology, it is more important how it is used and what the learners do with it; and (b) technology can be used to attract attention, but it is important to select the objects of attention carefully. Very loosely, those are the themes of this chapter.

ANIMATION IN LEARNING

My task is to discuss issues arising from the papers on individual differences and cognitive processes, that is those by Bétrancourt and Chassot; Hegarty and Kriz; Lowe; Mayer; Ploetzer, Bodemer, and Neudert; Schnotz and Rasch; and Schwartz, Blair, Biwas, Leelawong, and Davis. My comments concern five issues or themes. The first concerns the mental representation which learning with animation is intended to affect. The second is the involvement of learner-generated strategies: learners have many options in how to approach a complex learning task, and researchers and teachers need to deal with the resulting variance in performance. Two further issues are the role of attention, and the distinction between learning and performance. Finally, all of the papers share an interest in "real-world" learning; this is good, because it should lead to better educational practices, but it brings with it additional challenges. I make a few comments on these costs and benefits in the final section. But first some introductory comments on the importance of animations in learning, and the difficulties of relating cognitive processes and individual differences.

THE IMPORTANCE OF ANIMATIONS IN LEARNING

The authors of these chapters have commented on the ubiquity of visual displays in learning materials, and the increasing use of animated (dynamic) displays. Other research would be required to determine the reasons for the use of such displays, but I suspect that the reasons have more to do with cost (it will be cheaper to buy more computers – or let the students use their own – than to hire more faculty) and motivation (they'll pay more attention if their favorite cartoon characters move around the learning materials) than with cognitive theory (how well they learn). As with many educational innovations, the assessment of effectiveness will follow long after implementation. The technicians and programmers who are most able to design and produce the animations are the ones least trained to predict or understand their effects – this is the problem of the "technology-centered" approach that Mayer describes. Furthermore, any complex innovation is as likely to produce losers as winners; just as some learners will be advantaged by the innovation, other will be disadvantaged. In this way educational innovations are like environmental shifts in evolutionary psychology (see, e.g., Geary, 2005). Cognitive and instructional psychology has the responsibility to advise designers on optimal designs for animated learning environments, but also, assuming that the designers pay no more attention to such suggestions than usual, to advise learners on the best ways of dealing with such environments (and, if necessary, of avoiding them). The papers in this volume provide many examples of how healthy skepticism can help test particular materials and ideas, and how a coherent set of principles is beginning to emerge from the studies being done.

COGNITIVE PROCESSES AND INDIVIDUAL DIFFERENCES

Discussing cognitive processes and individual differences in one paper continues to present challenges. Cronbach (1957) observed that scientific psychology had two traditions, one *experimental* and the other *differential*; much the same point had been made by Ferguson (1954) a few years earlier. The two traditions have methodologically distinct cultures. The experimental tradition relies upon random assignment to distinct treatment groups, treatments that are relatively short in duration, and the analysis of variance to test hypotheses because the "effects" are generally orthogonal. Constructs come from theory, and are often measured by single variables whose reliability and validity are not investigated. Differences between participants are consigned to the error term, something to be minimized, or "disappeared" through the analysis of covariance. The differential tradition focuses instead upon those individual differences, relying upon broadly representative samples, correlations between variables, and factor analysis to discover underlying dimensions or constructs, whose reliability and validity are of great concern. Regression analysis is used to explore relations between constructs, or even "effects," but orthogonality of causal variables seldom occurs. Group differences, whether naturally occurring or artificially constructed, are inconveniences that are either ignored or tested ahead of time with the hope that they will be small enough to be ignored.

The methodological differences have been resolved through the recognition that analysis of variance and regression are both manifestations of the general linear model (e.g., Pedhazur & Schmelkin, 1991), and that it is often useful to include both treatment group and individual difference variables, and their interactions, in the same analysis. Not surprisingly there continue to be experimental studies that would have benefited from an added individual differences perspective, and *vice versa*. In the present group of papers, the combined approach is best represented by Hegarty and Kriz.

Theory differences between the two traditions were greater when Cronbach (1957) and Ferguson (1954) wrote, but many remain. The experimental tradition proposes and tests theoretical constructs without much concern that these constructs demonstrate stable variability among individuals. Consider for example working memory. The experimental approach has been to design tasks so that working memory, or different aspects of it, affect task performance; task differences, rather than individual differences, are the effects of interest, in that they *cause* different amounts of working memory to be available to the learner. The result has been the intricate models of working memory that are cited in some of these papers. Lacking to some extent has been a focus on whether some learners have *more of it* (whatever that might mean) or are more willing to use it, or whether the answers to these questions depend upon the circumstances. The differential approach, on the other hand, has worried less about the intricacies of working memory, and has instead tended to develop simpler and more robust measures that reveal stable individual differences. Lacking in this approach has been a concern for theoretical detail and for the effects of context. Individual differences theories are content to discuss relatively broad constructs such as intelligence, spatial ability, and cognitive strategy that have uncertain existence in theories of cognitive processes. Conversely, individual differences theories have been slow to embrace constructs that show low variability, or in developmental terms, slow growth (working memory space may be one example here). It is probably most helpful to see these theoretical traditions as complementary, and to aim to test particular theories in both traditions. There are many examples of research that has adopted this direction, especially those exploring the cognitive processes involved in intelligence (e.g., Sternberg & Pretz, 2005; Das, Naglieri, & Kirby, 1994; Kane & Engle, 2002). Cognitive load theory (van Merriënboer & Sweller, 2005; see also Schnotz and Rasch, this volume) is a good example of a fruitful marriage of the experimental and differential approaches – pre-existing individual differences in ability and prior knowledge are seen to mediate and moderate the effects of experimental manipulations.

Mental Representations

The papers dealing with individual differences and cognitive processing in this volume share, explicitly or implicitly, an underlying model of cognition that is multi- (or at least dual-) channel and in which the nature of the mental representation changes with depth of processing (see especially the paper by Mayer). As such, the focus on learning with animations presented here offers an intriguing arena in which to observe the complex interaction and integration of the processes proposed by theory. The dual-channel feature has roots extending back at least to Broadbent (1958) and Paivio (1971), but is best known more recently in the work of Baddeley (e.g., 1986). The depth aspect, indicating that the nature and content of mental representations differs with increased processing, relates to the work of Craik and Lockhart (1972) on levels of processing in memory, Johnson-Laird (1983) on mental models, Kintsch (1998) on situation models in text processing, Ericsson and Kintsch (1995) on long-term working memory, and Baddeley (2001) on the episodic buffer. As the processing becomes deeper, the modality-specific nature of the representations is lost, either being replaced by codes specific to the alternative modality (as when an image is verbally encoded) or by modality-free, or at least modality-interrelating, codes. The nature of the highest-level model is still unclear – are there two or more types of model, which are "inter-related" (whatever that may mean), or are there true cross-modal models that integrate information from both channels?

One of the main purposes of animation is to enhance or facilitate the accurate construction of such representations (Bétrancourt & Chassot, this volume). The formation of mental representations of either the verbal/descriptive or imaginal/depictive types comprises high-level cognitive processes – as such we should expect that individual differences in mental abilities and prior knowledge are associated with competence, though to some extent *provided* representations (in the form of adjunct aids) may compensate for weaker abilities or knowledge (Hegarty & Kriz, this volume). Schwartz et al. provide an intriguing example of the learner building an external mental representation of what they know, in a "Teachable Agent." Externalizing a mental representation forces the learner to be explicit, allowing the learner to test his or her knowledge and leading to learning opportunities; the presence of an agent (whether electronic, a peer, or even an instructor) to interrogate or interact with the learner intelligently is a further benefit.

This theoretical work provides an excellent basis for future empirical research. For me it raises question about the control of these cognitive processes. For example, to what extent is the progression of visual depiction to mental image to propositional description fixed or automatic, as opposed to being under the control of executive/strategic factors? To what extent do these executive/strategic factors comprise stable individual differences? What factors influence these individual differences, either in the individual's background or in the current instructional situation? Clearly there is variability, as not all images are verbally described, and not all verbal information is imagined, but can these decisions and the variability be predicted and controlled?

Depth is an interesting characteristic. Most instructors espouse depth as a goal, but it is often not clear what it entails. At different times depth can refer to abstraction, in which a more general feature is extracted from given information (with the likely loss of detail), or analysis, in which the conceptual foundation of the presented material is examined (with likely retention of detail), or even extension, in which the connections of the presented material to other information are made (with likely increase in detail) (see Bloom & Volk, 2006). The present focus on visual and verbal (or descriptive and depictive) channels further complicates this: greater depth, of all three sorts, can probably be attained in either channel and by crossing channels. These possibilities offer further effortful choices to learners. These choices and their success must surely depend upon the learners' prior knowledge (Hegarty & Kriz, this volume), including prior experience of learning in multi-media environments.

Strategies and the Control of Processing

The type of learning examined in these chapters is effortful; there may be little purpose in attempting to enhance effortless learning. As learning becomes more effortful, issues regarding strategies, willingness to exert effort, and cognitive (executive) control arise. Aside from the usual options that learners have to *not* read or to *not* pay attention, these multimodal learning situations present more options and further complexity, as noted by Ploetzer et al. First, they may, like text, force the processing of their meaning (For literate individuals, it is difficult to not process the meaning of presented words, thus the well-known Stroop effect; MacLeod, 1991). This is precisely why some interventions employ animations, so that students cannot avoid attending to them. This effect may be more true for relatively superficial meanings, deriving from lower-level heuristic processing (Geary, 2005). Second, however, when confronted with a complex graphic, the learner has many more options, and some of these depend upon specialized knowledge and ability. Consider for example a text with an accompanying graph, where the graph illustrates and specifies relations described in the text. Some learners may choose not to inspect the graph, and others may not recognize its relation to the text. Of those who do inspect it, some may encode it shallowly, either remembering it as a picture or interpreting it superficially ("a line going up"). Others may misinterpret it, for instance assuming that left-to-right in the graph corresponds to time, or that a line going up from left to right means improvement. Extracting deeper meaning from the graph, even for learners with the appropriate background knowledge and skill, may require more effort than they are willing to devote. Different types of graphics may appeal or not to different learners – those lacking background in mathematics and science may choose not to process graphs, whereas those without knowledge of art may avoid images of paintings. Learning preferences regarding visual and text information (e.g., Kirby, Moore, & Schofield, 1988) may influence the degree to which students engage with the material and the quality of the metacognitive strategies they employ.

Questions of strategy raise issues concerning knowledge of the tactics, skills, and abilities that strategies call upon, and about habitual learning strategies, or styles (e.g., Kirby, 1988). They also raise the issue of engagement: in real learning situations, learners may not be willing to engage in effortful processing, even if they believe that doing so will increase their learning and enhance their performance in a course. Students live in complex worlds with many competing demands on their time – it would be naive to think that they always do what is best for their learning!

Bétrancourt and Chassot described a number of qualitatively different strategies for inspecting text and graphics; such behavioral data are ultimately incomplete, because a seemingly inappropriate inspection pattern may make sense in terms of the mental model that the learner was constructing. To fully understand a strategy, one needs to know the basis of the learner's decisions at the time (which may be very difficult or impossible to uncover or reconstruct) and have a sense of the strategy's outcomes. Bétrancourt and Chassot made a step in the right direction by asking metacognitive questions after each navigation decision, but the learners' responses (wanted to proceed, curious, sought confirmation, and so on) seem too vague to relate to mental model construction. Learners may not be capable of more detailed verbalization, at least not during learning, and they may not be able to reconstruct their reasons if the questions are held until later. Perhaps more detailed options need to be presented, or some on-going external representation of the mental model needs to be made. In the absence of any outcome information, which Bétrancourt and Chassot did not report, it is difficult to evaluate the effectiveness of particular strategies.

Ploetzer et al. suggested that successful and unsuccessful learners adopt different strategies, but so far we do not have a good framework for describing the sequences of actions learners adopt when studying; until such a framework is created, we will have to rely upon more generic descriptions that may not suffice for instructional purposes. There is also the question whether strategies differences are the cause or the consequence of the learning differences. In either case, their conclusion that we need to develop guidelines for instruction in how to process complex or multimedia displays is valid.

Schwartz et al. provided a valuable tool, the Teachable Agent, with which to observe and encourage learners' strategies and initiative. Their evidence suggests that the "co-mingling" of student and Teachable Agent initiative increases learning – in that the Teachable Agent is the learner's own creation (to some extent), this may even be more valuable than having a teacher present.

Lowe showed an example in which learners have full control over the "running" of an animated display. Although in theory user-control should be the ultimate adaptation to individual strategies, Lowe's example demonstrates that complexity, and the mismatch between what learners know and do not know, may set limits on this. Too much control may increase cognitive load and even overwhelm some learners. Like Ploetzer et al., Lowe found and portrayed distinct strategies for inspecting the learning materials. In the absence of performance information, it is difficult to know which are the "best" strategies, and it may turn out that the best strategy depends on the individual's mix of abilities and knowledge. It seems likely, however, that piecemeal inspection is not likely to support comprehensive and deep mental model construction.

LEARNING STYLES

Learning styles can be conceived as habitual ways of approaching learning situations, ways that depend upon students' prior knowledge and abilities and the ways in which they interpret the current learning situation. Two senses of learning style are appropriate to mention here. First, because of the focus of these chapters on learning from text and graphics, it is important to consider learners with styles that prefer visual as opposed to verbal material (e.g., Kirby, Moore, & Schofield, 1988; Kirby 1993). Kozhevnikov, Hegarty, and Mayer (2002) argued for the existence of three visual-verbal styles, each based on distinct neuro-cognitive abilities: a verbal style for dealing with verbal material, a visual (iconic) style for dealing with and remembering static images, and a spatial style for processing relationships within graphic displays. The iconic style appears to be related to low spatial ability, whereas the spatial style is associated with high spatial ability. This suggests to me that when students learn in multi-modal learning environments, their efforts to do dual processing will fall into two pathways, one relating verbal or text information to static images, the other relating verbal information to more dynamic but more importantly more abstract, spatial mental representations. The first type of representation may be suited for certain tasks, such as relating a described journey to a depicted map, or remembering a painting for later description, or understanding that a line graph corresponds to a text statement that "gross domestic product is going up"; other tasks, for instance making relative distance judgments regarding a described journey from a supplied map, or recognizing figure-ground relationships in a painting, or comparing several graphs to see whether there is a relationship between GDP increases and employment, would seem to require the more spatial style. If the distinction between the visual and spatial styles holds up, then learners and instructional designers will have a challenge regarding how to deal with different types of learning information. One hopes that the distinction will not prove insurmountable, that learners will be able to excel in both.

It is difficult to determine which of the multimedia learning materials may have been subject to this type of learning style difference. One likely example is Lowe's weather maps: weather map features such as low-pressure systems do not have a constant shape, and so a more relational mental representation is required, more consistent with the spatial style. Ploetzer et al's graphical material would clearly favor the spatial style. Schnotz and Rasch's time-zone maps could be useful for investigating this issue: their simulation pictures perform the spatial transformations for the learner, perhaps placing less load on the processes of the spatial style than static pictures would. On the other hand, both their manipulation and simulation pictures are fairly abstract and unfamiliar representations of the Earth, and so may require considerable spatial visualization ability to relate the images to prior knowledge. Hegarty and Kriz's conclusion that spatial ability is only required when verbal and graphic information need to be integrated is provocative, and may tell us something about the higher levels of cross-modal mental model construction; on the other hand, it is possible that spatially complex animations, ones that might only be used with more advanced learners, may require spatial visualization, even in the absence of verbal material. Mayer's now-classic bicycle pump animation, and many of the other successful interventions, seem to minimize the need for spatial visualization ability or the spatial style. This may be ideal for less able, or low-prior-knowledge, learners, or for those lacking the spatial style; it is not clear if there is any negative consequence for those with high spatial visualization skills.

APPROACHES TO LEARNING

The second sense of learning style that is relevant concerns depth of processing (see also my earlier discussion of depth in the Mental representation section). A number of the current papers have referred to depth or quality of learning (e.g., Mayer's generative processing). Deeper learning, that which is coherent and extensive, which not only masters the content at hand but also supports transfer to more distant content, is the espoused goal of most education, though educational practices, from mass lecturing to multiple choice assessment, may undermine that goal (Biggs, 1999). Students too may sincerely espouse deeper learning goals, but not know how to achieve them, and may not even know that they do not know. At least two aspects of deeper learning are relevant, one being the cognitive structures that are or have been assembled (i.e., long-term memory schemas, mental models, situation models, etc.), and the other being the learners' orientation or approach to such learning. Biggs (e.g., 1993, 1999), Entwistle (e.g., Entwistle, McCune, & Walker, 2001), and Pintrich (2004) have shown that learners differ reliably in how they approach or conceptualize academic learning. Though the various authors describe different analytic systems (and none would be happy with the term *learning style*), I would summarize them as portraying learning conceptions in two dimensions, deep and surface. The more one demonstrates allegiance to the deep approach, the more one relates information, seeks meaning, and is intrinsically motivated by learning. The more one follows the surface approach, the more likely one is to fragment learning, rely upon memorization, and be extrinsically motivated. These two characteristics, deep and surface, mix in different proportions to form individual learners' conceptions of learning.

Ploetzer et al. observed strategy differences between their more and less successful learners that seem to reflect this difference in approach. Their less successful learners seemed to adopt a more superficial approach, going back to the instructional materials as soon as a problem was encountered, presumably to look for the specific solution. The more successful learners seemed to be more interested in constructing their own mental representation, apparently a deeper approach. Again it is not clear whether the strategy is the cause or the consequence of the learning.

Depth is an important goal of instruction, but effort is required. It is possible that excellent animations or other graphics make learning too easy, for some learners or in some situations. Though too much challenge may decrease engagement and learning, too little challenge may also decrease learning (see Schnotz and Rasch, this volume). I have a few further comments on this issue in the Learning and performance section.

Attention and Cognitive Load

One of the key, foundational insights of cognitive psychology is that attention is limited. It is very difficult to pay attention to more than one task at a time. Our only hopes in a complex world are to automate some tasks so that they can operate in the background, without absorbing the limited resource of conscious awareness, and to maintain focus as much as possible. Maintaining focus, and excluding or inhibiting irrelevant information, are the prerequisites for working memory, higher level cognition, and intelligence, and are the responsibility of the frontal lobes of the brain (Barkley, 1997, 2001; Geary, 2005; Kane & Engel, 2002). Good teaching manages learners' attention, and teaches learners how to manage their own (Mayer, this volume).

Animated learning materials have great potential power with respect to attention. Motion is inherently attention-grabbing (or at least this is an inherent characteristic of our visual systems), and the other tricks that designers employ (lighting, typographical, and graphical cues) are all intended to make one look. If where we look is where we *should* look, and if we know what to do with what we see, animation is supporting and perhaps enhancing learning. Naïve learners will not necessarily inspect the critical aspects of the display (Lowe; Ploetzer et al., this volume). One of the messages of these papers is that where media designers get us to look is not necessarily where a thoughtful instructor would want us to look. What is entertaining in not necessarily productive.

But attention is not enough. Unless the learner knows how to encode the inspected stimulus, any benefit will be fleeting (Ploetzer et al., this volume). Encoding here refers to the aspects of the stimulus, the dimensions on which to initially encode, and then subsequently recode. Graphic material can contain information that some learners will not know how to encode, or for which their normal way of encoding is not productive. Lowe's weather maps and Ploetzer et al.'s graphs are good examples of this problem, but others abound. Graphic conventions and symbols are almost as culturally specific as those of literacy are. Quantitative data graphs (line graphs, histograms) and flow charts are just two of the many kinds of graphical displays that learners often lack the skill and knowledge to encode appropriately. Initial encoding will be effortful or of limited success if the learner is not expert with the particular stimulus type.

Beyond the initial coding, further coding is required to compute deeper relations in the observed information (as when Lowe's participants notice a cold front or cyclone) and to relate the new information to what is stored in long-term memory. Of particular relevance here is the distinction between verbal and pictorial information, which applies to the externally presented information as well as to the internal descriptive (propositional) and depictive (analog or model-like) representations. As already mentioned, depth of processing (coding) often indexes quality of learning, and may be the prerequisite for transfer (see also the section on Learning and performance).

Related to the notion of attention is cognitive load, the load upon working memory that a particular instance of instruction has for a particular learner (see Mayer; Schnotz & Rasch, this volume). Much research has shown that working memory is strongly related to attention, inhibition, and general intelligence (e.g., Barkley, 1997, 2001; Geary, 2005; Kane & Engle, 2002). The responsibility of the competent instructor is to reduce the extraneous loads on working memory (see Mayer; Schnotz & Rasch, this volume). The goal of much learning-with-animations research is to manage attention and reduce extraneous load (Mayer, this volume).

But working memory is also an individual difference dimension: as Schnotz and Rasch argue persuasively, the same instructional instance will affect learners of different working memory capacity differently. Their working memory analysis shows how less able learners may benefit from reduced cognitive load or guidance. As indicated by a many of the present authors, however, there is great danger that the animations that are intended to assist the less able learners (those in greatest need of help) may be detrimental to their learning. This will happen if the animations encourage attention to the less important content, or if they place too much load (extraneous, but perhaps also germane) on working memory, or if the graphic displays call for more knowledge than the learners have, or require more effort than they are willing to invest (e.g., Ploetzer et al., this volume).

Schnotz and Rasch's analysis also provides a plausible account why simplified instruction may harm learning. There is the danger that animations, or other "user-friendly" interventions, will remove the challenge that had encouraged the learners to exert more effort and thus process information more deeply (e.g., McNamara, Kintsch, Songer, & Kintsch, 1996). The analysis of Schnotz and Rasch offers a means to understand the varying effects of instruction, and Mayer's principles of instruction provide guidance in improving instruction. However, it is important to remember that the actual learning is done by the learner – if for whatever reason that learner does not encode the right material and process it to the appropriate depth, the instruction will have failed. Learners need to learn how to learn from even poor instruction, and need to overcome any user-friendly aids that turn out to be harmful instead of beneficial for learning. There is clearly need for more research, and careful application in this area.

Learning and Performance

When we seek to change learners' behavior, it is important to keep in mind what we are trying to accomplish. In research studies, we typically want to change performance on some task, for instance a test about bicycle pumps, or time zone differences. We do not tend to ask questions about how durable this performance change is, or whether it contributes to other longer-term changes in capability. These can be seen as questions about transfer, across time or task (e.g., Barnett & Ceci, 2002). Kintsch (1994), for instance, has suggested that too many studies examine learning in a narrow sense (acquisition of information) rather than in a broader one (changes to long-term memory schemas that generate changes across tasks and into the future). Similar concerns should always be considered about instructional research, including the studies presented in this volume. It is possible that some graphic aids or animations facilitate (to use Schnotz and Rausch's term) performance, but do not contribute much to durable or generative learning. In a similar vein, the presence of graphics may increase the learner's sense of comprehension, or even actual comprehension, without necessarily augmenting the learner's capacity to act more competently in the future. A false sense of competence may even harm future action.

The acquisition of particular information is important in education, but it is far from the whole story. Because the shelf-life of many facts is getting shorter, and the availability of information is increasing exponentially through the internet, most educators would agree that other capacities and traits are of at least equal and probably greater importance. These would include the schema changes to which Kintsch (1994) referred, which constitute *generative* changes to our mental capacities, and increases in our ability to sift through information and select the best (*evaluative* changes). Deeper learning, as indexed by increased relevant processing and more sophisticated mental representations, may be the prerequisite for transfer (Barnett & Ceci, 2002; Kirby, 1989).

It is difficult to assess any study on these dimensions unless the appropriate data have been collected. And of course many researchers may not have these goals, and therefore feel no need to assess them. Among the chapters of this volume, Schwartz et al. offer some evidence of transfer to more regular learning environments, but I would like to see evidence of even further transfer, across time, content, and context.

Real-World Knowledge

Real-world knowledge cannot be controlled as easily as more artificial content; thus students enter with varying amounts of relevant knowledge.

Furthermore, the immense amount of work required to set up learning tasks leads researchers to include only a few tasks per study, most frequently one. By learning task I am not referring to the knowledge represented by a single item on a test, but rather to the content represented by a textbook chapter or a lecture. Accordingly, each learning task contains a huge amount of information, but is really only one instance drawn from a very large population of such instances. Idiosyncratic effects may abound, leading to variable results, or theories may be constructed addressing learning in general but only apply to the relatively narrow content on which the studies are based. Just as we would be unhappy with a study that did not have a large enough or representative enough sample of participants, we should start to worry about studies in which the *tasks* are not numerous or representative enough. The increasingly large number of independent studies represented by the papers of this volume, especially in the review papers by Mayer and Hegarty and Kriz, give cause for optimism that these effects are robust. However, one issue that remains concerns the role of prior knowledge. Theories of comprehension point to the critical role of prior knowledge in constructing meaning from text (e.g., Kintsch, 1998), and considerable research indicates that the lack of prior knowledge can impair comprehension and learning (e.g., Perfetti, Marron, & Foltz, 1996). Low knowledge is a common correlate of poor comprehension (Nation, 2005). In laboratory studies, we often try to minimize the effect of prior knowledge, but in the real world, prior knowledge may be as important as comprehension processes and instructional methods in determining consequences. We need to measure prior knowledge better and more often, and allow it to play its role more naturally.

Coda

The field of learning from animations, or more generally of learning from verbal and graphic information displays, is an active one, generating both empirical results and theoretical interpretations. The researchers are doing a good job of challenging old and new wisdoms, and of generating guidance for practitioners. Although I am sure that many learners continue to experience the less-than-optimal type of instruction that I experienced in introductory Chemistry, I am optimistic that their number is decreasing, and that the future holds even greater promise for improvement.

References

Baddeley, A. D. (1986). *Working memory*. Oxford, UK: Oxford University Press.
Baddeley, A. D. (2001). Is working memory still working? *American Psychologist, 56,* 851–864.

Barkley, R. A. (1997). Behavioral inhibition, sustained attention, and executive functions: Constructing a unifying theory of ADHD. *Psychological Bulletin, 121*, 65–94.

Barkley, R. A. (2001). The executive functions and self-regulation: An evolutionary neuropsychological perspective. *Neuropsychology Review, 11*, 1–29.

Barnett, S. M. & Ceci, S. J. (2002). When and where do we apply what we learn? A taxonomy for far transfer. *Psychological Bulletin, 128*, 612–637.

Biggs, J. B. (1993). What do inventories of students' learning processes really measure? A theoretical review and clarification. *British Journal of Educational Psychology, 63*, 1–17.

Biggs, J. (1999). *Teaching for quality learning at university.* Buckingham, UK: Open University Press.

Bloom, J. W. & Volk, T. (2006). The use of metapatterns and other broad concepts for research into complex systems of teaching, learning, and schooling. Manuscript submitted for publication.

Broadbent, D. E. (1958). *Perception and communication.* New York: Pergamon Press.

Craik, F. I. M. & Lockhart, R. S. (1972). Levels of processing: A framework for memory research. *Journal of Verbal Learning and Verbal Behavior, 11*, 671–684.

Cronbach, L. J. (1957). The two disciplines of scientific psychology. *American Psychologist, 12*, 671–684.

Das, J. P., Naglieri, J., & Kirby, J. R. (1994). *Assessment of cognitive processes: The PASS theory of intelligence.* New York: Allyn and Bacon.

Entwistle, N., McCune, V., & Walker, P. (2001). Conceptions, styles, and approaches within higher education: Analytical abstractions and everyday experience. In R. J. Sternberg & L. F. Zhang (Eds.), *Perspectives on thinking, learning, and cognitive styles.* Mahwah, NJ: Lawrence Erlbaum Associates.

Ericsson, K. A. & Kintsch, W. (1995). Long-term working memory. *Psychological Review, 102*, 211–245.

Geary, D. C. (2005). *The origin of mind: Evolution of brain, cognition, and general intelligence.* Washington, DC: American Psychological Association.

Ferguson, G. A. (1954). On learning and human ability. *Canadian Journal of Psychology, 8*, 95–112.

Johnson-Laird, P. N. (1983). *Mental models.* Cambridge, MA: Harvard University Press.

Kane, M. J. & Engle, R. W. (2002). The role of prefrontal cortex in working-memory capacity, executive attention, and general fluid intelligence: An individual-differences perspective. *Psychonomic Bulletin & Review, 9*, 637–671.

Kintsch, W. (1998). *Comprehension: A paradigm for cognition.* Cambridge, UK: Cambridge University Press.

Kintsch, W. (1994). Text comprehension, memory, and learning. *American Psychologist, 49*, 294–303.

Kirby, J. R. (1993). Collaborative and competitive effects of verbal and spatial processes. *Learning and Instruction, 3*, 201–214.

Kirby, J. R. (1989). Generality and specificity in strategy instruction. *Canadian Journal of Special Education, 5*, 179–186.

Kirby, J. R. (1988). Style, strategy, and skill in reading. In R. R. Schmeck (Ed.), *Learning styles and learning strategies.* New York: Plenum Press.

Kirby, J. R., Moore, P. J., & Schofield, N. J. (1988). Verbal and visual learning styles. *Contemporary Educational Psychology, 13*, 169–184.

Kozhevnikov, M., Hegarty, M., & Mayer, R. E. (2002). Revising the visualizer-verbalizer dimension: Evidence for two types of visualizers. *Cognition and Instruction, 20*, 47–77.

MacLeod, C. M. (1991). Half a century of research on the Stroop effect: An integrative review. *Psychological Bulletin, 109*, 163–203.

McNamara, D. S., Kintsch, E., Songer, N. B., & Kintsch, W. (1996). Are good texts always better? Text coherence, background knowledge, and levels of understanding in learning from text. *Cognition and Instruction, 14*, 1–43.

Nation, K. (2005). Children's reading comprehension difficulties. In M. J. Snowling and C. Hulme (Eds.), *The science of reading* (pp. 248–271). Oxford, UK: Blackwell.

Paivio, A. (1971). *Imagery and verbal processes*. New York: Holt, Rinehart and Winston.

Pedhazur, E. J. & Schmelkin, L. P. (1991). *Measurement, Design, and Analysis: An integrated Approach*. Hillsdale NJ: Lawrence Erlbaum Associates.

Perfetti, C. A., Marron, M. A., & Foltz, P. W. (1996). Sources of reading comprehension failure: Theoretical perspectives and case studies. In C. Cornoldi and J. Oakhill (Eds.), *Reading comprehension difficulties: Processes and intervention* (pp. 137–165). Mahwah, NJ: Lawrence Erlbaum Associates.

Pintrich, P. R. (2004). A conceptual framework for assessing motivation and self-regulated learning in college students. *Educational Psychology Review, 16*, 385–407.

Sternberg, R. J. & Pretz, J. E. (Eds.). (2005). *Cognition and intelligence: Identifying the mechanisms of the mind*. Cambridge, UK: Cambridge University Press.

van Merriënboer, J. J. G. & Sweller, J. (2005). Cognitive load theory and complex learning: Recent developments and future directions. *Educational Psychology Review, 17*, 147–177.

SECTION THREE

INTERACTIVITY AND LEARNING

9

Animated Pedagogical Agents

How Do They Help Students Construct Knowledge from Interactive Multimedia Games?

Roxana Moreno

INTRODUCTION

Animated pedagogical agents (APAs) are animated, lifelike characters designed to facilitate learning in computer-based environments (Baylor, 1999; Bradshaw, 1997; Johnson, Rickel, & Lester, 2000; Craig, Gholson, & Driscoll, 2002). The most sophisticated APAs advise and provide feedback to students (Towns, FitzGerald, & Lester, 1998) and even adapt intelligently to learner input by having their speech and behavior be contingent on the actions a learner takes (Clarebout, Elen, Johnson, & Shaw, 2002). Some examples of APAs currently in use are: *Adele*, a 2-D female character who provides advice, coaches, and tests students as they work through medical case studies (Shaw, Effken, Fajen, Garrett, & Morris, 1997; Ganeshan, Johnson, Shaw, & Wood, 2000); *Steve*, a 3 D male character who demonstrates procedural skills in virtual environments, monitors learners' actions and reacts accordingly (Johnson et al., 2000); *Cosmo*, a 3 D anthropomorphized robot who uses adaptive coaching to teach Internet packet routing (Lester, Towns, & FitzGerald, 1999); *WhizLow*, a childish-looking 3 D human who teaches programming skills by monitoring learners' misconceptions and providing relevant advice (Gregoire, Zettlemoyer, & Lester, 1999); and AutoTutor, a talking head designed to assist college students in learning an introductory computer literacy course (Graesser, Wiemer-Hastings, Wiemer-Hastings, & Kreuz, 1999). Although APAs clearly vary in their sophistication and design, they all share the fact of having a strong visual presence in an interactive computer environment and the purpose of enhancing learning (Moreno, 2005a).

Can APAs help students construct knowledge from interactive multimedia games? In the next sections, I derive two potential roles that APAs may have in promoting student learning according to a cognitive-affective theory of learning with media (CATLM; Moreno, 2005b): a motivational role, in which the agent promotes understanding by making the learning experience more interesting and a cognitive role, in which the agent promotes understanding by facilitating the cognitive processes involved in meaning making. The goal of this review is to distinguish between animated and non-animated properties of APAs and pinpoint their motivational and cognitive roles in promoting scientific understanding in a multimedia game. Concerning the agent's motivational role, I present a set of four studies that tested a *social-cue* hypothesis according to which, APAs that include social cues (such as having an animated visual representation and a human voice to communicate with the student), help students' learning by promoting interest in the learning task. Concerning the agent's cognitive role, I present a set of two studies that tested the *interactivity* and *guidance* hypotheses. According to the former, APAs enable active learning by creating interactive learning experiences between agent and learner. A second cognitive role of importance for promoting understanding in novice learners consists of APA's guidance. According to the *guidance* hypothesis, APAs facilitate learning by guiding novice students with explanatory feedback during the process of knowledge construction.

THE MULTIMEDIA GAME SCENARIO

Consider an environmental science simulation game presented on a desktop computer in which the learner goes on a space ship to a new planet. Upon arrival, an APA named Herman – an alien bug with human-like movements and an amusing voice (Lester, Stone, & Stelling, 1999), explains that the planet has certain weather conditions (e.g., heavy rain and low sunlight) and that the learner's job is to design a plant that will survive under such conditions. In this multimedia game, Herman has the following functions: (a) he introduces each new planet and its weather conditions to the student; (b) he asks the student to choose the roots that are appropriate for the weather conditions in that planet; (c) he gives feedback on students' choice of the root; (d) he asks the student to choose the stem that is appropriate for the planet; (e) he gives feedback on students' choice of the stem; (f) he asks the student to choose the leaves that are appropriate for the planet; (g) he gives feedback on students' choice of the leaves; and (h) he takes the student to a different planet with new weather conditions. For each of the choices of root, stem, and leaves, students are presented with the corresponding library of plant parts' graphics and names, and asked to click on one of the possible options to design their plant. Herman's feedback for students' choices consists of a verbal explanation in the form of narration.

The major aspects of the above-described game are intended to foster meaningful learning in at least three ways. First, by giving Herman a strong visual and auditory presence, students may become more interested in the learning task and in turn, process the learning materials more deeply. This is the *social-cue* hypothesis tested in Experiments 1 through 4. Experiments 1 and 2 compared the motivational and learning effects of having college students (Experiment 1) or middle school students (Experiment 2) interact with the botany multimedia game either with or without Herman's visual and auditory cues (image and voice, respectively). The subsequent two experiments examined the relative contribution to learning of each social cue (image versus voice) with two different agents. Experiment 3 used the fictional agent Herman and Experiment 4 used a non-fictional agent represented by a video clip of a real person in the same multimedia game.

A second way in which the botany multimedia game promotes learning consists of having students design the plants for each visited planet rather than observing the appropriate plant design for each planet. By having students learn by doing, they become more actively engaged in the learning experience (Anzai & Simon, 1979; Doctorow, Wittrock, & Marks, 1978; Moreno, Mayer, Spires, & Lester, 2001). This is the *interactivity* hypothesis. Experiment 5 tested this hypothesis by manipulating the level of learner interactivity and comparing the cognitive and motivational effects of students who were allowed to participate in the process of meaning making by selecting plant designs from the game (interactive treatment) or by having the APA choose the correct design with no student intervention (non-interactive treatment).

Third, by providing students with explanatory feedback on their choices, the botany multimedia game helps students reflect on their hypotheses and change possible misconceptions, such as their naïve theories on biology (Kuhn, 1989; Pintrich, Marx, & Boyle, 1993). This is the *guidance* hypothesis. For example, a learner may attempt to discover the relationship between the design of plants and the weather conditions with minimal guidance from the APA. However, although it might appear that the construction of meaning is most likely to occur when students are given freedom to explore a multimedia game without much direction, the *guidance* hypothesis suggests that this can overwhelm the novice learner (Moreno & Mayer, 2005; Moreno, 2004). Experiment 6 tested this hypothesis by comparing the cognitive and motivational effects of students who were guided in the process of meaning making through either the use of explanatory feedback (guidance treatment) or the use of corrective feedback alone (non-guidance treatment).

THE MOTIVATIONAL AND THE COGNITIVE ROLES OF APAS

Advances in computer and communication technologies have the potential for improving human learning, but all too often computers are used as static, high-tech books that fail to capture the learner's interest. According to interest theories of academic motivation, students need to be personally interested in the learning task to actively process instructional material and therefore learn more deeply (Dewey 1913; Renninger, Hidi, & Krapp, 1992). This thesis has been used to support the idea that educational technology, which offers opportunities to learn by exploring, collaborating, and reflecting on multiple knowledge representations, has great potential to foster understanding by making the learning experience more motivating and cognitively engaging (Jonassen, Peck, & Wilson, 1999). To better understand the relationship between motivation and cognition, I now present a model for learning with the multimedia botany game used in the reported studies according to a CATLM (Moreno, 2005b).

As can be seen in Figure 9.1, the instructional media consists of the APA explanations entering via the learner's ears plus the APA image and program graphics entering via the learner's eyes. Learners then need to actively select and organize the verbal and non-verbal information from the game and connect it with each other. For example, verbal explanations concerning why plants in low sun environments need to be designed with large leaves has to be connected with its corresponding non-verbal information such as plant graphics showing how a plant with small leaves dies as a result of not generating enough food through the process of photosynthesis. As can be seen in the model, learning takes place when connected verbal and non-verbal information is represented into a mental model and integrated with the learner's prior knowledge. However, how much is learned will depend on two additional factors. First, students need to be motivated enough to devote the necessary attentional resources to actively process the new information delivered by the media. The role of non-cognitive factors in learning is depicted in Figure 9.1 by the upward arrows connecting students' motivation and affect to the cognitive processes that are essential for learning to occur. For example, in the case of the botany multimedia game, if learning with the presence of an animated agent is perceived as more interesting than learning without his presence, this will produce positive learning effects by influencing students to spend more effort on the learning task (Tang & Isaacs, 1993; Lester, Towns, & FitzGerald, 1999). Second, according to a CATLM, learners may use their self-regulation skills to control their motivation, affect, and cognitive processing. For example, when learners are aware of the strengths and limitations of

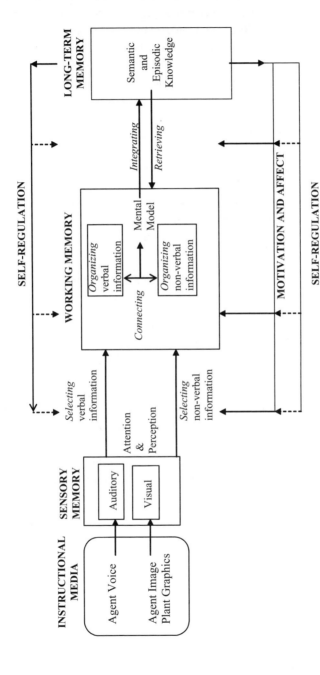

FIGURE 9.1. A Cognitive-Affective Model of Learning with the APA Botany Game.

their knowledge and/or strategies they are able to regulate their own learning
by planning and monitoring the cognitive processes needed for understanding (Bruning, Schraw, & Ronning, 1999). In addition, when learners become
aware of either their lack of motivation or their negative emotions during
learning (i.e., fear of failure, anxiety, etc.), they are able to regulate their own
learning by using self-management techniques to control their feelings and
increase their engagement in the learning task (Albert & Troutman, 1999;
Heward, 2003). The role of self-regulation in learning is depicted in Figure 9.1
by the two sets of dotted arrows operating directly over cognitive processes and
non-cognitive factors. Lastly, although not depicted in Figure 9.1 explicitly, a
CATLM assumes that learning is highly dependent on individual differences.
For example, differences in learners' prior knowledge (Kalyuga, Ayres, Chandler, & Sweller, 2003; Moreno, 2004; Tuovinen & Sweller, 1999) and traits such
as cognitive styles and abilities (Moreno & Durán, 2004; Plass, Chun, Mayer,
& Leutner, 1998) may affect how much is learned with specific media.

HOW DOES THE ANIMATED PROPERTY
OF APAS HELP LEARNING?

Despite the fact that there has not been adequate research on how exactly
game environments should be designed to realize their learning potential (De
Jong & Van Joolingen, 1998), a promising technology that has many advocates consists of presenting animated life-like pedagogical agents (Moreno,
2005a). How does the animated property of APAs help learning? Rieber (1990)
identified four common uses for animation in his review of the literature:
(a) directing students' attention to relevant portions of the screen; (b) representing information that may be otherwise hidden or too complex to understand with words alone or static pictures alone such as the steps of a procedure,
the movements of a machine, the dynamics of a natural event, or the relationships between abstract or theoretical concepts; (c) enhancing practice and
mastery of concepts through direct manipulation of graphic objects; and (d)
increasing cosmetic appeal.

According to this classification, whereas the first three functions of animations are to promote learning by helping students select, organize, and integrate the new information with prior knowledge (i.e., a cognitive role), the
fourth function of animations is to mediate cognitive processing by increasing
students' engagement (i.e., a motivational role). Consequently, the animated
property of APAs may have three different functions in learning: to direct students' attention to relevant information by using deictic gestures (i.e., such
as using gaze or arm movements); to represent procedural information with

facial or body movements that might be otherwise too complex to learn with verbal explanations alone (i.e., such as modeling how to operate a machine); and to motivate students by presenting animated engaging sequences.

How do the different functions of the animated property of the agent relate to a CATLM? First, when the agent's animation directs students' attention to relevant portions of the computer screen, learning is enhanced by helping students in the selection process depicted in Figure 9.1. Second, when the agent's animation models a procedure with a facial or body demonstration, learning is enhanced by using dual-code instruction (Paivio, 1986), that is, by creating connections between verbal and non-verbal knowledge representations. Third, if the function of the agent's animation is solely to increase motivation, learning may be enhanced indirectly, by promoting students' engagement in the learning task.

In summary, when investigating the effectiveness of APAs it is important to distinguish between the cognitive and motivational function of the agent's animated property to better understand how animations may contribute to learning. Furthermore, it is necessary to not confound the cognitive and motivational effects of the animated property of APAs and those of the non-animated properties of APAs such as the instructional method used to teach the lesson (i.e., scaffolding, direct instruction, discovery). Finally, because agent-based multimedia games usually include dynamic representations of the system to be learned, special caution needs to be given to distinguishing between the cognitive and motivational effects of agent animations and those of other animations not included in the APA itself. To illustrate these distinctions further, I now offer a few examples from the APA research.

An example of an APA with the cognitive function of directing students' attention is *PPPersona*, who uses his arm to point to relevant multimedia materials in technical and non-technical lessons (Van Mulken, André, & Muller, 1999). Van Mulken and colleagues asked college students to learn either with or without the animated *PPPersona* agent. To make agent and no-agent conditions equivalent in their cognitive function, the no-agent condition included an arrow that served the same function of selecting students' attention than the APA's arm. Results showed no significant recall or comprehension differences between conditions, suggesting that although the animated property of the agent can be used to help select information, its value is no greater than that of equivalent non-agent signaling procedures.

An example of an animated agent whose function is to demonstrate procedural knowledge is Baldi®, a three-dimensional talking head agent who serves as a language tutor. The goal of this animated agent is to produce visible speech via accurate lip movements to help deaf and hard of hearing children perceive and understand messages (Massaro, 2004). Although a limitation of this work is the lack of adequate controls for the specific type of learning support that the agent provides, evidence for the cognitive and motivational effectiveness of this APA stems from the observation that children who learned with Baldi® have persisted in some of the lessons until they were mastered, even when they were not required to do so.

An example of an animated character that is used to promote learning by increasing student motivation is the one used in the present study: Herman. More specifically, Lester and colleagues (1999) investigated the *persona* effect: the finding that the presence of an APA in a learning environment has a positive effect on student's perception of their learning experience, which in turn, promotes learning (Lester et al., 1999; Mitrovic & Suraweera, 2000). To this end, middle school students were asked to learn about plant design by interacting with Herman in one of five different types of explanatory presentations: (a) principle-based animation and voice advice plus task-specific advice; (b) principle-based animation and voice advice alone; (c) principle-based voice advice alone; (d) task-specific advice; and (e) no advice. To assess learning and motivation, students were asked to complete a pre-post test and a program rating questionnaire, respectively. Because the affective scores were overall high and all conditions showed increase on post-test performance, the researchers concluded that Herman had produced a persona effect. However, similar to the case of Baldi®, a limitation of this work is the lack of adequate controls in the study's design (i.e., a static agent or no agent condition).

Finally, a useful example to help discriminate between the cognitive function of agent-based animations and non-agent based animations is the study conducted by Craig and colleagues (2002). In this study, the researchers examined the cognitive function of pedagogical agent animations by comparing college students' learning about science with an APA in three conditions. One group was presented with an agent whose animated gestures selected students' attention to portions of the computer screen, a second group learned with a static agent, and a third group was not presented with a visual agent. An additional goal of this research was to examine the cognitive function of the animation of the scientific system to be learned. Therefore, for each agent condition (i.e., animated, static, no-agent), some students learned with sudden onset highlighting around key elements of the system, others learned with animations of the system, and others learned with static pictures of the system. Results showed no differences between the different agent conditions on students' learning. However, the onset highlighting and animations of the system led to the best learning outcomes, suggesting that non-agent animations are most effective to direct students' attention during learning.

THE SOCIAL-CUE AND INTERFERENCE HYPOTHESES

A review of the literature reveals that the APA function that is mostly emphasized is motivational (Lester et al., 1999; Mitrovic & Suraweera, 2000; Moundridou & Virvou, 2002). Furthermore, the idea that APAs can play an important motivational role in learning has relied mostly on anthropomorphism – the fact that people unconsciously ascribe mental states to computers and are quite inclined to relating to and communicating with other people (Reeves & Nass, 1996). A direct consequence of taking an anthropomorphic stance in instructional design has been that of embedding animated characters that range from cartoon-like to realistic in many interfaces. This broad implementation dates as early as 1987, when Apple Computer introduced a bow-tied young male agent to carry out tasks for an environmental researcher.

More specifically, according to the *social-cue* hypothesis, because the teaching process is an inherently social process involving communication between teacher and learner, educational games should present an APA with strong visual and auditory social cues to promote interest in learning. This hypothesis is based on empirical findings that people respond socially to computer interfaces themselves even when very few social cues are included (Nass & Moon, 2000; Reeves & Nass, 1996) and anecdotal evidence indicating that users strongly prefer to interact with others (Heeter, 1992) across a wide range of media products (Reeves & Nass, 1996). Social presence has also been argued to facilitate persuasion (Fogg & Tseng, 1999) and sales in e-commerce (Moon, 1998). As Van Mulken and colleagues (1998) state: "the main reason for personification is that it is believed to render human-computer interaction more human-human like, more social" (p. 54). Two predictions can be drawn from the *social-cue* hypothesis. First, the prediction that students who learn with a lifelike APA that has a visual cue (image) and an auditory cue (voice) will outperform those who learn with a multimedia game that has identical graphics and explanations but where the image and voice of the agent have been removed. Second, the prediction that students who learn with a lifelike APA that has more social cues (image and voice) would outperform those who learn in an identical multimedia game where the APA presents less social cues (image alone or voice alone).

Can the animated property of APAs hurt learning? It is important to note that the use of APAs in instructional technology does not go without opposition. According to APA opponents there is no need to engage in the costly development of animated human-like characters, especially if people tend to treat the computer as a social agent even when no human representation exists (Erickson, 1997; Nass, & Steuer, 1993). Moreover, it has been argued that APAs might hamper motivation and learning in at least two ways. First, the social cues represented in the APA may lead to wrong expectations about its behavior therefore creating confusion, disappointment, and frustration (Norman, 1994; Shneiderman & Maes, 1997; Wilson, 1997). Second, the animated representation of the agent may result in cognitive overload or distraction (Clark, 2003; Moreno & Flowerday, 2006; Walker, Sproull, & Subramani, 1994). For example, Mayer (2001) has documented the learning deficits experienced by learners who are overloaded by adding interesting but conceptually irrelevant material to a computer-based lesson. Evidence from research on this premise indicates that adding entertaining but irrelevant sentences to a text hurts students' retention of the core material (Garner, Gillingham, & White, 1989; Renninger, Hidi, & Krapp, 1992), that adding entertaining illustrations and text to a scientific explanation hurts students' retention and transfer of the core material (Harp & Mayer, 1997, 1998), and that adding entertaining video to a multimedia presentation hurts learning (Mayer, Heiser, & Lonn, 2001). A second way in which agent animations may hurt learning is by forcing students to divide their visual attention between the agent and other competing graphics that are essential to understand the computer lesson, a case of split-attention (Moreno, 2005a; Paas, Tuovinen, Tabbers, & Van Gerven, 2003). In sum, according to this opposite view, APAs may hinder motivation and interfere rather than facilitate the learning process. The purpose of Experiments 1 through 4 was to test this *interference* hypothesis against the *social-cue* hypothesis in an interactive multimedia game on environmental science.

EXPERIMENTS 1 AND 2: AGENT VERSUS NON-AGENT ENVIRONMENTS

Method and Procedure

The participants in Experiment 1 were 44 college students who lacked prior knowledge on botany as measured by a botany questionnaire. Twenty-four participants served in the no-APA group and 20 participants served in the APA group (Moreno et al., 2001, Experiment 1). The participants in Experiment 2 were 48 seventh-grade students from an urban middle school. Twenty-four students served in the APA group and 24 students in the no-APA group (Moreno et al., 2001, Experiment 2). The purpose of Experiment 2 was to replicate Experiment 1 in another study involving younger learners. Consistent with Massaro (2004), we were interested in examining the hypothesis that the presence of the APA would have a strong effect on children's engagement.

For example, in his research, children who learned with an APA persisted in some of the lessons until they were mastered, even when they were not required to do so.

The two versions of the computer game for the APA and no-APA groups had identical explanations and graphics for the teaching of botany concepts as previously described in the multimedia game scenario section. The goal of the game is to teach students how to design plants that would survive in different weather conditions. Students in the no-APA group received no social cues during their interactions. Explanations were presented as on-screen text and they were not presented with the visual image of an agent. Students in the APA group had words and graphics identical to those in no-APA group but were presented with the image of the fictional agent Herman (visual social cue) who provided spoken explanations (auditory social cue) rather than on-screen text explanations.

After students interacted with the respective program, they were given a retention test, a seven-page problem-solving test, and a program-ratings sheet (see Moreno et al., 2001 for a detailed description of the materials). The retention test involved students writing down as many plant part designs as they could remember. The problem-solving transfer test consisted of designing the root, stem, and leaves for five hypothetical planets not used during their learning with the multimedia game (questions 1 to 5) plus identifying the weather conditions in which two hypothetical plants could survive (questions 6 and 7). The program-ratings sheet asked participants to rate on a 10-point scale their level of motivation, interest, understanding, the friendliness of the program, and the perceived difficulty of the material.

Experiment 1 Results

Separate one-way ANOVAs were conducted on each dependent measure (retention, transfer, and program ratings). The mean number of items correctly recalled by the APA group was not significantly different than the mean number of correctly recalled items by the no-APA group. This result is not surprising because students in the APA and no-APA groups received identical factual information consisting of the same verbal and visual representations of plant part designs. However, as predicted by a *social-cue* hypothesis, students in the APA group produced significantly more correct solutions on transfer problems than students in the no-APA group ($p < .005$). In addition, the APA group rated their motivation to continue learning and their interest in the material significantly higher than the no-APA group ($p < .01$). No significant differences were found in their ratings of how understandable, helpful, or difficult the program was.

Experiment 2 Results

As in Experiment 1, separate one-way ANOVAs were conducted on each dependent measure (retention, transfer, and program ratings). The mean number of correctly recalled items by the APA group was not significantly different than the mean number of correctly recalled items by the no-APA group but students in the APA group produced significantly more correct answers on the transfer test than did students in the no-APA group ($p < .005$), a similar finding to that of Experiment 1. Additionally, as in Experiment 1, the APA group rated their interest in the material significantly higher than the no-APA group ($p < .005$). However, groups did not differ in their motivation to continue learning (which was high for both) or the rest of the program ratings. The results of these two studies are consistent with a *social-cue* hypothesis by demonstrating an *APA effect* on transfer and interest. The findings support a CATLM according to which learning with APAs that give spoken explanations can encourage students to learn more deeply by making multimedia games more interesting.

EXPERIMENTS 3 AND 4: VISUAL VERSUS AUDITORY-AGENT CUES

Method and Procedure

Experiments 1 and 2 provided evidence in favor of using APAs with visual and auditory social cues. The goal of Experiments 3 and 4 was to examine the relative contribution of each social cue (image versus voice) to learning. The affective and learning outcomes of two groups of students were compared using the same dependent measures as in the previous experiments. One group learned with the botany game by listening to the narrated explanations (N) of the agent either with or without the image (I) of the agent (groups IN and –IN, respectively). Another group learned with the botany game by reading identical explanations as on-screen text (T) either with or without the image of the agent (groups IT and –IT, respectively). That is, each participant served in one cell of a 2 × 2 between-subjects factorial design, with the first factor being modality of the verbal information (N or T) and the second factor being whether or not the agent's image was displayed on the computer screen (I or –I). In Experiment 3 (Moreno et al., 2001, Experiment 4), 64 college students who lacked prior knowledge in botany learned by interacting with the fictional APA used in Experiments 1 and 2. There were 15 participants in the IT group, 17 participants in IN group, 16 participants in the – IT group, and 16 participants in the – IN group. The materials and procedure were identical to those used in Experiments 1 and 2.

Experiment 4 had an identical design to that of Experiment 3 with the exception that the fictional character Herman was replaced by a close-up video of a real person (Moreno et al., 2001, Experiment 5). The video was recorded so that the human agent looked directly at the student during the instructional communication and the words used by the human agent were identical to those of the fictional agent used in Experiment 3. Seventy-nine college students who lacked prior knowledge in botany learned by interacting with the human agent in one of four conditions. There were 19 participants in the IT group, 19 participants in IN group, 21 participants in the –IT group, and 20 participants in the –IN group. The materials and procedure were identical to those of Experiments 1 and 2.

Experiment 3 Results

For each dependent measure (retention, transfer, and program ratings), a two-factor ANOVA was conducted with the modality of the verbal information (T versus N) and the presence or absence of the agent's image (I versus –I) as between-subject factors. Students presented with the image of the APA did not rate the lesson more favorably, recall more, or show better transfer to solve problems than students not presented with the image of the APA. On the other hand, the narration groups recalled significantly more than the text groups ($p < .005$); gave significantly more correct answers in the transfer tests than the text groups ($p < .0005$); and gave significantly higher interest ratings than the text groups ($p < .005$). There were no other significant differences in students' ratings and no interaction between image and modality.

Experiment 4 Results

Similar to the pattern of results found in the third study, students presented with the image of the human agent did not rate the lesson more favorably, recall more, or show better transfer to solve problems than students not presented with the image of the agent. However, the narration groups recalled significantly more than the text groups ($p < .005$); gave significantly more correct answers in the transfer tests than the text groups ($p < .0001$); and gave significantly lower difficulty ratings than the text groups ($p < .05$). There were no other significant differences in students' ratings and no interactions between image and modality.

Taken together, the findings of our first four studies do not support the *social-cue* hypothesis for the animated property of the agent but rather show that it is the voice of the agent that positively affects students' affective and learning outcomes. I call this a *modality effect* on retention and transfer: Students who learn with the voice of an APA recall more and are better able to use what they have learned to solve problems than students who are given identical explanations as on-screen text. According to the social-cue hypothesis, the modality effect is the result of adding social cues to the instructional messages contained in the lesson. These social cues help learning by making the lesson more motivating to students than having to read on-screen text. Experiment 3's finding that students rated the computer game as being more interesting lends support for this hypothesis. However, it is important to point that there are at least two other interpretations for the modality effect.

According to Liberman (1995), the modality effect can be attributed to the naturalness of the speech medium. Evidence for this hypothesis is: (a) written language is not a universal phenomenon and in our evolutionary history is fairly recent with many languages not even having a written form; (b) speech comes earlier in the history of the individual but written language comes later, if at all; (c) although speech must be learned, it need not be taught but reading and writing need to be taught formally; (d) there are brain mechanisms that evolved with language and are specialized for speech but no brain specialization for reading-writing as such exists; and (e) although text can be easily missed if we fail to consciously direct our attention to reading, speech usually can not be missed due to the invasive character of sound. In sum, contrary to the case of narration, which is human's more natural communication medium, "reading requires mental concentration and effort" (Norman, 1993, p. 244). Experiment 4's finding that students rated the computer game as being easier when it uses narration rather than on-screen text is consistent with this interpretation (Anderson & Craik, 1974).

Finally, a third explanation for the modality effect is that the superiority of presenting simultaneous narrations and graphics over simultaneous text and graphics is caused by an expansion of effective working memory capacity. That is, students are more likely to make referential connections and build a coherent mental model when, rather than splitting their limited visual attention between words and pictures, they can use the auditory channel to process the verbal information and the visual channel to process the non-verbal information (Mousavi, Low, & Sweller, 1995; Mayer & Moreno, 1998, 2003; Moreno &

Mayer, 1999). In summary, although our data supports the social-cue hypothesis for presenting the agent's voice, which relies on motivational influences on learning, it also supports alternative cognitively based hypotheses. How do the different motivational and cognitive aspects of voice processing interact to produce the modality effect? More research should be conducted to empirically answer this question and provide a better explanation for APA's modality effect.

THE COGNITIVE ROLE OF NON-ANIMATED APA PROPERTIES

One of the assumptions underlying a CATLM (Moreno, 2005b) is that learning occurs when students actively construct a coherent knowledge representation by way of a limited capacity working memory. More specifically, a successful learning process includes the following three cognitive processes (shown in Figure 9.1 in italics): (a) selection of relevant verbal and non-verbal information (Paivio, 1986); (b) organization of verbal and non-verbal information into a mental model or representation; and (c) integration of the new model with existing knowledge (Pressley et al., 1992).

How can APAs foster the cognitive processes of selection, organization, and integration of multimedia materials by novice learners? In answering this question, we are faced with the challenge of designing instruction that seeks to encourage students to be cognitively active yet minimizes any unnecessary cognitive load. According to cognitive load theory, when students have low prior knowledge in a domain, cognitive load will be high because no relevant schema is available to process the new information (Sweller, 1999). When discussing the different ways in which the animated property of APAs may help students' learning I presented one method to help reduce students' cognitive load: using the agent's gestures to direct students' attention to relevant information from the computer screen.

In the next section, I propose two additional methods that can be embedded in an APA to foster learning. However, the effectiveness of these methods does not rely on the animated property of APAs and, therefore, they can be implemented even without the visual presence of the pedagogical agent. First, to increase meaningful interaction with the multimedia materials, APAs can offer mixed-initiative environments (Lester et al., 1999), where students learn by actively participating with the agent in the process of meaning making. Second, to minimize the cognitive load inherent to learning a new topic in an interactive multimedia game, the APA may facilitate students' selection, organization, and integration of materials by providing explanatory feedback on their choices.

THE INTERACTIVITY AND GUIDANCE HYPOTHESES

According to a CATLM, the cognitive function of the APA during the process of knowledge construction plays a crucial role in promoting student learning. For example, instructional methods that encourage students to connect the new information with their existing knowledge will promote deeper learning by increasing cognitive activity. Which type of instructional methods can be embedded in APAs to facilitate or enable the cognitive processes involved in meaning making? One way in which an APA can help students in the process of meaning making is to promote students' interaction and manipulation of the learning materials by mixed-initiative designs (Lester et al., 1999). This is the *interactivity* hypothesis. By allowing students to select answers before explanations are provided, APAs allow them to learn by doing (Anzai & Simon, 1979). According to Anderson (1983), a central part of the learning process occurs when students attempt to apply the instructional material to solve problems for themselves. This hypothesis was tested in Experiment 5 by comparing the affective and learning outcomes of students who learned with the multimedia game in two conditions: by designing a plant for each environment before listening to the agent's explanations (design or D group) or by observing an appropriate plant design chosen by the agent and listening to the agent's explanation for that choice (no design or –D group).

Another promising way to promote learning is by facilitating the process of organization and integration of the new materials through APAs guided feedback while students interact with the learning environment (Mark & Greer, 1995). The basis of the *guidance* hypothesis is that the free exploration of highly complex environments may generate a heavy cognitive load that is detrimental to learning (Sweller, 1999). This is particularly important in the case of novice learners, who lack proper schemas to integrate the new information with their prior knowledge (Tuovinen & Sweller, 1999). Therefore, according to the *guidance* hypothesis, a more structured environment for novices, such as one where an APA facilitates students' meaning making by presenting explanatory feedback for the correctness or incorrectness of their choices, will reduce cognitive load and facilitate the building of a coherent model of the system to be learned (Moreno, 2004). In our botany game, students' freedom to explore the many plant designs consisted of giving them the opportunity to interrogate the available visual and verbal information. However, due to the fact that students lacked prior knowledge in the botany domain and that the number of variables to be considered during problem solving was cognitively demanding (three root, stem, and leave variables, respectively) we hypothesized that this exploration would be overwhelming.

Because the explanatory feedback treatment used in Experiment 6 provided students with principle-based explanations for their plant design choices, it was centrally concerned with steering the learner towards better targeted interrogation and to minimize a trial and error process of learning. Similar to past research on discovery learning, we expected students who received information on the correctness of their choices alone to become frustrated and eventually fail to infer the principles to be learned (Brown & Campione, 1994; Hardiman, Pollatsek, & Weil, 1986; Mayer, 2004). Experiment 6 tested this hypothesis by comparing the affective and learning outcomes of students who were able to manipulate the plant parts and discover the principles of plant design either with or without guiding principle-based feedback (groups G and no-G, respectively).

The following predictions can be drawn from the above section. First, according to the *interactivity* hypothesis, students who are able to participate in the process of knowledge construction by designing a plant for each learning trial will outperform those who learn with a multimedia game that has identical graphics and explanations but where the opportunity to interact has been removed. Second, according to the *guidance* hypothesis, because the students used in the reported set of experiments lack prior botany knowledge, those who are offered explanatory feedback for their problem-solving choices will outperform those who learn with corrective feedback alone.

EXPERIMENTS 5 AND 6: TESTING THE INTERACTIVITY AND GUIDANCE HYPOTHESES

Method and Procedure

In Experiment 5, 18 college students participated in group D and 20 students participated in group –D (Moreno et al., 2001, Experiment 3). In Experiment 6, 23 college students participated in group G group and 26 participants in group –G (Moreno, 2004, Experiment 1). The procedure and materials were identical to those used in Experiments 1 and 2 except that, for Experiment 5, the –D version of the multimedia game was modified to exclude the opportunity to design the plant before listening to the APA's explanations and, for Experiment 6, the –G version of the game was modified to replace the explanatory feedback with corrective feedback alone. In each experiment, comparisons were made between the two groups on measures of retention, transfer, and program ratings.

Experiment 5 Results

Students in group D recalled significantly more ($p = .01$) and gave more correct answers in transfer tests ($p < .05$) than students in group –D. Both groups gave comparable program ratings. These findings are consistent with past study strategy literature (Elliot, McGregor, & Gable, 1999), where it is found that students learn deeper from becoming engaged in an active search for meaning (Anzai & Simon, 1979). The results support the cognitive-guide role for APAs and the *interactivity* hypothesis by showing that an important role that APAs may have in multimedia learning is to provide mixed-initiative, participatory environments to encourage the deep processing of the instructional materials.

Experiment 6 Results

For Experiment 6, students who were presented with explanatory feedback (guidance treatment), recalled significantly more information about the plant library ($p = 0.005$), gave significantly more correct answers on the transfer test ($p < .0001$), and rated the multimedia game as being less difficult ($p = .01$) and more helpful in understanding the subject matter ($p = .01$) than those who were not presented with explanatory feedback. Conversely, both groups rated their levels of motivation and interest comparably. In sum, Experiment 6 demonstrated a *guidance effect* in agent-based multimedia games: Novice students achieve better retention, transfer, and rate the instructional program as being more helpful and less difficult when the agent provides guidance in the form of explanatory feedback rather than corrective feedback alone.

DISCUSSION

The purpose of this chapter was to make three important distinctions when examining the effectiveness of APAs in multimedia games. First, we need to distinguish the two potential roles that APAs may play in fostering learning from interactive multimedia games: a motivational role, in which APAs promote understanding by making the learning experience more interesting and a cognitive role, in which APAs promote understanding by facilitating the cognitive processes involved in meaning making. Second, we need to distinguish the role that the animated and no-animated properties of the agent has in promoting students' learning. Third, we need to distinguish between the motivational and cognitive functions of the animated property of the APA and those of the animations that are not based on the APA.

To examine the motivational role of APAs, I presented a set of four studies that tested the *social-cue* hypothesis according to which, including visual and auditory cues of APAs in educational games promotes students' interest and learning. Therefore, the focus is on the motivational and learning effects of the animated and voice properties of the agent. To examine the cognitive role of APAs, I presented a set of two studies that tested the *interactivity* and *guidance* hypotheses according to which, it is not the amount of social cues included in an educational game or how anthropomorphic the agent is portrayed but rather how APAs facilitate students' cognitive processing that fosters learning. Therefore, the focus of the second set of studies is on the motivational and learning effects of the non-animated properties of the agent.

Experiments 1 and 2 demonstrated that, compared to multimedia games that do not include social cues in the environment, games that include the image and voice of an APA are rated to be more interesting and promote retention and problem-solving transfer. However, when the relative contribution of image and voice were investigated in Experiments 3 and 4, what showed to be the driving force underlying students' deeper understanding was the presentation of the APA's explanations via narration (Moreno et al., 2001). Although this modality effect may be interpreted as supportive of a *social-cue* hypothesis according to which, the additional social cues included in the human voice increases students' motivation to learn, the benefit of the APA's voice may also rely on a more efficient use of working memory (Penney, 1989; Mayer & Moreno, 1998; Moreno & Mayer, 1999; Mousavi, Low, & Sweller, 1995) and the naturalness of the speech medium (Liberman, 1995). Therefore, more research is needed to better understand the underlying cognitive and affective mechanisms that are responsible for the modality effect.

On the other hand, the reported findings do not support the widespread idea underlying the *social-cue* hypothesis that the main function of the animated property of an APA resides on the ability to motivate and engage students by providing more social cues in a multimedia game. However, because the findings do not support the *interference* hypothesis either, they suggest that, similar to the case of the modality effect, the motivational role of APA's animated property is an area that is ripe for further research and theory building.

The results from Experiments 5 and 6 emphasize the cognitive role of the non-animated property of pedagogical agents in multimedia learning. Both, allowing students to interact with the APA by testing plant design hypotheses and having an APA provide explanatory feedback for students' problem-solving interactions, proved to have significant learning effects. An interesting result was that students who learned with or without the interactive or guidance treatments did not report different levels of motivation or interest. That is, consistent with a cognitive-guide thesis, the results of Experiments 5 and 6 suggest that the way that APAs help students' learning resides on the cognitive and not the affective variables that are associated with a CATLM. More specifically, three cognitive functions that pedagogical agents (animated, static, or not visual) may have are: First, presenting explanations in the form of speech rather than text (Moreno & Mayer, 1999; Moreno et al., 2001). By doing so, APAs offload students' limited visual working memory, which is severely taxed by the need to select, organize, and integrate the game's visual representations. A second cognitive function is that of creating participatory rather than non-participatory presentations (Moreno et al., 2001). By having students try to make sense of the materials with agent-learner interactive problem-solving experiences, the process of learning becomes cognitively engaging (Jonassen, Peck, & Wilson, 1999). Third, APAs should provide guidance in the form of explanatory feedback when novice students interact with multimedia games (Tuovinen & Sweller, 1999). According to a CATLM and cognitive load theory, when students lack sufficient prior knowledge to process the new multimedia materials in a meaningful way and no guidance is embedded in the design, cognitive overload is likely to occur (Moreno, 2004, 2005b; Sweller, 1999).

On the practical side, this research has direct implications for instructional design. More specifically, the present review of empirical work reveals the following principles to be embraced in the development of agent-based multimedia:

Modality principle: APAs should communicate with the learner with spoken words. Students are better able to understand multimedia explanations when words are presented as speech rather than on-screen text (Moreno et al., 2001).

Interactivity principle: APAs should be designed to promote students' interaction and manipulation of the learning materials by mixed, agent-student initiative designs that allow students to select answers before receiving explanations or to ask questions during learning (Lester et al., 1999).

Guidance principle: APAs should provide principle-based explanations during learning, especially when teaching novice learners who lack proper schemas to guide them in the selection of relevant new information (Tuovinen & Sweller, 1999).

Cost-efficient principle: Finally, an important practical implication of this chapter is that there is no need to waste costly resources on developing APAs if the agent's image or animations do not directly serve the educational objective of the lesson. Although APA research fails to report the relative cost and benefit of agent and no agent treatments, the design of animated agents is presumably more expensive than the design of agent-less or static agent multimedia environments (Clark, 2003).

Are there any other cognitive roles that the animated image of a pedagogical agent may have? Although a recent review of past research on APAs has failed to find an image effect (Moreno, 2005a), it is clear that the visual presence and animations of APAs in the reviewed studies was overwhelmingly directed towards increasing student motivation. The few studies where the animated property of the agent was aimed at helping students' cognitive processing had either inconclusive results or lacked appropriate research designs. Therefore, further developments and evaluations of APAs whose animated property is designed with a specific instructional function are encouraged. For example, if the role of the animated agent is to demonstrate or model a procedure, a suggestion for future research is to examine the learning contribution of APAs in domains such as physical education, dance, or technical training. Furthermore, a fruitful direction for future research on APAs is that of extending current research by systematically investigating the motivational and cognitive roles of their animated property in different learning domains and for a diversity of student populations and agent representations.

References

Alberto, P. & Troutman, A. (1999). *Applied behavioral analysis for teachers* (4th ed.). Upper Saddle River, NJ: Merrill/Prentice Hall.

Anderson, J. R. (1983). *The architecture of cognition.* Cambridge, MA: Harvard University Press.

Anderson, C. M. B. & Craik, F. I. M. (1974). The effect of a concurrent task on recall from primary memory. *Journal of Verbal Learning & Verbal Behavior, 13,* 107–113.

Anzai, Y. & Simon, H. A. (1979). The theory of learning by doing. *Psychological Review, 86,* 124–140.

Baylor, A. L. (1999). Intelligent agents as cognitive tools for education. *Educational Technology, 39*(2), 36–40.

Bradshaw, J. M. (Ed.). (1997). *Software agents.* Menlo Park, CA: AAAI Press / MIT Press.

Brown, A. L., & Campione, J. L. (1994). Guided discovery in a community of learners. In K. McGilly (Ed.), *Classroom lessons: Integrating cognitive theory and classroom practice* (pp. 229–270). Cambridge, MA: The MIT Press.

Bruning, R., Schraw, G. J., & Ronning, R. R. (1999). *Cognitive psychology and instruction.* Upper Saddle River, NJ: Prentice-Hall.

Clarebout, G., Elen, J., Johnson, W. L., & Shaw, E. (2002). Animated pedagogical agents: An opportunity to be grasped? *Journal of Educational Multimedia and Hypermedia, 11*(3), 267–286.

Clark, R. E. (2003). Research on web-based learning: A half-full glass. In Bruning, R., Horn, C. A., & PytlikZillig, L. M. (Eds.), *Web-based learning: What do we know? Where do we go?* (pp. 1–22). Greenwich, CT: Information Age Publishing.

Craig, S. D., Gholson, B., & Driscoll, D. M. (2002). Animated Pedagogical Agents in Multimedia Educational Environments: Effects of Agent Properties, Picture Features, and Redundancy. *Journal of Educational Psychology, 94*(2), 428–434.

De Jong, T. & Van Joolingen, W. R. (1998). Scientific discovery learning with computer simulations of conceptual domains. *Review of Educational Research, 68*, 179–201.

Dewey, J. (1913). *Interest and effort in education.* Cambridge, MA: Houghton Mifflin.

Doctorow, M., Wittrock, M. C., & Marks, C. (1978). Generative processes in reading comprehension. *Journal of Educational Psychology, 70*, 109–118.

Elliot, A. J., McGregor, H. A., & Gable, S. (1999). Achievement goals, study strategies, and exam performance: A mediational analysis. *Journal of Educational Psychology, 91*, 549–563.

Erickson, T. (1997). Designing agents as if people mattered. In Bradshaw, J. M. (Ed.). *Software agents.* Cambridge, MA: MIT Press.

Fogg, B. J. & Tseng, H. (1999). The elements of computer credibility. In *Proceedings of the CHI '99 Conference on Human Factors in Computing Systems* (pp. 80–87). New York: ACM Press.

Ganeshan, R., Johnson, W. L., Shaw, E., & Wood, B. (2000). Tutoring diagnostic problem solving. In G. Gauthier, C. Frasson, & K. van Lehn (Eds.), *Proceedings of the Fifth International Conference on Intelligent Tutoring Systems.* Berlin: Springer-Verlag.

Garner, R., Gillingham, M., & White, C. (1989). Effects of "seductive details" on macroprocessing and microprocessing in adults and children. *Cognition and Instruction, 6*, 41–57.

Gregoire, J. P., Zettlemoyer, L. S., & Lester, J. C. (1999). Detecting and correcting misconceptions with lifelike avatars in 3D environments. In *Proceedings of the Ninth World Conference on Artificial Intelligence in Education* (pp. 586–593). Le Mans, France: AE-ED-Society.

Graesser, A. C., Wiemer-Hastings, K., Wiemer-Hastings, P., & Kreuz, R. (1999). AutoTutor: A simulation of a human tutor. *Journal of Cognitive Systems Research, 1*, 35–51.

Hardiman, P., Pollatsek, A., & Weil, A. (1986). Learning to understand the balance beam. *Cognition and Instruction, 3*, 1–30.

Harp, S. F. & Mayer, R. E. (1997). The role of interest in learning from scientific text and illustrations: On the distinction between emotional interest and cognitive interest. *Journal of Educational Psychology, 89*, 92–102.

Harp, S. F. & Mayer, R. E. (1998). How seductive details do their damage: A theory of cognitive interest in science learning. *Journal of Educational Psychology, 90*, 414–434.

Heeter, C. (1992). Being There: The subjective experience of presence. *Presence, 1*(2), 262–271.

Heward, W. (2003). *Exceptional children* (6th ed.). Upper Saddle River, NJ: Merrill/Prentice Hall.

Johnson, W. L., Rickel, J. W., & Lester, J. C. (2000). Animated pedagogical agents: Face-to-face interaction in interactive learning environments. *International Journal of Artificial Intelligence in Education, 11*, 47–78.

Jonassen, D. H., Peck, K. L., & Wilson, B. G. (1999). *Learning with technology: A constructivist perspective.* Upper Saddle River, NJ: Merrill.

Kalyuga, S., Ayres, P., Chandler, P., & Sweller, J. (2003). The expertise reversal effect. *Educational Psychologist, 38*, 23–31.

Kuhn, D. (1989). Children and adults as intuitive scientists. *Psychological Review, 96*, 674–689.

Lester, J. C., Towns, S. G., & Fitzgerald, P. J. (1999). Achieving affective impact: Visual emotive communication in lifelike pedagogical agents. *International Journal of Artificial Intelligence in Education, 10*(3–4), 278–291.

Lester, J. C., Stone, B., & Stelling, G. (1999). Lifelike pedagogical agents for mixed-initiative problem solving in constructivist learning environments. *User Modeling and User-Adapted Interaction, 9*, 1–44.

Liberman, A. M. (1995). The relation of speech to reading and writing. In de Gelder, B., and Morais, J. (Eds.), *Speech and reading: A comparative approach.* Hillsdale, NJ: Lawrence Erlbaum Associates.

Mark, M. A. & Greer, J. E. (1995). The VCR tutor: Effective instruction for device operation. *Journal of the Learning Sciences, 4*, 209–246.

Massaro, D. W. (2004). A framework for evaluating multimodal integration by humans and a role for embodied conversational agents. *Proceedings of International Conference on Multimodal Interfaces '04*, (pp. 24–31). State College, PA: Association for Computing Machinery.

Mayer, R. E. (2001). *Multimedia learning.* New York: & Cambridge University Press.

Mayer, R. E., Heiser, J., & Lonn, S. (2001). Cognitive constraints on multimedia learning: When presenting more material results in less understanding. *Journal of Educational Psychology 93*, 187–198.

Mayer, R. E. & Moreno, R. (2003). Nine ways to reduce cognitive load in multimedia learning. *Educational Psychologist, 38*(1), 43–52.

Mayer, R. E. & Moreno, R. (1998). A split-attention effect in multimedia learning: Evidence for dual processing systems in working memory. *Journal of Educational Psychology, 90*, 312–320.

Mitrovic, A. & Suraweera, P. (2000). Evaluating an animated pedagogical agent. *Lecture Notes in Computer Science, 1839*, 73–82.

Moon, Y. (1998). Intimate self-disclosure exchanges: Using computers to build reciprocal relationships with consumers. *Working Paper for Harvard Business School.*

Moreno, R. (2005a). Multimedia learning with animated pedagogical agents. In R. Mayer (Ed.), *Cambridge Handbook of Multimedia Learning* (pp. 507–524). New York: Cambridge University Press.

Moreno, R. (2005b). Instructional technology: Promise and pitfalls. In L. PytlikZillig, M. Bodvarsson, & R. Bruning (Eds.), *Technology-based education: Bringing researchers and practitioners together* (pp. 1–19). Greenwich, CT: Information Age Publishing.

Moreno, R. (2004). Decreasing cognitive load for novice students: Effects of explanatory versus corrective feedback on discovery-based multimedia. *Instructional Science, 32*, 99–113.

Moreno, R. & Durán, R. (2004). Do multiple representations need explanations? The role of verbal guidance and individual differences in multimedia mathematics learning. *Journal of Educational Psychology, 96*, 492–503.

Moreno, R. & Flowerday, T. (2006). Students' choice of animated pedagogical agents in science learning: A test of the similarity attraction hypothesis on gender and ethnicity. *Contemporary Educational Psychology, 31*, 186–207.

Moreno, R. & Mayer, R. E. (2005). Role of guidance, reflection, and interactivity in an agent-based multimedia game. *Journal of Educational Psychology, 97*, 117–128.

Moreno, R. and Mayer, R. E. (2004). Personalized Messages that Promote Science Learning in Virtual Environments. *Journal of Educational Psychology, 96*, 165–173.

Moreno, R. & Mayer, R. E. (1999). Cognitive principles of multimedia learning: The role of modality and contiguity effects. *Journal of Educational Psychology, 91*, 358–368.

Moreno, R., Mayer, R. E., Spires, A. H., & Lester, J. C. (2001). The case for social agency in computer-based teaching: Do students learn more deeply when they interact with animated pedagogical agents? *Cognition and Instruction, 19*(2), 177–213.

Moundridou, M. & Virvou, M. (2002). Evaluating the personal effect of an interface agent in a tutoring system. *Journal of Computer Assisted Learning, 18*, 253–261.

Mousavi, S., Low, R., & Sweller, J. (1995). Reducing cognitive load by mixing auditory and visual presentation modes. *Journal of Educational Psychology, 87*, 319–334.

Nass, C. & Moon, Y. (2000). Machines and mindlessness: Social responses to computers. *Journal of Social Issues, 56*(1), 81.

Nass, C., & Steuer, J. S. (1993). Voices, boxes, and sources of messages: Computers and social actors. *Human Communication Research, 19*, 504–527.

Norman, D. A. (1993). *Things that make us smart: Defending human attributes in the age of the machine.* Reading, MA: Perseus Books.

Paas, F., Tuovinen, J. E., Tabbers, H., & Van Gerven, P. W. M. (2003). Cognitive load measurement as a means to advance cognitive theory. *Educational Psychologist, 38*, 63–71.

Paivio, A. (1986). *Mental representations: A dual coding approach.* Oxford, England: Oxford University Press.

Penney, C. G. (1989). Modality effects and the structure of short-term verbal memory. *Memory and Cognition, 17*, 398–422.

Pintrich, P. R., Marx, R. W., & Boyle, R. A. (1993). Beyond cold conceptual change: The role of motivational beliefs and classroom contextual factors in the process of conceptual change. *Review of Educational Research, 63*, 167–199.

Plass, J. L., Chun, D. M., Mayer, R. E., & Leutner, D. (1998). Supporting visual and verbal learning preferences in a second language multimedia learning environment. *Journal of Educational Psychology, 90*, 25–36.

Pressley, M., Wood, E., Woloshyn, V., Martin, V., King, A., and Menke, D. (1992). Encouraging mindful use of prior knowledge: Attempting to construct explanatory answers facilitates learning. *Educational Psychologist, 27*, 91–109.

Reeves, B. & Nass, C. (1996). *The media equation: How people treat computers, television, and new media like real people and places.* Stanford, CA: CSLI Publications.

Reiber, L. P. (1990). Animation in computer-based instruction. *Educational Technology Research and Development, 38*, 77–86.

Renninger, K. A., Hidi, S., & Krapp, A. (Eds.). (1992). *The role of interest in learning and development.* Hillsdale, NJ: Lawrence Erlbaum Associates.

Shaw, R., Effken, J. A., Fajen, B., Garrett, S. R., & Morris, A. (1997). An ecological approach to the on-line assessment of problem-solving paths: Principles and applications. *Instructional Science, 25*, 151–166.

Shneiderman, B., & Maes, P. (1997). Direct manipulations vs. interface agents: excerpts from debates at IUI '97 and CHI '97. *Interactions, 4*, 42–61.

Sweller, J. (1999). *Instructional design in technical areas.* Camberwell, Australia: ACER Press.

Tang, J. C. & Isaacs, E. (1993). Why do users like video? Studies of multimedia-supported collaboration. *Computer-Supported Cooperative Work: An International Journal, 1*, 163–196.

Towns, S., FitzGerald, P., & Lester, J. (1998). Visual emotive communication in lifelike pedagogical agents. In *Proceedings of the Fourth International Conference on Intelligent Tutoring Systems* (pp. 474–483), San Antonio.

Tuovinen, J. E. & Sweller, J. (1999). A comparison of cognitive load associated with discovery learning and worked examples. *Journal of Educational Psychology, 91*, 334–341.

Van Mulken, S., André, E., & Müller, J. (1998). The persona effect: How substantial is it? In H. Johnson, L. Nigay, and C. Roast (Eds.), *People and Computers XIII, Proceedings of HCI '98* (pp. 53–66). London: Springer.

Walker, J. H., Sproull, L. & Subramani, R. (1994). Using a human face in an interface. In B. Adelson, S. Dumais & J. Olson (Eds.), *Human Factors in Computing Systems: CHI '94 Conference Proceedings* (pp. 85–91). New York: ACM Press.

Wetzel, C. D., Radtke, P. H., & Stern, H. W. (1994). *Instructional effectiveness of video media.* Hillsdale, NJ: Lawrence Erlbaum Associates.

Wilson, M. (1997). Metaphor to personality: the role of animation in intelligent interface agents. In *Proceedings of the IJCAI-97 Workshop on Animated Interface Agents: Making them Intelligent.* Nagoya, Japan.

10

Young Learners' Control of Technical Animations

Jean-Michel Boucheix

INTRODUCTION

This chapter deals with the effect of user control on learning from technical animations. First, the concept of user controllability is explored and possible reasons for the varied research findings concerning its effectiveness in supporting learning are considered. Second, an empirical study is reported in which young learners studied the operation of gear systems from animated instruction featuring different levels of user control. Finally, results of the study are discussed and related to processing constraints that may influence the educational effectiveness of user controllable animations.

CHALLENGES IN LEARNING FROM ANIMATIONS

Recent research challenges the widespread assumption that animations are intrinsically superior to static graphics for developing understandings of dynamic processes (Bétrancourt & Tversky, 2000; Bétrancourt, 2005; Hegarty, Narayanan, & Freitas, 2002; Lowe, 2004, 2005; Schnotz, 2005; Tversky, Bauer-Morrison, & Bétrancourt, 2002). For example, Mayer, Hegarty, Mayer, and Campbell (2005) compared the effectiveness of presenting different types of content via sequences of paper-based static pictures (accompanied by texts) with presenting the same content via computer-based narrated animations. No advantages were found for animations across the four content types examined (lightning storms, toilet cistern, ocean waves, and car brakes). In some cases, retention results for the sequences of static depictions were superior to those for the animated illustrations (waves, brakes), while in other cases, transfer test results for static pictures were superior (lightning, cistern).

The author would like to acknowledge the invaluable assistance of Ana Morais and Adeline Thanane.

A number of explanations have been advanced to account for such findings (Bétrancourt, 2005; Lowe, 2004; Schnotz & Lowe, 2003; Lowe & Schnotz, in press; Tversky, Bauer-Morrison, & Bétrancourt, 2002). A common thread linking these explanations is that problems can occur when the information processing requirements of using a particular animation to carry out a specific learning task do not match the individual learner's capacities. For example, such problems may occur when the animation depicts its subject matter with a high degree of *behavioral realism* (Lowe & Schnotz, in press). If realistic portrayal of the referent situation's behavior results in a very rapid flow of dynamic information and simultaneous presentation of a multiplicity of changing system states, this may pose processing difficulties for learners.

Four broad sources of potential challenges in learning from animations that have been described in the literature are (i) perceptual difficulties encountered due the temporal characteristics of animation; (ii) attentional difficulties related to split attention effects; (iii) conceptual difficulties concerned with the level of abstraction and deficiencies in prior knowledge; (iv) cognitive difficulties arising from low spatial abilities. Such difficulties reflect the fact that human perceptual and cognitive processes are limited in their capacity to deal with dynamic information. This is exemplified by the well-known difficulty painters working before the advent of photography had in producing accurate depictions of galloping horses due to the rapid visual transformations involved.

Perceptual difficulties can be a consequence of the speed at which key events are presented to the learner. For example, very fast or very slow changes within the animated portrayal could produce perceptual errors that in turn lead to cognitive misinterpretations of the depicted events. In addition, difficulties could arise from split attention effects that occur within the animated display due to simultaneous changes taking place in widely distributed regions of the depiction. In this case, Lowe (2003) suggests the operation of an intra-picture split attention effect between individual pictorial components that differs from the classical split attention effect between text and picture. Learners who lack prior knowledge relevant to the specific subject matter portrayed in an animation may have difficulty in conceptualizing the presented information at a level appropriate to the task requirements. For example, Lowe (1999) found that meteorological novices characterized the dynamic information shown on an animated weather map in terms of visually obvious extrinsic changes rather than the more subtle intrinsic changes. Cognitive difficulties in learning from animations may also arise for those with low spatial abilities due to factors such as their inability to coordinate the necessary mental manipulations with the changing external spatial information depicted by the animation (see Hegarty & Waller, 2005)

Allowing users to control the presentation regime of an animation gives them opportunities to address such difficulties. For example, user controllable animation may help learners to lessen perceptual processing difficulties by letting them adjust the playing rate to make the animation more "apprehendable" (Tversky, Bauer-Morrison, & Bétrancourt, 2002). In this regard, the research of Mayer, Hegarty, Mayer, and Campbell (2005) raises the issue of whether a computer-based animation with narration is fully comparable with a paper-based series of static diagrams with written text. In both conditions of that study, participants were given the same amount of time to learn the subject matter. However, in the animated version, the animation itself was not controllable by the learner but rather its playing regime was fixed by the system. In contrast, processing a series of diagrams with text is a highly controllable activity because the learner is able to make self-paced transitions between text and diagrams (Hegarty, 2005). Controlling an animation itself allows individuals to regulate the presentation's various playing characteristics in ways that have the potential to benefit learning.

USER CONTROL OF THE ANIMATION

Controllable versus Non-Controllable Animations

The possibility that user control over the course of an animation could assist learners in processing dynamic visualizations more effectively has received increasing attention from researchers (e.g., Boucheix & Guignard, 2005; Boucheix & Schneider, submitted; Garg, Norman, Spero, & Maheshwary, 1999; Garg, Norman, & Sperotable, 2001; Lowe, 1999; Mayer & Chandler, 2001; Schwan & Riempp, 2004; Tassini & Bétrancourt, 2003). In such research, learners are typically given control over three main aspects of the animation: speed, direction, and continuity (Lowe, 2003). Having control of these aspects has the potential to benefit learner processing of dynamic information in various ways. Controlling animation speed could diminish perceptual, and to some extent, attentional difficulties. This may be especially helpful to learners when many and varied depicted components change at the same time (as in the animated weather maps studied by Lowe, 1999), or when two causal chains are involved (as with the toilet cistern device studied by Narayanan & Hegarty, 2002). Control over direction and continuity could be beneficial at the level of conceptual integration or comprehension. For example, it gives learners the option of interrupting the animation at crucial stages to view one of its single frame as a static graphic, or to compare different phases to verify the transition between key fixed states. These control activities give learners themselves a role in shaping temporal aspects of how the main steps of the depicted content are presented. From this analysis, it appears that user control should be highly beneficial because it allows learners to adapt an animation's presentational characteristics to their own processing capacities and to the information processing demands of a specific task.

The effects of using a somewhat restricted form of user control over animation has been studied by Mayer and Chandler (2001) with respect to multimedia instruction about the development of lightning storms. In that study, learners could control the speed with which slides containing narrated animated were presented, but had no control over the individual animated segments contained within those slides. One version gave participants control over the slide presentation regime while for the other version the speed and course of presentation were fixed. A better level comprehension resulted from the controllable condition than from the fixed condition but this difference was limited to the transfer task. Using the same basic level of control over the speed of slide presentation, Boucheix and Guignard (2005) compared a non-controllable version of an animated lesson (text and dynamic or static illustrations) about mechanical functioning with a controllable version (auto-presentation of the different slides, allowing participants to replay the animation). The controllable version led to better comprehension results for a delayed retention test. A positive effect for the animated version of the lesson, compared to the static one, was significant only for the controllable condition.

The effects of giving learners more extensive control over the course of a dynamic depiction have also been investigated. Schwan and Riempp (2004) studied how user control of video presentation affected participants' learning of knot tying skills. In the controllable condition, participants could stop, reverse, forward, or replay the video as well as change its presentation speed. In the non-controllable version, speed and duration of the videos were fixed and they could only be restarted from the beginning. Compared with the non-controllable videos, the controllable presentations required a much shorter learning period to reach criterion performance. Participants in the controllable condition often made use of the various control facilities to vary the way information was presented. In the medical domain, Garg, Norman, Spero, and Maheshwary (1999) studied medical students' learning of spatial anatomy with 2D and 3D rotating objects. Views of the carpal bones in the hand were presented as a 3D object whose rotation could be either controlled or not by learners in the different experimental conditions. There was a significant positive effect when learners had control over rotation. The authors suggested that the use of self controlled multiple view representations, such as dissected samples, skeletons, plastic, and computer models, are an effective method of improving this type of learning. However, they found that spatial abilities affected performance within the 3D condition. Control of an animated rotating object has also been found to enhance the learning of those with low spatial abilities (Garg, Norman, & Sperotable, 2001).

However, full control of the animation itself is not always *optimal for learning*. In the case of complex tasks or systems about which the learner lacks prior knowledge, novice subjects may not be able to employ control features of the animation effectively. For example, in the domain of *meteorology*, Lowe (2003, 2004) found that novices' interrogation of a user controllable weather map animation was largely ineffective because they tended to focus upon features that were perceptually salient, rather than thematically relevant. Consistent with these results, Kriz and Hegarty (2004) found that students with low prior knowledge were unable to construct adequate models of how a novel device works using controllable animations, whereas this problem tended not to occur for students with high domain knowledge. In studies of undergraduate students' learning about brain synapse mechanisms, Bétrancourt and colleagues compared non-controllable, partly controllable, and fully controllable versions of animation instruction (Bétrancourt & Réalini, 2005; Tassini & Bétrancourt, 2003). They found that user control over the animation did not produce superior comprehension performance. Rather, better results were obtained with the non-controllable version. The next section explores possible reasons for the apparent contradictions among the findings discussed in this section.

Features of User Control

Several reasons can be suggested to account for the mixed findings on the effectiveness of user control in learning from animations. First, some of the previous research investigated the extreme cases only, essentially comparing full user control with no control at all, and so was perhaps too narrow in scope. Further, because the features of the animated materials employed in the experimental studies differed widely (in terms of speed, realism, etc.), the nature of the user control also varied across studies. The effect of the *degree of control* on learning has received little systematic investigation to date. For example, levels of control that are intermediate between complete user control and complete system control have been neglected. The effect of *directness of control* has also not received sufficient consideration. Second, very different tasks have been used in the various studies; procedural tasks, comprehension tasks, prediction tasks, and so on, and this may also help to explain the diverse findings. Third, very different levels of prior knowledge and spatial abilities were involved in the different studies.

The degree of control that learners are given over the animated system could affect both learner performances and learner activities. In the case of a high level of user control, learners determine the animation's presentation regime and how the displayed content is segmented into units. If the material is segmented inappropriately, this could lead to flaws in subsequent processing operations. The potential for such difficulties increases with the complexity of the subject matter involved and is also likely to be greater when the learner lacks sufficient prior knowledge of the depicted content. However, as discussed above, giving the learner too little user control may also be problematic due to perceptual and attentional difficulties that can result.

Some intermediate level of control may provide a better match between the processing capacities of the learner and the demands of learning from animation. For example, perhaps some features of the dynamic process are likely best controlled by the learner whereas others should be fixed by the presentation system. One possibility is that the main macro steps of the device could be system driven whereas the control of the animation's course within those main fixed steps could be learner driven. Findings from several recent empirical studies tend to support use of such an approach. In Schwan and Riempp's (2004) study of knot tying, participants made extensive use of the pause function to temporarily stop the animation. It seemed that they needed to halt the continuous animation in order to extract crucial steps in the procedure. Studies involving interrogation of animated meteorological information by Lowe (2003, 2004) found that static pictures were sometimes chosen in preference to the display of a continuous flow of dynamic information. It may therefore be inappropriate to give low prior knowledge learners complete control over animation. Rather, it is possible that a carefully chosen blend of controllable and fixed features could provide an optimal sharing of control between the learner and the system. For example, novice learners may benefit by having the natural functional constraints of the system fixed (i.e., the main functional steps and their boundaries, the key states of a continuous movement, and the overall movement directions) but being given control over the specific behavior or particular course of the animation within such constraints.

Boucheix and Schneider (submitted) compared three degrees of control over a dynamic pulley system similar to that used in the work of Hegarty (Hegarty 2004; Hegarty & Just, 1993). In addition to non-controllable and fully controllable versions of the system, a version with an intermediate degree of control was used. In this version, boundaries of three main functional states of the pulley system were fixed but participants could use the computer mouse to "pull" on the pulley system's rope to make it operate. This intermediate condition was found to significantly benefit participants with low spatial abilities. It therefore seems important to consider not only the degree of controllability over the course of the animation as a whole, but also control over the different component elements of the system.

Another feature common to much previous research about user control of animations is that learners were required to manage control of the animation indirectly. For example, control typically required the operation of an array of video-like buttons or slider generally situated at the bottom of the screen (to pause, play, fast forward, rewind, speed up, or slow down the animation). In this type of situation, learners face the task of monitoring the control system while processing the animation. In order to manage these two tasks, they need to invoke strategies such as working very parsimoniously by taking only occasional glances at the control area and inferring what happens between glances. This monitoring activity is a secondary task that could prejudice learning due to a spilt attention effect, particularly for learners with low spatial abilities or those who lack prior knowledge about the depicted domain.

Using a more direct form of device control could help to prevent possible negative effects on learning related to monitoring the animation's control system. Direct control over the elements of the device itself could provide a closer coupling between the learner and the system's functioning. With mechanical systems, for example, learners could, via the computer's mouse, have a more direct quasi-physical experience of rotating the gear wheels and lifting the load. Providing this form of direct device control could thus largely eliminate the added processing costs associated with manipulating the animation indirectly.

Task Content and User Control

Another possible reason for the contradictory findings regarding user control is the type of content used in the experimental learning tasks. Performing simple concrete procedures such as knot tying is a very different task from understanding complex abstract concepts such as meteorological processes. The nature and conceptual level of human information processing demands facing learners in these very different types of task are not comparable. For example, in the knot tying task studied by Schwan and Riempp (2004), learners could readily evaluate their total informational requirements for imitating the procedure displayed on the screen. Actions relevant to successful tying of the knot were all explicitly depicted (there are no hidden concepts) so that learning this task in large part involves remembering and ordering these actions. However, in the case of learning how to predict meteorological markings on weather maps (Lowe, 2005), evaluation of the informational needs relies on an abstract, conceptually driven interpretation of what is happening on the weather map. There is a wide range of tasks that lie between these extremes of concrete procedures on one hand and abstract interpretation in terms of physical variables on the other. Successful performance across this range is likely to be related to the directness and degree of control that educational animations provide to support each type of task. Both an intermediate level of control and a more direct control interface have the potential to enhance task performance.

Signaling Techniques to Improve User Control Properties

Despite the apparent potential of the possibilities canvassed in the preceding section, the actual benefits obtained from more sophisticated systems of user control may be limited for learners with low spatial abilities or those who are lacking in relevant prior knowledge. Previous research comparing understandings developed from animated versus static pictures found no real evidence that animations are more effective than static diagrams for helping learners with low spatial abilities (Hegarty, 2004, 2005; Hegarty & Waller, 2005). It is also possible that more sophisticated user control over animations would be detrimental to learning due to the inherent processing demands involved in taking advantage of that facility. One aspect that is crucial to effective processing of animations is the learner's success in detecting and extracting task-relevant information in the changing display. Such detection and extraction are often challenging for those who lack prior knowledge because they are typically ill-equipped with respect to " . . . where to look, how to look, and what to notice" (Lowe, 2001). This difficulty is exacerbated in the case of events that take place in unpredictable locations or along unfamiliar trajectories. In the domain of meteorology, learners can have difficulties in taking proper advantage of user control because they lack the prior knowledge necessary to exploit the available information (Lowe, 2004).

Because learners lacking prior knowledge don't know which temporal and spatial locations in the animation are most likely to contain thematically relevant information, their attention tends to be directed to features that are most conspicuous at the expense of those that are most relevant. For this reason, it may be that prudent addition of appropriate signaling techniques for directing learner attention to key aspects of the animated information would benefit comprehension of complex systems. In principle, such cueing techniques have the potential to compensate for negative perceptual effects by steering learner attention towards high relevance aspects of the display. In this way attention could be directed towards crucial regions of the depiction and focused upon particular elements that need to be noticed at different times during the animation's progress. For example, graphic entities such as distinctive arrows or colored dots could cue relevant perceptual features whereas precise verbal information could provide conceptual support that facilitates explicit processing of key dynamic information. Cues could also help the learner make connections between an animation and its accompanying text (Mautoné & Mayer, 2001; Hegarty & Steinhoff, 1997; Huck & Floto, in press; Shah, Mayer, & Hegarty, 1999). However, the nature of the signaling used should be sufficiently congruent with the animation for interference effects to be avoided (Bétrancourt, 2005).

Experimental Overview and Hypothesis

The experiment reported here investigated the effect of three different levels of animation controllability on learning about gear functioning (Hegarty, 1992; Hegarty & Just, 1993; Hegarty, 2004). Both the degree and directness of controllability were varied with a non-controllable condition and two controllable conditions. One of these allowed very direct control over the gear wheels whereas the other was considerably more indirect. Two signaling conditions were also incorporated by presenting the material with or without attention-directing cues (arrows, dots, words). It was hypothesized that controllable conditions, especially those allowing direct user control, would benefit comprehension of gear system functioning overall. However, for learners with low spatial abilities and/or little prior knowledge, such control would be prejudicial to comprehension performance due to the additional processing demands involved. In those cases, the presence of attention directing cues would be expected to increase potential benefits from controllability.

METHOD

Participants

A total of 129 French primary school children (69 fourth grade and 60 fifth grade) with a mean age of 10.8 years participated to the study and were tested individually in their schools.

Experimental Design

Two factors manipulated in the experiment were the level of animation controllability and the presence of signaling cues. Non-controllable, indirectly controllable, and directly controllable versions of the animation were used with or without the presence of signaling. Between 20 and 24 participants were included and equally distributed in each of the six conditions (see below). Two control factors were spatial ability and level of prior knowledge (see below).

General Procedure

The experiment consisted of four phases. First, participants' spatial abilities and levels of prior knowledge about gear systems were evaluated in order to balance the different experimental groups. These tests were administered collectively several weeks before the experiment (see below). According to their performance on these tests, students were grouped for the different experimental conditions (see below). In the second phase, participants studied the lesson individually on a computer. The third phase, consisting of a comprehension test, followed immediately. The final phase in which participants completed a pencil and paper post test took place approximately a week later and was a parallel form of the pre test.

Materials

The multimedia lesson on gear systems comprised 24 slides delivered on a 17-inch computer screen and created with Macromedia Director version 8.5. Figure 10.1 shows a representative selection of images from this lesson. It should be noted that each of the slides was self-contained with respect to its animation. That is, the animated material was confined with individual slides and did not extend across successive slides. Further, any control of these animation segments was also provided on a slide-by-slide basis.

Each slide presented an animated depiction of one or two gear systems, some of which included a motor. All slides contained a small amount of explanatory text. Four main aspects were successively explained in the lesson. The first concerned the configuration of a gear system's component elements. The second covered the direction in which these individual gear system elements rotated. The third aspect dealt with the rotation speed of the gears as a function of their diameter in terms of the number of teeth involved. For this third part of the lesson, the slides portrayed two gear systems, each lifting a bucket of water. These gear systems were composed of two toothed wheels of different sizes whose positions were reversed in the two versions (Figure 10.1). The fourth aspect concerned the mechanical effect, i.e. the force applied by the gearing system to lift the load. Slides dealing with this aspect showed animated characters (imps) trying to lift a heavy bucket of water (Figure 10.1). The text

Here is a two-wheeled gear system, a big wheel (A) and a small (B). With the help of the green arrows, notice the direction of rotation of wheel A and wheel B.

Using the scrolling bar, look at the direction of rotation of the big wheel and then of the small wheel.

1- A simple gear system, no-control or direct control condition, cued

2- A simple gear, indirect control condition, uncued

The rack and pinion Gear

In the rack and pinion gear, the wheel drives a notched bar to transform rotation into rectilinear motion.

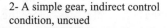

The worm screw shaft

The worm screw shaft can drive a wheel positioned at right angles to it. This gear is slower than the others but is able to move heavier loads.

3-A more complex gear, no-control or direct control condition, cued

4- Complex gear, no-control or direct condition, cued

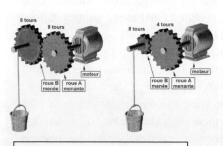

How many turns does the wheel B make when the wheel A makes one turn?

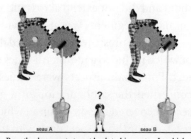

Rox, the dog, wants to get back to his master. In which bucket, A or B, should he ride, if he does not want his master to become tired?

5- Two-gear systems, no-control or direct control condition, cued

6- Two-gear systems, no-control or direct control condition, cued

FIGURE 10.1. Example of illustrations from the animated lesson.

on each slide was a maximum of two short sentences and was the same in the different experimental conditions.

Method

The task was described then participants told that after the lesson, they would answer questions on what they had understood and remembered about gear systems. The whole lesson was studied once and the participant could control the pace of progress through the series of slides using a "next" button situated at the bottom of each screen (Figure 10.1). Depending on the experimental condition, participants could or could not control the animation delivered on the individual slides. Study time (total, and for each slide) and the number of interactions the participant had with the animations were automatically recorded. During the learning session, the experimenter was seated near the participant and recorded any relevant behavior.

Studied Factors

Scale of Control of the Animation

In the non-controllable (NC) version of the lesson, when the learner clicked on the gear system, the animation played for its entire course with no opportunity to stop, pause or rewind. However, once the animation had reached its end, learners could replay it and do this as many times as they wished. In the direct control condition (DC), the participant could use movements of the computer mouse to 'directly' move, turn, or change the speed of each gear wheel. In the indirect control version (IC) the participant could adjust the overall speed of the animation (and thus indirectly also the rotation and speed of the gears) by using the mouse to move a horizontal scrolling control bar. The learner could also use this control bar to stop the animation, rewind it, or change its speed. Forty-four participants were assigned to the IC group, 40 to the DC group, and 45 to the NC group.

Signaling Cues

In the signal condition (Signal+), three types of signals appeared across 10 slides. The first was an arrow pointing in the direction of the gear's rotation (Figure 10.1). The second was a tachometer set next to each gear wheel and indicating the number of turns it was making. The third was a short sentence that directed the learner to look at relevant aspects in the animation (e.g., "look at gear A" or "look at the two wheels A and B and compare their speeds"). When the illustration was static, the "look at" instructions were replaced by corresponding "imagine" instructions. These brief verbal cues were in addition to the explanatory text provided with the slides, but not delivered at the same time. Whereas the verbal cues were intended to direct attention to specific objects and events that could appear, the graphic cues on or near objects (arrows, tachometers) were intended to direct attention to behavior (turning direction, number of turns). In the no-signal condition (Signal-), none of the cues described above were present. Sixty-three participants were placed in the signal condition and 66 in the no-signal condition.

Controlled Factors

Levels of Prior Knowledge

On the basis of pre-test scores, participants were divided into three groups according to their prior knowledge: L1, low; L2, medium; and L3, high. L3 contained 38 participants, L2 contained 46 participants and L1 45. The participants of each group were the most equally as possible distributed across the six conditions. Matching across group prior knowledge variable was confirmed by ANOVA and Neuman Keuls statistical tests: no differences at the pretest scores were found across the six conditions, as well for the simple effects as for the interactions between factors (control, signaling, and prior knowledge group).

Spatial Abilities

Spatial abilities were measured in order to examine if this capacity would influence the effectiveness of user control on learning from the animation. As a further control measure, participants reading abilities were also determined using a standard test (see below for details).

Dependent Measures

Participants' learning was evaluated using both an immediate comprehension task and in terms of the learning gain as indicated by change in performance between the pre-test and post-test. A third measure was the time participants took to complete the lesson. The nature of the tests used will now be elaborated.

Pre-test, Post-test, and Immediate Comprehension Test

Pre-test and Post-test

The pre-test consisted of 15 paper-based multiple-choice questions and problem solving tasks concerning the concepts explained in the lesson. Each question came with an illustration. Topics covered were the composition and operation of the gears, their directions of rotation, their relative speeds, and the forces involved. The contexts of the questions and the types of problems to be solved were more varied than in the situations used for the multimedia lesson. Questions asked ranged from naming parts of the gearing system (e.g., *"on the picture, indicate where the gears are"*) to deciding which gear ratio would be more or less advantageous for cyclists (e.g., *"in which condition will it be the hardest for the cyclist to reach to top of the hill?"*). The post-test was a parallel form of the pre-test. In both tests, each answer or part answer as appropriate was awarded one point, with those for calculations scoring half a point to give a maximum possible total of 40 points. The total scores were converted to percentage correct to give a comprehension score for each participant.

Immediate Comprehension Test

Each participant answered orally a total of 15 questions, in three categories, with the experimenter recording the answers. The categories were (i) comprehension questions requiring recall of information about gears and their operation, (ii) transfer (inference) questions covering concepts from the lesson but in slightly different contexts and requiring application to solve problems, and (iii) explanation questions for each concept covered in the lesson in which the student had to orally justify his answers on the comprehension and transfer questions. Total scores were converted to percentage correct.

Spatial Abilities Measures

The spatial ability test consisted of 40 items organized into four subtests and is based on a spatial working memory task by Shah and Myaké (1996). It requires recognition of spatially manipulated letters and objects. This test has been used successfully in previous research (Boucheix & Guignard, 2005) and is highly correlated with a classical spatial aptitude test (Primary Mental Aptitude; Thurstone, 1964). Test scores were transformed into proportions of correct answers and a median split used to allocate participants into high and low spatial ability groups. Sixty three participants belonged to the low spatial ability group and 66 belonged to the high spatial. Participants from these two levels were equally distributed across the different experimental conditions. The reading test used (Lefavrais, 1967) is a timed individual reading aloud task that provides a global measure of reading ability expressed as one of five levels. The levels attained by participants were used to assign scores on a five-point scale that were used to distribute them equally across the different experimental conditions. Matching across all measured abilities and group

Low spatial

High spatial

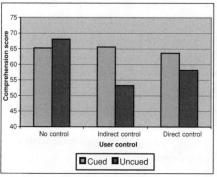

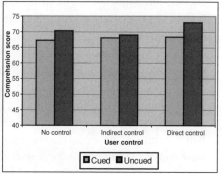

FIGURE 10.2. Comprehension scores as a function of user-control, signaling, and spatial abilities.

variables was confirmed by ANOVA and Neuman-Keuls tests to compare all the experimental conditions.

RESULTS

We will describe the results in three steps. We will first examine the learning performances for the immediate comprehension task. Then, we will analyze the differences between pre and post-test results. Finally, we will investigate the relation between comprehension scores and study time.

Immediate Comprehension Test

User Control and Spatial Abilities
The participants' performances on the immediate comprehension test are shown in Figure 10.2.

An ANOVA revealed no significant main effect for the level of user control (M No Control = 67.7, N = 45, SD = 12.46; M Indirect Control = 64, N = 44, SD = 15.56; M Direct Control = 65.8, N = 40, SD = 13.54; $F(2,117) = 0.80$; $p = .45$) and no significant main effect for the signaling cues (M Cued = 66.35, N = 63, SD = 12.65; M Uncued = 65.28, N = 66, SD = 15.07; $F(1, 117) = 0.20$; $p = .66$), whereas the main effect of the spatial ability was significant (M Low spatial = 62.3, N = 63, SD = 13.42; M High spatial = 69.33, N = 66, SD = 13.84; $F(1, 117) = 8.3$; $p = .005$). Learners with high spatial abilities out-performed learners with lower spatial ability. The interaction between user control and spatial ability is not significant ($F(2,117) = 1$, $p = .37$) and the interaction between cueing and spatial ability approached significance ($F(1, 117) = 2.60$, p $= .109$). Separate analyses for each spatial ability level revealed different performance patterns as a function of control and signaling cues. When learners had low spatial ability and when no signaling cues were available, indirect user control condition appeared to have negative effects in comparison to the dynamic condition without control (M Low spatial-IC = 54.88, SD = 17.25, N = 11; M Low spatial-NC = 67.23, SD = 12.3, N = 13; $F(1, 117) = 6.83$; p $= .01$). When signaling cues were presented, we found no effect of user control. It seems that guidance of attention when processing the animation could compensate for the cognitive and operative difficulties under the full control condition. When learners had high spatial abilities, there were no significant differences between the three levels of control nor between the two level of signaling. In this group, we found no hints on difficulties of the control condition and the learners obviously did not need guidance of their attention.

User Control and Prior Knowledge

Participants were tested for their prior knowledge by the pre-test and were categorized according to three levels: L3, High (M = 63.10; N = 38), L2, Medium (M = 42.64; N = 46), and L1, Low (M = 24.8; N = 45). Prior knowledge was (relatively) correlated with spatial ability (r = .34; p < 01). Table 10.1 shows the pattern of comprehension test scores of learners with high, medium, or low prior knowledge for the different control conditions and for signaling versus no signaling. The pattern of results is similar to the results described above. An ANOVA revealed no significant main effect for user control (F (2, 111) = 0,53, p = 0,58), a significant effect of prior knowledge (F(2, 111) = 5,03, p = .006), and an interaction between prior knowledge and signaling (F(2,111) = 4.07; p = .019). For learners with low prior knowledge, availability of signaling cues improved comprehension. The other interactions are not significant.

Learning Gains Between Pre- and Posttest

User Control and Spatial Abilities

The results obtained from the gains between pre-test and post-test (differences between post-test and pre-test performance) are presented Figure 10.3.

An ANOVA with the factors control, signaling cues and spatial ability showed no significant main effect for user control (*M* IC = 22.05, N = 44, *SD* = 14.92; *M* DC = 24.62, N = 40, *SD* = 15.64; *M* NC = 26.7, N = 45, *SD* = 14.12; F (2, 117) = 1.31; *p* = .27). However, similar to the results of the immediate comprehension test, participants with no control seemed to

TABLE 10.1. *Comprehension Scores – (Mean and SD) as a Function of Prior Knowledge, User Control, and Signaling Cues*

	High Prior Knowledge (N = 38)			Medium Prior Knowledge (N = 46)			Low Prior Knowledge (N = 45)		
	No Control N = 11	Indirect Control N = 14	Direct Control N = 13	No Control N = 19	Indirect Control N = 16	Direct Control N = 11	No Control N = 15	Indirect Control N = 14	Direct Control N = 16
Signaling	72.50 (5.77)	64.04 (10.29)	70.83 (7.56)	64.50 (10.40)	63.60 (13.76)	65.41 (26.52)	64.21 (14.17)	75.33 (15.40)	63.63 (8.62)
No-signaling	74.93 (13.13)	75.00 (15.67)	75.17 (9.70)	68.82 (13.04)	61.90 (17.67)	67.56 (11.32)	64.34 (15.22)	51.52 (15.18)	55.50 (13.31)

Low Spatial   **High Spatial**

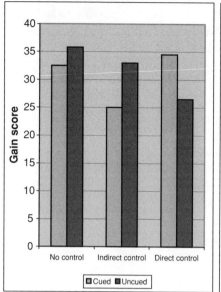
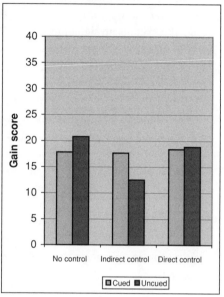

FIGURE 10.3. Mean gains from pre-test to post-test as a function of spatial ability, control, and cues.

perform slightly better. The same overall tendency appeared for signaling cues (M Cued = 24.3, N = 63, SD = 14.20; M Uncued = 24.6, N = 66, SD = 15.63; F (1, 117) = 0.01; p = .90). The gains obtained by the participants with low spatial abilities were higher than the gains attained by the participants with high spatial abilities (M low spatial level = 31.22, N = 63, SD = 13.86; M high spatial level = 17.67, N = 66, SD = 12.56; F(1, 117)= 32.30; p < .0001).

When learners had low spatial abilities but received signaling cues, participants with direct user control had a marginal higher mean learning gain of 34.13 (N = 11, SD = 13.10) than those with indirect user control of 25 (N = 11, SD = 16.44) (F (1, 117) = 2.74; p = .10). When learners had high spatial abilities, the learning gains appeared to be better in the no-control condition, particularly when signaling cues were absent (M IC = 12.50, N = 13, SD = 11.77; M DC = 18.86, N = 11, SD = 13.57; M NC = 21.00, N = 11, SD = 14.04) but these differences failed to be significant (F (1, 117) = 2,30; p = . 13). To summarize, the gains between the pre-test and the post-test clearly indicate a strong learning effect. However, learner control did not have an influence on these learning gains.

User Control and Prior Knowledge

Table 10.2 shows the pattern of learning gain scores of participants with high, medium or low prior knowledge for the different control conditions and for signaling versus no signaling. An ANOVA revealed neither a significant main effect for user control (M IC $= 21.65$, N $= 44$, SD $= 14,92$; M DC $= 23.32$, N $= 40$, SD $= 15,64$; M NC $= 25.39$, N $= 45$, SD $= 14.12$; $F(2, 111) = 0.82$; $p = .44$) nor a significant main effect of signaling ($MCued = 23.52$, N $= 63$, SD $= 14.20$; $MUncued = 23.32$, N $= 66$, SD $= 15.63$; $F(1,111) = .01$; $p = .95$). However, prior knowledge had a highly significant effect on learning gains (M low $= 31.18$, N $= 45$, SD $= 12.97$; M medium $= 24.6$, N $= 46$, SD $= 15.89$; M high $= 14.57$, N $= 38$, SD $= 9.84$; $F(2,111) = 15.09$; $p < .0001$). In a further step, we used the sum of the 10 post-test sub-scores (which were related to rotation direction, speed, mechanical effect) as dependent variable and analyzed its relation to the level of control, the availability of signaling cues and prior knowledge. This analysis revealed a marginally significant effect of user control ($F(2, 111) = 2.64$; $p = .056$). Participants in the dynamic non-control condition outperformed participants in the indirect control condition ($t(111) = 2.41$; $p < .02$).

Study Time

Our results suggest that in learning from animation, user control is not always beneficial for comprehension, that is, for integrating information about a dynamic mechanical device. The lack of a learning benefit seems to occur especially when learners cannot rely on signaling cues, which would guide their visual attention and cognitive processing. This raises the question, what might be the reasons for this result pattern. A preliminary answer seems to be possible based on the analysis of the study times for the different versions of the gear lesson.

The mean study times and the total comprehension scores (immediate comprehension plus learning gain between pre- and post-test) under the different learning conditions are shown in the Table 10.3. The data indicate that the lesson took much more time under the condition of direct control than under the non-control condition (M IC $= 851.5$ sec, SD $= 303.20$, N $= 44$; M DC $= 1060$ sec., SD $= 340.82$, N $= 40$; M NC $= 712$, SD $= 219.22$, N $= 45$ $F(2, 117) = 16.61$; $p < .0001$). Furthermore, the most interactive direct manipulation of the gears required the highest study time. Differences between the different levels of control regarding study time appeared to be especially pronounced for the participants with low spatial abilities, but the interaction between spatial ability and level of control is not significant $F(2,117) = 1.31$, $p = .27$). More

TABLE 10.2. *Mean Gains (and SD) from Pre-test to Post-test as a Function of Prior Knowledge; Control and Signaling Cues*

	High Prior Knowledge (N = 38)			Medium Prior Knowledge (N = 46)			Low Prior Knowledge (N = 45)		
	No Control (N = 11)	Indirect Control (N = 14)	Direct Control (N = 13)	No Control (N = 19)	Indirect Control (N = 16)	Direct Control (N = 11)	No Control (N = 15)	Indirect Control (N = 14)	Direct Control (N = 16)
Cued (N = 63)	16.25 (6.37)	19.86 (8.19)	13.95 (12.38)	23.75 (20.50)	19.68 (14.38)	23.75 (14.01)	31.25 (10.24)	27.5 (19.10)	34.43 (13.10)
Uncued (N = 66)	12.70 (8.67)	10.53 (9.37)	14.10 (12.13)	34.09 (14.17)	18.43 (16.56)	27.91 (16.61)	34.28 (13.89)	33.88 (13.16)	25.75 (11.54)

TABLE 10.3. *Mean Study Time and Mean Comprehension Score as Function of Spatial Abilities and User Control*

	Low Spatial (N = 63)			High Spatial (N = 66)		
	No Control (N = 23)	Indirect Control (N = 22)	Direct Control (N = 18)	No Control (N = 22)	Indirect Control (N = 22)	Direct Control (N = 22)
Study time (sec)	687.7	859.2	1133.8	736	843.7	986.1
	(207.80)	(294.04)	(387.54)	(232.14)	(195.64)	(289.93)
Total Comprehension score	65	59.2	58.8	71.6	68.8	71.6

specifically the analysis for each spatial group (see Table 10.3) show that: the differences between indirect control and direct control were highly significant for the low spatial ability group ($F(1,117) = 9.28$; $p = .003$), whereas they were relatively slight for the high spatial ability group ($F(1,117) = 2.93$; $p = .09$). The differences between direct control and non-control condition were highly significant, especially when spatial ability was low (low spatial ability: $F(1,117) = 25.34$; $p < .0001$); high spatial ability: $F(1,117) = 9.19$; $p = .003$). The difference between the indirect control condition and the non-control condition was significant when spatial ability was low ($F(1,117) = 4.28$; $p = .041$), but not when spatial ability was high ($F(1,117) = 1.67$; $p = .20$). Finally, positive effects of signaling cues were marginally significant only when spatial ability was low (M Cued, Low spatial = 939. 28, SD = 335.66, N = 32; M Uncued, Low spatial = 803.70, SD = 345.97; $F(1,125) = 2.9$; $p < .10$).

Regarding the comprehension scores, the non-control group showed the best performance with the shortest study time. The possibilities and requirements of operating the animation under the condition of direct interactive control lead the learners to spend a very long time on the lesson. However, the increased learning time and the high amount of interaction did not lead to better comprehension. Participants with indirect control showed the lowest comprehension scores and a longer study time than participants in the non-control condition ($F(1, 126) = 6.90$; $p < .01$). The direct control condition did not lead to a significant improvement of comprehension, but resulted in a very high study time as compared to the non-control condition ($F(1, 126) = 31$; $p < .0001$) or to the indirect control condition ($F(1, 126) = 8.57$; $p = .005$). These differences were entirely due to the different forms of user control, because correlations between comprehension scores or learning gain scores and study times were either negative or close to zero and in all cases not significant. The correlation between immediate comprehension and study time was $r(129) = -.17$ ($p > .10$). The correlation between learning gain between the pre-test and the post-test and study time was $r(129) = .02$ ($p > .10$).

DISCUSSION

This research investigated the effect of degree of control and levels of directness of the control on young children's learning from animations. Neither direct nor indirect control over the course of the animations led to overall benefit. On the contrary, there were indications that, compared to non-controllable continuous animation, user control may have negative effects for certain types of learners. The lesson study time increased markedly with controllability and in some cases this was associated with inferior learning performance. These results are consistent with those found by Bétrancourt and Réalini (2005) and Lowe (2004) in very different content domains. Further, the consequences of requiring learners to exercise control are reminiscent of findings about learning with hypermedia (e.g., Kerwin, 2004) in which an interactive hyperlinked web site did not produce performance superior to a conventional linear organization of the information. Nevertheless, it is also clear from other evidence such as the previously mentioned research of Schwan and Riempp (2004) that in some circumstances, user control can be highly beneficial for learning. The negative findings concerning the effectiveness of control obtained in the present study suggest that particularities of individual investigations in this area need to be closely considered.

First, the specific nature of the control system provided might permit manipulations that interfere with the central comprehension task. In such circumstances, operation of the control facility could affect the level at which animations are processed. For example, with direct control over the gear wheels, the learner's processing resources could be largely focused on the level of carrying out actions such as turning the wheels of the gear system with the mouse. In this case, "learning-by-doing" could disturb comprehension level processing because focusing on the action level and the results of actions competes with the deeper processing of the animation, particularly with respect to concepts that are less obvious. Perhaps this is why, with direct control, performance was lower when signaling cues were absent. In the indirect control condition, manipulation of the system of control itself is less involving but the use of the scrolling bar system can produce a split attention effect between the control and processing of the animation.

Second, with controllable conditions, the shaping of micro-steps in the depicted process depends on user actions. Given this freedom, it is perfectly possible for individuals to use the control facility in ways that are poorly suited to the requirements of a specific learning task. For example, the learner could manipulate the animation too quickly, explore just part of the full animated sequence, or play the animation only once. Such deficiencies in an interrogation regime are likely to be particularly damaging when learners who are novices in the depicted domain are faced with complex dynamic content. Under these circumstances, the result of control over the animation could be conceptual misinterpretations that arise because superficial aspects of the display are extracted rather than information that is fundamental to building high-quality mental models (Lowe, 2004).

The findings reported here suggest that controlling animations has a particular performance penalty for those with low spatial abilities or little prior knowledge. For these types of learners, using the system of control introduces an added task involving substantially increased processing demands that they are poorly equipped to handle. Control that is supposed to help learners actually has the effect of impairing learning performance. These findings run counter to the prevailing conviction amongst many designers of educational animations about the utility of interactivity in multimedia learning. Learners who lack relevant prior knowledge tend to have limited capacity for productive interrogation of user controllable animations so cues may be beneficial in helping them locate relevant information and understand the changes they perceive. However, it appears that learners with a high level of prior knowledge are less in need of such additional cues. A high degree of control that allows novices to personally monitor and shape the course of the animation could impair understanding of the concepts portrayed if they are unsupported. By focusing on the superficial perceptual features of the display, novices tend to neglect crucial conceptual aspects of animated information (Lowe, 2003) such as the meaning of perceptually subtle feature transformations. Further, as research into perceptions of trajectories has demonstrated (Kaiser, Proffitt, Whelan, & Hecht, 1992), learner control may actually provoke misinterpretations about matters such as causality relations (Boucheix, Lowe, & Soirat, 2006).

However, a balanced view of the potential of user control for assisting learning requires that animations with two kinds of task goals should be distinguished: (i) animations intended to support a deep understanding of conceptual changes or mechanisms and (ii) animation to support learning by doing of procedural tasks. In the case of procedural tasks, like those in the Schwan and Riempp study (2004), learners would be able to evaluate their information needs quite readily. Essentially, such tasks involve imitation and recall of actions portrayed in the videos. Learning to faithfully imitate a knot-tying procedure should be facilitated by a high level of control over depiction of the micro steps and the associated gestural and motor activity involved in task execution. However, free control of an animation may not be beneficial for other types of learning task in which a key goal is the deep understanding of the concepts underlying complex dynamic processes (for example the mechanism of volcanic eruption, Rebetz, Sangin, Bétrancourt, & Dillebourg, 2004, or meteorological prediction, Lowe, 2005).

Implications for Design

Ideally, the provision of user control for educational animations should be designed to have minimal impact on the central task of comprehending to-be-learned subject matter. Negative effects of the demands imposed by user control appear likely to be more marked for learners with low spatial abilities and for those who lack relevant background knowledge. In order to counter-act the often-dominant influence that purely perceptual aspects of dynamic visualizations have on their processing, it seems advisable to provide support for such learners in the form of appropriate attentional cues and interpretative guidance. This direction should be designed to help focus learner processing on information that is most relevant to the task requirements.

Further research is needed to deepen our understanding of how learn-ers interact with animations and many fundamental questions remain to be addressed. For example, a distinction could be made between two ways of con-ceptualizing the control of animations. To date, research has tended to focus on control over the *external* presentation of the material that is to be learned (for example, whether the animation is controllable or not). However, another way to conceptualize control is in terms of the level of cognitive processing that learners engage in when they interact with presented animations. This form of control could be introduced by a system that asks questions designed to engage the learner at a particular level of conceptual processing. In this approach, the animation then functions as a source of direct verification for specific aspects of the learning task – a more *internal* form of control. Other fruitful areas for investigation include the nature of "online" processing that occurs during learning from animations and how designers might best share control between the system and learners. Devising effective ways of balancing these two loci of control poses major challenges for designers of animated learning materials and interesting questions for researchers.

References

Bétrancourt, M. (2005). The animation and interactivity principles in multimedia learning. In R. E. Mayer (Ed.), *The Cambridge Handbook of Multimedia Learning* (pp. 287–296). New-York: Cambridge University Press.

Bétrancourt, M. & Réalini, N. (2005). Le contrôle sur le déroulement de l'animation. *11ème JETCSIC; 17* Juin, Nice.

Bétrancourt, M. & Tversky, B. (2000). Effect of computer animation on user's performance: a review. *Le travail humain, 63*(4), 311–329.

Bétrancourt, M., Dillenbourg, P., & Clavien, L. (2007). Reducing cognitive load in learning from animation: impact of delivery features. In J.-F. Rouet, R. K. Lowe & W. Schnotz (Eds.), *Understanding Multimedia Documents*.

Bogacz, S. & Trafton, J. G. (2007). Understanding dynamic and static displays: using images to reason dynamically. *Cognitive Systems Research*.

Boucheix, J. M. (2003). Simulation et compréhension de documents techniques: le cas de la formation des grutiers. *Le Travail Humain, 66*, 3, 252–282.

Boucheix, J. M. & Guignard, H. (2005). Which animation condition can improve text comprehension in children? *European Journal of Psychology of Education, 20*(4), 369–388.

Boucheix, J. M., Lowe, R. K., & Soirat, A. (2006). On line processing of a complex technical animation: Eye tracking investigation during verbal description. In, *Proceedings of the EARLI-SIG 2 Congress*, University of Nottingham, September.

Boucheix, J. M. & Schneider, E. (submitted). Designing "apprehendable" animation features to enhance animation in multimedia comprehension: integrated micro-steps format and user control.

Catrambone, R. & Fleming Seay, A. (2002). Using animation to help students learn computer algorithms. *Human Factors, 44*(3), 495–511.

Garg, A. X., Norman, G., & Sperotable, L. (2001). How medical students learn spatial anatomy. *The Lancet, 357*, 363–364.

Garg, A. X., Norman, G. R., Spero, L., & Maheshwari, P. (1999). Do virtual computer models hinder anatomy learning? *Academic Medicine, 74*, 87–89.

Hegarty, M. (1992). Mental Animation: Inferring Motion From Static Displays of Mechanical Systems. *Journal of Experimental Psychology: Learning, Memory, & Cognition, 18*(5), 1084–1102.

Hegarty, M. (2004). Mechanical reasoning by mental simulation. *Trends in Cognitive Sciences, 8*(6), 280–285.

Hegarty, M. & Just, M. A. (1993). Constructing mental models from texts and diagrams. *Journal of Memory and Language, 32*(2), 717–742.

Hegarty, M. (2005). Multimedia learning about physical systems. In R. E. Mayer (Ed.), *The Cambridge Handbook of Multimedia learning* (pp. 447–466). New-York: Cambridge University Press.

Hegarty, M. & Kozhevnikov, M. (1999). Types of visual-spatial representations and mathematical problem solving. *Journal of Educational Psychology, 91*(3), 684–689.

Hegarty, M. & Sims, V. K. (1994). Individual differences in mental animation during mechanical reasoning. *Memory & Cognition, 22*, 411–430.

Hegarty, M. & Steinhoff, K. (1997). Individual differences in the use of diagrams as external memory in mechanical reasoning. *Learning and Individual Differences, 9*, 19–42.

Hegarty, M., Kriz, S., & Cate, C. (2003). The roles of mental animations and external animations in understanding mechanical systems. *Cognition and instruction, 21*(4), 325–360.

Hegarty, M., Narayanan, N. H., & Freitas, P. (2002). Understanding machines from multimedia and hypermedia presentations. In J. Otéro, J. A. Léon, & A. C. Graesser (Eds.). *The psychology of Science Text Comprehension* (pp. 357–384). Mahwah, NJ: Lawrence Erlbaum Associates.

Hegarty, M., Quilici, J., Narayanan, H. N., Holmquist, S., & Moreno, R. (1999). Multimedia instruction: lessons from evaluation of theory-based design. *Journal of educational multimedia and hypermedia, 8*, 119–150.

Hegarty, M. & Waller, D. A. (2005). Individual differences in spatial abilities. In P. Shah and A. Myake (Eds.), *The Cambridge Handbook of visuo spatial thinking* (pp. 121–169). New York: Cambridge University Press.

Huck, J. & Floto E. (to be published). Signaling effects in multimedia learning. *International Journal of Human-Computer Studies.*

Kaiser, M. K., Profitt, D. R., Whelan, S. M., & Hecht, H. (1992). Influence of animation on dynamical judgments. *Journal of experimental Psychology: Human Perception and Performance, 18*, 669–690.

Kerwin, M. L. (2004). Evaluation of a computer based instructional package about eating disorders. *Computers in Human Behavior, 6*(1), 25–41.

Kriz, S. & Hegarty, M. (2004). Constructing and revising mental models of a mechanical system: The role of domain knowledge in understanding external visualizations. In, K. Forbus, D. Gentner, & T. Regier (Eds.), *Proceedings of the 26th Annual Conference of the Cognitive Science Society.* Mahwah, NJ: Lawrence Erlbaum Associates.

Lefavrais, P. (1967). *Test de L'Alouette, Manuel et tests.* Editions du Centre de Psychologie Appliquée (ECPA). Paris.

Lowe, R. K. (1999). Extracting information from an animation during complex visual learning. *European Journal of Psychology of Education.* Special Issue: Visual Learning with New Technologies, *14*(2), 225–244.

Lowe, R. K. (2001). Understanding information presented by complex animated diagrams. In, J-F. Rouet, J. J. Levonen, & A. Biardeau (Eds.), *Multimedia learning: Cognitive and instructional issues* (pp. 65–74). London: Pergamon

Lowe, R. K. (2003). Animation and learning: selective processing of information in dynamic graphics. *Learning and instruction, 14*, 257–274.

Lowe, R. K. (2004). Interrogation of a dynamic visualization during learning. *Learning and Instruction, 14*, 257–274.

Lowe, R. K. (2005). Multimedia learning of meteorology. In R. E. Mayer (Ed.), *The Cambridge Handbook of Multimedia Learning* (pp. 429–446). New York: Cambridge University Press.

Lowe, R. K. & Schnotz, W. (in press). Traitements cognitifs et fonctions pédagogiques des animations. In, J-M. Boucheix, & J-F. Rouet (Eds.). *Les animations graphiques et leurs effets dans le cadre des technologies d'apprentissage.*

Mautoné, P. D. & Mayer, R. E. (2001). Signaling as a cognitive guide in multimedia learning. *Journal of Educational Psychology, 93*, 377–389.

Mayer, R. E. (2001). *Multimedia learning.* Cambridge: Cambridge University Press.

Mayer, R. E. (Ed.) (2005). *The Cambridge Handbook of Multimedia learning.* New York: Cambridge University Press.

Mayer, R. E., & Chandler, P. (2001). When learning is just a click away: does simple user interaction foster deeper understanding of multimedia messages. *Journal of Educational Psychology, 93*, 390–397.

Mayer, R. E., Hegarty, M., Mayer, S., & Campbell, J. (2005). When static media promote active learning: Diagrams versus animations in multimedia instruction. *Journal of Experimental Psychology: Applied, 11*, 256–265.

Narayanan, N. H. (2007). Designing multimedia explanations of causal and dynamic systems. In J.-F. Rouet, R. K. Lowe & W. Schnotz (Eds.), *Understanding Multimedia Documents*.

Narayanan, H. N. & Hegarty, M. (2002). Multimedia design for communication of dynamic information. *International Journal of Human-Computer Studies, 57*(4), 279–315.

Rebetz, C., Sangin, M., Bétrancourt, M., & Dillenbourg, P. (2004). Effects of collaboration in the context of learning from animations. In *Proceedings of EARLI SIG Meeting on Comprehension of text and Graphics: Basic and Applied Issues*, September, 9–11, Universita de Valencia: Valencia, Spain, 187–192.

Schwan, S. & Riempp, R. (2004). The cognitive benefits of interactive videos: learning to tic nautical knots. *Learning and Instruction, 14*, 293–305.

Schnotz, W. (2005). An integrated model of text and picture comprehension. In, In R. E. Mayer (Ed.), *The Cambridge Handbook of Multimedia learning* (pp. 49–70). New York: Cambridge University Press.

Schnotz, W. & Lowe, R. K. (2003). External and Internal representations in multimedia learning. *Learning and Instruction, 13*, 117–123.

Shah, P., & Myaké, A. (1996). The separability of working memory resources for spatial thinking and language processing: An individual differences approach. *Journal of experimental Psychology, 125*, 4–27.

Tassini, S. & Bétrancourt, M. (2003). Le contrôle sur l'animation influence-t-elle le niveau d'efficacité cognitive de l'animation. *Neuvièmes Journées JETCSIC*, 21 juin: Dijon.

Thurstone, L. L. & Thustone, T. G. (1964). *Batterie Factorielle P.M.A* (Aptitude Mentales Primaires, 11–17 ans). Paris: ECPA.

Tversky, B. (2005). Functional significance of visuo-spatial representations. In, P. Shah and A. Myaké (Eds.), *The Cambridge Handbook of visuo-spatial thinking* (pp. 1–34). New York: Cambridge University Press.

Tversky, B., Bauer-Morrison, J., & Bétrancourt, M. (2002). Animation: can it facilitate? *International Journal of Human-Computer Studies, 57*, 247–262.

11

Turning the Tables

Investigating Characteristics and Efficacy of Student-Authored Animations and Multimedia Representations

Teresa Hübscher-Younger and N. Hari Narayanan

INTRODUCTION

Providing multiple perspectives on complex concepts can promote deeper learning. This principle, in its simplest form, can be seen at work if one opens up any popular textbook on a complex topic in science or engineering. One will find textual descriptions of concepts and ideas interspersed with symbolic (e.g., equations) and graphical (e.g., diagrams or photographs) representations. An animation has the capacity to present dynamic aspects of a situation directly and explicitly. It is another way of presenting multiple perspectives to a learner, one that is particularly well suited to verbally explaining and visually illustrating complex procedures (e.g., computer algorithms) and dynamic processes (e.g., meteorological events). In fact, animations can be considered to be a special case of multiple representations in which a series of pictures are fluidly presented, along with other representations such as sounds and spoken words.

There is a wealth of literature on the educational benefits of animations as well as multiple static representations. For instance, Cox and Brna (1995) found that whereas only 17% of students solving analytical reasoning problems tended to use multiple representations, those who did performed better. In our work on learning in the complex domain computer science, we found that students learn more about an algorithm from interactive visualizations that presented a suite of multiple representations – animations integrated with

This material is based upon work supported by the National Science Foundation (NSF) under grant REC-9815016. This chapter was prepared with NSF support while the second author was serving at NSF. However, any opinions, findings, and conclusions or recommendations expressed are those of the authors and do not reflect the views of NSF. Authors are grateful to the editors for reviewing the chapter and providing constructive criticisms that helped significantly improve the clarity and flow of ideas.

hypertext explanations – than from lectures and descriptions of algorithms in a style that is typically found in textbooks (Hansen, Narayanan, & Hegarty, 2002). We also discovered from ablation experiments that learning is negatively impacted when animations are selectively removed from this suite of multiple representations (Hansen & Narayanan, 2000).

Providing multiple perspectives on a complex concept involves more than providing multiple representations of the same information. Learning is enhanced when representations that differ not only in modality but also in information content, with both redundancy and differentiation of information, are made available to the learner. For instance, pictures, by their very nature, present a different perspective on the subject matter than text. Mayer (2001) found that comprehension improved when text and graphics were presented side by side instead of one after the other. One possible reason for the effectiveness of animations in explaining dynamic concepts and processesis that animations typically employ both verbal narratives and consecutive visuals, presented simultaneously, to explain things that change over time.

Another argument for the potential benefits of exposing a learner to multiple perspectives arises from Lakoff and Johnson's theory of concept formation (1999). They argue that metaphor is the basis for all concept formation. According to their theory, abstract concepts are derived from multiple metaphors interacting and emphasizing different aspects of the concept. This suggests that analogical or metaphoric explanations can produce a richer understanding of an abstract concept than literal explanations. Although we are not aware of research that directly tests this conjecture, our ablation experiments with algorithm visualizations revealed that students who viewed animated analogies of algorithms prior to viewing literal animations of the algorithms learned more than students who only saw the literal animations (Hansen & Narayanan, 2000). For example, an algorithm for sorting numbers can be illustrated with an analogy of organizing playing cards. But note that, like the algorithm, the analogy is also dynamic. It is difficult to capture the essence of such an analogy with a static picture or a verbose description as well as an animation can. Animations are multiple and fluid representations that can not only illustrate a complex and dynamic process to a learner, but also show analogies and metaphors that allow learners to connect the dynamics of the process or concept being learned to their existing background knowledge or everyday experience.

Despite these advantages, traditional classroom instruction on algorithms mostly relies on static representations created by experts – text and diagrams found in textbooks, and verbal descriptions and pictures spoken, written or drawn by the teacher. Another issue is that animations or other kinds of multiple representations may not always lead to successful learning. For instance, Lowe (1999) found that novices viewing weather animations focused more on perceptually salient aspects than on thematically significant aspects. Novices may not have sufficient knowledge to identify and attend to semantically important aspects of a representation. Another possibility is that even when multiple representations are presented to learners, they may choose not to use all available representations in the learning process. Even if they do, the added cognitive effort of translating between representations may negatively impact learning (Ainsworth, Bibby, & Wood, 1998). Similarly in the case of animations, the cognitive effort of mapping between the pictorial elements of the animation and the domain concepts they represent may impede learning. Surely, there are many aspects of learning from animations and multiple representations that are in need of further research.

These problems can perhaps be avoided by having learners themselves construct, share, and discuss expository representations of the concepts they are learning. For example, if students are asked to build animations of weather phenomena they are learning about, they are likely to make aspects of the meteorological domain that are thematically salient to them also appear perceptually salient in their animations. If they create multiple representations to explain complex concepts, and share, discuss, and evaluate each other's representations, all representations may be equally understood and inter-representation translation may no longer be a problem.

Furthermore, constructionist theories of learning hold that learning will be deeper if students develop and share their own diverse understandings of a concept. If all students gain their understanding from the same expert-created representations, they will likely develop a uniform understanding rather than a diverse set of insights. This raises the question of whether the diversity of representations that students learn from can be increased by having students create explanatory representations instead of relying solely on instructor and textbook provided representations. Extant literature contains many studies of the efficacy of animations and other kinds of representations created by expert teachers and researchers. However, studies on the characteristics and efficacy of student-created representations are much less numerous. Therefore, the focus of this chapter is on characterizing student-authored expository representations and the learning that results from authoring and evaluating representations. We use the term "representation" broadly, to include both dynamic representations, such as animations, and static ones, such as pictures. Thus our focus is not on learning from animations per se, but on learning from multiple representations that include animations. We describe investigations of whether college students of computer science naturally tend to use all available representations while trying to understand an algorithm, and the characteristics of expository representations that they themselves create to explain algorithms to their peers.

The rest of this chapter presents summaries of three studies that investigated the following questions. When students engage in their natural or habitual learning practices and study an algorithmic concept, do they effectively use all available representations? The first study reported here uncovered students' tendency to converge on one explanatory representation rather than use all available representations. It also revealed a limitation of the most common representations students use in learning: static representations such as text and pictures found in textbooks, and words and diagrams spoken, written, or drawn by the teacher. Such representations may be inadequate, in comparison to dynamic representations (i.e., animations), to accurately and completely portray all aspects of a complex dynamic process.

If instead of studying representations provided by a teacher or textbook, students are asked to create, share, and critique explanatory representations of a complex concept amongst themselves, what kinds of representations will they build – animations, static graphics, textual narratives, or combinations of these styles? How diverse will these representations be? If this exercise in constructivism is repeated multiple times in class over a semester, how will the nature and styles of representations change over time? Will students learn from the activity of authoring and evaluating explanatory representations? The second and third study addressed these issues.

STUDENT USE OF MULTIPLE REPRESENTATIONS IN TRADITIONAL INSTRUCTION

We address the aforementioned questions in the context of undergraduate student learning in the domain of computer algorithms. Algorithms are fundamental and abstract procedural concepts in computer science. These concepts are generally considered to be difficult to learn and teach. Because data and algorithms do not have physical manifestations, it is difficult for someone to "observe" an algorithm or to "show" someone how the procedure operates on and transforms data. To explain these concepts, textbooks and teachers often rely on verbal explanations and graphical representations of data, and how data changes over time as a result of an algorithm operating on it. This difficulty has also given rise to researchers developing various kinds of algorithm animations during the last two decades (see Hundhausen, Douglas, & Stasko, 2002, for a survey). Despite the fact that first such animations were designed in the early eighties, algorithm animations remain in the realm of research and are not yet widely used in college level algorithm instruction. The teaching of algorithms at the undergraduate level still primarily depends on static pictorial and textual representations available in textbooks and created by teachers. So our first study looked at the way multiple representations drawn from traditional instruction are used by a group of college students majoring in computer science during an algorithm studying exercise.

Study I

Method

This was a qualitative observational study of natural or habitual learning practices of students engaged in studying an algorithm. Sixteen students from a university department of computer science and software engineering who were enrolled in an introductory algorithm analysis course volunteered to participate in the study, in return for extra course credit. Their sex, race, work experience, previous schooling, nationality, and age varied considerably. Based on their reports that they typically study for this course in small groups, they were split into six groups of two to three students each. Students were grouped together based on what times they were available for the study, and so we grouped students together who had never met and who did not normally study together.

The course instructor was videotaped explaining the Quick Sort algorithm. The videotaped lecture resembled the lectures the students normally attended, that is, it was presented by their instructor, who used only a white board and markers, his usual method of presenting the material. This videotape was shown to the students during the study session. The instructor provided a printed lecture summary. This summarized the material he presented in the lecture, and also contained a step-wise description of Quick Sort. This summary was given to the students before they watched the lecture. The students also brought the course textbook, which they normally use to study for the course, to the session. Thus, the following multiple representations were available to the students: descriptions and diagrams explaining the algorithm in the textbook, the instructor's lecture, a diagram he drew on the whiteboard during the lecture, the notes students made while watching the videotaped lecture, the teacher's lecture summary and a step-wise description of the algorithm.

The experimenter ran a session for each of the six groups separately. In each session, after an introduction to the study, the group watched the videotaped lecture. They were allowed to take notes. After watching the video, they were

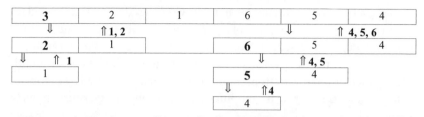

FIGURE 11.1. A recursion tree diagram showing how the Quick Sort algorithm makes recursive calls with different inputs extracted from the original input.

given a set of questions about the algorithm and asked to study the algorithm using any of the materials available and then answer the questions. While the students were studying the algorithm and answering questions, they were videotaped. The experimenter also observed student activities and interactions, and made notes. After the session, the experimenter collected any notes or pictures students made and conducted a short interview of the group or the individuals in the group separately. These interviews were used to collect the students' thoughts about the session and to understand how they normally study algorithms.

Results

We expected to see students using multiple representations that were available to them in order to answer the questions. Videotapes, observations, and interview responses revealed that students in this study chose to consider a single pictorial representation presented by the instructor, a recursion tree diagram (Figure 11.1), over all the other representations presented or available to them for understanding the algorithm. This graphical representation became central to their understanding of the algorithm. They acted as if they would be able to understand everything about the algorithm by using this one representation, and subsequently reasoned with this representation to come up with answers to the questions. Consequently, they failed to correctly answer questions that required information not available in this diagram.

The instructor explicitly said while presenting this representation that all he was showing using this representation was one, albeit central, aspect of the algorithm, its pattern of recursive executions. The lecture and the pseudocode given to the students covered other equally critical aspects of the algorithm. Nevertheless, students did not pay attention to the limitation of this graphical representation, that it only presented a partial (i.e., only shows snapshots of one aspect of the algorithm's dynamics) and high-level (i.e., without details of dynamic operations on individual data items carried out by the algorithm) static view of the algorithm's execution.

All students realized when they encountered questions about algorithm steps not explicit in the recursion tree diagram, that their understanding of the algorithm was incomplete. But instead of reaching out to other representations and explanations available to them, they struggled to construct answers to such questions based on their understanding of the algorithm from the recursion tree diagram. The information to answer these questions was available to them from various representations in their textbook. Most students observed did not seek information from the textbook to supplement their understanding from the instructor provided representation. They convinced each other that they did not need to use other available representations to answer the questions, and on occasion even decided not to accept correct answers that some group members derived from other representations.

Discussion

One detriment to learning revealed by this study was *premature convergence*: students converged on one representation and understanding of the algorithm too early in the learning process, without considering other available representations. We suspect that all groups converged on the recursion tree diagram as their representation of choice because it was presented and discussed extensively by the instructor in the videotaped lecture (thereby making it an authoritative representation), not because it provided the most complete explanation. This observation is consistent with Milgram's studies on student obedience to authority (Milgram, 1963, 1965).

An undesirable result of this convergence was that despite realizing that information needed to answer some questions could not be derived from this one representation, students attempted to construct answers rather than seek additional information from other representations available to them. Mulholland and Eisenstadt (1998) note a similar phenomenon happening with novice users of software visualizations. They argue that when students discover a mismatch between a software visualization and their assumptions, they work to reinterpret the visualization, so that it is consistent with their expectations, rather than investigate the disparity further. Clearly, the tendency to privilege one representation over others is problematic.

A second impediment to learning, *groupthink* (Janis, 1967), was manifested by all of the groups. Often the groups would convince themselves that explanations based on a faulty understanding of the algorithm were in fact correct.

Even when students were observed accessing other representations such as descriptions and diagrams from their course textbook, it was clear that they became frustrated in trying to integrate those with the instructor's descriptions and diagram. Thus, *information integration* – successfully combining information from multiple representations – was observed to be another learning difficulty.

TURNING THE TABLES: HAVING STUDENTS AUTHOR AND EVALUATE THEIR OWN ANIMATIONS AND MULTIMEDIA REPRESENTATIONS

One approach to addressing the three problematic aspects of student learning practices identified in the previous study – premature convergence, group-think, and information integration – is for instruction to emphasize one complete and accurate representation of each concept. However, it is almost impossible for one static representation – a textual description or a diagram – to capture all aspects of complex and dynamic concepts such as algorithms accurately and completely. Any single representation of a complex algorithm, even when accurate, is likely to be incomplete. This is precisely why students' choice of a single representation to focus on in the previous study led to incomplete learning. On the other hand, narrated animations can simultaneously explain and illustrate the detailed and time-varying behaviors of even the most complex algorithms. Perhaps students might have learned more, and answered the questions more accurately, had the instructor used an animation instead of a static picture like Figure 11.1 to illustrate the behavior of the Quick Sort algorithm over time. A strong case can indeed be made for the development and integration of animations into algorithms curricula, and for using animations as central representations in lectures.

Despite the expressive power of animations, research in the field has shown that algorithm animations (Byrne, Catrambone, & Stasko, 1999), and animations in general (Tversky, Morrison, & Bétrancourt, 2002), do not always provide learning benefits. Our prior research (Hansen, Narayanan, & Hegarty, 2002) demonstrated that animations have to be embedded within a larger context of multiple explanatory representations in order to be educationally effective. However, efficaceous algorithm visualizations in which multiple synchronized animations are integrated with hypertext explanations, and which ask students questions and allow them to make predictions, are extremely time consuming to design and produce (Hansen, Narayanan, & Hegarty, 2002).

An alternative approach is to encourage students to first *individually* create, and then *collectively* share and evaluate their own animations and other kinds of explanatory representations of concepts prior to teaching them the concepts in a classroom lecture. Because this makes a plethora of representations created by a group of peers available to each student, no single representation is likely to be considered more authoritative than the others. This can possibly counteract student's tendency to seek out and latch onto one representation. Because representation authoring is done individually and subsequently discussed and evaluated by the entire class collectively, groupthink may be less of a problem. The act of individual authoring, and the common prior knowledge, culture, and social experience shared by students, can possibly make integrating information from one's own and others' representations easier than integrating information from representations created by experts outside the peer group.

Learning from a large set of diverse student-created representations may lead to a richer, more connected concept of an algorithm than learning from a small set of instructor and textbook provided representations. As Cox and Brna (1995) argue, multiple representations are more effective for problem solving than relying on a single representation for answering all questions, and people vary considerably in how able they are to use and understand different types of representations. So a diverse set of representations is likely to better match the different cognitive and learning styles of students.

We implemented such an approach in an algorithms course and conducted two studies to investigate student learning and characteristics of student-created representations. In these studies, students authored, shared, and evaluated each other's algorithm animations and other multimedia algorithm representations. To facilitate the sharing and evaluation of representations, we designed a computer supported collaborative learning tool called CAROUSEL. This tool allows students to store and share their representations with each other and to evaluate these representations. More details on CAROUSEL can be found in (Hübscher-Younger & Narayanan, 2003). Students could upload their representations, in the form of text, images, audio files or animations, to CAROUSEL, which displayed these items on the web so that other students could log in and view each representation and rate it using a set of pre-determined criteria.

Given the increasing prevalence of animations in electronic learning materials and the web, students are likely to be familiar with animations as explanatory representations. Existing software such as Macromedia Flash makes authoring simple animations relatively easy. Moreover, as discussed in the introduction to this chapter, animations are well suited to explaining the dynamics of algorithms. Therefore, we expected to find that students learned fromcreating and sharing animations and other multimedia representations that were quite different from the static textual and pictorial representations found in textbooks and classroom blackboards.

Study II

Method

Twelve students from the same university department who were enrolled in an introductory data structures and algorithms course volunteered to participate in the study, in return for extra course credit. The study occurred over four weeks with three different algorithms (Fibonacci Number Series algorithm, Selection Sort algorithm, and Merge Sort algorithm) presented as course assignments with three identical stages. In the first stage, the student participants were given a printed step-wise description of an algorithm, and asked to study and understand it themselves. Following this, each participant was asked to create an explanatory representation, that is, one that explains the algorithm to someone else. This representation could involve text, pictures, video, animations, sounds, or speech in any combination. The student then used CAROUSEL to store the representation and to exhibit it to all other students in the volunteer group. This activity took place over a one-week period.

After all representations were online and visible to everyone in the group, the students started the second stage, in which each student reviewed and evaluated all representations (except one's own) using CAROUSEL. To evaluate representations, students used a form in CAROUSEL asking them to rate the following six characteristics of each representation using a five-point Likert scale.

- Usefulness (How central was this representation to your understanding of the algorithm?)
- Understandability (How easy was this representation to understand?)
- Salience (How well did this representation point out the important features of the algorithm?)
- Familiarity (How familiar were you with the content of the representation?)
- Pleasure (How much did you enjoy the way this representation communicated the algorithm?)
- Contiguity (How well did this representation connect with the other representations of this algorithm?)

Fibonacci algorithm representation 7

The Marble Statues

There was once an old salesman who had just acquired a large inventory of marble statues. Almost all the statues were different sizes, ranging from very small to some that were so big the salesman could hardly lift them.

Thinking to make his fortune with these statues, the salesman rented a small shop on the main street, and bought a shelf to display some of his statues to the public. Unfortunately, once he got the shelf to his shop he realized that although the shelf was very strong, it wasn't very stable. He found that if the items on the shelf were unbalanced, then the shelf would eventually begin to lean until it finally toppled over.

Unable to afford a new shelf, the salesman hit upon an idea. He searched through his inventory of statues until he found two one pound statues. He placed one statue on each end of the shelf to keep it balanced, but after looking at it for awhile decided that the shelf looked to bare. So he searched through his inventory until he found a two pound statue. He placed the two one pound statues on one end of the shelf, and balanced it out with the two pound statue on the other end. Now satisfied, he made up a sign, and opened his shop for business.

Later that day, a woman came into his shop and was quite taken by the two one pound statues on the shelf. She wanted to buy both statues, but couldn't afford them. Eventually, she made up her mind, and decided to just buy one of the statues. The salesman gladly wrapped up the statue for her and took her money.

Although he was happy to have finally made a sale, this caused a bit of a problem for the salesmen. Now his shelf was no longer balanced, and he could already see that it was leaning slightly. He searched and searched through his inventory for another one pound statue to replace the one he had sold, but the closest he could get was a three pound statue.

FIGURE 11.2. Part of a metaphoric story representing a recursive algorithm for calculating the Fibonacci Number Series.

These raw ratings and their average values provide a set of peer measures for the *perceived quality* of a representation. This activity took place over a one-week period. After the week for the evaluating task was over, the students took a post-test that examined their understanding of the algorithm. This was the third stage. Any classroom discussion of an algorithm used in this study occurred only after this post-test.

Results

A total of 36 representations were created by 11 of the 12 study participants. Students constructed a variety of representations, differing both in style and content. Some students submitted pure text containing elaborate metaphorical stories that illustrated what an algorithm computes, such as a story about a shopkeeper who used the Fibonacci series to balance his shelf of statues (Figure 11.2). Others produced entertaining animations that illustrated the mathematical basis of an algorithm, such as the "Dancing Hampsters" (spelling in context) showing the Fibonacci series (Figure 11.3). Most representations were of a walkthrough style, giving an example of a data set and showing how it would change over time as the algorithm operated on it.

For two of the three algorithms that were used in this study, positive correlations between creating and sharing a representation and post-test scores were found ($r = .635$, $p = .07$; $r = .663$, $p = .05$). This suggested a positive relationship between authoring/rating representations of algorithms and understanding the algorithms; however, this does not necessarily indicate a strong causal relationship.

Media use by students was categorized using integers 1 to 4, with 1 being the use of only text, 2 being the use of graphics and text, 3 being the use of 2D animation or other graphics/text/speech combinations and 4 being the use of 3D animation or hypermedia (i.e., hyperlinked graphics/text/speech combinations). Multiple logistic regression analysis techniques were then employed to look at how the use of these different kinds of media in the representations affected student ratings of representation characteristics. Media use had a marginally significant effect on student ratings of all six characteristics: usefulness, understandability, salience, familiarity, pleasure, and contiguity, G^2s $(3, 237) = 7.8, 15.4, 6.6, 7.6, 7.8$, and 15.2, respectively, $ps < 0.1$.

Another interesting result was a convergence observed over the four weeks in representation characteristics. For the first algorithm approximately 64% of the representations were text only, 9% were text and graphics, 9% included animations and sound, and 18% had more complex media. For the second algorithm, the number of text-only representations decreased (37%), those with graphics increased (50%), and the use of animations and complex media decreased (13%). For the third and last algorithm, only text representations (57%) and representations with graphics (43%) were used (Figure 11.4).

The experimenter rated all representations on a scale of 1 to 5, with 1 being a rating for representations that are least like a textbook or classroom explanation and 5 being a rating for representations that are most like a textbook or classroom explanation. These ratings increased over time with each new algorithm: the first algorithm had an average rating of 3.4, the second 3.9, and the third 4.7. So, over time, students created representations that were increasingly similar to conventional or familiar styles.

Furthermore, the average of all the ratings the students gave each representation was significantly positively related to the rating of how similar that representation was to a textbook or classroom explanation ($F(1, 24) = 3.9$, $p = .06$). Multiple linear regression analysis techniques were used to explore how the ratings of the representations' similarity to textbook or classroom explanations were related to the student ratings of different characteristics.

Now that the audience is prepared,

ON WITH THE HAMPSTERS!!!

FIGURE 11.3. An entertaining animation produced to represent a recursive algorithm for calculating the Fibonacci Number Series.

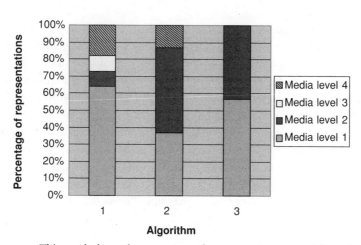

FIGURE 11.4. This graph shows the percentage of representations created for each algorithm at each media level in Study II. The media levels are defined as follows: level 1 is text only, level 2 contains text and graphics, level 3 includes 2D animation or sound, and level 4 uses 3D animation or hypermedia.

The similarity ratings' relations to students' ratings of usefulness, salience and contiguity were positive and significant ($F(1,24) = 6.5, 6.0$, and 10.6 respectively, $p < .05$).

Discussion

Discussion of the results of this study can be structured around several questions. When students are given the freedom to create their own expository representations instead of being handed expert-created representations, do they generate a diverse set of multiple representations? Do students use a variety of media in their representations? How does media use impact perceived quality of representations? Are student-authored representations similar to, or different from, conventional or familiar styles? How does similarity to conventional or familiar styles impact perceived quality of representations? Do they learn from authoring and evaluating each others' representations? Our expectations were that students would create a wide variety of representations with animations and multimedia, and that they would rate media-rich representations to have higher quality. We assumed that the representations they generated would contain both conventional and non-conventional styles without either kind being dominant, and expected to find learning benefits from the acts of creating and evaluating representations. We did not have a priori expectations regarding the impact of conventional styles on perceived representational quality.

For the first algorithm assignment, students created representations that contained text, graphics, animations, and sound. They employed a variety of styles, perspectives and media in their representations. Media use had a significant effect on student ratings of the six characteristics: usefulness, understandability, salience, familiarity, pleasure, and contiguity. Adding graphics to text had a positive effect on all rating dimensions except familiarity. Adding animation or sound to representations with text and graphics had a positive effect on all rating dimensions except contiguity. Interestingly, adding more complex media types such as hypermedia and/or 3D animation always led to a large negative effect on the ratings. Student-authored representations were initially very different from conventional styles found in textbooks. But over time, students created representations that were increasingly similar to familiar styles (i.e., text and graphics, with no animations). The rating of this similarity to conventional representations was positively related to students' overall ratings of representations and their specific ratings of usefulness, salience and contiguity. In other words, how similar a representation was to a textbook or classroom explanation positively influenced not only the overall rating of that representation, but also student ratings of how useful that representation was to their understanding of the algorithm, how well that representation pointed out the salient features of the algorithm, and how well it was contiguous with (built upon) the other representations for that algorithm. Correlations between creating and rating representations and post-test scores suggested that authoring and rating representations was positively related to learning (for two of the three algorithms students saw in this study).

Study III

Method

This was a replication of study II with more algorithms, more students and over a longer period of time. There were three other differences. First, the *contiguity* rating was replaced by a rating of *originality* (How much did this representation differ from the other representations?). This was done because students reported having a difficult time understanding how exactly they were supposed to evaluate contiguity. Besides, we felt that the contiguity rating might have inadvertently encouraged students who initially produced animations and other kinds of representations to converge over time to static representational styles in Study II. Another reason for this convergence might have been CAROUSEL's display of average ratings each representation received on each characteristic, compelling students to mimic styles that received high average scores in a previous assignment. So the system was revised to hide this information. To prevent students from mimicking representational styles of top students in the class, the system was changed to hide author information and present the representations anonymously for peer evaluation. Finally, a pre-test was added to each algorithm representation assignment.

Sixty students in an introductory algorithm analysis course participated in this study. The study was conducted over 12 weeks with nine algorithm representation assignments: Fibonacci algorithm, Exponentiation algorithm, Binary Search Tree Node Insertion algorithm, Leftist Heap Merge algorithm, Selection Sort algorithm, Merge Sort algorithm, Quick Sort algorithm, Disjoint Set Find algorithm, and Depth-First Search algorithm. Each assignment included taking a pre-test and the three stages of study II.

Results

A total of 196 representations were created by 36 of the 60 participants. Representations that used text and static graphics to wallk the reader through the

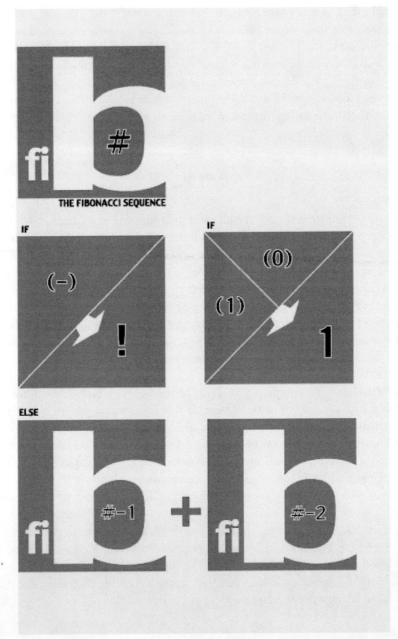

FIGURE 11.5. A creative representation of how to recursively compute the Fibonacci Number Series.

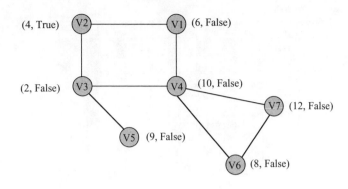

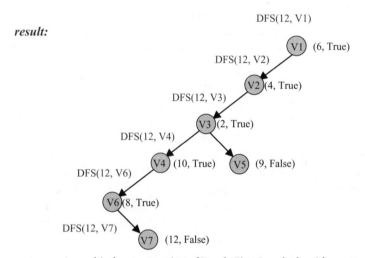

FIGURE 11.6. A graphical representation of Depth-First Search algorithm execution.

sequence of an algorithm's operations on data were prevalent (60%). However, there was not a convergence to this style over time, and there was no significant difference in the number of such representations across the assignments. There were plenty of other styles of representations that focused on aspects of algorithms that had not been represented at all in the first study, such as control flow charts, interactive representations that illustrated algorithm efficiency, creative representations of key aspects of an algorithm (e.g., Figure 11.5) and graphical representations of execution results (e.g., Figure 11.6).

Creating and evaluating algorithm representations clearly aided learning. Students involved in the study improved their scores from pre-test to post-test by 30% on average. Test scores were normalized by dividing raw scores

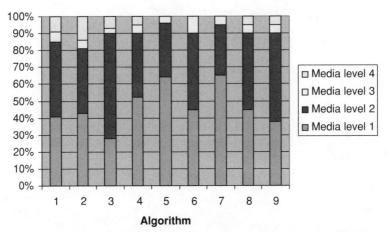

FIGURE 11.7. This graph shows the percentage of representations created for each algorithm at each media level in Study III. The media levels are defined as in Figure 11.4.

by the maximum score attained by any student on a test for a particular algorithm. Some students did not create representations, as participation in any part of the activities associated with each algorithm was voluntary. The mean for the normalized post-test scores for the students who did not create a representation was 46% and for the students who did create one was 57%. The mean for the normalized learning scores for the students who did not create a representation was 25% and for those who did create one was 31%. These differences were significant: ($F(1,327) = 14.4$, $p < .001$) for post-test scores and ($F(1,327) = 3.63$, $p = .058$) for learning scores. Learning score of a student was calculated as his or her pre-test to post-test score improvement.

When multiple linear regression analysis techniques were used to look at how whether someone did or did not create a representation and the algorithm being covered affected normalized learning scores, it was found that the model was significant ($F(9,318) = 3.37$, $p < .001$). Creating a representation had a significant positive effect on learning when the choice of algorithm was controlled for ($F(1,318) = 5.025$, $p = .026$).

The representations in this study converged less on a type, style and choice of topic than in study II. There was not a significant difference between the media the students chose to work with during each assignment and certainly no trend towards a particular style as can be seen in Figure 11.7.

Figure 11.7 shows the percentage of representations created for each algorithm at each media level in Study III. The media levels are defined as follows: level 1 is text only, level 2 contains text and graphics, level 3 includes 2D animation or sound, and level 4 uses 3D animation or hypermedia.

Media use had a significant effect on all six dimensions of student ratings: usefulness, understandability, salience, familiarity, pleasure, and originality, $F(3, 205) = 12.9, 9.6, 9.16, 10.6, 29.07, 37.79$, respectively, $ps < 0.0001$.

As in study II, the experimenter rated each representation for similarity to conventional or familiar styles on a scale of 1 to 5. Although the representations significantly differed in this similarity rating across the 9 algorithm assignments ($\chi^2(32, N = 206) = 62.4, p = .001$), there was not a trend toward the representations becoming more similar to the representations used in class. The average ratings of similarity for the 9 algorithms were 2.47, 2.96, 2.64, 2.9, 3, 2.95, 3.1, 3.25, and 2.47 respectively.

Multiple linear regression analysis techniques were used to explore how the ratings of the representations' similarity to textbook or classroom explanations were related to the average student ratings of different characteristics. The similarity ratings' relation to students' ratings of usefulness, understandability, and salience were positive and significant ($F(1,205)= 4.56, 5.25$, and 9.65 respectively, $p < .05$). The similarity ratings' relation to students' ratings of pleasure and originality were negative and significant ($F(1,205) = 4.09$ and 16.6 respectively, $p < .05$).

Discussion

Did students employ a variety of styles and perspectives in their representations in this study? We expected to see diverse representations that included animations as well as other media, and predicted that the changes we made in the method would prevent convergence toward conventional styles. Indeed, the representations in this study converged less on a type, style and choice of topic than in Study II. Students used more styles and conventions in their representations than students in the previous study. Their representations included animations, sound, graphics, and text. They also represented aspects of algorithms that were not addressed by any of the representations from the previous study. There was not a convergence to any particular style, such as the walkthrough style, over time. Thus, students maintained their individual styles throughout the course of the study instead of converging. This is a clear difference from the previous study. We believe that convergence was prevented and representational diversity preserved by the use of the dimension "originality" instead of "contiguity" in the rating scheme, and due to hiding the authorship and ratings of representations during the course of the study.

Did students use a variety of media in their representations? How did media use impact perceived quality of representations? Consistent with our expectations, students did use a variety of media, including animations, and maintained their individual styles thorough the nine assignments. Media use had an effect on all six dimensions of student ratings: usefulness, understandability, salience, familiarity, pleasure, and originality. Adding graphics to text improved the rating of all characteristics. Adding sound and/or animation to a representation with graphics and text improved average ratings of pleasure, originality and understandability. Adding hypermedia (representations produced in this study did not include 3D animations) improved usefulness, understandability, salience, and familiarity ratings but decreased pleasure and originality ratings.

Did students create representations that are similar to conventional or familiar styles? How did similarity to conventional or familiar styles impact perceived quality of representations? As predicted, there was not a trend toward the representations becoming more similar to the representations used in class. The average of all the ratings the students gave each representation was not significantly positively related to the rating of how similar that representation was to a textbook or classroom explanation, unlike what we found in the previous study. The similarity ratings' relation to students' ratings of usefulness, understandability and salience were positive and significant, as reported in the prior section. In other words, student ratings of how useful the representation was, how understandable it was, and how well it pointed out the important aspects of the algorithm were positively influenced by how similar that representation was to their classroom and textbook conventions. The similarity ratings' relation to students' ratings of pleasure and originality were negative and significant. That is, students rated a representation higher in pleasure and originality, if it differed from their classroom conventions. It seems familiar styles and conventions did influence how students perceived the quality of representations. Unconventional representations were considered to be more original and pleasurable, but conventional representations were considered to be more useful, understandable, and salient.

Did students learn from authoring and evaluating each others' representations? We expected, based on the results of Study II, that authoring and evaluation would lead to better learning than evaluation alone. Students who participated in this study improved their score from pre-test to post-test by 30% on average. Creating and evaluating algorithm representations clearly aided learning. Although all participants rated representations, some students only evaluated others' representations and did not create any of their own, because participation in any part of the activities associated with each algorithm was voluntary. The mean for the normalized post-test scores for the students who did not create a representation was 46% and for the students who did create one was 57%. The mean for the normalized learning scores for the students who did not create a representation was 25% and for those who did create one was 31%. So creation and evaluation of representations led to better learning than evaluation alone.

GENERAL DISCUSSION

Research on learning from multimedia and animations in the domain of algorithms has for the most part focused on expert created animations (Naps et al., 2002). Even when investigating student created representations, researchers (e.g., Stasko, 1997; Hundhausen & Douglas, 2000) have not focused on quantitative as well as qualitative analyses of whether students learn from constructing, sharing and evaluating each other's representations. Neither have they attempted to characterize the nature of student-authored representations in terms of diversity by looking at the variety of static and dynamic multimedia representations students create. These aspects are unique to the research presented in this chapter.

This work was motivated by a study in which we observed the learning strategies of computer science undergraduates learning algorithms in groups and with multiple available representations. This study revealed a tendency of students to focus on a single explanatory representation provided by the teacher as the means to learn an algorithm, even though other representations were available to them. This led us to explore the benefits of having students create, share and critique their own expository representations such as pictures and animations in two subsequent studies. In these studies, students represented algorithms using animations and a variety of other media and styles. Their representations included metaphoric stories involving only text, entertaining animations with sound and three-dimensional graphics, as well as more conventional text and graphics combinations that walked a reader through an example and explained the steps of an algorithm. Students evaluated each other's representations by rating them on Likert scales of six characteristics: usefulness, understandability, salience, familiarity, pleasure, and contiguity/originality.

Analyses of pre-test and post-test scores indicated that representation authoring and rating helped students develop a deep understanding of algorithms. Students who constructed their own representations and evaluated those of others, and students who only evaluated others' representations, learned from these activities. But those who authored representations learned more than those who did not.

Use of multiple media in representations had a significant effect on the ratings representations received on all six characteristics. In general, we found that students rated representations with text and graphics higher than text only representations, and rated representations with sound and/or animation higher than representations with only text and static graphics. But no consistent evidence indicating that the addition of more complex media further improved perceived quality of representations was found. In short, students rated media-rich representations such as animations higher than unimodal (text) and bimodal (text + graphics) representations.

Despite the positive effect that adding animation to an explanatory representation had on student ratings, and despite the initial set of student representations containing close to 30% animated representations (algorithm 1, Study II, Figure 11.4), students eventually converged to a static representational style (text and diagrams explaining the algorithm in a walkthrough style, similar to representations in their textbook) over the course of several weeks and algorithm assignments in the first study that looked at student-constructed representations. Thus, there was a loss of diversity in style and perspective over time. We suspected that this occurred because students might have mimicked the representational styles of top students in the class or styles that received high overall ratings, and also because one rating dimension (contiguity) emphasized conformity. So we changed this rating dimension to one that emphasized non-conformity (originality), prevented students from seeing the ratings representations received in prior assignments until the end of the semester, and hid author information. As expected, convergence did not occur in the next study (Study III).

Although the representations students created in Study III were more diverse, and their styles did not converge to a textbook-like style over time, a majority of the representations remained static in format and walkthrough in style. Representations with animations stayed at or below 20% for all algorithms (Figure 11.7). This small percentage was contrary to our expectation of higher production of animations. This expectation was based on the advantages of animations as explanatory representations of complex and dynamic procedures like algorithms. Students produced animations at a lower rate despite the fact that animations provide opportunities for explanation of dynamic processes that are not available with static representational forms. It was surprising that an intrinsically dynamic form of representation (i.e., animation) was used so little by the student authors to explain an intrinsically dynamic process (i.e., algorithm).

There are several possible explanations. The most obvious one is that constructing animations, even with excellent software support, takes more time and effort than writing text and drawing pictures. An alternate explanation is that perhaps students felt that walkthrough style representations that employed explanations and illustrations conveyed key aspects of algorithms well enough, and the additional expressive power of an animation was not worth the cost of producing one. A third explanation is that even when the learning activities involve only representations created by themselves and their peers, students are influenced by conventional and familiar representational styles (what they see in the textbook and hear in the classroom). This influence could be seen in the representations students authored and in how they rated their peers' representations. Student authored representations received an average rating of at least 2.5 on a similarity (to conventional and familiar styles) scale of 1 to 5 in every algorithm assignment in both Study II and III. In the third study, a majority of the representations employed a walkthrough style – walking the reader through an example illustrating the operations of an algorithm on a sample data set – that is commonly employed in textbooks and by instructors. Students in general rated these representations higher in usefulness, understandability, and salience. On the other hand, representations differing from conventional and familiar styles received higher ratings of originality and pleasure.

In spite of the predominance of conventional styles, students did produce representations with diverse styles and perspectives. There were metaphorical stories, entertaining animations, creative graphical representations of the steps, executions and results of algorithms, algorithm efficiency comparisons, web calculators that showed algorithm results, and so on. Giving students free rein to create their own explanatory multimedia generated animations and other varieties of explanations that are absent in typical algorithm instruction based on textbooks and lectures.

Our findings have some pedagogic implications for teaching and learning complex and dynamic concepts. The activities of creating, sharing, and evaluating explanatory representations do facilitate learning, and ought to be encouraged. Intentional design choices in instruction and supporting technology can counteract students' tendency to converge on a representation or style, and lead to improved diversity of representations in both style and content. A large percentage of representations created by students in our studies conformed to the style used by textbook authors and instructors. This is not necessarily detrimental to learning, but we suggest that it is important for students to create and/or peruse representations that employ styles and perspectives different from what is seen in the textbook or provided by the instructor. Thus for example, encouraging students to create their own animations (which are not found in textbooks or commonly employed by teachers) of complex procedural concepts may enhance learning in an otherwise traditionally delivered course.

References

Ainsworth, S. E., Bibby, P. A., & Wood, D. J. (1998). Analysing the costs and benefits of multi-representational learning environments. In H. Spada, P. Reimann, P. Bozhimen & T. de Jong (Eds.) *Learning with Multiple Representations*. Oxford: Elsevier Science, pp. 120–134.

Byrne, M. D., Catrambone, R. C., & Stasko, J. T. (1999). Evaluating animations as student aids in learning computer algorithms. *Computers & Education, 33*, 253–278.

Cox, R. & Brna, P. (1995). Supporting the use of external representations in problem solving: the need for flexible learning environments. *Journal of Artificial Intelligence in Education, 6*(2), 239–302.

Hansen, S. R. & Narayanan, N. H. (2000). On the role of animated analogies in algorithm visualizations. *Proceedings of the Fourth International Conference of the Learning Sciences*. Hillsdale, NJ: Lawrence Erlbaum Associates, pp. 205–211.

Hansen, S. R., Narayanan, N. H., & Hegarty, M. (2002). Designing educationally effective algorithm visualizations: Embedding analogies and animations in hypermedia. *Journal of Visual Languages and Computing, 13*(3), 291–317.

Hübscher-Younger, T. & Narayanan, N. H. (2003). Constructive and collaborative learning of algorithms. *Proceedings of the SIGCSE Technical Symposium on Computer Science Education*. New York: ACM Press, pp. 6–10.

Hundhausen, C. D. & Douglas, S. A. (2000). Using visualizations to learn algorithms: Should students construct their own, or view an expert's? *Proceedings of the IEEE Symposium on Visual Languages*, IEEE Computer Society Press, pp. 21–28.

Hundhausen, C. D., Douglas, S. A., & Stasko, J. T.2002. A meta-study of algorithm visualization effectiveness. *Journal of Visual Languages and Computing, 13*, 259–190.

Janis, I. (1967). *Victims of Groupthink: A Psychological Study of Foreign Decisions and Fiascoes*. Boston, MA: Houghton Mifflin.

Lakoff, G. & Johnson, M. (1999). *Philosophy in the Flesh: The Embodied Mind and its Challenge to Western Thought*. New York: Basic Books.

Lowe, R. K. (1999). Extracting information from an animation during complex visual learning. *European Journal of the Psychology of Education, 14*, 225–244.

Mayer, R. E. (2001). *Multimedia Learning*. New York: Cambridge University Press.

Milgram, S. (1963). Behavioral study of obedience. *Journal of Abnormal and Social Psychology, 67*, 371–378.

Milgram, S. (1965). Some conditions of obedience and disobedience to authority. *Human Relations, 18*, 57–76.

Mulholland, P. & Eisenstadt, M. (1998). Using software to teach computer programming: past, present and future. In J. Stasko, J. Domingue, M. H. Brown & B. A. Price (Eds.), *Software Visualization: Programming as a Multimedia Experience*. Cambridge, MA: MIT Press, pp. 399–408.

Naps, T., Roessling, G., Almstrum, V., Dann, W., Fleischer, R., Hundhausen, C., Kohonen, A., Malmi, L., Mchally, M., Rodger, S., & Valazquez-Iturbide, J. A. (2002). Exploring the role of visualization and engagement in computer science education. *ACM SIGCSE Bulletin*, Volume 35, Issue 2, June 2002.

Stasko, J. T. (1997). Using student-built algorithm animations as learning aids. *Proceedings of the 28th SIGCSE Technical Symposium on Computer Science Education*. New York: ACM Press, pp. 25–29.

Tversky, B., Morrison, J. B., & Bétrancourt, M. (2002). Animation: Can it facilitate? *International Journal of Human-Computer Studies, 57*, 247–262.

SECTION FOUR

INSTRUCTIONAL ISSUES

12

Enriching Animations

Barbara Tversky, Julie Heiser, Rachel Mackenzie,
Sandra Lozano, and Julie Morrison

ANIMATIONS

Appeal of Animations

Animations have enormous appeal. They capture the eye and the mind: the eye because it is naturally directed to change and the mind because it is naturally primed to make sense of the new. Animations change just as the world changes, so animations seem truer to life. Their success in telling stories has been nothing short of astounding; the number of hours people spend watching TV, movies, and video is surpassed only by the number of hours they work or sleep. Animations have these attractions and more for learning. They can portray change over time far more vividly than static images or words, from demonstrating dance steps, magic tricks, and golf swings to depicting weather, embryonic development, molecular bonding, operating a computer, and pendulum swings.

Failures of Animations

What has been surprising and discouraging is that dozens of studies comparing animated graphics to static ones for teaching change over time have not shown advantages to animated graphics across a broad range of content (for a review, see Tversky, Morrison, & Bétrancourt, 2002). What have been taken as successes of animations have typically been confounded. In some studies, animations have been compared only to text or to static graphics that

The authors are grateful to Ric Lowe and Wolfgang Schnotz for helpful and detailed feedback on an earlier version. Portions of the research reported were supported grants ONR Grants NOOO14-PP-1-O649, N000140110717, and N000140210534, and NSF REC-0440103 to Stanford University.

didn't contain the same information. In other studies, animations were interactive, that is, students could stop and start and reverse the animation, but the control conditions were not. Interactivity is known to facilitate learning and understanding, at least in part because it requires active construction and testing of hypotheses by learners, another strategy known to improve learning. But so far, clean comparisons between animated and static graphics conveying the same information have not been encouraging for animations. This presents a challenge to animation aficionados, ourselves among them.

Caveats

Some qualifications for the claim are in order. The animations that have not proved to be superior to their static equivalents have typically shown the operation of a system or a process or an algorithm from beginning to end. They are meant to convey structural or more commonly causal, functional, or conceptual content, often in educational settings. Animations are used for many other ends. They are common in computer interfaces to maintain real-time spatial or temporal continuity, and for that, they may be helpful. Animations meant to convey manner or timing of actions or movements, such animations to teach different patterns of fluid flows or the subtle movements of magic tricks may indeed convey those better than the alternatives. Animations such as virtual tours may be valuable for showing what things look like, especially from different perspectives. Animations that are invented and used in exploring phenomena and data that are not understood, often by experts in pursuit of organization and understanding, may be useful. Creating animations may confer benefits to the creators, may increase their own understanding of phenomena through the design decisions that need to be made. Expertise in the specific content and animation may make some animations effective. Our focus is in animations meant to convey more than spatial or temporal continuity, more than what things look like, but less than advanced expertise; our interest is in animations conveying for relative novices, the kinds of information that typical animations in educational settings convey, changes in structure, process, and function.

What is an Animation and What Could Animations Be?

Loosely defined, an animation is a changing graphic display. Although there are numerous ways that graphic displays can change, the typical animation changes continuously in time and shows the operation of a system from start to finish, at the same temporal and spatial grain, from the same temporal, spatial, and conceptual perspective. In general, animations use primarily structural graphic information, without enhancing or highlighting that information. Changing these implicit procedures for animations may make them more effective, just as changing these aspects of static graphics improves static graphics (e.g., Tversky, 2001). There is research encouraging this idea.

Supplementing an animation with a narrative increases its' effect (Mayer & Anderson, 1991; Mayer & Sims, 1997). Narratives provide several benefits: one is to focus learners on the important parts and the important changes in the animation; a second is to provide an explanation of what is happening. Animations can focus and explain using graphics, supplemented by symbols, including language. A simple animation, successive highlighting of segments of a single diagram, proved to be effective in instilling a mental model, a perspective for organizing the information, even when it did not improve learning (Bétrancourt & Tversky, in press). Moving arrows provided a better hint for transferring previous knowledge in problem solving than static arrows (Pedone, Hummel, & Holyoak, 2001). The arrows weren't in any context and weren't expressing literal movement, but rather, using movement abstractly to suggest movement. In all these cases, the animations were simple, but each suggests ways that animations could be enriched.

Thus, although the research comparing animated and static graphics has been discouraging, there is reason to hope that properly designed animated graphics may yield benefits above and beyond equivalent static graphics. Designing effective animated graphics requires understanding first why animations have failed and then why certain static graphics succeed. We begin with principles for designing effective graphics, developed out of analysis and research on static graphics. We use these to suggest why many animations have failed to surpass static graphics.

Principles of Good Graphics: Congruence and Apprehension

The conclusion that so far, animations have not proved to be superior to informationally equivalent static graphics in teaching structural or conceptual content is met with surprise, dismay, disbelief, even anger. The resistance is understandable. Animations are viewed as more realistic, that is, more like real life. The presumption is that closer to life is better. Animations appear to satisfy the Congruence Principle of good external representations (Tversky et al., 2002), according to which the structure and content of an external representation should match the structure and content of the desired mental representation. Animations use change in time to convey change in time, a natural, compatible correspondence, often the core of the information to be conveyed. This presumption will soon be challenged, but first let us consider whether typical animations fulfill another principle of good graphics, the Principle of Apprehension.

Many who try to figure out what is happening in animations, animations given by the real world as well as animations designed by educators and computer scientists, soon realize that animations fail the Apprehension Principle of good graphics (Tversky et al., 2002), according to which an external representation should be readily and accurately perceived. Too much happens too fast. Static graphics can be inspected and reinspected. Until stop-gap photography (Muybridge, 1955, 1957), generations of painters portrayed horses galloping incorrectly; the exact pattern of movements of four legs galloping is to complex to be apprehended in real time. Yet, even simple animations, portraying a slowly moving path of a simple geometric figure, are no better than static motion paths in teaching rules of navigation (Morrison & Tversky, 2001). What's more, people do not always correctly perceive even simple motion paths; for example, straight paths of moving objects are perceived as more horizontal or vertical than they actually are (Shiffrar & Shepard, 1991; Pani, Jeffres, Shippey, & Schwartz, 1996). Selection of the correct motion path from animations of several possible motion paths of a pendulum or falling object does not guarantee correct production of the motion path (Kaiser, Proffitt, Whelan, & Hecht, 1992).

From this, two animation aphorisms: Seeing isn't perceiving. Perceiving isn't understanding. Users often know animations are inadequate even when designers do not. Users often ignore a readily available animation, preferring some other means of learning. Experience may matter. Prior to using an animation of a set of simple navigation rules, students thought an animation of rules would be helpful, but after using it to try to understand them, they no longer preferred animated graphics to static ones (Morrison, 2002). After learning, their preferences mirrored the relative effectiveness of the tools: graphics and text better than text alone, but no differences between static and animated graphics.

Events are Thought of Discretely

Given the failure of even animations that are perceptually simple, that is, animations that should be readily apprehended, let us reconsider whether animations in fact conform to the Congruence Principle. True, animations can use time to portray processes that occur in time, change over time. But how do people actually think about events that occur in time? When asked to describe ordinary events that take place in time, such as making a bed or assembling a saxophone, people describe them as sequences of steps (Zacks, Tversky, & Iyer,

2001). People think about such events hierarchically, and organized around objects and actions on objects. At the higher level of organization, each step is distinguished by a separate object – top sheet, bottom sheet, and pillow cases, for making the bed – or separate object part, for assembling the saxophone. At the fine level, each step is distinguished by an articulated action on the same object: spreading the sheet, tucking in each corner, smoothing the sheet. Each step is recognized as a breakpoint in the sequence of action by observers, and it turns out that the breakpoints are the points at which there are bursts of motion (Martin, Tversky, & Lang, in press). Hence, the breakpoints are not uniformly distributed across time, but rather cut up action at points of highest change. Similarly, people think of the action of complex systems, such as a pulley, as a directed sequence of steps from beginning to end: the first pulley goes clockwise, the second, counterclockwise, and so on (Hegarty, 1992). The exact placement of the pulleys and the distances between them are ignored. Navigating the world is another everyday event that is thought of discretely, as a sequence of turns at nodes, typically landmarks or street corners (Denis, 1997; Tversky & Lee, 1998, 1999). The exact distances between nodes and the exact angles of turns are not essential, only approximations. The structure of events performed by hands, then, is a sequence of actions on objects, and the structure of events performed by feet is turns at landmarks, actions at objects; both can be abstracted nodes and links (Tversky, Zacks, & Lee, 2004). The important conclusion from this is that if animated events are thought of as a sequence of discrete steps, then the congruent way to present them is as such. The technique of having observers segment ongoing action, for example, animations, can prove valuable for finding the critical steps.

This is not to say that *all* events are readily conceived of as a set of discrete steps, but just that many are. For some events, like patterns of weather or movements of tectonic plates, determining the boundaries of steps is not at all straightforward. Nonetheless, apprehending weather patterns from animations is difficult for novices, and even for experts (Lowe, 1996, 1999). In their actual work of predicting, experts do not use animations, preferring other forms of information (Trafton, personal communication, 2003). Moreover, descriptions of weather phenomena by experts are discretized, often by landmarks, spatial and temporal. Weather is reported for discrete time periods at discrete places.

Misconceptions from Animations

Visualizations, including animations, aren't always a benefit. Just as for language, there are gradations of quality. Like other visualizations and like metaphors, animations can mislead; they can create misunderstandings. The experiments in which observers recognized animated motion paths correctly but reproduced them incorrectly are suggestive (Kaiser et al., 1992). Science educators worry that their students take visualizations too literally; for example, interpreting colors and shapes in visualizations as the colors and shapes of things that are being represented, rather than as idealization in the case of shapes or symbolic in the case of colors. There is an additional pitfall in animations, especially abstract ones, such as movements of molecules and particles. People are known to interpret movements of geometric figures as having causality, agency, and even intention. Properly staged, triangles and squares moving in a sparse environment can be seen as chasing, bullying, hiding, even talking (e.g., Gelman, Durgin, & Kaufman, 1995; Heider & Simmel, 1944; Martin & Tversky, in press). This bias to impose causality, agency, and intention to motion of abstract figures can yield misinterpretations. For example, students watching movements of crowds of molecules, balls of different colors, tumbling, coming apart, coming together, tend to see some of the molecules "pushing" others so that they will join (Tasker, 2003).

STATIC GRAPHICS

In the larger domain of external tools to augment thinking, animations are recent. Graphics are ancient, invented and reinvented by children and adults in communities all over the globe (e.g., Tversky, 1996). Maps, cave paintings, and petroglyphs are widespread examples. People creating and using graphics in communities for generations refine them. The depictions become streamlined and schematized in the sense that essential information gets sharpened, even distorted, and irrelevant information drops out. Not only does information drop out, but non-representative information, such as names, symbols, boxes, and arrows, gets added in the service of communication. Maps make an excellent paradigm as they seem to be ubiquitous. In many, roads get schematized to lines, roads get straighter, turns sharper, and only critical features of the environments are retained, and they are depicted schematically, or by name (Tversky, 2000). An analysis of some successful static graphics developed throughout the ages can inform design of animations.

How Maps Communicate

Maps provide many different useful messages (e.g., Tversky, 2000). Maps of various forms have been invented and reinvented across time and space. As such, they have undergone generations of informal user-testing: people have produced them, used them, and refined them to improve communication.

Maps are made for various purposes, for walking, for locating significant landmarks, for driving, for weather, for hiking, for understanding spread of pollen, population, disease, for planning battles, parades, evacuations, for displaying earthquake faults, forestation, temperature, rainfall, watersheds, and more. For each of these purposes, different information is needed. A good map presents the information needed and omits the irrelevant information, which only clutters, distracts, confuses. Even after clutter is removed, some significant information may not be visible, so it is enlarged. For example, many maps meant for drivers are at a scale where roads would not be visible. Scale is violated in order to show roads or other features of importance. Maps, then, not only omit some information, they also distort other information. But maps do more than that, they also add information: arrows for troop movements on battle maps, isobars for weather maps, colors for topographic maps, symbols for churches, museums, markets, or railroad stations in tourist maps.

Altogether, maps, in particular, and diagrams in general, are good for showing structure. They use spatial elements to convey spatial elements, spatial relations to convey spatial relations (e.g., Tversky, 1995). But the success of various kinds of maps indicates that they do not need to portray space proportionately; on the contrary, violating metric accuracy is part of their success. Another part of their success is communicating more than just structure; maps communicate features that would not be visible, like precipitation and population; they express function and process, like disease spread and earth movements. They do this by adding extra-pictorial devices like symbols, but also like arrows, boxes, brackets, and lines, devices whose geometric and Gestalt properties give clues to their interpretations in context (Tversky, Zacks, Lee, & Heiser, 2000). Importantly, among the extra-pictorial devices that maps rely on are words. Maps and other effective graphics are mixed media. It's hard, and ineffective as well, to do everything in pictures, even when you add visual symbols.

Highlighting, Exaggerating, and Distorting the Relevant; Omitting the Irrelevant

In short, maps, and other effective static graphics, play tricks with space; they are far from 1-to-1 mappings of the world onto paper. Why not play tricks with space in animations? And why not play similar tricks with time? Most animations are linear in time; they may be in real time or they may slow or speed time, but they don't play with temporal scale the way that common static graphics play with spatial scale. As we have seen, events in time have critical steps that are not uniformly distributed in time. Maps don't just expand and compress space; they also discretize it. Spontaneously produced route and area maps could be analog; they could preserve distance, direction, and shape, but they do not, they are not analog, and they do not need to be analog to be useful, as they are used in contexts that disambiguate the underspecified or distorted information (Fontaine, Edwards, Tversky, & Denis, 2005; Tversky, 2003). Maps play with perspective as well. Tourist maps, for instance, superimpose frontal views of landmarks on overviews of roads. Animations could do that; stop and start, show views and actions selectively; change spatial scale and perspective, change temporal scale and perspective. They could combine non-linear and discontinuous uses of time with non-linear and discontinuous uses of space.

Adding Extra-Pictorial Information

Maps and other effective graphics also add extra-pictorial features that communicate concepts that structure cannot, such as arrows, lines, brackets, boxes, or blobs. Arrows are particularly useful: they call attention, reference, provide temporal order, indicate causality, express motion paths and motion manner, and convey outcomes (e.g., Heiser & Tversky, 2002; Tversky, 2005). Animations could do all that, and more.

Enriching animations in the hope of making them more effective is more than a matter of borrowing successful devices from static graphics; it is also a matter of developing devices that work in animations. Another source of inspiration comes from the creativity poured into comics (e.g., Gonick and Smith, 1993; McCloud, 1994), cartoons, animated films, advertisements, video games, and computer graphics. Here we look for inspiration for devices to improve animations from three research projects we are involved in.

SUGGESTIONS FROM RESEARCH

Diagram Narratives

In principle, animations tell stories; they are narratives. Another way to tell a story diagrammatically is a sequence of static graphics. This, too, is an ancient device; think, for example, of pictorial histories such as those in Egyptian tombs, on Trajan's Column, in Aztec codices, on the Bayeux Tapestry, on stained glass windows. Another is a single complex graphic that has a linear reading. Contemporary examples range from scientific visualizations and assembly instructions to graphic novels (McCloud, 1994). Useful devices for enriching animations may come from studying narratives conveyed by static graphics. What kinds of stories do they tell? What devices do they rely on? In order to find answers, we conducted a survey of diagram narratives in college textbooks across a wide range of sciences, chemistry, geology, and biology (MacKenzie, 2004). We wanted to know what sequences of diagrams are meant to convey, and how they convey it. What general themes are expressed? What steps are distinguished? How is each step portrayed? How are the links between steps established? How is abstract information conveyed? How are the depictions schematized, and what extra-pictorial techniques are used? We won't address all those questions here. Instead, we focus on the types of narratives diagrams relate and on the extra-pictorial devices they use.

Here are most of the stories that diagram narratives tell, some appearing together:

- *Change over time; cycle or process from beginning to end; implication, consequences.* Some examples: the rock cycle, the circulatory system, the life cycle of a butterfly, the election process, Napoleon's campaign on Russia, how to operate a copy machine, how to assemble a piece of furniture, how to perform a magic trick, flow diagrams, decision trees.
- *Structure to function/behavior.* Some examples: an engine, a cell, a leaf.
- *Large to small/ whole to parts (partonomy).* Some examples: a tree, a computer, a city,
- *Variations of a type (taxonomy).* Some examples: architectural styles, kinds of roses, diseases of the skin.
- *Different views.* Some examples: a building (inside or out), the ocean floor, the human body.

Enriching Diagrams with Extra-Pictorial Devices

The first narrative type, change over time, is the prototypical case for animation. Large to small/whole to parts is also a natural candidate for animation, in particular, for zooming, and different views and variations of a type are naturals for panning. Graphics, animated or still, depict appearance and structure readily. Conveying change over time, function, consequences, outcomes, and other abstract content is less direct. To express abstractions, most narratives of these types are enriched with extra-pictorial symbolic graphic devices. Zooming is often conveyed by insets or a combination of brackets and lines. Brackets and lines are also used for change of perspective. These extra-pictorial devices, notably lines, arrows, boxes, blobs, and bars, often have meanings that are readily inferred from their geometric or Gestalt properties and context (Tversky et al., 2000).

Lines and Arrows

Prominent among extra-pictorial devices are lines and arrows. Both can refer or point or label. Lines link, establish relationships. A network of lines is ideal

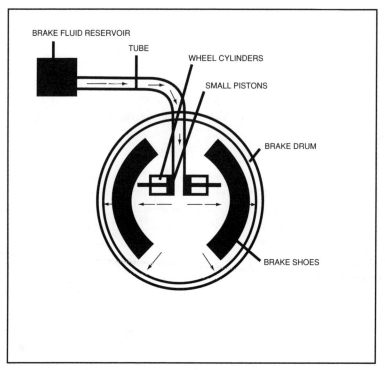

FIGURE 12.1. Car brake with arrows. Adapted from Mayer and Gallini (1999), with permission.

for organizing hierarchies, such as language families or the animal kingdom or the parts of a tree. Arrows are asymmetric lines, establishing asymmetric relationships. So arrows are excellent for conveying change over time, for sequencing, for conveying causality, direction and manner of motion, consequences, outcomes, and more, perhaps too good.

The power of arrows in diagrams is demonstrated in a study in which students were asked to describe what is conveyed in diagrams of a bicycle pump, a pulley system, or a car brake with or without arrows, such as those in Figures 12.1 and 12.2. When diagrams had no arrows, participants gave structural descriptions, the spatial arrangement of the parts. When diagrams had arrows, participants gave functional descriptions, the processes and causal consequences from start to finish. Conversely, when participants were given structural descriptions, they produced diagrams without arrows, but when given functional descriptions, they produced diagrams with

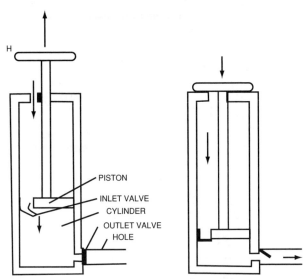

FIGURE 12.2. Bicycle pump with arrows. Adapted from Mayer and Gallini (1999), with permission.

arrows (Heiser & Tversky, 2002). In this context, mechanical devices, people readily understand and produce arrows to convey change over time, sequence, causality.

Interpreting arrows and other devices is not always immediate. Lines and arrows, and other graphic devices, have multiple meanings, as do the words whose meanings are similar, *link* or *association* or *relationship*. Carefully crafted context can disambiguate meanings of depictive symbols just as they can disambiguate meanings of words. Our survey, however, has turned up many examples that are not well crafted. In the diagram depicting movement of DNA in Figure 12.3, arrows are used to *label* the cell wall opening and the foreign DNA, to indicate *movement* of the foreign DNA, and to indicate the *consequences* of the process.

Similarly, the meanings of the arrows in the diagram of the rock cycle in Figure 12.4 are not at all clear. Some of the clearer ones seem to be processes that link start states with end states, for example, the arrow at bottom center seems to indicate that metamorphic rock turns into magma by melting, which in turn is a consequence of heat and pressure. What is especially confusing in this diagram is that it depicts a coherent place, albeit one with cross-sections carved out, and it is hard to ignore the more typical use of arrows in places as indicating movement.

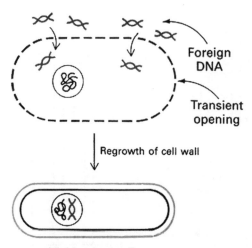

FIGURE 12.3. Movement of DNA. From Stryer, p. 139, Figure 6–36 (1995). Used with permission.

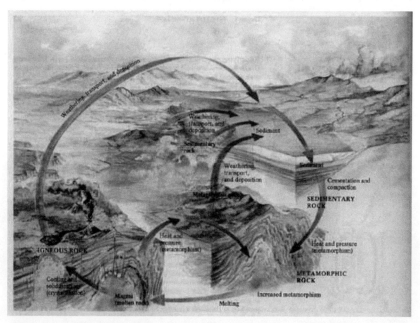

FIGURE 12.4. Rock Cycle. From Chernicoff, p. 14, Figure 1–9 (1995). Used with permission.

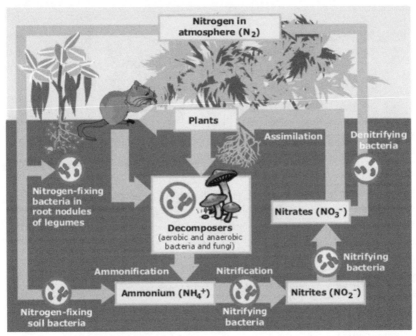

FIGURE 12.5. Nitrogen Cycle. From http://www.epa.gov/maia/html/nitrogen.html

Problematic as it is, the processes the arrows represent are labeled. Not so in Figure 12.5's visualization of the nitrogen cycle. Here the boxes appear to be processors and the arrows the processes that carry the products from processor to processor. However, at least one of the processors is depicted but not named, animals, and the processes, which differ for each arrow, are rarely named.

The point of this exercise is not to show that static diagrams have their share of problems because in fact, all of these problems are fixable. The point of the exercise is to show some of the devices used to convey change over time that are not animations Let's look at another example of a change-over-time narrative: how to put something together. To the dismay of many do-it-yourselfers, many things that need assembly come with an exploded diagram, as in Figure 12.6. Exploded diagrams have the advantage of showing the decomposition while showing the whole and preserving the spatial relations of the parts. However exploded diagrams typically fail to provide the sequence of assembly, do not show the method of attachment, and all too often are at a uniform scale, so that small parts are not discernible. This diagram uses guidelines not to indicate

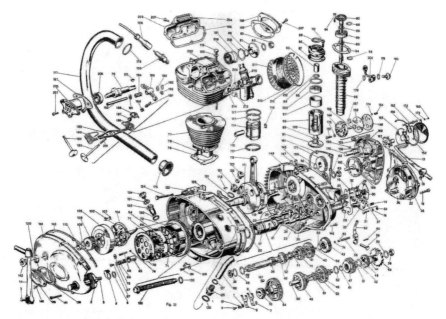

FIGURE 12.6. Exploded Diagram of a Motorcycle Engine. From http://www. ducatimeccanica.com

points of attachment, which does need indicating, but rather to label parts with numbers; the key to the numbers is inconveniently elsewhere.

Step-by-Step, Perspective, Action

We thought users would have better ideas for visualizations of assembly (Heiser et al., 2004; Tversky et al., in press). We asked students to assemble a TV cart using the photograph on the carton as a guide. After assembling, students produced instructions for assembly. Spatial ability, as measured by a mental rotation task (Vandenburg & Kuse, 1978), accounted for not only speed and accuracy of assembly, but more significantly, for quality of diagrams. Those lower in spatial ability often only produced menus of parts, and did not show assembly. Some showed assembly steps, but with insufficient visual information about attachment operations, as in the left diagram of Figure 12.7. Those high in spatial ability tended to produce step-by-step perspective drawings that showed assembly actions, typically using arrows and guidelines, as in the right diagram of Figure 12.7. These are the key design features: step-by-step, action, perspective of action. The diagram by the high spatial participant also imposes a narrative structure on the diagram: it clearly indicates the separate

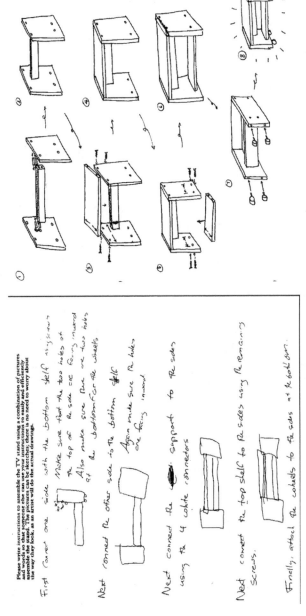

FIGURE 12.7. Assembly Instructions by Low Spatial Participant (Left) and High Spatial Participant (Right).

277

steps, and it highlights the finished product. Many others included part menus at the beginning, visually indicating the starting state.

The next set of studies was aimed at evaluating the different kinds of instructions produced by the first group. New participants assembled the TV cart and then evaluated a range of instructions. Those produced by high ability participants, step-by-step action perspective diagrams, received the highest ratings by participants of both high and low ability. In yet another study, highly rated diagrams facilitated performance of low ability participants, but had no effect on high ability participants, who needed only the photograph on the box to successfully assemble the TV cart.

Extra-Pictorial Devices

Together, these findings provide strong support for the inclusion of extra-pictorial devices in visualizations. Extra-pictorial devices such as arrows, boxes, and guidelines are especially useful for conveying information that is not easily conveyed in depictions. Depictions are ideal for conveying structure; they show the essential parts of an object, device, or system in their proper spatial relations. But all too frequently, the information designers wish to convey in visualizations is dynamic in some way, the behavior of an organ or organism, the function of a device or system, the consequences of a set of operations or procedures. In order to do so, diagrams need extra-pictorial devices. Additional extra-pictorial devices our survey has uncovered include boxes or brackets combined with guidelines or arrows to indicate zooming, enlargement, or change of perspective. Animations have been used to achieve those ends as well. Useful as extra-pictorial devices are in static graphics, they are rarely used in animated ones.

Narrative Structure

Similarly, animated graphics rarely superimpose a narrative structure. A narrative structure facilitates understanding and structures learning. It conveys to users or learners the beginning or initial state, it anticipates the end state, it differentiates the sequence and the steps required to achieve the end state, and it highlights the end state. Interestingly, verbal explanations, for example, those in textbooks, typically impose a narrative structure.

Demonstrations

If someone were to produce an animation to show how to assemble the TV cart, we suspect that they would animate the good diagrams, that is, they would show the parts coming together from the assembly perspective, using change over time to convey change over time. But would this be how human demonstrators would show others how to assemble the TV cart? Or would it be the most effective way of conveying assembly? The need to enrich animations is further supported by observing people demonstrating how to do something for others. We asked students to assemble the TV cart, and then to make a video showing others how to assemble it (Lozano & Tversky, 2004). One group of participants was told not to use language, as the video was meant for non-English speakers; this group relied primarily on gestures. Another group was free to use both language and gestures. A control group simply reassembled the TV cart. What distinguished assembly to instruct from pure assembly? For one thing, demonstrators made sure that the parts to be attached and the attachment actions were visible to the camera, even when this made assembly far more awkward. This parallels the earlier result on good static visualizations: they present the perspective of assembly action, showing both parts and connections. In addition, both groups made wide use of gestures, primarily pointing and exhibiting, but also modeling the assembly. They tended to point to small parts, usually connectors, and to exhibit larger parts, holding them up to the camera. As for all communication, redundancy is used to facilitate. Speaking demonstrators more often than not accompanied their speech with gestures. When allowed to use language, demonstrators accompanied their actions with clear verbal markers of steps and with caveats, things to be careful of during assembly. Those limited to gestures also marked steps and conveyed caveats, though less frequently as these are harder to express in gestures. In other words, demonstrators imposed a narrative structure on the assembly, a beginning, the initial state showing the parts, a middle, clearly marked steps, and an ending, the final state.

Remarkably, many of the critical aspects of assembly were more in evidence in the group restricted to gestures than in the group allowed to use speech as well. Gesture-only demonstrators made nearly all assembly actions visible to viewers whereas gesture and speech demonstrators made only about two-thirds of their assembly actions visible to viewers. Gesture-only demonstrators pointed and exhibited more than gesture and speech demonstrators. Both groups of demonstrators used gestures to create models, that is, three or more related gestures. The speaking demonstrators only modeled the structure of the TV cart, whereas those demonstrators restricted to gesture, modeled assembly action as often as they modeled cart structure. Frequently, the modeling was a preview of assembly action.

A subsequent project found parallel results for explaining routes (Lozano and Martin, 2005). Those restricted to gesture pointed to landmarks and traced paths, as if from above. They switched perspective to a viewpoint embedded in the environment to indicate the actions travelers need to take, for example, turning. They added a narrative structure by first orienting the listener in the environment, then organizing route segments into groups, summarizing them, and finally, clearly indicating the final destination.

Parallels among Words, Pictures, and Gestures

Many of the gestures people add to assembly actions in order to demonstrate how to assemble parallel pictorial and extra-pictorial devices used in highly rated visual instructions. Points are like lines, they can refer, label, or direct attention, and perhaps more. Exhibits also function to refer, but they can do more. Exhibits implicitly describe, they show what something looks like, just as depictions and verbal descriptions can do. Modeling structure is like structural diagrams, and modeling action is like action diagrams. Performing assembly actions so that they are visible to viewers parallels drawings that depict the perspective of assembly. Each of these communicative functions has a parallel in language as well, structure, action, and perspective. Human communication is remarkably flexible. Despite differences in these modalities, many important meanings can be conveyed in words, gestures, or sketches.

The lessons to be applied to animations from demonstrations, then, are quite similar to those derived from productions of visual instructions: break action into clear steps. show the action of each step from the perspective of the viewer; give previews; add caveats; impose a narrative structure. We have already observed that animations rarely do more than show the perspective of action.

LESSONS FOR DESIGNING EFFECTIVE ANIMATIONS

We began with the bad news that animations meant to teach don't do it better than equivalent static graphics. There are explanations, of course. Animated graphics are hard to perceive, too much changes too quickly. Animated events are typically conceived as sequences of discrete steps. Nevertheless, the hope remains that the proper animation has yet to be designed. There is reason for that hope. Most animations are continuous in time, with animated time proportional to "real" time. Similarly, most animations are continuous in space. Most animations simply depict; they do not add non-depictive communicative devices, most significantly, explanations.

Analysis of successful static graphics quickly reveals that they do more than depict and that they do not map space or time continuously. Take a paradigmatic example, route maps, sketches designed to tell others how to get from A to B. They are sequences of actions at nodes, turns at landmarks. To convey that information, they distort and eliminate other information. Exact distances, exact angles of turns, exact shapes of landmarks aren't needed. Nor are streets and landmarks not on the route. Sometimes extra-pictorial information is added. If static graphics play tricks with space and time, why shouldn't animated graphics do the same?

Hints for ways to supplement and amplify animated graphics to increase their efficacy have come from a review of three projects that we are involved in. The first is a survey of static graphics meant to convey change over time and other narratives animated graphics are used to convey. Static graphics discretize the actions in time to critical steps. They link the steps with arrows and lines, and other extra-pictorial devices. The depictions of the steps and the uses of the arrows and lines are not always clear. Arrows, for example, have a range of meanings, referring, attracting attention, suggesting sequence, movement, change, causality, implication, outcome, and more. Frequently, a single visualization will use several meanings of an arrow or a line without disambiguating them. In a second project, we examined one domain in detail, visual instructions for assembling an object produced by experienced users. This more restricted domain also elicited extra-pictorial devices, notably arrows and lines. In this context, the meanings of the extra-pictorial devices were far clearer. The third project examined demonstrations of object assembly, contrasting them to assembly alone. Demonstrations of assembly differ considerably from actions of assembly. Demonstrations discretize actions into clear steps, each corresponding to a large object part. They supplement assembly actions with language and gestures that serve several purposes: to separate steps, to indicate parts to be assembled, to preview action, and to demonstrate action and desired structure. Animations that are continuous in space and time rarely adopt these practices that humans do when teaching. It is time to "teach" animations, and these practices have potential.

There is yet another task that animations can learn, one suggested both by the narratives accompanying animations in the work of Mayer and Sims (1994) and by the narratives in plain vanilla science textbooks. The narratives explain. Most animations just show. Showing isn't explaining. If seeing the sequence of steps were sufficient for understanding, then we'd all be a lot smarter.

A Third Animation Aphorism: Showing isn't Explaining

What makes a good explanation? Many things. Explaining a process can be supplemented with analogies to other processes, with enlargements of subprocesses, with different views, with examples, with data showing consequences, with contrasting processes that differ in crucial ways. These aspects of good explanation can be done visually as well. It entails carefully designing each frame of a visualization, and linking the frames in a deliberate manner that is clear to learners. Much as a well-crafted graphic novel links its' frames, using language as well as graphics (e.g., Gonick & Smith, 1993; McCloud, 1994). Returning to maps, you can think of a good explanation as a good route from here to there, with distinctive and informative landmarks and clear paths from landmark to landmark. Like an effective route map, an animation doesn't have to preserve temporal or spatial continuity. Just like good explanations and good maps, animations can include other views, other scales, other examples, other processes; they can use language and extra-pictorial devices to connect them. Animations can exaggerate and minimize and distort and highlight information. Animations can slow down, speed up, and stop for a moment to let learners absorb and study the current frame. Those frames can be preselected to be informative, the breakpoints in a continuous sequence. There is no guarantee that shifting focus from showing to explaining will produce animated graphics that are effective, but it does look promising.

References

Bétrancourt, M., and Tversky, B. (In press). Simple animations for organizing diagrams. *International Journal of Human Computer Studies*.

Chernicoff, S. (1995). *Geology: An introduction to physical geology*. New York: Worth.

Denis, M. (1997). The description of routes: A cognitive approach to the production of spatial discourse. *Cahiers de Psychologie Cognitive, 16*, 409–458.

Edgerton, S. Y. (1991). *Heritage of Giotto's geometry*. Ithaca, NY: Cornell University Press.

Fontaine, S., Edwards, G., Tversky, B., and Denis, M. (2005). Expert and non-expert knowledge of loosely structured environments. In D. Mark and T. Cohn, Editors, *Spatial information theory: Cognitive and computational foundations*. Berlin: Springer.

Gelman, R., Durgin, F., and Kaufman, L. (1995). Distinguishing between animates and inanimates: Not by motion alone. In D. Sperber, D. Premack, and A. J. Premack, Editors, *Causal cognition: A multidisciplinary debate*. Pp. 150–184. Oxford: Clarendon Press.

Gonick, L., and Smith, W. (1993). *The cartoon guide to statistics*. New York: Harper Collins.

Hegarty, M. (1992). Mental animation: Inferring motion from static displays of mechanical systems. *Journal of Experimental Psychology: Learning, Memory, and Cognition, 18*, 1084–1102.

Hegarty, M., Narayanan, N. H., and Freitas, P. (in press). Understanding machines from multimedia and hypermedia presentations. In J. Otero, J. A. Leon & A. Graesser, Eds. *The psychology of science text comprehension*. Hillsdale, NJ: Lawrence Erlbaum.

Hegarty, M., Quilici, J. Narayanan, N. H., Holmquist, S. and Moreno, R. (1999). Designing multimedia manuals that explain how machines work: Lessons from evaluation of a theory based design. *Journal of Educational Multimedia and Hypermedia, 8*, 119–150.

Heider, F., and Simmel, M. (1944). An experimental study of apparent behavior. *American Journal of Psychology, 57*, 243–259.

Heiser, J., Phan, D., Agrawala, M., Tversky, B., and Hanrahan, P. (2004). Identification and validation of cognitive design principles for automated generation of assembly instructions. *Proceedings of Advanced Visual Interfaces '04*. Pp. 311–319 ACM.

Heiser, J. and Tversky, B. (2002). Diagrams and descriptions in acquiring complex systems. *Proceedings of the Cognitive Science Society*. Mahwah, NJ: Lawrence Erlbaum Associates.

Heiser, J. and Tversky, B. (2004). Characterizing diagrams produced by individuals and dyads. In T. Barkowsky (Editor). *Spatial cognition: Reasoning, action, interaction.* Pp. 214–223. Berlin: Springer-Verlag.

Kaiser, M. K., Proffitt, D. R., Whelan, S. M., and Hecht, H. (1992). Influence of animation on dynamical judgments. *Journal of Experimental Psychology: Human Perception and Performance, 18*, 669–690.

Lozano, S. C. and Tversky, B. (2004). Communicative gestures benefit communicators. *Proceedings of the Cognitive Science Society*. Mahwah, NJ: Lawrence Erlbaum Associates.

Lozano, S. C. and Tversky, B. (2005). Gestures convey semantic content for self and others. *Proceedings of the Cognitive Science Society*. Mahwah, NJ: Lawrence Erlbaum Associates.

Lowe, R. K. (1996). Background knowledge and the construction of a situational representation from a diagram. *European Journal of Psychology of Education, 11*, 377–397.

Lowe, R. (1999). Extracting information from an animation during complex visual processing. *European Journal of the Psychology of Education, 14*, 225–244.

MacKenzie, R. (2004). Diagrammatic narratives: Telling scientific stories effectively with diagrams. Master's Dissertation, Department of Psychology, Stanford University.

Massironi, M. (2002). *The psychology of graphic images: Seeing, drawing, communication.* Mahwah, NJ: Lawrence Erlbaum Associates.

Martin, B., Tversky, B., and Lang, D. (In press). Making sense of abstract events: Building event schemas. *Memory and Cognition.*

McCloud, S. (1994). *Understanding comics.* New York: Harper Collins.

Mayer, R. E. and Anderson, R. B. (1991). Animations need narrations: An experimental test of a dual-coding hypothesis. *Journal of Educational Psychology, 83*, 484–490.

Mayer, R. E. and Gallini, J. K. (1990). When is an illustration worth ten thousand words? *Journal of Educational Psychology, 82*, 715–726.

Mayer, R. E. and Sims, V. K. (1994). For whom is a picture worth a thousand words? Extensions of a dual-coding theory of multimedia learning. *Journal of Educational Psychology, 86*, 389–401.

Mijksenaar, P. and Westendorp, P. (1999). *Open here: the art of instructional design.* London: Thames and Hudson.

Morrison, J. B. (2002). How goals affect evaluations of animation effectiveness. In W. Gray and C. Shunn (Editors), *Proceedings of the 24th Annual Meeting of the Cognitive Science Society* (p. 1022). Mahwah, NJ: Lawrence Erlbaum Associates.

Morrison, J. B. and Tversky, B. (2001). The (In) effectiveness of animation in instruction. In Jacko, J. and Sears, A. (Editors), *Chi 001: Extended Abstracts.* Pp. 377–378. Danvers, MA: ACM.

Muybridge, E. (1955). *The human figure in motion.* New York: Dover

Muybridge, E. (1957). *Animals in motion.* New York: Dover.

Pani, J. R., Jeffres, J. A., Shippey, G. T., and Schwartz, K. T. (1996). Imagining projective transformations: Aligned orientations in spatial organization. *Cognitive Psychology, 31*, 125–167.

Pedone, R., Hummel, J. E., & Holyoak, K. J. (2001). The use of diagrams in analogical problem solving. *Memory and Cognition, 29*, 214–221.

Shiffrar, M. M. & Shepard, R. N. (1991). Comparison of cube rotations around axes inclined relative to the environment or to the cube. *Journal of Experimental Psychology: Human Perception and Performance, 17*, 44–54.

Stryer, L. (1995). *Biochemistry.* 4th Edition. New York: W. H. Freeman.

Tasker, R. (2003). Personal communication.

Trafton, G. (2003). Personal communication.

Tversky, B. (1995). Cognitive origins of graphic conventions. In F. T. Marchese (Ed.). *Understanding images.* (pp. 29–53). New York: Springer-Verlag.

Tversky, B. (2001). Spatial schemas in depictions. In M. Gattis (Ed.), *Spatial schemas and abstract thought.* Pp. 79–111. Cambridge: MIT Press.

Tversky, B. (2000). Some ways that maps and graphs communicate. In Freksa, C., Brauer, W., Habel, C and Wender, K. F. (Eds.), *Spatial cognition II: Integrating abstract theories, empirical studies, formal methods, and practical applications.* Pp. 72–79. New York: Springer.

Tversky, B. (2003). Navigating by mind and by body. In C. Freksa, W. Brauer, C. Habel, K. F. Wender (Editors), *Spatial Cognition III: Routes and Navigation, Human Memory and Learning, Spatial Representation and Spatial Reasoning.* Pp. 1–10. Berlin: Springer Verlag.

Tversky, B. (2005). Functional significance of visuospatial representations. In P. Shah & A. Miyake (Eds.), *Handbook of higher-level visuospatial thinking.* Cambridge: Cambridge University Press.

Tversky, B., Agrawala, M., Heiser, J., Lee, P., Hanrahan, P., Phan, D., Stolte, C. and Daniele, M.-P. (In press). Cognitive design principles for automated generation of visualizations. In G. Allen (Editor), *Applied spatial cognition.* Hillsdale, NJ: Lawrence Erlbaum Associates.

Tversky, B. and Lee, P. U. (1998). How space structures language. In C. Freksa, C. Habel, & K. F. Wender (Eds.), *Spatial Cognition: An interdisciplinary approach to representation and processing of spatial knowledge.* (pp. 157–175). Berlin: Springer-Verlag.

Tversky, B. and Lee, P. U. (1999). Pictorial and verbal tools for conveying routes. In Freksa, C., & Mark, D. M. (Eds.). *Spatial information theory: cognitive and computational foundations of geographic information science.* (pp. 51 64). Berlin: Springer.

Tversky, B., Zacks, J. M., and Lee, P. (2004). Events by hand and feet. *Spatial Cognition and Computation, 4*, 5–14.

Tversky, B, Zacks, J., Lee, P. U., and Heiser, J. (2000). Lines, blobs, crosses, and arrows: Diagrammatic communication with schematic figures. In M. Anderson, P. Cheng, and V. Haarslev (Editors). *Theory and application of diagrams.* Pp. 221–230. Berlin: Springer.

Vandenberg, S. G. and Kuse, A. R. (1978). Mental rotations. A group test of three-dimensional spatial visualization. *Perceptual motor skills, 47*, 599–604.

Zacks, J., Tversky, B., and Iyer, G. (2001). Perceiving, remembering, and communicating structure in events. *Journal of Experimental Psychology: General, 130*, 29–58.

13

A Comparison of How Animation Has Been Used to Support Formal, Informal, and Playful Learning

Yvonne Rogers

INTRODUCTION

Animation has been used in formal, informal, and playful learning contexts to facilitate comprehension, understanding and reflection in different ways. Much of the research to date has been concerned with its efficacy in an educational context, in particular, as a cognitive aid to facilitate the comprehension of difficult and complex subjects (Scaife & Rogers, 1996). There has been less attention paid to how it can be used to promote more informal kinds of learning activities. The purpose of this chapter is to begin to take stock, comparing and contrasting how animation is being used to support different learning processes and activities.

A well-known benefit of using animation in an instructional context is its ability to visually depict changing information, which is usually imperceptible, in a variety of abstracted and simplified ways. The trajectories of objects and dynamical processes, especially those that can not be seen by the naked eye, are visually depicted in ways that explicitly show how something happens or works. For example, processes that change very rapidly or slowly can be animated to appear in slow motion (e.g., a bullet being fired) or speeded up (e.g., a plant growing). Dynamical processes that are hidden from view can also be made visually explicit such as blood circulating around the body or a tree taking up minerals from the soil.

Historically, animation has its roots in the entertainment world, being used in the film and cartoon industries, as a way of explicitly visualizing a narrative, with the aim of making it accessible and engaging, especially for young children. Various animation techniques have been developed, such as movement

Thanks to Blaise Cronin and Paul Brna for their reflective comments on an earlier draft. Special thanks to Greta Corke for designing the abstract animations for the Hunting of the Snark game.

blur and exaggerated actions and behaviors (e.g., Thomas & Johnston, 1981). The explicit changes in movement provide visual cues that can make it easier to work out a character's inner thoughts, feelings and motivations. In so doing, comprehension of the unfolding narrative can be facilitated.

Drawing from the lessons used by cartoonists, interaction designers have started to use animation to create agents that serve a variety of functions at the computer interface (e.g., Kline & Blomberg, 1999). In particular, they have been developed as learning companions in computer-based tutoring environments (e.g., Lester et al., 1997) and as virtual agents in interactive narratives (e.g., Bates et al., 1994). A goal has been to determine whether animating characters can engage and motivate students to learn about a given topic. A further concern has been to see whether using animation encourages students to reflect more about different aspects of a narrative.

A further use of animation, that has begun to be experimented with recently, is to investigate how it can support playful learning (Scaife & Rogers, 2005). Playful learning in this context means engaging children in playful activities, that at the same time enables them to learn a variety of skills and abstract concepts, such as how to tell a complex story, how to share, how to understand the rules of a game, how to cause phenomena to happen, and understand why this is the case (Bruner, 1979; Resnick, 2002; Scaife & Rogers, 2005). Playful activities are viewed as physical, familiar and enjoyable, and include creating buildings out of blocks, manipulating art and craft materials, going on a treasure hunt and chasing others. In these settings, animation is used to represent aspects of what is being searched, created and manipulated, such as a character's motives, moods and personality or to convey the effects of a physical action. This application of animation is similar to how it has been used in the other informal learning settings, insofar as the aim is to promote interpretation and reflection in children. Where it differs is in the mechanisms and representational format used: the animations are triggered in response to the user's physical interactions with an artefact or their actions in a physical space (as opposed to interacting with an agent via a software package) and are designed to be simple, abstract, and to suggest (as opposed to being obvious and clear), in order to provoke children into reflecting upon what they mean with respect to their physical actions or manipulations of an artefact. Hence, rather than making the mapping between referent and representation obvious or easy to read; the animations are designed to be 'harder' to work out, and, in so doing, allowing for multiple interpretations – in the same way abstract paintings are meant to.

The purpose of this chapter is to explain how animation is being used in different learning settings. It considers how effective the animation is and which learning processes are being supported. It also provides design implications and outlines its suitability for different learning activities and age groups. To begin, a critique of how animation has been used in instructional contexts is provided. This is followed by an overview of how it has been used to support informal learning and then playful learning. It must be stressed, however, that research in the latter is nascent and exploratory. Projects that the author has been involved in are used to illustrate its potential rather than presenting a critique of the literature, as is done in the previous two sections on animation in formal and informal settings. In conclusion, it compares how animation has been used to explicitly depict invisible processes to make them *easier to understand* versus using it to suggest possible underlying processes, making them *more ambiguous to understand*.

THE USE OF ANIMATED DIAGRAMS
IN INSTRUCTIONAL SETTINGS

Much of the research on learning with animations in instructional settings has been concerned with identifying the benefits and problems of using a specific kind of animation, namely animated diagrams, to depict abstract processes in an instructional setting (Price, 2002). A main objective has been to determine whether this graphical form is effective at aiding comprehension and to consider why this might be so. Typically, difficult-to-understand, science-based topics are chosen for this treatment, where complex systems, having multiple variables that co-vary spatially and temporally, are dynamically represented. Examples include Newton's laws, car mechanics, the circulatory system, weather patterns and electronic circuitry. The animations are designed to support middle school upwards, and university students.

Effectiveness

A key property of an animated diagram is its ability to explicitly convey interdependent relationships and dynamic processes over time and space. In contrast, a static diagram can only depict a snapshot and hence the dynamic aspects of the process being conveyed remain implicit. This suggests that animated diagrams should be more effective than static diagrams in facilitating learning and problem solving, because the dynamical information is explicitly conveyed. The empirical evidence supporting this thesis, however, is inconclusive. Although a few studies have reported better task performance for animations compared with static diagrams (e.g., Park & Gittelman, 1992; Rieber, 1989), when the methods used in each of the studies are more closely examined, it can be seen that the differences in performance are most likely to have been caused by a lack of control between the two conditions, especially in terms of informational equivalence. For example, Morrison et al. (2000) found that in all the studies they examined the animation condition had a superior visualization, providing extras details.

Learning Process Being Supported

There is a distinct lack of theoretical explanations of how the learning process is supported through using animations (Scaife & Rogers, 1996). Instead, various suggestions have been put forward as to what cognitive processing takes place when animations are observed. One hypothesis is that an animated diagram provides the information necessary for learners to construct rich mental models of the depicted systems that have both structural and functional aspects (e.g., Park & Gittleman, 1992). By this is meant that the external and internal representations are assumed to have the same characteristics. The development of such mental models is assumed to take place through a process of 'information pick-up' where the explicitly portrayed spatio-temporal changes are internalized. In so doing, the resultant internal representation (i.e., the mental model) is thought to mirror the external representation. The mental model is further assumed to provide the basis for 'mental animation' to take place, where the dynamic parts of the system are simulated in the mind. In contrast, the mental models that develop from observing static diagrams are assumed to be poorer because the information pick-up from observing them is less.

Although an appealing proposition, this line of argument has a number of flaws. First, it falls into the trap of what is called the 'resemblance fallacy' (Scaife & Rogers, 1996) where it is assumed that the structure of an external representation, be it a static diagram, animation or other form, is preserved when it becomes a 'mental representation.' However, because we cannot observe the nature of any putative mental representation it is impossible to determine what form it might take. Thus, we cannot say mental animation results from observing an external animation and a mental diagram results from observing a static diagram. Second, although it may be possible to memorize and mentally 'play back' certain dynamical aspects of what has been perceived in an external animation it does not follow that it provides a better cognitive basis from which to make inferences about the underlying processes (Lowe, 1999). This is to assume that a 'richer' mental model develops from a 'richer' form of information that, in turn, provides a better basis from which to solve problems. Simply, there are too many missing gaps in the 'more is more' argument. For example, although a learner may be able to read off certain movements from an animated diagram and remember those (e.g., something flows into something else in a clockwise manner) this, by itself, is not sufficient to make judgments about how a system functions, other than at a perceptual level (e.g., the movement of component X is clockwise). A deeper level of cognitive processing is needed to 'transform' and integrate the external animation with existing knowledge, and to be able to make inferences about the function of the system. It is not clear how and if people can do this when using animations.

If anything, having to infer the nature of the dynamic changes of the system being represented in a static diagram would seem to involve a deeper level of cognitive processing, requiring domain knowledge to make predictions about what might happen. Moreover, this active form of processing of the external representation is, arguably, more likely to result in a deeper understanding and a better basis from which to make inferences (Rogers, 1999). Thus, the alternative hypothesis – that interacting with static diagrams results in deeper cognitive processing and 'richer' mental representations being formed – is more likely to be the case.

It is not surprising, therefore, to see increasing skepticism about the benefits of using animated diagrams in learning (e.g., Lowe, 1999; Morrison et al., 2000; Price, 2002). Some have even argued that animation is detrimental to the learning process. Stenning (1998), for example, suggests that using animation as a learning aid makes it harder for learners to understand the underlying process because of the additional memory load required when trying to keep track of its transient form. Because an animation, by definition, consists of a sequence of fleeting images, it means that the images have to be held in memory to be perceived, so that the ones that have been just viewed can be processed in conjunction with the newly arriving ones. The need to constantly integrate the stream of changing images is thought to involve a heavy perceptual load (Stenning, 1998; Price, 2002), which is not the case when comprehending a static diagram, because it consists of a singular, persistent image. Moreover, a static diagram's persistence means that it is continuously available for inspection and re-inspection, which is not so with animated diagrams. Even when an animation can be continuously replayed, its evanescence means that the viewer always has to integrate the fleeting images to comprehend what is being conveyed. Although relatively simple dynamical processes (e.g., a wheel spinning) can be mentally animated, it is virtually impossible for people to mentally animate more complex processes that have a number of simultaneous components moving (e.g., the circulatory system). Quite simply, we do not have the mental capacity to do so.

So what do learners do when confronted with a complex animation? Lowe (1999) found differential effects in terms of what aspects of an animation are attended to, suggesting people find it difficult to perceptually follow the elements of an animation. One consequence is that only a superficial understanding is gleaned. As commented by Kaiser and colleagues (1992, p. 686) "our perceptual appreciations do not spontaneously form the basis of our conceptual understanding of dynamics." It is not surprising, therefore, that a number of studies have shown how learners find it difficult to answer questions about the processes depicted in the animation they have just observed (e.g., Hannafin & Phillips, 1987; Jones & Scaife, 2000; Morrison et al., 2000). Price (2002) also notes how students observing an animated diagram of the circulatory system, that depicted the different way blood flowed in and out of the heart and lungs, found it very difficult to make inferences from it. As a coping strategy, they chose to stop the animation when making their inferences.

Design Implications

The ability of animations to abstract from and simplify a complex process can be exploited to good effect. They are likely to be suitable when used in an instructional context for students from 12 years upwards. The key is to understand that animation, as a representational format, is good at visually showing dynamic processes but it places high cognitive demands on the user. Thus, a good strategy is to design simple animations that convey specific processes or features of a system, rather than designing complete animations that depict all the interdependent processes of a system at the same time. It can make it easier for the learner to focus their attention on the different aspects of a system and to gradually build up their knowledge of the system by integrating over time how the different components relate to one another. In so doing, far less cognitive demands are likely to be made on the learner than when trying to attend to and relate multiple changes that happen simultaneously in different regions of a complete animation (Lowe, 1999). As pointed out by Kaiser and colleagues (1992, p. 671), an animation can be designed to "temporally parse a multi-dimensional problem into unidimensional components." Computer-based animation offers a flexible way of doing this by dynamically highlighting changes in one dimension or component of a system, while 'freezing' the rest of the diagram. Integrating the different animated parts of the system may require considerable cognitive processing to accomplish, but it is, arguably, what underlies 'deeper' learning and the development of knowledge.

In addition, an effective strategy is to add interactivity to a computer-based animated diagram, enabling students to explore the different components of the system in their own time. This can be achieved by providing a control panel that enables learners to switch different animations on and off and to speed them up or slow them down. For example, students can be given the opportunity to choose to see how blood enters the heart from the body by selecting the animation of the relevant part of the diagram. They can then choose to look at another animated section such as how oxygen exits the lungs. In so doing, learners can focus their attention on comprehending individual processes in relation to the whole, and by referring back to the different aspects build up an understanding of how the different parts relate to each other.

By designing animations to function interactively, cognition can be 'off-loaded' onto the external representation in a way that makes it possible for learners to both perceive what is going on in the animation while at the same time comprehend the diagram in relation to the underlying process. Moreover, enabling the learner to interact with the external representation while also problem-solving – instead of having to observe the animation all in one go and then try to solve problems based on whatever is internalized – is a much better way of using an external representation as a learning resource (Rogers, 1999). The learner can continuously switch between the various cognitive processes involved in perception, comprehension, and problem solving.

In sum, it would appear that animated diagrams are generally limited in their ability to facilitate the learning of complex dynamical processes. Although they may be effective at highlighting and illustrating certain aspects of a process, like flow, they are not a good form of external representation from which to make inferences. Instead, they appear to encourage a form of 'passive' learning, in the sense that a learner's attention focuses largely on trying to follow the various parts of an animation without necessarily comprehending them in relation to what is being represented. A more effective use of animated diagrams is to visually convey only a limited amount of information at a given time that can be controlled and manipulated by the learner in various ways.

THE USE OF ANIMATED AGENTS AND VIRTUAL CHARACTERS IN INFORMAL LEARNING

Designing animated characters to appear at the interface has become increasingly popular in interaction design (Sharp et al., 2007). Here, we consider how they have been used in informal learning contexts, as companions that motivate and guide the learner through a piece of educational software, and, as virtual actors that are part of an interactive narrative, manipulated by the users to change the direction of the story. Typically, animation is used to suggest agents' and virtual characters' underlying emotional, motivational and intentional processes through conveying their overt behavior and facial expressions in exaggerated and simplistic ways. An objective is to provide a highly engaging and accessible means by which to understand the mapping between the external representation (i.e., the animated character's behavior and actions) and the underlying intentions and motives (e.g., anger, jealousy, altruism) that cause them and vice versa.

Effectiveness

Learning companions have been designed to encourage reflection and artic-ulation and to increase a learner's motivation (Chou et al., 2003; Goodman et al., 1998; Hietala & Niemirepo, 1998). Typically, they appear in an animated cartoon form as part of the computer interface. An example is 'Herman the Bug' who was designed to help students learn about biology (Lester et al., 1997). In particular, it was designed to be a talkative, quirky insect that flew around the screen and dived into plant structures to provide problem-solving advice to students. When providing an explanation, it exhibited a range of ani-mated activities, including walking, flying, shrinking, expanding, swimming, bungee jumping, acrobatics, and teleporting. Studies of Herman have shown it to be effective at directing children's attention to relevant information, sustaining their interest in the course material and helping them to carry out online activities. They appear to do so by motivating and maintaining interest:

> . . . these lifelike autonomous characters cohabit learning environments with stu-dents to create rich, face-to-face learning interactions. This opens up exciting new possibilities; for example, agents can demonstrate complex tasks, employ loco-motion and gesture to focus students' attention on the most salient aspect of the task at hand, and convey emotional responses to the tutorial situation. (Johnson, Rickel, & Lester, 2000, p. 47)

Animated agents have also been designed as part of an interactive game, play, or other online narrative, where their behavior and/or emotions are controlled directly by users. For example, the Woggles were designed as a group of animated characters that inhabited a virtual playground, which children could control using various sliders at the interface (Bates, 1994). They appeared on the screen as differently colored, bouncy balls, each having animated facial expressions. Moving a slider or combination of them caused a change in the Woggle's movement (e.g., it bounced less), facial expression (no longer smiled) and the extent to which it was willing to play with the other Woggles. For example, moving a particular Woggle's slider to a 'scared' position on an emotional scale causes it to behave scared, hiding behind objects, and its facial expressions to appear frightened, with startled eyes and open mouth.

The animation makes explicit the virtual character's underlying emotions and moods through the use of color, shape, and movement. Changes to the internal states of a character that a child makes are easy to infer from the animated character's overt behavior. This use of interactivity in conjunction with animation has been found to encourage children to create more sophisticated stories and to reflect upon different aspects of a narrative (Scaife & Rogers, 2001). For example, in the virtual PUPPET play environment, young children (4–8 years) could change the dialogue and emotional states of various animated characters, such as a farmer, a sheep and a cow, by selecting facial expressions (e.g., smiling, cross), body movements (e.g., walking slowly) and recording what the characters would say and then watching their scripted play being acted out at the interface. It was found that the children developed a sophisticated level of understanding of each new drama before it unfolded and were able to reflect upon this afterwards (Marshall et al., 2002). In particular, they were capable of understanding the varying attitude of the agents and how this affected the behavior of the others, for example, the farmer becoming grumpy and annoyed because the pig had been mischievous and let the sheep out of its pen.

Learning Process Being Supported

So what learning process is being supported when children interact with animated agents? Is it the same for when animated agents are used as learning companions versus when they are used as virtual characters in an interactive narrative? In both instances, it appears that the use of animated agents results in a highly engaging user experience, enabling children to more readily understand what is being said, acted out and being asked for. The animation used to represent the agents is visually compelling and this may be a major factor in motivating students to learn and/or infer the motives and intentions of the characters in their interactions with other characters on the screen. Moreover, just like in real life, seeing an agent get excited can be infectious, stimulating learners to, likewise, get excited. Lester et al. (1997) claim that the lifelike quality of animated characters creates a 'persona effect,' having a strong impact on the student's perception of their learning experience. Moreover, they claim that the greater the persona effect the more captivating the presence the learning companion will have. This is thought crucially to be what motivates students to interact more frequently with the educational software. In increasing inter-action with the agent it is thought, too, that reflection and self-explanation are stimulated.

But is it the animation that is making the difference or interacting with a virtual agent? Both play a role in facilitating learning, but the persona effect is most likely to arise for learning companions and virtual characters, that are animated at the interface rather than those presented as static images who have no visible presence at the interface (i.e., where the advice or dialogue appears in the form of speech bubbles or as text). A study by Baylor and Ryu (2003), comparing static images and animated versions of a learning agent, found that the animated versions were rated as being more engaging and credible. Using animation enables expressions, emotions, and other lifelike qualities to be depicted more effectively. The findings of another study of children's reactions to virtual characters, showed that they preferred and more readily understood the expressions of cartoon-like characters rather than human-like ones (Scaife & Rogers, 2001). The cartoon-like representations used appear to make the character's personality and qualities more transparent and easier to read.

Design Implications

Animation can be effectively used to design virtual characters that are moti-vating and engaging, and that will enable children to believe in them and to understand their motives. Techniques that have been developed in the film industry, namely, the use of simple and exaggerated expressions and behaviors make this possible. For young children (up to 12 years), creating characters that are cartoon-like rather than human-like can result in a more effective persona effect, provided they are life-like.

USING ANIMATION TO ENCOURAGE CREATIVITY AND REFLECTION IN PLAYFUL LEARNING

A potential downside of using cartoon-like animations, however, is that chil-dren learn to attribute a fixed set of emotions, moods, and so on, to the set of animated behaviors and actions they see at the interface. For example, they may learn to read a character's exaggerated smiling behavior as always indicating it is happy or their flapping of arms as always being angry. In so doing, their understanding of a narrative becomes locked into to certain way of reading character's overt behaviors. Although this may not be problematic, because such informal learning experiences help children learn to read and understand social situations, the way animation is being used in this context is fixed. There may be other ways that animation can be used to broaden children's minds, especially in terms of promoting more creative and imaginative interpretations of animated characters or events.

Thus, in addition to using animation to make obvious the underlying motives, intentions and emotions of a virtual character, it is suggested that animation can be used to make underlying processes *less* obvious but nonetheless more intriguing. Children (and adults) can be encouraged to interpret ambiguous representations in multiple and creative ways, rather than simply 'reading off' what is given at face value, and in so doing, develop a deeper understanding of what is being represented (Gaver et al., 2003; Rogers et al., 2000). An underlying assumption is that by thwarting easy interpretations (such as those invoked by lifelike animated cartoon characters) children can be forced to use their imagination more.

Animations have begun to be experimented with, as a representational format to encourage children's imagination, as part of mixed reality games. Mixed reality is defined as "views of the real world combined in proportion with views of a virtual environment" (Drascic & Milgram, 1996, p. 123), where the experience is designed to enable children to move between the virtual and the physical seamlessly and seamfully, and in so doing promote reflection on what is happening. In particular, by blurring the boundaries between the physical and virtual, mixed reality environments can be designed to provoke users into experiencing them to re-evaluate their notions of reality and fiction (Koleva et al., 2000). Mixed reality games that have been designed for children have coupled familiar physical actions (e.g., walking, waving, and running) with unexpected digital events, depicted through using abstract animations, via PDAs or other displays (Facer et al., 2004; Rogers et al., 2005). The animations are used to show partial, changing and uncertain information, for example, the energy levels or emotional states of imaginary characters or animals in a virtual world. These appear in different spatio-temporal locations in the physical environment, triggered by the various physical actions of the children.

One of the earliest forays into using mixed reality to support playful learning was the Hunting of the Snark game (Rogers et al., 2002). The objective was to enable children to reflect during and after playing the game, to be able to integrate their fragmented experiences of the game and subsequently explain it as a narrative to others. The game was designed to be played in a large open space where an imaginary creature is purported to be roaming around. Small groups of young children (6–8 year olds) have to gather evidence about the nature of the creature when they happen upon it in different parts of the physical space. The game is a nod to Lewis Carroll's poem in which a group of adventurers describe their encounters with a never really found fantasy creature. Similarly, in the mixed reality game, the Snark never shows itself in its entirety, but reveals aspects of itself, for example, its likes/dislikes, personality, and so forth, depending on what the children do in different 'activity spaces'. These include flying with the Snark in the sky, exploring a cave with it and feeding it at a well. A special multimedia camera was provided to enable the children to capture their experiences with the Snark and to subsequently aid them in their reflections after the game.

Glimpses of the Snark's inner states, personality traits, moods or emotions were conveyed as brief animations that were in the form of trajectories of colored shapes. These abstractions were intended to make the children think about what caused an animation and what it meant, rather than read off a pre-determined state.

The basic building block used in all the animations was a square that was multiplied and combined, using different colors, in various ways (see Figure 13.1 for an example). The trajectories of colored blocks appeared in the different spaces, such as swimming in water, moving around corners, slithering along flat surfaces, and traversing through surfaces. A central part of the playful learning involved in the Snark game was to work out which physical action caused an animation to occur and why. For example, in the flying activity space, the children initially have to work out which arm movements to flap to make the Snark appear and disappear. They then need to interpret what the animated colored forms mean, that change their shape and size, in relation to their flying movements.

Effectiveness

An evaluation of the Snark mixed reality game showed that the children who took part in it were fascinated both by the various representations of the Snark that appeared and how their actions caused them to materialize (Rogers et al., 2002). This increased their level of interest in the physical activities and the physical environment, promoting a desire to continue to play the Snark game and explore further. Moreover, at the end of the game the children came up with complex narratives of what it was and why it behaved in the way it did. The children were very open about their interpretations, sharing their reflections with each other of the Snark's behavior in relation to their actions and interactions with it.

However, in our attempts to make the animations uncertain and ambiguous, some depictions had more 'obvious' meanings than others and were more

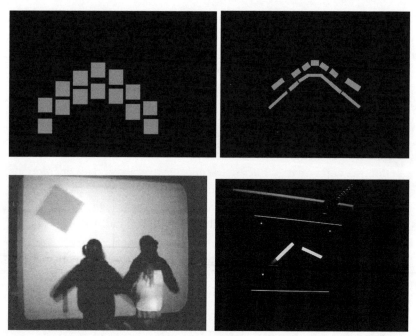

FIGURE 13.1. Four snapshots of the abstract animations used to represent the Snark's inner states. The top two images are expressions conveyed on the water's surface after being fed a food item. The bottom two images are responses made by the Snark in the sky when the children flap their arms together in certain ways.

uniformly interpreted. Those that had less obvious meanings resulted in more varied interpretations by the children. For example, the like/dislike sounds and animations of the Snark following eating a piece of food at the well were uniformly interpreted, whereas the animations of the Snark responding to their walking over the ground in a cave were perceived quite differently by the children.

Learning Process Being Supported

The coupling of different physical actions and animations that have to be discovered and interpreted enable children to combine and recombine the known and familiar in new and unfamiliar ways. This approach provides an impetus for creativity while also promoting reflection within children, that in turn can stimulate awareness and enhance learning (Price et al., 2003).

A question this nascent research raises is what function does the animation serve in facilitating playful learning. In the context of a mixed reality game, it provides vague and ambiguous information about something unknown, that is suggestive enough to enable children to understand and attribute meaning to it in relation to the physical action that triggered it. The coupling between a child's physical actions and the system's responses (e.g., the Snark revealing part of its personality) can help children build up a complex mental model of an unfolding narrative, that they can embellish as they interact more and in different ways as the game progresses.

Design Implications

When designing playful learning experiences, like mixed reality games, simple, abstract animations can be successfully used to encourage interpretation and reflection. Using simple abstract shapes that are suggestive of an event, character trait, etc., can invite children to use their imagination to make creative inferences about the underlying causes and intentions, and to piece together fragments of a complex narrative. However, for this to happen, the game needs to be designed to not have right or wrong answers, but where children are free to associate the information they find with what they know. In so doing, children can focus on understanding and interpreting what the animations mean to them in the context of their physical activities, rather than trying to work out the 'correct' answer proposed by someone else.

If the animations are designed to be too abstract, however, they run the risk of being overlooked and given no meaning at all. This is most likely to happen if the animations are too obscure or are too decoupled from the physical action. One way of circumventing this possibility is to design simple animations that are closely coupled with physical actions that make sense in the particular setting they occur.

Mixed reality games are best suited for young children (up to the age of 10), because this age group can easily suspend their disbelief and become engrossed in the make belief. They can also be designed for older children, where the animations are used to represent the presence or absence of other players and to show patterns and trends of unfolding data and information. Again, it is suggested that they are likely to be most effective when designed as simple abstract forms, especially if the goal is to encourage the players to make sense of uncertain situations.

In sum, animations designed for playful learning experiences should be simple and suggestive, inviting multiple interpretations of an underlying state or event that is coupled with various physical actions. The couplings can be designed to change over time to prevent them from becoming too predictable, for example, the Snark may respond differently to the same food item it is fed, depending on how hungry or full it is. To enrich the experience, other forms of representations can be used to provide feedback (e.g., tactile, auditory) that can also be combined with the visual animation. But, the additional representations should be used parsimoniously so as to avoid making the digital event or response to lifelike and easy to read.

DISCUSSION AND CONCLUSIONS

The research reviewed here suggests that animation can be used to facilitate comprehension and understanding in different learning contexts, supporting different learning processes. On the one hand, it can be used to explicitly show what are normally invisible processes, enabling students to more readily infer how complex systems work or the underlying intentions, personality, or moods of a virtual character/ learning companion. On the other hand, it can be deliberately designed to make it more difficult for children to infer what is happening, with the intention of encouraging them to work harder (and use their creativity) to figure out what the animation is representing within the context it appears.

The success of using animations in instructional settings has been mixed. This was considered partly due to certain kinds of animated diagrams, that have been used, being too complex, making it difficult to perceive and comprehend them. It was suggested that the most effective form of animations to use are those that are simple and interactive, that the child can have control over when learning about a dynamic process.

Animations that have been used to represent the personality or emotional states of characters in informal learning settings appear to have been more successful. Part of the reason for this difference is the cognitive overhead involved in perceiving the different forms of animation and the demands of the learning task. Animated diagrams appear to require more cognitive effort to perceive and comprehend. This is thought partially to be due to the level of familiarity with the representational format used and the underlying referent. Children are largely unfamiliar with the genre of animated diagrams used and also with the unfamiliar and difficult concepts that have been mapped onto. In contrast, they are much more familiar with the cartoon-style of animation, having been exposed to it on TV, video games, and comics, from an early age. They are also more likely to be familiar with the underlying narrative structures that are being represented.

Animations can also be used in more playful learning settings to encourage children to use their imagination and creativity more when interpreting the meaning of events with respect to their ongoing physical activities. This involves designing couplings between action and representation that surprise and are ambiguous rather than being explicit and obvious. By using animation in this seemingly, counter-intuitive way, new opportunities are opened up for augmenting and supporting learning that moves beyond the way it has traditionally been used in formal and informal learning contexts. Instead of making it easier to 'read' off information it can be used to make it more difficult and, in so doing, extend children's minds.

References

Bates, J. (1994). The role of emotion in believable agents. *Communications of the ACM, 37(7)*:122–125.

Baylor, A. L. & Ryu, J. (2003). Does the presence of image and animation enhance pedagogical agent persona? *Journal of Educational Computing Research, 28(4)*, 373–395.

Bruner, J. S. (1979). *On Knowing*. Cambridge, Mass.: Belknap Press of Harvard University Press System.

Chon, C., Chan, T. & Lin, C. (2003). An approach of implementing general learning companions for problem-solving. *IEEE Transactions on Knowledge and Data Engineering, 14(6)*, 1376–1386.

Drascic, D. & Milgram, P. (1996). Perceptual issues in augmented reality. *Stereoscopic Displays and Applications VII and Virtual Reality Systems III*, SPIE Vol. 2653, 123–134.

Facer, K., Joiner, R., Stanton, D., Reid, J., Hull, R., & Kirk, D. (2004). Savannah: mobile gaming and learning. *Journal of Computer Assisted Learning, 20*, 399–409.

Gaver, W. W, Beaver, J., & Benford, S. (2003). Ambiguity as a resource for design. In *Proc. of CHI '03*. New York: ACM Press, 233–240.

Goodman, B., Soller, A., Linton, F., & Gaimari, R. (1998). Encouraging Student Reflection and Articulation Using a Learning Companion. *International Journal of Artificial Intelligence in Education, 9*, 237–255.

Hannafin, M. J. & Phillips, T. L. (1987). Perspectives in the design of interactive video. *Journal of Research and Development in Education, 21(1)*, 44–60.

Hietala, P. & Niemirepo, T. (1998). The Competency of Learning Companion Agents. *International Journal of Artificial Intelligence in Education, 9*, 178–192.

Johnson, W. L., Rickel, J. W., & Lester, J. C. (2000). Animated Pedagogical Agents: Face-to-Face Interaction in Interactive Learning Environments. *International Journal of Artificial Intelligence in Education, 2000(11)*, 47–78.

Jones, S. & Scaife, M. (2000). Animated Diagrams: An Investigation into the Cognitive Effects of using Animation to Illustrate Dynamic Processes. In M. Anderson & P. Cheng (eds) *Theory and Applications of Diagrams. Lecture Notes in Artificial Intelligence*, 1889, Berlin: Springer-Verlag, 231–244.

Kaiser, M., Proffitt, D., Whelan, S. & Hecht, H. (1992). Influence of animation on dynamical judgements. *Journal of Experimental Psychology: Human Perception and Performance, 18*, 669–690.

Kline, C. & Blumberg, B. (1999). The art and science of synthetic character design. In *Proceedings of The AISB 1999 Symposium on AI and Creativity in Entertainment and Visual Art*, Edinburgh, Scotland. 1999.

Koleva, B., Schnadelbach, H., Benford, S. & Greenhalgh, C. (2000). Traversable interfaces between real and virtual worlds. In *Proc. CHI'2000*. New York: ACM Press. 233–240.

Lester, J. C., Converse, S. A., Kahler, S. E., Barlow, S., Stone, B. A., & Bhogal, R. (1997). The Persona Effect: Affective impact of animated pedagogical agents. In *Proceedings of CHI'97*. New York: ACM, 359–402.

Lowe, R. (1999). Extracting information from an animation during complex visual learning. *European Journal of Psychology of Education* Vol. XIV, 2, 225–244.

Marshall, P., Rogers, Y., & Scaife, M. (2002). PUPPET: a virtual environment for children to act and direct interactive narratives. In *Proceedings of the 2nd International Workshop on Narrative and Interactive Learning Environments*, Edinburgh, August 6–9th 2002, 8–15.

Morrison, J. B., Bétrancourt, M., & Tverksy, B. (2000). Animation: Does it facilitate learning? In *Spring Symposium, Smart Graphics*, Stanford, CA: AAAI, 53–60.

Park, O. & Gittleman, S. S. (1992). Selective use of animation and feedback in computer based instruction. *Education Technology Research & Development, 40*(4), 27–38.

Price, S. (2002). Diagram representation: The Cognitive Basis for Understanding animation in education. *Dphil dissertation*. University of Sussex.

Price, S., Rogers, Y., Scaife, M., Stanton, D., & Neale. H. (2003). Using 'Tangibles' to promote novel forms of playful learning. *Interacting with Computers, 15*(2), 169–185.

Resnick, M. (2002). Rethinking learning in the digital age. In G. Kirkman (Ed.) *The Global Information Technology Report: Readiness for the Networked World*. New York: Oxford University Press.

Rieber, L. P. (1989). The effects of computer-animated elaboration strategies and practice on factual and application learning in an elementary science lesson. *Journal of Computing Research, 5*(4), 431–444.

Rogers, Y. (1999). What is different about interactive graphical representations? *Learning and Instruction, 9*, 419–425.

Rogers, Y., Price, S., Randell, C., Stanton-Fraser, D., Weal, M., & Fitzpatrick. G. (2005) Ubi-learning: Integrating outdoor and indoor learning experiences. *Comm. of ACM, 48*(1), 55–59.

Rogers, Y., Scaife, M., Harris, E., Phelps, T., Price, S., Smith, H., Muller, H., Randell, C., Moss, A., Taylor, I., Stanton, D., O'Malley, C., Corke, G., & Gabrielli, S. (2002). Things aren't what they seem to be: innovation through technology inspiration. In *Proceedings of DIS2002*. New York: ACM, 373–377.

Scaife, M. & Rogers, Y. (1996). External cognition: How do graphical representations work? *International Journal of Human-Computer Studies, 45*, 185–213.

Scaife, M. & Rogers, Y. (2001). Informing the design of a virtual environment to support learning in children. *International Journal of Human-Computer Studies, 55*, 115–143.

Scaife, M & Rogers, Y. (2005). External cognition, innovative technologies and effective learning. In P. Gardenfors and P. Johansson (eds.) *Cognition, Education and Communication Technology*. Hillsdale, NJ: Lawrence Erlbaum Associates. 181–202.

Sharp, H., Rogers, Y. & Preece, J. (2007). *Interaction Design: Beyond Human Computer Interaction 2nd Edition*. New York: John Wiley & Sons.

Stenning, K. (1998). Distinguishing Semantic from Processing Explanations of Usability of Representations: Applying Expressiveness Analysis to Animation. In (eds.) J. Lee, *Intelligence and Multimodality in Multimedia Interfaces: Research and Applications*, AAAI Press.

Thomas, F. & Johnson, O. (1981). *The Illusion of Life: Disney Animation*. New York: Hyperion.

14

A Unified View of Learning from Animated and Static Graphics

Wolfgang Schnotz and Richard Lowe

INTRODUCTION

Recent advances in technology have provided a wide variety of possibilities for incorporating animation in computer-based learning environments. In a very general sense, the term 'animation' can refer to any display element that changes its attributes over time. Taken this broadly, examples such as words that fly across the screen or objects that vibrate, blink, or change their color would be regarded as animations (Wright, Milroy, & Lickorish, 1999). In this chapter, we use the term in a more restricted sense. We define 'animation' as a pictorial display that changes its structure or other properties over time and which triggers the perception of a continuous change. Our definition includes examples of dynamic visualization such as pictorial displays that present objects continuously from different perspectives, show the assembly of a complex object from its parts, present the functioning of a technical device such as a bicycle pump, display the dynamic behavior of a meteorological system, or model the co-variation of variables in a graph (Bodemer, Ploetzner, Feuerlein, & Spada, 2004; Hegarty, Narayanan, & Freitas, 2002; Lowe, 2004; Mayer, 2001, 2005; Mayer & Moreno, 2002; Schwan & Riempp, 2004).

Although the use of animation has been enabled and stimulated by technology, our definition excludes technical considerations such as the number of frames per second and whether or not the pictorial display is computer generated. However, our definition does include video (cf. Baek & Layne, 1988; Bétrancourt & Tversky, 2000). Steven Spielberg's film "Jurassic Park" demonstrated that viewers cannot distinguish sequences generated by computer from those filmed in a conventional studio. Although these differences in

This work was supported by Research Grant 'Visual Communication of Knowledge' of Ministry of Research, Education and Culture of Rhineland-Palatina, Germany, and Australian Research Council Discovery Grant DP0451988.

how sequences were generated may be important from a technical perspective, they are obviously of no psychological relevance to the viewer.

On the one hand, animations are frequently considered as inherently superior to static pictures. Whereas static pictures display only *visuospatial* information, animations display *temporal* information as well. Accordingly, animations can be considered as more informative, more natural or more 'authentic' than the corresponding static pictures. Thus, it is very tempting to assume that learning from animation will be more effective than learning from static pictures. On the other hand, learning from animation can also be seen as more demanding because more information has to be processed and this imposes a higher cognitive load on the learner's working memory (Sweller, van Merriënboer, & Paas, 1998).

These two views encapsulate the prevailing tendency to emphasize differences between animated and static graphics rather than to consider their commonalities. From a technological perspective, there may well be clear differences between static and animated pictures with regard to the physical nature of the representation. However, from a psychological perspective, they are fundamentally linked in terms of the human information processing capacities that operate upon them both during learning. Our evolutionary history has given us a perceptual and cognitive system that is well equipped to cope with world in which change is part of the normal condition. The highly dynamic environment in which we live usually includes both temporally stable and temporally changing components. In our everyday lives, we do not continually compartmentalize our environment into static and dynamic parts. Rather, we deal with these components in an integrated and flexible manner as we continually construct a coherent functional mental representation of the world around us. Even when we move through a static environment, our visual field is continuously changing. The flux of our everyday experience is thus a seamless blend of changing and unchanging stimuli without fixed boundaries between static and dynamic components. On this basis, it seems difficult to justify a sharp distinction between learning from animated and learning from static pictures, and there appears to be little reason to assume that animations are necessarily easier or more demanding than static pictures.

In this chapter, we will therefore argue for a more unified approach to dealing with animations and static pictures. The basis for this argument is that animations and static pictures are not fundamentally different from a psychological point of view because animated and static pictures are processed by the same perceptual and cognitive system. Given that this system has evolved by interacting with a complex environment containing an ongoing blending of both dynamic and stable stimuli, the same set of basic perceptual and cognitive principles should underlie learning from both types of representation. It follows that the principles for using animation effectively are not fundamentally different from those for using static pictures and that the former can be considered as an extension of the latter. With regard to educational practice, we suggest that designers and developers of learning resources should not consider animation as something totally different in a qualitative sense and that therefore requires totally new design principles. Rather, they could learn from our history's rich legacy of visual communication in order to understand and apply underlying principles that are common to static and animated graphics. With regard to educational theory, we suggest that researchers should not 're-invent the wheel' by considering learning from animation as a fundamentally different branch of scientific analysis. Rather, they should view this topic as closely related to other research on visual communication.

The chapter is organized as follows. First, we give a short overview of the history of visual communication and classify animation as one element within this history. Second, we describe different types of animation and the functions of animation in the display of static and dynamic content. Third, we describe animations with regard to their spatial and temporal structures with a special focus on the types of patterns displayed and on principles for the categorization of events. Fourth, processing of animation is analyzed both on the perceptual level and on the cognitive level with regard to limited processing resources and the necessity of directing those resources in order to align perceptual and cognitive processing as far as possible.[1] Fifth, we analyze learning with user-controlled animations with regard to their potential for improving comprehension or learning as well as their requirements in terms of the learners' expertise and processing capacities. Finally, we draw some conclusions for further research into learning from animation and for the practical application of animations to teaching and learning.

HISTORY OF VISUAL COMMUNICATION

The creation of realistic pictures as a means of communication is a relatively recent phenomenon in human history. Famous early examples are the cave paintings found in Northern Spain that are estimated as being up to 20,000 years old. Although we do not know exactly what function was intended for these paintings, it seems reasonable to assume that pictures were used very

---

[1] Whereas the term "cognitive processing" is often used in a broad sense including both perceptual and conceptual processing, we will use the term "cognitive processing" in a more narrow sense that entails only higher order processing above the perceptual level.

early as a tool for communication. For example, their purpose could have been to inform others about an unknown object or an event. Once established as a tool for communication, the further development of drawing and painting proceeded along a number of different pathways. One line of development had the general aim of producing highly realistic depictions. Painters such as Canaletto and Spitzweg were famous for their skill in capturing subject matter with such a level of accuracy and detail that it gave the observer an illusion of looking upon reality through a window. Renaissance architect L. B. Alberti based his theory of painting explicitly on this metaphor. He considered a picture as a surrogate for a real window providing a view on an external reality. The skill in realistic depiction so painstakingly developed by generations of artists was made redundant by the invention of color photography which made it possible for anyone to create realistic pictures. A second line of development in visual representations did not aim at pictorial realism but instead had a very different communicative purpose. Its goal was to emphasize selected aspects of the presented content that were important and in so doing make visual communication more efficient. In this respect, the development of written languages shares some characteristics with this second line of pictorial development. Written language introduced segmentation techniques such as full-stops, paragraphs, headings, and subheadings as well as signaling techniques such as different font types, type sizes, and colors. Similarly, drawing and painting introduced various techniques such as simplification, highlighting, and color coding in order to shape the observers' perceptual and cognitive processing. The use of pictures that were carefully selected and specially designed for the purposes of teaching and learning was given particular attention by Comenius, the seventeenth-century educator who emphasized the role of envisioning in learning. A third line in development of visual communication is far more recent. Charts and graphs, often referred to as 'logical pictures,' were introduced by the British economist William Playfair in the second half of the eighteenth century. In this type of picture, direct perceptual similarity with a designated referent has essentially been abandoned in favor of capturing information about subject matter that cannot be directly perceived. Because of their power to represent more abstract types of content, they have been widely adopted by educators and the media (Schnotz, 2001).

How does animation fit into this pattern of pictorial development? Animation is widely considered to be a modern development that emerged as a result of technological advances. Film technology, the first practical means of presenting 'moving pictures' to be widely adopted, was invented only just over 100 years ago. It was followed by video and most recently by computer-based animation. However, a closer examination reveals that from a psychological point of view, animation is not as new as its modern technological incarnation would suggest. Today's high-tech animations have various low-tech predecessors. Oriental shadow puppets that display moving silhouettes on a paper screen could be regarded as an early form of animation. If one accepts the notion of a 3 D animation, the movements of marionettes on a stage could also be considered as a form of animation. Further examples would be animated mechanical toys or automata, such as the fluttering and singing birds built some centuries ago by skilled inventors to amuse their royal patrons. The recipients seem to have been as fascinated by the new technology of mechanical animation of their time as we are today by computer-based animation. Whereas many of the early mechanical animations were made for entertainment, others were used for educational purposes. Examples include dynamic models of the solar system and the presentation of religious or mythological events through moving figures displayed on a public clock.

As was the case with the development of drawing and painting, realism was – and still is – a source of seemingly endless fascination for those who produce animations. In earlier times, artisans competed to make mechanical toys for entertaining their royal patrons as realistic as possible. Similarly, many of today's computer-based animations try to portray their dynamic subject matter with a high degree of realism. However, as was the case with static graphics, the emphasis on realism in animations corresponds to only one line of development. Animations can also be used in situations where visual realism is not the ultimate goal. This other line of development applies animation techniques for representational and directive purposes in order to make visual communication more efficient by emphasizing specific aspects of the depicted content. This application is analogous to the well established use of various graphic techniques for increasing the explanatory power of static depictions (Lowe, 2005). However, the corresponding development of techniques for the beneficial manipulation of animations is still in its infancy. For static pictures, many and varied techniques have been invented, refined, and used successfully over a very long period. Unfortunately, this is not the case with animation because of its comparatively short history. Today's animations are too often designed simply to be aesthetically pleasing and to present dynamic content as realistically as possible. Due to the paucity of research-based knowledge about what is required to make animations educationally effective, current approaches to the design of instructional animations are largely intuitive. However, for animations to be truly effectively in fostering learning, a principled approach to their design and development is needed that systematically applies research findings on how learners process and comprehend graphic information.

TYPES AND FUNCTIONS OF ANIMATION

Over its short history, animation has until quite recently been mainly used for entertainment. Accordingly, many established uses of animation tend to have an affective purpose. Media designers too often assume that the affective impact of animation on learners' motivation and engagement will necessarily increase learning. However, a simplistic adoption of affectively-oriented design principles from the entertainment industry ignores the fact that there is far more to successful instruction than having learners motivated and engaged. Indeed, it is even possible that because a medium is normally associated with entertainment, our entrenched attitudes about its undemanding 'recreational' nature could sometimes have negative effects on learning. A well-known example is the association of text with studying and of television with entertainment: 'text is tough, television is easy' (Salomon, 1994). Similarly, the association of animation with entertainment and the resultant triggering of inappropriate attitudes can invoke processing strategies that are inadequate for learning. Although we acknowledge the potential of an affective or motivational role for animation, this chapter will go beyond these aspects and focus on animations designed to support learners' perceptual and cognitive processes in order to enhance their comprehension and learning.

Static and Dynamic Content

Those who design learning media often seem to assume that the temporal characteristics of an external visual representation should correspond to those of the represented content. This would imply that static pictures should be used to display static content because they lead to the construction of a static mental model, whereas animated pictures should be used to display dynamic content because they lead to the construction of a dynamic mental model. Although this line of thinking may have some superficial appeal, a more detailed consideration reveals serious flaws in such an assumption. On the one hand, static pictures are not limited to supporting the construction of static mental models; they can also be the basis for constructing dynamic mental models (Hegarty, 1992). On the other hand, animations are not limited to supporting the construction of dynamic mental models but can also lead to the construction of static mental models.

Examples of static pictures that lead to the construction of dynamic mental models are presented in Figure 14.1. The upper panel of the figure is a pictogram of a tennis player. Although the picture is static, most observers cannot avoid making dynamic inferences about the player's movement on the

FIGURE 14.1. Static displays of movements: Pictogram of a tennis player (top) and sequence of pictures of an accelerating motorbike (bottom).

court. The lower panel of the figure presents a series of static pictures showing the different locations of an accelerating motorbike after 0 sec, 5 sec, 10 sec, and 15 sec with the corresponding velocity vectors. Although the pictures are static, they allow learners to construct a dynamic mental model of the motorbike's acceleration. Other examples include a snapshot of a horse clearing a hurdle or of a kangaroo during a hop. Extensions of the presented temporal frame can also be found in safety advertisements. For example, a static picture that shows a child chasing a ball on the street where a car is approaching allows the viewer to infer an upcoming accident. Static pictures can depict richer information about the temporal change than is available in a simple snapshot by combining different events from a dynamic sequence and placing them at separate locations within a single frame. Such a 'temporal collage' requires sequential reading. Examples of this technique are frequently found in comic book dialogues where a question from one character and the answer by another character are combined into one and the same frame (McCloud, 1994). The inclusion of a time axis in a single realistic picture can also be found in scientific visualizations. An example is shown in Figure 14.2 where

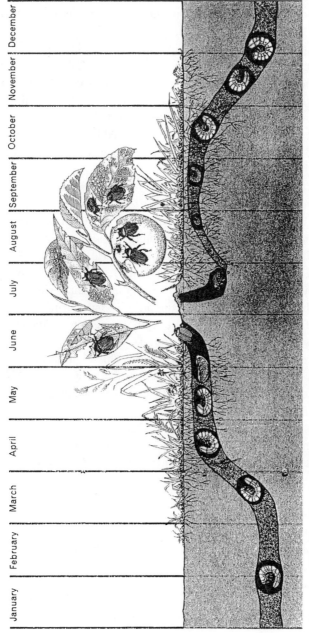

FIGURE 14.2. Combination of a realistic picture with a time-axis. The display shows the life cycle of the Japanese beetle (from Tufte, 1983). Reprinted with permission.

horizontal space contains an implicit time axis in order to represent the life cycle of the Japanese beetle (from Tufte, 1983). The picture requires a 'dynamic' reading in order to construct a dynamic mental model of the animal's behavior.

Various techniques have been developed for static graphics to indicate mental animations that viewers need to generate in order to fully comprehend the depiction. The addition of arrows is one of the most widely used techniques and these ancillary entities can serve a variety of different functions within a graphic. Arrows are frequently used to mark out divisions at a specific time interval with the direction of movement indicated by the arrow's pointing direction and the speed of the movement by the arrow's length. A related technique is the use of dots 'left' by a moving object along its path (like Hansel and Gretel dropping pieces of bread on their way from home into the deep forest). When these dots a placed at regular time intervals, their placement indicates the path, and their distance indicates the speed of movement (but not its direction). Figure 14.3 shows an example of this technique from the physics learning software Thinkers' Tool (White & Horwitz, 1987). A further related technique is the display of multiple static pictures consisting of a series of snapshots at regular time intervals showing different states within an event. This approach can be used to show the unfolding of actions such as the hop of a kangaroo. If one combines such a series with the metaphor of fading memories by showing the 'older' snapshots in a fainter color, the series of static pictures also signals the direction of movement. This additional information could further help to guide the viewer's construction of a dynamic mental model. The examples cited here indicate that it is not uncommon to construct dynamic mental models from static pictures.

The reverse is also possible; animations can lead to the construction of static mental models. Examples would be video clips explaining how a complex object such as a Greek temple or the Sydney Harbor Bridge is composed from its parts. In this case, animation is used to overcome specific weaknesses of static pictures with respect to displaying the composition of complex objects. This weakness of static pictures arises from the usual practice of presenting the subject matter only in its final, completed state. As Taylor and Tversky (1992) have observed: "A drawing does not need to be comprehended until it is completed, so that the order in which elements are drawn is not part of the communicative act." A static picture therefore typically provides relatively little guidance regarding the most appropriate order for its analysis or how the displayed content should be decomposed into parts and subparts. However, animations can furnish such guidance by directing the learner's visual attention and cognitive processing in appropriate ways.

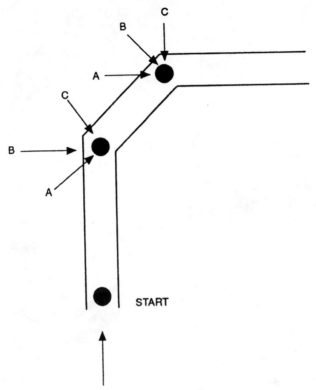

FIGURE 14.3. Static display of a movement's path and speed in the computer based learning environment 'Thinker's Tool' (White & Horwitz, 1987). Reprinted with permission.

Complex objects may be decomposed into a hierarchy of parts and subparts. Such decomposition can be regarded as a fundamental activity in the process of learning because it provides the raw material for building hierarchically organized mental representations (McNamara, Hardy, & Hirtle, 1989; Narayanan & Hegarty, 2002). Learners use a hierarchical structuring approach when processing a display in order to build a mental representation of what is depicted externally. As objects undergo progressive hierarchically decomposition, different levels of granularity emerge. An animation showing how a complex object is 'logically' assembled usually deals with how the object's main parts are put together and therefore operates at a relatively high level of the information hierarchy (i.e., with low granularity). Such assembly of a structure from its components signals the relations amongst these components more clearly than presenting the complete structure from the outset. In this respect, animation can provide direct guidance for the process of mental model construction. Alternatively, animation may be used for analytical purposes

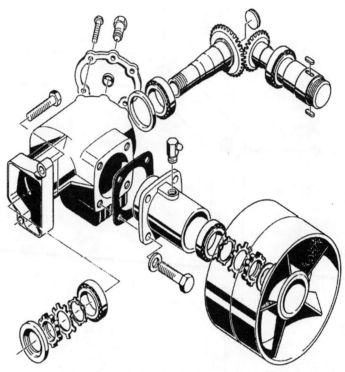

FIGURE 14.4. Assembly of a technical device shown as an explosion picture (from Ball-staedt, S. P., 1997). Wissensvermittlung. Die Gestaltung von Lernmaterial. Weinheim: Beltz, PVU. Reprinted with permission.

by showing the progressive breaking down of a complete structure into its parts and by displaying the relations between them. Animations that depict the assembly or decomposition of complex subject matter can therefore provide learners with explicit information about its structure. In contrast, with most static pictures responsibility for the type and order of subject matter decomposition lies largely with the learner. It is also possible to signal the appropriate type of decomposition in a static graphic by means of a so-called explosion picture such as is shown in Figure 14.4. However, such depictions are unable to provide the direct temporal information about sequencing that is available with the animated alternative.

When animations are used to depict dynamic content, they provide an external analog representation of the temporal changes that occur in the referent situation. The depicted situations may range from natural processes (such as the drifting of a continent, the hopping of a kangaroo, or a chameleon's catching of an insect), to technical processes (such as the functioning of a tyre pump, the operation of a four-stroke engine, or the tying of a specific sailing knot). The degree of *behavioral* realism (Lowe, 2006) in these various types animations is not necessarily correlated with their degree of *visuospatial* realism. For example, in current educational practice, animations often depict their subject matter diagrammatically (i.e., with a low degree of visuospatial realism) and yet use a high degree of behavioral realism so that changes in the animation closely parallel changes in the referent situation.

A special case of visualizing a system's dynamics is the use of explanatory animations to show causal relations. These animations are intended to help learners construct causal mental models that allow them to explain or to predict the behavior of the system. A causal relation in the real world becomes apparent through a directed co-variation of attributes. Such a directed co-variation exists when change in a specific attribute of one entity systematically results in change in a specific attribute of another entity. For example, when the movement of a bicycle pump handle from its upper to its lower position is followed by a flow of air from the pump cylinder, the first event is characterized as the cause of the second (i.e., the change in the handle's position *causes* a change in the position of the air). Because co-variation occurs in time, animations can be used to explain cause and effect. If such animations are user-controllable, they can even offer learners the opportunity to manipulate cause-effect relationships. But again, animation is not the only instructional approach that is capable of providing such causal explanations. In the case of our bicycle pump example, a pair of static pictures showing the two key states of the pump's handle and of the pumped air could be sufficient for learners to construct a satisfactory dynamic mental model, provided they have the capacity to infer the intervening processes. This model would then allow them to explain or predict the pump's behavior. To summarize, there is no necessary one-to-one relationship between the static or dynamic characteristics of content and the use of static or animated pictures for its depiction. Rather, static pictures can display both static and dynamic content, and this also holds for animations.

Representational Function and Directive Function of Animation

Irrespective of whether animations are used to display static or dynamic content, they can serve two basic functions: a representational function, and a directive function. When animations have a close similarity with the referent in terms of appearance and behavior, they have a representational function. They provide a direct way of representing temporal changes through explicit depiction of how a system alters over time, either by changes in the positions of its component entities in space (*translations*) or by changes in attributes of those entities such as size, shape, or color (*transformations*) (Lowe, 2003). On a more abstract level, the direct display of changes over time is also possible by animating logical pictures such as bar graphs. Rather than representing their subject matter via pictorial similarity, logical pictures depict their referents on the basis of more general structural commonalities (i.e., based on analogy). In this case, change in a visual attribute over time (the height of a bar in a graph, for example) would depict the change of a more abstract attribute (a company's monthly turnover, for example). An animation also has a representational function when it displays the assembly of a complex static object, such as a Greek temple or the Sydney Harbour Bridge, from its components. In this case, the animation serves to represent the complex static object in a way that clarifies its spatial structure. The representational function of animation described here has the effect of making information of relevance to a learning task more accessible.

However, merely having access to relevant information does not guarantee that the learner will attend to the spatial and temporal regions in which that information is located, especially if the contents of these regions are of low perceptual salience. In such circumstances, animations can be used for a different purpose – to enhance perceptual and cognitive processing of relevant information by means of their directive function. Making use of this directive function of animation involves directing the learner's visual attention to task-relevant features of the displayed information by adding dynamic highlighting techniques (for example, by flashing). Such visual cueing devices can increase the perceptual salience of parts as well as their attributes or relations so that they are more likely to attract the viewer's attention. Other techniques for attracting viewers' attention include zooming, panning, exaggeration, and simplification. In some cases, the directive function of animation derives from its representational function. For example, entities that are in reality closely related may nevertheless be widely separated in space and distributed across the display so that their physical locations hide the intimate link between them. Animations can be used to move these entities closer together or realign them with respect to relevant corresponding features so that their spatial arrangement better reflects their underlying conceptual relationship. In this case, the animation has a directive function because task-relevant comparisons are facilitated through this repositioning. The result is that similarities and differences between the entities become more noticeable.

Enabling and Facilitating Functions of Animation

Because conscious information processing requires some working memory capacity, it always imposes demands, a so-called 'cognitive load,' on the learner's working memory (Sweller & Chandler, 1994; Sweller, van Merriënboer, & Paas, 1998). Animation can be considered as a means to manipulate cognitive load and this in turn can have various effects. Two of these are the *enabling effect* and the *facilitating effect* (Schnotz & Rasch, this volume). We first consider the enabling effect. Imagine a task is so difficult that its processing requirements exceed the learner's working memory capacity. In this case, the learner would find it impossible to process the task successfully. However, if the cognitive load associated with the task were to be reduced so that it fits within the learner's working memory capacity, successful performance of the task becomes possible. Thus, the enabling effect involves a reduction of cognitive load such that processes become possible which otherwise would have remained impossible. We turn now to the facilitation effect. Imagine that a task can be performed by the learner but to do so requires most of working memory capacity. In this case, processing the task successfully is likely to be very difficult. However, if the cognitive load associated with the task is reduced so that it requires less working memory, successful task performance is facilitated. Thus, the facilitating effect involves a reduction of cognitive load that makes otherwise difficult processes easier. Both the enabling effect of animation (previously impossible processes become possible) and the facilitating effect of animation (possible, but difficult processes become easier) result from a reduction of cognitive load.

For example, if an animation allows an object to be shown from many different perspectives that could not be provided with a static picture, then the animation has an enabling function. This is because it enables a learner to perform a greater amount of productive, task-related cognitive processing than could be accomplished with a static picture. Animations can also display dynamic processes. These animations could have a facilitating function by providing external support for the corresponding mental simulations thus making these mental processes easier to perform. Individuals with high learning prerequisites seem to benefit primarily from the enabling function, whereas individuals with low learning prerequisites seem to be affected primarily by the facilitating function of animations (Schnotz & Rasch, this volume).

SPATIAL AND TEMPORAL STRUCTURES IN ANIMATION

Because the world around us exists in space and because events within this world occur in time, our everyday environment continually presents us with both spatial and dynamic information. Our perceptual and cognitive system evolved to maximize our chances of surviving in this world. It is therefore finely tuned to an environment that usually contains a blend of stable and changing components by being very well adapted to process both spatial and dynamic information.

When considering the way we process animated and static pictures, it is useful to think about the world around us as a 3D spatial structure that changes over time. It can therefore be conceptualized as a $3 + 1$-dimensional structure that includes three spatial dimensions and one temporal dimension. Both animations and static pictures present spatial information on what is effectively a flat, 2D structure (such as a screen, for example). This means that in terms of their spatial structure, animations and static pictures are strictly speaking 2D, even if it is possible for an observer to infer a 3D scenario from them. Because animations are pictures that change over time, they not only have a 2D spatial structure (a characteristic they share with static pictures) but also have the additional dimension of time. On this basis, animations can be considered as having a $2 + 1$-dimensional structure, with two spatial dimensions and one temporal dimension. When considered in this way, animations can be treated as an 'elaboration' of static pictures in which a 2D spatial structure is extended into a $2 + 1$-dimensional spatial-temporal structure. This $2 + 1$-dimensional structure of animations can be visualized as a stack of frames ordered in a temporal sequence with only one frame presented at any point in time (Figure 14.5). Analysis of such a $2 + 1$-dimensional structure can be undertaken from a spatial perspective by slicing it in a cross-sectional direction, or from a temporal perspective by slicing it in a longitudinal direction. The cross-sectional slices reveal spatial information (i.e., spatial patterning), whereas the longitudinal slices reveal dynamic information (i.e., temporal patterning).

Spatial-Temporal Invariants and Dynamic Contrasts

Compared to static pictures, animations provide additional (i.e., temporal) information. However, the mere presence of this additional information does not necessarily mean that the amount of information that actually needs to be processed is correspondingly higher. This is illustrated in the case of an animation showing a constantly swinging pendulum. Although the animation provides spatial as well as temporal information, the behavior of the pendulum itself is invariant in that it follows a regular and highly predictable pattern. The invariants presented in this situation are quickly grasped by the observer and further observation of the pendulum's behavior adds no new information.

The world around us includes innumerable examples of spatial-temporal patterns that repeat cyclically and thus contain invariance, such as people walking, horses galloping, dogs running, or kangaroos hopping. Our perceptual

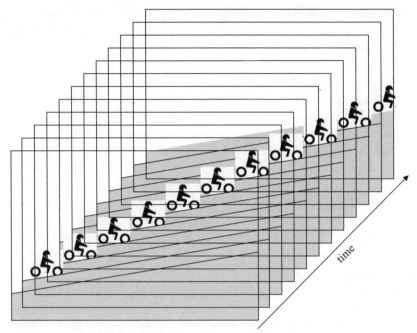

FIGURE 14.5. Visualization of the $2 + 1$-dimensional spatial temporal structure of animations by a stack of frames ordered in a temporal sequence. The example displays a motorbike going up a hill. Only one frame is presented at any point in time.

and cognitive systems are well equipped to detect such invariants and to encode them into specific dynamic schemas. These schemas represent typical (most frequently experienced) spatial-temporal patterns that help us to process dynamic information extremely efficiently. It should be noted that the concept of invariant temporal patterns does not imply that there is *no* movement or change in time. Rather, it covers situations in which the *pattern* of movement or change is constant. Even if everything in our visual field is moving, specific relations between certain elements can nevertheless be stable and these constitute an invariant spatial-temporal pattern that can be grasped by the appropriate dynamic schema. For example, if a kangaroo is hopping across a field, the animal's shape and its position in space are continuously changing. Nevertheless, the repeated sequence of states ('prepare – jump – fly – land – prepare – jump – fly – land – etc.') remains invariant.

Spatial-temporal invariants play an important role not only in the perception and cognition of dynamics, but also in their practical mastery. Such invariants are sometimes deliberately created as a means of dealing with a dynamic target system more effectively. A common strategy for creating and taking advantage of invariants involves synchronization with the target system. Some predators, for example, once they are closely aligned with their prey synchronize their motion with that of their prey. In this way, they minimize the relative movement between the two systems (predator and prey) and thus create a spatial-temporal invariant before they attack. This has a facilitating effect because the number of spatial relations between the two systems that remain constant in time is maximized during this short period. Other examples are the horse-riding bandit seen in old movies who adapts his horse's speed to the speed of the train before he jumps onto it, the photographer who pans a still camera to capture a high-speed action shot, and the rifle-shooter who tracks a flying clay pigeon before firing. In all these cases, an alignment is produced between two systems through a synchronization of their spatial-temporal patterns. Such alignment requires the active creation of spatial-temporal invariants within a highly dynamic environment by an agent (predator, bandit, photographer, shooter) involving his/her perceptual, cognitive, and motor systems.

As demonstrated some time ago by Marey (1874), dynamic schemas play a crucial role in the recognition of movement. If a person dressed in black but wearing lights at the shoulders, elbows, hands, hips, knees, and feet is standing still in front of a wall covered by black velvet, it is impossible to recognize that this is a human being. Rather, the observer sees only a seemingly arbitrary distribution of light spots. As soon as the person starts walking, however, the observer immediately recognizes the presence of a human figure. The invariant pattern in the movement of the lights is sufficient to activate the appropriate dynamic schema so that the dynamic display can be recognized as a person walking. In addition to having such dynamic schemas for the detection of human movements, we also possess schemas that encapsulate various movement patterns for other animals. For example, we can readily distinguish different types of horse gait such as walking, trotting, and galloping. The generic knowledge about typical movement patterns represented in these schemas includes expectations about subsequent or prior movements that allow us to anticipate what will happen or to make retrospective inferences about what might have happened. Because such dynamic schemas represent highly typical spatial-temporal patterns, we can also use them to infer other information about movements we observe. For example, we can readily detect even a slight limp in a person's walk and so infer that s/he has an injured leg. Our inference is based both on the fact that the movement is atypical and that it deviates from the expected pattern in a specific way.

Gestalt psychologists have shown that in the field of spatial patterns, one can distinguish between configurations (*Gestalten*) of different qualities, between 'good' and 'bad' gestalts (Wertheimer, 1938). The notion of different gestalt qualities can be explained by today's cognitive psychology in terms of the extent to which an observed external pattern corresponds to an internal pattern stored by a (perceptual or cognitive) schema that represents the pattern of a 'good gestalt.' Similar gestalt phenomena can be found with regard to dynamic material and may be explained in a similar fashion. Spatial-temporal patterns can also be conceptualized as 'good' or 'bad' gestalts, depending on how well they correspond to the pattern encoded by the relevant schema. For example, the recognizable moving pattern of lights attached to a human figure referred to above can be considered as a good spatial-temporal gestalt, whereas an arbitrary, uncoordinated movement of the same set of lights would be a bad gestalt. Similarly, the running of a four-legged dog would correspond to a better spatial-temporal gestalt than the running of a dog with only three legs.

According to Gestalt psychology, good gestalts tend to be more salient, which implies that they provide a better figure-ground-distinction (i.e., the distinction between a gestalt and its environment) than bad gestalts. Furthermore, it is hypothesized that good gestalts are easier to encode in memory and easier to retrieve from memory than bad gestalts (cf. Brewer & Nakamura, 1984; Ohlsson, 1984a, 1984b). These benefits are assumed to apply not only to the spatial field where we find object-based gestalts, but also to the spatial-temporal field where we find event-based gestalts. We can assume that the specific pattern included in a dynamic schema as a spatial-temporal invariant defines what is considered as a good dynamic gestalt and what is considered as a bad gestalt. Salience rules derived from Gestalt psychology allow us to predict which objects are likely to be more salient and which objects are likely to be less salient in the spatial field. In a similar way, salience rules allow us to predict which events are more or less salient in the spatial-temporal field (c.f. Lowe, 2004). A general salience rule for events might be that the better the gestalt quality of an observed spatial-temporal pattern (i.e., the better it corresponds to the typical pattern stored in the appropriate schema), the more likely it is to become salient, that is, that the better its figure-ground-distinction will be.

The salience of a configuration of elements in the spatial field (i.e., an object-based gestalt) depends among other things on *visual contrast* – on the extent to which its perceptual attributes differ from those of its surroundings. For example, a single black object will stand out amongst many white ones. Similarly, the salience of a configuration of elements in the spatial-temporal field (i.e., an event-based gestalt) depends on how its dynamic attributes differ from those of its surrounding context. Frequently, this context (i.e., the ground) is stable, whereas the salient configuration (i.e., the figure) is animated. However, it would be wrong to assume that static objects in a display would only ever function as the ground for the perception of moving figures. It is also possible for this type of figure-ground-relationship to be reversed. Imagine that a rock stands out from a field of grass that is swaying in the wind. Although the grass is moving and the rock is stable, the rock is seen as the figure and the grass as the ground. As this example demonstrates, it is not the amount of movement that is psychologically important. Rather, it is the figure-ground distinctions that are to be made, and these distinctions are made on the basis of *dynamic contrasts* (Lowe, 2003).

Dynamic contrast can be essential for the figure-ground distinctions involved in object recognition. For example, if an eagle is hunting a rabbit running through a field of moving grass, the eagle is able to make a *dynamic figure-ground* distinction between the moving rabbit and the moving grass. The running rabbit contributes one specific dynamic pattern in the scene and this movement is invariant in a relative sense. The grass contributes a second very different type of dynamic pattern and this is also relatively invariant. Because of the considerable difference between these the two patterns, there is a clear contrast between them. This dynamic contrast helps the eagle to detect and catch the rabbit, even if the rabbit and the grass have a very similar color and texture so that visual contrast is minimal.

Avoidance of dynamic and visual contrast is therefore a key issue for camouflage where animals reduce their perceptibility as much as possible in order to protect themselves from predators. The Leafy Seadragon, for example, is a marine creature with a bizarre form due to the leaf-like appendages on its body that mimic seaweed and provide superb camouflage. Its texture and color make the creature nearly invisible, but only as long as it stays still. As soon as it moves, it becomes visible due to dynamic contrast with its environment. The various subparts of the creature move at the same speed in the same direction and therefore have a 'common fate' in space and time. Gestalt psychology considers 'common fate' to be one of a number of gestalt-creating factors. Therefore in the case of the Seadragon, a moving figure is perceived in front of a relatively stable ground, and this figure is revealed as the creature. In other words, the creature's movement is characterized by a dynamic (spatial-temporal) invariant which differs from the dynamic invariants of its environment and therefore constitutes a dynamic contrast. In order to keep this dynamic contrast as low as possible, the Leafy Seadragon moves very slowly through the water. Similarly, birds such as the Great Bittern hide when standing in moving grass by swinging to-and-fro in time with the grass. They minimize dynamic contrast by synchronizing their micro-movements with the movements of their environment.

Principles of Temporal Categorization

In her analysis of principles of categorization, Eleanor Rosch and her co-workers have shown that the perceived world includes natural discontinuities which suggest themselves as boundaries of categories (Rosch, 1978). The practical usefulness of categories therefore depends on the extent to which they grasp these natural discontinuities in the perceived world. The instances within a category are, despite some differences, relatively similar to the other instances within the category. However, comparison between instances within the category and instances outside the category reveals low similarity and many differences. Within the category of birds, for example, instances such as robins, doves, ducks, hawks, emus, and so on show considerable similarity despite various differences, whereas comparing instances within the category and instances outside the category such as robins with dogs, emus with sharks, and so on tends to reveal differences rather than similarities. In other words, provided that the category grasps the natural discontinuities of the perceived world, there is a high continuity of attributes within a category and a high discontinuity of attributes at its border. Within a category, an instance can be nominated (sometimes real, sometimes fictitious) that best represents the category as a whole and can therefore be considered as its prototype. In Europe and in America, for example, a robin would be a good candidate for the prototype of the 'bird' category, whereas in Australia, a cockatoo could be considered more suitable as the bird prototype. The different instances of a category can be distinguished according to their typicality or similarity to the category's prototype (Rosch, 1978).

These principles of categorization apply not only to objects in space, but also to events in time (Zacks & Tversky, 2001). Events can be decomposed from a top-down perspective into sets of subordinate events at progressively finer levels of detail. The ultimate result of this decomposition can be considered as a sequence of an infinite number of states that corresponds to the ongoing flow of continuous temporal change. From a bottom-up perspective, the states within the ongoing flow of temporal change can be categorized into events at different levels of granularity. At each level, there are boundaries that separate the events from each other based on natural spatial-temporal discontinuities between the events and their predecessor and successor events. These boundaries between events are analogous to the boundaries between categories of objects mentioned above. Accordingly, the different states within an event are more similar to each other than they are to states outside (i.e., before or after) the event.

Consider, for example, the preparation of a meal such as tomatoes with mozzarella. One can distinguish different phases or macro-level events in this process: washing the tomatoes, cutting the tomatoes, distributing the tomato slices on a plate, cutting the mozzarella, covering the tomato slices with mozzarella slices, and dressing. The states within one phase are much more similar to each other than they are to the states of another phase in the process. For example, the states within the cutting of tomatoes phase are more similar to each other than they are to the states of the washing or the tomato-distributing phases. It is therefore possible to identify continuities and discontinuities within the temporal flow of states and the discontinuities suggest themselves as the boundaries between different events or phases in the ongoing flow of states.

The segmentation of a flow of states into events can be easy or difficult. It would be easy to carry out this segmentation in the case of preparing tomatoes with mozzarella. Segmentation would also be easy in the case of a chameleon catching an insect where the beginning of the event is marked by the departure of the chameleon's tongue from its mouth and the end is marked by the tongue's arrival on the insect. Each of these individual events is clearly distinct from its predecessor event or successor event due to marked spatial-temporal discontinuities. The events are also highly salient because of their stark dynamic contrast with the rest of the scenario. In other cases, segmentation is more difficult. Consider, for example, the hopping of a kangaroo in which there is continuous flow from 'prepare' to 'jump,' from 'jump' to 'fly' and from 'fly' to 'land,' at least with regard to the body shape of the kangaroo. Despite the boundaries being less sharp because natural movements are typically characterized by fluent transitions, this activity can nevertheless can be segmented into a sequence of events such as 'prepare,' 'jump,' 'fly,' and 'land.'

Within an event, it is possible to find among the component states one specific state that is, on average, most similar to all other states within the event. This state with the highest average similarity to the other states of the event can therefore be considered as prototypical because it is the best representative of all states within the event. It also functions as a prototype state at a more inclusive level because it is the best representative of the event as a whole (among all its states). Imagine that the prototype state of an event within an animation is captured as a 'snapshot' and then presented as a static picture. In this case, the static picture (which is ordinarily shown for only a minimal amount of time somewhere in the flow of the animation) can be considered as a 'key frame' within the animation with regard to this specific event. Because the key frame represents the most typical state within this event, it would allow (if presented as a static picture) a suitably knowledgeable observer to infer a maximum of other states comprising the event.

Let us return to the mozzarella example. Cutting of the tomatoes begins with all tomatoes uncut and ends once they are all cut. An intermediate state, when about half of the tomatoes have been cut, could be used to represent the whole event and so considered as its prototype. A static picture of this state – as the best representative of 'cutting tomatoes' – could then act as a key frame. It would allow the inferences to be made that there must have been a state when all tomatoes were uncut and that there will be a state when all tomatoes are cut. It would also allow inferences to be made about all the states in between. In the example of a hopping kangaroo, the key frame of the prepare-phase would show the kangaroo crouching ready to spring. The key frame of the jump-phase would show the kangaroo having stretched its legs as far as possible with its feet still on the ground. The key frame of the fly-phase would depict the kangaroo high in the air with its feet beneath. The key frame for the land-phase would show the kangaroo hitting the ground with its feet stretched forward. The pictogram of a tennis player shown earlier in Figure 14.1 of course provides another example of how a static key frame can be used to represent dynamic information. It has been chosen as a key frame to represent the sport of tennis because it depicts a typical state within an event that frequently occurs during tennis matches.

We suggest that identifying the most typical state within an event and representing it as a key frame could play an important role in the construction of dynamic mental models when learning from animations or from static pictures. Our justification for this suggestion is that such a condensation would provide a highly parsimonious way to mentally represent crucial event-related information that is consistent with the way object-related information is understood to be represented. With natural categories of objects, the prototype of a category tends to be especially well encoded in memory as the best representative of the category and it also allows other category members to be inferred. If events are dealt with in a similar way, we could also assume that key frames tend to be especially well encoded in memory. This is because they depict the most typical states within events and are therefore good candidates for allowing us to infer as many other states within the corresponding event as possible.

The segmentation of the ongoing flow of states into discrete events and the parsimonious representation of each of these events by its own prototypical key frame is a way of chunking continuous temporal information. In general terms, chunking has the effect of condensing information and so allows it to be encoded efficiently in memory by subsuming a set of items under a super-ordinate item. The items comprising the subsumed set are interrelated by, for example, gestalt factors such as proximity, similarity, or common fate, or by causality, finality or other kinds of relations that hold for the whole set of items. Chunking reduces the information to be stored in memory because the whole set of subordinated items can be inferred from the super-ordinate item via these relations on the basis of prior knowledge. The process of inferring the whole set of items from the corresponding superordinate item constitutes 'unpacking' the chunk.

Chunking has both extensional and intensional aspects. The extensional aspect concerns the issue of *what* belongs to the chunk. It implies the drawing of a virtual boundary around the items that are included in the chunk. In a shopping list, for example, the chunk 'dairy' may includes items such as 'milk,' 'butter,' 'cheese,' and 'cream.' The intensional aspect concerns the issue of *how* the items are related to each other. It refers to the invariants defining the content of the chunk – a specific pattern of relations that holds for the whole set of included items. In the example of the chunk 'dairy,' these relations may include 'produced from raw milk' or 'to be found in the diary-section of a supermarket.' Because a chunk is defined intensionally by an invariant pattern describing the content of the chunk, and because schemas contain such invariant patterns as descriptions of their referents, it follows that schemas provide possible descriptions for chunks. As a consequence, the act of chunking can be conceptualized as a schema-driven process in which elements that can be subsumed under the same schema are good candidates for chunking. As we have mentioned above, schemas can also be seen as the basis of gestalt perception because their internally stored patterns describe 'good gestalts.' Accordingly, gestalt perception can be considered as a schema-driven process as well as a form of chunking because the gestalt elements are economically subsumed under the same super-ordinate unit referred to as the corresponding 'gestalt.'

From the previous analysis, we can conclude that as well as spatial chunks, there are also temporal chunks that are formed by segmentation of the flow of states into specific events and are held together by specific relations between states or events in time. In a manner similar to spatial chunking, temporal chunking subsumes a sequence of temporally related states under a super-ordinate event or a set of temporally related events under a super-ordinate, higher-order event. With regard to its extensional aspect, temporal chunking segments the ongoing flow of states into events by introducing appropriate inter-event boundaries. In the case of preparing tomatoes with mozzarella, temporal chunking groups a specific sequence of states under the 'cutting tomatoes' phase, a segment of the overall preparation process that starts when all tomatoes are uncut and ends when all tomatoes are cut. With regard to its intensional aspect, temporal chunking interrelates the states within an event by specific relations. In the case of preparing tomatoes with mozzarella, temporal chunking relates the states of the 'cutting tomatoes' phase by an iterative operation 'cut one more slice' applied as long as possible.

Like spatial chunking, temporal chunking can be assumed to provide benefits both for encoding information about dynamic of events in memory and for retrieving this information from memory. Further, the process of creating temporal chunks is likely to be driven by dynamic schemas that encapsulate typical spatial-temporal patterns. Accordingly, an observer segments the ongoing sequence of states into chunks on the basis of dynamic schemas. These chunks can then be represented in memory by prototypical states as their best representatives. Finally, these states can be used as nuclei for the reconstruction of the whole set of dynamic information from memory because they allow other states of the event to be inferred.

In a manner similar to the way that most complex objects can be decomposed into a hierarchy of parts and sub-parts, behaviors can usually be decomposed into a set of hierarchically related events and sub-events (Graesser, 1978; Hacker, 1986). Eating in a restaurant, for example, can be decomposed into being seated, ordering, eating and drinking, paying, and leaving (Schank & Abelson, 1977). Similarly, the movement of a kangaroo can be subdivided into hops which can in turn be further subdivided into component movements of specific body parts. In other words, macro-events are composed of a series of embedded micro-events. This embedding of micro-events within macro-events results in a hierarchy of dynamics that ranges across different levels, from temporal microstructures through to temporal macrostructures.

Macro- and micro-events are frequently associated with different kinds of movements that combine into complex patterns. For example, when a kangaroo is hopping about, it performs a translation in moving from one place to another. This overall change in the kangaroo's external spatial relation to its environment is a macro-event. Embedded within this macro-event are micro-events such as the kangaroo's individual hops that together produce the animal's movement across space. These micro-events are characterized by cyclic changes in the kangaroo's form, that is, repeated transformations in its internal spatial relations or properties. Other possible types of transformations that can occur in different situations include changes in visual attributes such as size, shape, color, or texture. These can be the result of growth, distortion, or specialized processes such as the metamorphosis from a caterpillar via a pupa to a butterfly. According to the hierarchy of dynamics discussed above, a single animation can depict multiple levels of change. However, these various levels are not necessarily of equal importance. For some purposes, the macro-changes are more important than the micro-changes. For example, an ecologist interested in comparing the global movements of kangaroos during the day and the night will concentrate on macro-changes – their translations across space. In this case, the micro-changes involving transformations of a kangaroo's body are not important. For other purposes, the micro-changes are important. For example, an animal physiologist interested in the biomechanics of kangaroo locomotion would place far more importance on micro changes in a kangaroo's body parts than on the macro-changes occurring during its wanderings.

PERCEPTUAL AND COGNITIVE PROCESSING OF ANIMATION

Animations give learners the opportunity to perceive temporal changes directly from an external pictorial representation whereas static pictures of dynamic content require learners to infer the temporal changes. In this respect, animations present more information, namely temporal as well as spatial information, than do static pictures. Nevertheless, learning from an animation not necessarily more demanding is *per se* than learning from a static picture. The ease with which displayed temporal patterns can be grasped depends on the extent to which the learner is equipped with the appropriate perceptual and cognitive schemas. As mentioned earlier, the human perceptual and cognitive system has developed as an adaptation to a highly dynamic environment. It is therefore very well suited to processing information from both spatial and temporal patterns in the surrounding world by the application of well-adapted perceptual and cognitive tools. We have suggested that such tools include hierarchically organized dynamic schemas representing typical temporal patterns of different granularity. These allow us to anticipate changes in the environment, to chunk temporal patterns so as to represent them in a condensed, parsimonious way, and to 'unpack' these chunks by inferring the encoded patterns from a minimum of information on the basis of the individual's perceptual and conceptual prior knowledge.

For the same reason, not all information about a dynamic event has to be obtained from its direct, immediate perception. Individuals can anticipate and elaborate movements via top-down processing based on their perceptual and conceptual prior knowledge without having to observe the movement in detail. This means that even if animated pictures *contain* more information than static pictures, learners will not necessarily actually *extract* more information from them. For example, consider a situation in which learners need to construct a dynamic mental representation from an animation that provides an explicit representation of the relevant dynamic information. Despite this information being available, learners may not bother to make much use of the external animation if they are already equipped with appropriate internal resources. If learners are so equipped, they can instead infer the relevant temporal patterns and perform the required mental simulation (as a 'mental animation') primarily on the basis of their dynamic schemas as they would do for static depictions. Of course, this is not to say that the direct display of a dynamic situation cannot be helpful for constructing a dynamic mental model. Construction of such a mental representation on the basis of a static depiction can be very demanding and prone to error, particularly if the learner lacks prior knowledge of the subject matter (Lowe, 1999b). In this case, presenting a well designed animation may be highly beneficial for learning. We only want to make clear that even in the case of constructing a dynamic mental representation of dynamic subject matter, using an animation is not necessarily better than using static pictures.

On one hand, animations are potentially beneficial for learning because they supply explicit dynamic information that is available to be read directly from the display. On the other hand, however, animations can also impose perceptual and cognitive costs on the learner due to the transitory nature of the presented information (Lowe, 1999a, 2003). Media design therefore needs to balance very carefully the relative benefits and costs of using animation or static pictures. Because perception is selective and cognitive processing capacity is limited, there is even the possibility that there will be a trade-off between processing of spatial patterns and processing of temporal patterns (Lowe & Pramono, 2006). In this case, information about temporal patterns could be processed at the expense of information about spatial patterns, and vice versa. In the following sections, we consider both perceptual processing and cognitive processing of animation

Perceptual Processing

Selectivity of Visual Perception

Human perception is based on essentially pre-attentive and data-driven bottom-up processes that are guided by highly automated visual routines operating relatively independent of prior knowledge (Neisser, 1976; Ullman, 1984). A fundamental characteristic of our visual perception is its extreme selectivity. Only part of our surroundings can be included in our visual field, and only a small portion of that visual field, the area of foveal vision, can capture information at sufficiently high resolution for it to be subsequently processed in detail by working memory (Baddeley, 1992). Within the area of foveal vision, the sensitivity for spatial patterns is again limited because the eye cannot make distinctions below a certain visual angle (Sekuler & Blake, 1994). The information processed by foveal vision is said to be in the focus of visual attention and this corresponds to what the individual is looking at. Because visual perception is so selective, visual attention is highly limited.

When viewing a static picture, the focus of visual attention can wander across a permanently available display. The learner is thus able to interrogate the visual display systematically without time constraints and so accumulate information via successive eye fixations. This interrogation process benefits from peripheral vision through which information is gathered about the wider visual context and so serves to identify possible regions for further specific fixations (Radach & Kennedy, 2004). The learner is therefore able, in principle at least, to grasp more and more of the pictorial information until all task-relevant aspects of the visual display have been processed and represented in working memory (Kosslyn, 1994; Sims & Hegarty, 1997). However, when viewing an animation, the situation is different. The viewer is confronted with a series of frames, each of which is made available for only a fraction of a second. Because of this limited display time, information that was available at one moment may become unavailable an instant later. The highly selective nature of visual perception means that successful learning from animation therefore relies on directing visual attention to the right place at the right time. An inevitable consequence of the selectivity in processing spatial information is that by focusing on one area of an animated display, other areas do not receive attention. Because of the fluent nature of animation, it follows that any transient information not receiving attention is necessarily lost.

Research on reading and visual learning generally assumes a close relationship between perception and cognition. This closeness is reflected in the eye-mind assumption and in the immediacy assumption (Carpenter & Just, 1981; Radach & Kennedy, 2004). According to the eye-mind assumption, the information grasped by the eye is *directly related* to the information cognitively processed in the human mind (effectively in working memory). This means the eye usually fixates information that seems to be of relevance to current cognitive processing requirements. According to the immediacy assumption, perceptual information grasped by the eye is *immediately* further processed by the cognitive system. In other words, perceptual information is – except for extremely short intervals – not stored in a buffer for later cognitive analysis.

Rather, because of limited storage and processing capacities of the perceptual and cognitive system, perceptual information is processed immediately and used as far as possible as soon as it is available. In essence, the eye-mind assumption and the immediacy assumption taken together hypothesize that perception and cognition are very closely coupled, both spatially and temporally.

Because visual attention is highly selective, one can think of it as 'cutting out' only a part of the visual display at each moment in time for further information processing. The specific part of the display that is cut out at any particular instant depends on where the visual attention is being directed at that moment. As the focus of visual attention changes over time due to eye movements, different regions are cut out from the information display during successive instants. Recall the earlier characterization of animations as information displays with a $2 + 1$-dimensional structure (2 spatial dimensions and 1 temporal dimension). Based on this characterization, the operation of selective visual attention during the viewing of an animation can be considered as the continuous cutting-out of attentional regions from the information display as the animation progresses. Taken together, the series of attentional regions that link through successive frames of the animation form an 'attentional core' which results from the varying selective attention 'tunneling' through the complete set of information that is available over the animation's course. Figure 14.6 illustrates the concept of such an attentional core running through the $2 + 1$-dimensional structure of an animation. The attentional core that an individual learner cuts out during viewing an animation provides the raw material for the learner's further cognitive processing.

Potentially negative consequences of the high selectivity of visual attention when learning from animation may be ameliorated by reducing an animation's playing speed. Such speed reduction allows for a larger total attentional region per frame of the $2 + 1$ structure and so a more extensive attentional core overall. Nevertheless, a fundamental and unavoidable constraint on learning from animation remains; the attentional core will always be *less* than the *whole* block of information presented by the $2 + 1$-dimensional structure. Because of the constraints on the capacity of our perceptual system to process visual information, the attentional core can encompass only *some part* of the complete set of information contained in an animation. As a consequence, only this part feeds into further cognitive processing which in turn greatly limits the amount of raw material that is available for mental model construction. This is not necessarily a problem for learning. Consider an ideal case in which (i) the learner has already scanned the static components within the animation,

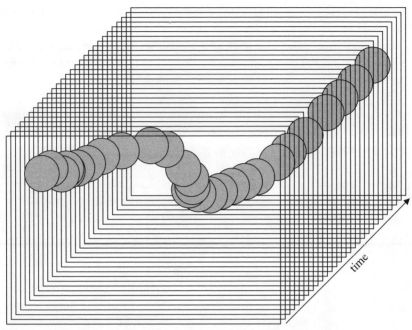

FIGURE 14.6. Example of the selective visual attention during viewing of an animation. Due to the selectivity of perception, an attentional region is cut out from each information display. These regions form an attentional core, which 'tunnels' through the complete 2 + 1 -dimensional set of information and which forms the raw material for the learner's further cognitive processing.

(ii) only one part of the display changes over time, (iii) the learner's eyes focus exactly on this part, and (iv) the information presented in this part neither overwhelms the perceptual processing capacities nor exceeds the cognitive capacities of working memory. Under these perfect conditions, the learner should indeed be able to grasp all the relevant information despite his/her limited processing capacities and despite the fluent nature of the animation. However, the reality of what learners face when they encounter an animation is usually very different. If several parts of the visual field are changing simultaneously (a far more likely scenario than that presented in our ideal case), a split of the learner's attention within the depiction is required (Lowe, 1999a). Because the human eye cannot focus different parts of a visual display simultaneously, focusing on one part of the animation means that relevant information displayed simultaneously in other parts is necessarily neglected. Research on multimedia learning has so far focused on split attention in situations in which different representations such as written texts and pictures are presented simultaneously and the learner's eyes have to switch between different representations (Mayer, 2001, 2005; Mayer & Moreno, 1998; Sweller, 1999). In contrast to this *inter*-representational split of visual attention, learning from animation can require an *intra*-representational split of visual attention (Lowe, 1999a). The split of attention between different parts of an animation can have negative consequences for comprehension and learning. It follows that external instructional guidance and internal strategies of learners for directing their visual attention are likely to be extremely important in learning from animation.

The sensitivity of human visual perception is limited not only for spatial patterns, but also for temporal patterns. Although we have a high general sensitivity for movements, this sensitivity operates only within a very specific speed range. Outside that range, we are simply unable to resolve dynamic information. For example, on the one hand, we cannot see the growing of a plant unless its growth is speeded up in an animation. This manipulation can be considered as a 'temporal zooming out' that brings the extremely slow process into the range of the human eye's sensitivity for change. On the other hand, we cannot determine just how a chameleon 'shoots' an insect with its tongue unless the action is slowed down because the whole process lasts for only a few hundredths of a second. An animation that uses slow motion in this way can be considered as providing a 'temporal zooming in' that brings the extremely fast process within the range of the human eye's sensitivity for change.

Animations can be run at different speeds, and depending on their speed, can emphasize different levels of a system's dynamics (Lowe, 2006). As a result, perceptual biasing can be produced such that if the animation speed is high, macro-events tend to be more salient than micro-events. The overall effect of this type of biasing is that the macro-structure of the dynamic information is emphasized at the expense of its micro-structure. Conversely, if speed is low, micro-events become more salient than macro-events and, thus, the microstructure of the dynamic information is emphasized. It follows that one should consider playing animations several times at different speeds in order to enable learners to perceive different levels of a system's dynamic information. Further, one should carefully consider the best presentation speed to begin with and how speed should then be varied as the learning episode progresses.

Directing Visual Attention

The constraints imposed by the conjunction of our highly selective visual perception and the fluent nature of animation makes it crucial that the learner's visual attention is directed to the right place at the right time. One way to direct a learner's visual attention is by verbal descriptions (e.g., 'The figure above shows...') or by directive verbal instructions (e.g., 'Look in the top right of the figure above and notice...'). Both types of verbalization can guide the learner about when to look, where to look, and what to notice. As has been repeatedly demonstrated in multimedia learning research, verbal guidance by synchronized spoken text ('narration') can lead to better learning from animation than verbal guidance by written text because spoken text avoids inter-representational split of attention, maximizes opportunities for providing temporal contiguity, and allows more working memory capacity to be allocated to the process of learning than is the case for written text (Mayer, 2001, 2005; Moreno & Mayer, 2002; Sweller, 1999).

The learner's visual attention can also be directed by manipulating the perceptual salience of information depicted within a display. Because visual perception is to a large extent automated and pre-attentive, it is difficult for an observer to ignore a highly conspicuous object or event. Accordingly, a learner's attention can be guided by visual cueing, that is, by making the relevant aspects perceptually more dominant. In static pictures, various graphical devices such as arrows, circles, boxes and forms of highlighting that rely on visual contrast can be used to direct the viewer's attention towards what is relevant. These same devices can also be used for direction of attention within an animation. However, animation provides further devices to direct the observer's visual attention that take advantage of the perceptual effect of dynamic contrast. As already mentioned, the human visual system is tuned to focus on figures that contrast with their grounds. Figure-ground contrast can be applied not only to static properties, but also to dynamic ones. Accordingly, dynamic contrasts can provide powerful visual cueing for guiding perceptual processing. Although such dynamic cues are capable of directing learner attention to what is relevant, unfortunately they can also direct attention to irrelevant information. For this reason, it is important that attentional cues from the dynamic characteristics of an animation are properly aligned with their thematic relevance. One way to correct such alignment is to increase the salience of relevant components by altering dynamic contrasts within the animation. This approach is similar to that used with static pictures where the salience of objects can be increased through visual signaling that exaggerates key aspects of their appearance by manipulating visual contrasts. The corresponding approach for an animation would be to exaggerate dynamic contrasts by manipulating differences in behavior between the figure and its ground.

Spatial and Temporal Granularity

Pictures can represent their subject matter at different levels of detail. If they contain a higher level of detail, they tend to have a more realistic appearance than pictures with a lower level of detail. The level of detail in a picture can be described in terms of its spatial granularity which refers to the size of the display elements from which the picture is composed. High spatial granularity (fine-grained display) gives the impression of high visuo-spatial realism, whereas low spatial granularity (coarse-grained display) gives the impression of low visuo-spatial realism. Modern high-resolution photography allows very high visuo-spatial granularity which makes pictures look very realistic. In contrast, a pixilated photograph in a daily newspaper or the extremely coarse-grained display of a human face used to obscure the person's identity has a low visuo-spatial granularity that makes the picture look less realistic. The degree of perceived visuo-spatial realism is not infinitely variable. On the one hand, realism increases with granularity only up to a specific level because the human eye is unable to discriminate between adjacent items if their visual separation is below a certain threshold angle. Spatial granularity above this critical level is therefore not detectable by the human eye and does not contribute to a higher degree of realism. On the other hand, pictures with lower spatial granularity can be smoothed by the observer's perceptual schemas, but only to a limited extent. The picture in Figure 14.7 represents a Salvador Dali painting. When seen from a distance, observers eventually notice that the picture includes a portrait of Abraham Lincoln with an extremely low granularity. A further decrease of granularity would destroy the picture's function as a visuospatial representation.

Animations can vary not only in their spatial granularity but also in their temporal granularity. A high number of frames per second corresponds to a high temporal granularity, whereas a low number of frames per second corresponds to a low temporal granularity. In contrast to spatial granularity which affects how realistic we consider a picture's *appearance* to be, temporal granularity affects the realism of an animation's *behavior*. Provided that the temporal characteristics of the presented dynamic information correspond to legitimate changes in the depicted subject matter, high temporal granularity gives the impression of a high degree of behavioral realism, whereas low temporal granularity gives the impression of a low degree of behavioral realism. The degree of perceived behavioral realism is not infinitely variable. On the one hand, the perceived behavioral realism can increase only up to a specific level because above a specific threshold of frames per second, the human eye is unable to discriminate between successive frames. At the usual motion picture

FIGURE 14.7. Salvador Dali painting including a portrait of Abraham Lincoln of very low granularity. Reprinted with permission from Verwertungsgesellschaft Bildung-Kunst.

speed of 24 frames per second, viewers perceive the display as continuous change without discriminating individual frames. Temporal granularity above this frame rate is not detectable by the human eye and therefore makes no additional contribution to behavioral realism. On the other hand, viewers can cope with low temporal granularity through perceptual schemata which to

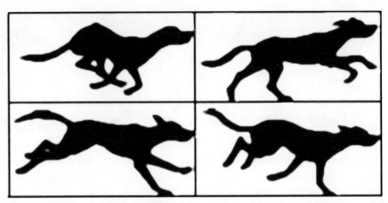

FIGURE 14.8. Sequence of four frames showing a running dog. If the frames are presented by an animation at a speed of 0.17 seconds per frame (i.e., 6 frames per second), the display is seen as dog's run despite of a very low temporal granularity.

some extent allow them to 'smooth' a coarse-grained animation. For example, a looped sequential display of the four frames shown in Figure 14.8 at a speed of 6 frames per second still allows us to recognize that the dog is running despite the extremely low temporal granularity. However, if the granularity were to be reduced still further by removing one or two frames, we would no longer perceive the presentation as normal continuous dog movement.

Note that the degree of perceived behavioral realism depends not only on how many frames per second are used, but also on the correspondence between the temporal characteristics of the display and the temporal characteristics of reality. If the duration of the displayed events equals the actual or expected duration of the corresponding real events, the animation will appear more realistic than if these durations differ appreciably. For example, if the running dog animation were to be greatly speeded up, its movement would appear to be unrealistic. Conversely, if the animation were to be slowed down to a display rate of 1 frame per second, we would perceive single frames rather than ongoing movement.

Temporal granularity is also a key consideration in the portrayal of dynamics via a series of simultaneously displayed static pictures. In this case, granularity corresponds to the number of key frames used to represent a dynamic event. For example, in the upper panel of Figure 14.9, a kangaroo's hop is displayed with low granularity by using only four frames (prepare – jump – fly – land) whereas in the lower panel, the hop is displayed at a higher granularity by a series of eight frames. With the low granularity depiction, the viewer must make extensive inferences about the kangaroo's transformation between one key frame state and the next. With a higher granularity, the need for such

FIGURE 14.9. Visual display of a kangaroos hop with low granularity by a series of 4 static pictures (top) and with high granularity by a series of 8 static pictures. The low granularity display requires more inferences, but is more realistic with regard to the length of the hop. The reduction of inferential requirements by a higher granularity display is obtained at the expense of its representational function, and vice versa.

inferences is reduced because more information about incremental changes involved in the transformations is available to be read directly from the display. However, there is a trade-off here in which reduction of the inference problem occurs at the expense of distorting of spatial reality. This is because the larger number of adjacent frames makes the hop appear much longer than it really is. Varying the number of frames in this way means that a benefit gained in terms of inference is obtained at the expense of a representational cost, and vice versa. Furthermore, using a greater number of pictures can also make comparisons between specific key states more difficult. This is because the high granularity means that these states are more distant from each other with a consequent reduction of intra-pictorial spatial contiguity (cf. Mayer, 2001; Sweller, Paas, and van Merrienboer, 1998). Using an animation instead of a series of static pictures would prevent the types of representational problem raised here. However, the transient nature of an animation has the negative consequence of making comparisons between states much more difficult. This difficulty arises because only one state at a time can be perceived directly in the visual display so that any other state to be used for comparison has to be retrieved from long-term memory (Lowe, 1999a). The transient nature of an animation can thus pose considerable challenges, especially for learners who lack background knowledge about the depicted subject matter.

How realistic should animations be in order to best serve learners' needs? Because designers like to take advantage of latest cutting-edge developments to simulate reality as closely as possible, animations are frequently highly realistic. However, the quest for a high degree of visuo-spatial realism (degree of spatial detail) and behavioral realism (degree of temporal detail) is not necessarily advantageous for learning. Animations with a high degree of spatial and temporal detail run the risk of learners failing to extract information relevant to the construction of high quality dynamic mental model. This risk is likely to be particularly severe for learners who lack domain-appropriate background knowledge. The question of how much detail should be included in an animation depends on the instructional objective and the target audience. If the aim is to develop an understanding of the causal functioning of a complex device and if the learners being targeted lack relevant prior knowledge, a simplified display with low spatial and temporal detail is likely to be better than a highly realistic display. This was demonstrated for static pictures by Dwyer (1978) and also seems likely be the case with animated pictures. However, if the aim is to prepare learners to interact with real life environments, at some stage they will need to work with displays whose degree of realism is sufficient to ground the learner's conceptual knowledge in the world as it is normally perceived.

Cognitive Processing

We assume that when learners try to understand an animation (as opposed to merely perceive it), they engage in the cognitive task of constructing a mental model of the depicted content. To be effective, the nature of the mental model so constructed should reflect the nature of the content being represented (a static model for static content or a dynamic model for dynamic content). Whereas perceptual processing is largely pre-attentive and bottom-up, cognitive processing is attentive and depends on learner intentions as well as prior knowledge. It includes both bottom-up processes and top-down processes that are driven by cognitive schemas in which the individual's prior knowledge is implemented (Kintsch, 1998; Neisser, 1976).

Because cognitive schemas represent spatially and temporally invariant patterns on a higher level of abstraction than perceptual schemas, these higher order schemas can be used to construct dynamic mental models of behaviors or events. As a result, complex activities such as visiting a restaurant can be understood with the help of a cognitive schema (or 'script') consisting of a set of hierarchically organized sub-schemas. In this restaurant example, these sub-schemas deal with the various behaviors that patrons exhibit during their visit (Schank & Abelson, 1977). Central to the process by which understanding develops in this type of situation is the construction of a coherent dynamic mental model consisting of a hierarchically structured sequence of behavioral chunks (e.g., being seated, ordering, etc.). An animation displaying dynamic content provides explicit spatial and temporal information about the referent behavior or event that is, in principle at least, available to be used for the construction of a dynamic mental model. Mental model construction can be considered as a schema-driven structure mapping process in which perceived spatial-temporal patterns in the animation are mapped onto spatial-temporal patterns in the mental model (Gentner, 1983; Schnotz, 1993).

Spatial and Temporal Inferences

When viewing static pictures, we often make spatial inferences about things outside the displayed spatial frame (Lowe, 1994). For example when viewing a snapshot of some cyclists competing in the Tour de France, we assume that the street they are racing along will continue beyond the section shown, and that other riders outside of the current picture frame would be positioned in front of and behind the displayed cyclists. Similarly, we make temporal inferences about events that precede or succeed the currently displayed events. For example, we assume that the cyclists shown riding along the street when the picture was taken would have been riding through another part of the route some minutes before. Our capacity to make such temporal inferences also allows us to use static pictures for constructing dynamic mental models, as was already demonstrated by the pictogram of a tennis player in Figure 14.1. It is important to note that these cycling and tennis examples relate to simple, everyday subject matter for which specialist background knowledge is not required in order to make the necessary temporal inferences. However, if a static graphic is complex and portrays specialized subject matter, novices in the depicted domain are unlikely to make appropriate inferences because they lack background knowledge about the wider temporal context (see Lowe, 1996).

Dynamic inferences that people make about objects on the basis of static pictures are often constrained by intrinsic front-to-back orientation cues in the shape of these objects, and by the individual's prior knowledge. For example, we know that most animals (kangaroos, lizards, sharks, etc.) move in the direction their head is facing, and that inanimate objects such as rockets fly in the direction of their pointed ends. Thus, even without explicit dynamic information, we can infer that the movement of these items will most likely be in a particular direction relative to their structure (Lowe & Pramono, 2006). Although these generalized inferences can occasionally be erroneous (crabs typically move sideways, ant lions mostly move backwards), they are usually a best guess across a broad class of objects. Prior knowledge also allows us to infer changes of size and form as, for example, in the growth of plants.

When learners see an animation, it is no longer necessary for them to make some of these inferences about changes over time because the changes are shown explicitly. It follows that animations reduce the need to make temporal inferences, something which may be especially difficult for some learners.

However, animations can also make other cognitive processes more difficult. With a static picture, learners can repeatedly interrogate the visual display at their own pace in order to extract and understand all relevant information. In contrast, animations are transient displays and their fleeting nature means that the processing regime involved is intrinsically more demanding. If different states from a dynamic sequence are to be compared (Lowe, 1999a), the processing demands imposed by animations can be far greater than imposed by static depictions of those states. This is because the learner has either to hold the previous state in working memory or to retrieve the previous state from long-term memory in order to make the required comparison with the subsequent state. Comparison of different states can therefore be more difficult with their successive presentation via an animation than with their simultaneous presentation via a static display.

Although animations have the advantage over static pictures of reducing the need for temporal inferences, some temporal inferences beyond those events that are explicitly depicted in the animation may be required for mental model construction, especially if the animation is not fully realistic with regard to its temporal aspects. As already mentioned, a high degree of behavioral realism is not necessarily advantageous for learning. If an animation were to be fully realistic in terms of its behavior, key aspects of the presented dynamic material may be difficult to extract because of a perceptually inappropriate depiction speed or because they are swamped by other low relevance dynamic information. This suggests that presenting animations at non-realistic speeds could facilitate the building of high-quality mental models. One possibility is that a very fast process containing key information for mental model construction would be made more accessible and given more emphasis by presenting the process more slowly than it really happens (temporal 'zooming-in'). Alternatively, very slow processes could be speeded up (temporal 'zooming-out') in order to make the changes more apparent and activate the learner's cognitive schemas. Further, long periods of a process during which little new information is provided could be abbreviated by omitting the least informative parts and condensing the process into a more parsimonious and efficient representation. For example, instead of showing the full 10 minutes of hand pumping required to inflate a tire, an animation could be restricted to representing just a few token strokes. This condensation would be sufficient to represent the whole process and trigger the construction of a perfectly satisfactory dynamic mental model in which omitted parts of the process were readily inferred by the learner on the basis of prior knowledge. The perceptual information provided by an animation therefore does not always need to correspond to a strict one-to-one mapping with the real process it depicts. If learners are able to make inferences based on their prior knowledge, they should be able to construct a satisfactory mental model despite being provided with graphic information that has undergone substantial temporal manipulation.

The reason why animations are not inherently better than static depictions for the construction of dynamic mental models seems to be closely related to the nature of these models. As we have already mentioned, we do not consider dynamic mental models to consist of an endless series of 'mental snapshots' with high temporal granularity. Rather, we assume that these models are constructed from specific key states. Recall that the continuous flux of states can be segmented into meaningful units, and that each of these can be represented by the most typical (or key) state within the corresponding event. Key states capture a maximum of relevant information about their corresponding events and are mentally represented as cognitive schemas in long-term memory. They are easier to encode in long-term memory than a fuller representation of the dynamic referent and are subsequently easier to retrieve. They are therefore especially useful for the reconstruction of the whole sequence of states and events from memory. In other words, key states serve a framework role for the construction of dynamic mental models or for the mental simulation of the referent events by running the mental model.

From this perspective, it is therefore quite possible that a series of static pictures could sometimes be a better basis for constructing a dynamic mental model than an animation. This of course relies on the learner being equipped with the prior knowledge necessary to infer and interpolate the required further information. Static pictures of key states can be considered as ultimately condensed temporal chunks that can be used to construct or reconstruct the corresponding dynamic mental model of the whole sequence of states and events. When detailed comparisons between different states within a process are less important, the use of an animation seems to be more advantageous. In this case, the key states within the process can also be signaled to the observer by having the animation stop at appropriate frames. This should be beneficial when deeper interrogation of those especially informative states within the whole sequence is required. Pauses in an animation should therefore be placed strategically to facilitate such intensive processing where it is required. These pauses could not only help the learner to subdivide the animation into meaningful parts, but could also provide some time for a 'cognitive wrap-up' in the process of mental model construction. As Mayer and Chandler (2001) have shown, inclusion of pauses can significantly reduce the extraneous cognitive load of understanding an animation and so enhance learning. When working memory is not yet ready for the input of further information, displaying the animation too quickly would force the learner to ignore some of the visual information.

Pictorial and Verbal Guidance of Cognitive Processing

We have seen that the transitory nature of animations can make their processing especially demanding in terms of precisely where and when the learner's attention must be focused. It follows that using an appropriate pace of presentation, shaping learners' cognitive processing, and guiding of their strategies for directing visual attention are extremely important in learning from animation.

Both pictorial and verbal guidance have the potential to influence the cognitive processing that occurs during learning from animation. Pictorial guidance typically involves manipulating the animated display in order to produce bottom-up effects on perceptual processing. In learning from visuals, the information extracted from the display at the level of perceptual processing provides the raw material upon which mental model construction is ultimately based. The perceptual qualities of an animation can support the construction of an adequate mental model if they steer the learner's attention to relevant information. However, the perceptual qualities can also hinder mental model construction if the attentional cues they provide do not correspond with the thematic relevance of the information. One can assume that when pre-attentive perceptual processing results in a spatial-temporal structure that is consistent with the structure of the required mental model, the process of constructing that mental model and subsequent comprehension of the referent will be facilitated. In other words, the perceptual characteristics of an animation should ideally be aligned as closely as possible with the conceptual requirements of mental model construction. Pictorial guidance of conceptual processing in learning from animation can employ types of approaches for directing viewer attention that are similar to those used in static pictures. These include the use of arrows, circles, boxes, and other forms of signaling that make relevant aspects more salient. However, animations can also take advantage of additional cueing opportunities such as the use of dynamic contrast to guide the learner's visual attention, or the stopping of an animation at key states as mentioned above.

If the perceptibility of information and its thematic relevance are poorly aligned, learners who are novices (and therefore lack background knowledge about the depicted domain) can have difficulties in locating the informative regions and in detecting the crucial changes that occur within those regions

(Lowe, 1993). Their lack of knowledge prevents them from top-down direction of attention to what is thematically relevant rather than to what is perceptually salient. Instead, their exploration is dominated by bottom-up processing with their visual attention tending to be attracted by features that are perceptually conspicuous, irrespective of their actual thematic relevance. As a result, their cognitive processing will be driven primarily by the perceptual attributes of the display and these are likely to be a poor basis upon which to construct the required dynamic mental model. In contrast, domain experts can invoke knowledge-based top-down processing so that they are less subject to inappropriate influences from perceptual salience. Background knowledge allows them to direct their exploration productively and to concentrate on information of high thematic relevance regardless of its perceptual salience. Accordingly, domain experts' exploration and cognitive processing is more likely to be strategic.

Another type of pictorial guidance for cognitive processing is the use of animation to reveal the segmentation of a complex object by assembling the object from its parts. In this case, guidance of cognitive processing corresponds to a pictorial given-new-strategy. As Haviland and Clark (1974) have shown for verbal communication, an author or speaker continuously signals to his/her listeners or readers by his/her utterances about what they already know (i.e., what is 'given') and what aspects they should elaborate with new information. Similarly, an animation that shows the assembly of a complex object from its parts signals the observer as to what is already 'given' and what is 'new.' The parts that have already been introduced by the animation are presented as static objects, whereas new parts are introduced and added to the assembly by moving them into the picture.

As well as being influenced by pictorial guidance, cognitive processing in learning from animation can also be influenced by verbal guidance through accompanying descriptions or directions. For example, descriptive accompaniments such as 'In this animation, you see . . . ', or directive instructions such as 'Look in the top left-hand corner the animation and observe . . . ' can provide verbal guidance for cognitive processing of thematically relevant information. Whereas verbal guidance of perceptual processing will focus on the visual aspects of the display, verbal guidance of conceptual processing will focus on the understanding of more fundamental semantic relationships. This guidance should be given by synchronized spoken text rather than by a written text in order to avoid splitting visual attention and to maximize temporal contiguity so as to benefit from the modality effect in multimedia learning (Mayer, 2001, 2005; Sweller, 1999).

USER-CONTROLLABLE ANIMATIONS

With static pictures, individuals have great freedom to regulate their own learning because they can control the sequence in which they process information, the continuity of that processing, and its pace. With conventional 'fixed-play' (system controlled) animations, the situation is very different. When the display system controls the presentation of information rather than the user, the learner is faced with processing the information under an externally imposed regime. In this situation, learner control over processing is very limited because aspects such as sequencing, continuity, and pace are predetermined. One way to give learners more freedom to shape their processing is to provide user-controllable animations (Narayanan & Hegarty, 1998). It is easy to equip an animation with facilities such as a set of video-like controls that allow individual learners to alter the playing regime. More advanced techniques provide further opportunities for learners to interrogate animations and interact with them in a variety of ways. For example, learners can be given the opportunity to zoom in and out on various regions of the display while the animation is in progress, or click hotspots that alter the course of its presentation. Compared to system-controlled animations which present a sequence of frames just once with a fixed set of play parameters, user controllable animations offer far greater flexibility in perceptual and cognitive processing. In this respect, it seems that user control has the potential to make learning from animation less challenging and more effective by providing a level of freedom far closer to what individuals have in learning from static pictures.

Advantages of User Control

If the presentation rate of an animation is too high or too low, the dynamic information it contains lies beyond the upper or lower limits of the learner's perceptual capacity. In these cases, the relevant information is simply not perceived and the learner is unable to acquire the raw material necessary for further cognitive processing and mental model construction. However, even if the presentation rate of an animation is well within the limits of perceptual capacity, the learner may still be challenged. This is because the limited capacity of the cognitive processing system constrains the amount of information that can be processed per unit time. If the presentation rate is too high so that excessive information is presented within a specific time interval, the learner must be selective about which information to process in order to align information extraction with processing capacity (Lowe, 2001). User control offers learners the possibility to manipulate an animation's display rate in order to adapt the presentation regime to processing capacity limits. In an extreme case, control of playing speed can convert the dynamic presentation into a series of static pictures that can be explored individually in a stepwise manner in order to extract their visuo-spatial detail.

The density of relevant information can vary considerably throughout the course of an animation. During some periods of the animation, the amount of information that needs to be extracted may be well within the limits of processing capacity, whereas during other periods the amount of information may exceed what can be processed within the time available. User control provides learners the opportunity to vary the intensity with which they interrogate different segments of an animation. Segments of low relevance can be skipped or glossed over by fast-forwarding through the material, whereas segments of high relevance can be given intense scrutiny. If segments are so dense with information that it is impossible to extract everything of relevance in a single pass, the learner can play through these segments repeatedly. In this way, learners can concentrate their processing on those periods of the animation that contain information of most relevance to the learning task.

By allowing learners to play through an animation several times, user control provides them with the opportunity to extract information cumulatively. This possibility for revisiting information repeatedly gives the learner a processing advantage similar to that offered by static pictures. However, simply making repeated passes through an animation with the same playing speed is not necessarily a good strategy for learning. Animations usually contain multiple levels of dynamic information due to the hierarchical embedding of micro-events within macro-events. The relative perceptibility of information at these different levels varies according to the rate at which it is presented. At higher playing speeds, the macro-dynamic information tends to become more conspicuous, whereas at lower playing speeds, the micro-dynamic information becomes more salient (Lowe, 2006). In other words, different playing speeds would produce different profiles of perceptual salience that in turn may influence the level of information likely to be attended to by the learner. Multiple playings of an animation at different speeds therefore have the potential to reveal different levels of the overall dynamic structure. Merely playing an animation repeatedly at the same speed may reveal little additional information, especially when the animation has a hierarchical multi-level structure. However, if an animation is played repeatedly but at different speeds, the learner has the opportunity to extract various levels of dynamic information and so construct a coherent, multi-layered dynamic mental model of the subject matter.

Strategic Use of Control

User control appears to offer various potential benefits for learning. However, simply providing a learner with a high degree of user control does not ensure that such control will be exercised to good effect. In order for user control to be of real educational benefit, learners must be able to exercise that control strategically and so use the available exploratory freedom effectively in a goal-directed manner. For example, consider the case in which a learner adapts the rate of information presentation to fit within the limits of human perceptual and cognitive capacities. This could be done by slowing down in segments with high information density and by speeding up in segments with low information density. However, this first requires that the learner is able to identify the informational characteristics and relative significance of these segments. Similarly, in order to benefit from repeated passes at different speeds through an animation with a multilayer dynamic information structure so as to make both macro-changes and micro-changes salient, the learner must be aware that the animation has a hierarchical structure and be able to interrogate this structure effectively.

For user control to benefit learning, it must be used strategically. Making decisions about how an animation should be used while engaging in learning from the animation and monitoring learning effectiveness compounds the demands on the learners' limited processing resources. Given that animations themselves may already be demanding on these resources, the processing capacity available would probably be insufficient to meet all requirements satisfactorily. This is especially likely for novices because they lack knowledge about the subject matter, often have only a limited repertoire of processing strategies, and may have difficulties in selecting interrogation strategies that are appropriate. These deficiencies are likely to limit their exploration of the animation and the range of their cognitive processing.

CONCLUDING REMARKS

The analysis presented in this chapter raises important issues about learning with animation for both research and educational practice. With regard to research, our analysis suggests that some of the recent approaches in the field of learning with graphics are based on unwarranted conceptual distinctions between static and animated depictions. It is unlikely that the research questions generated on the basis of these distinctions will prove very fruitful in advancing our understanding of how people learn with graphics. Too often, researchers and practitioners seem to use a simplistic characterization of static and animated pictures that limits their consideration of these representations to broad questions of relative educational effectiveness. This can generally be traced back to a preoccupation with differences in their external characteristics and associated technology. Our analysis suggests that it is very difficult to justify a sharp distinction between animation and static pictures from a psychological point of view. As a consequence, it is probably unhelpful to limit our consideration to broad brush issues such as whether learning from animations is inherently better than learning from static pictures (see also Tversky, Morrison, & Bétrancourt, 2002). In essence, what an animation does is to add a further dimension – the temporal one – to those that already need to be considered when learning from static pictures. This should be regarded as involving an extension of the factors that need to be considered in designing educational visualizations, not a move to a qualitatively different design space. It is certainly true that animations allow learners to perceive temporal changes directly from pictorial representations whereas with static pictures they are required to infer temporal changes. However, both kinds of depictions are processed by the same perceptual and cognitive system according to the same set of perceptual and cognitive principles. Human perceptual and cognitive processing capacities have developed over the course of our evolutionary history as an adaptation to a highly varied environment in which stable and changing stimuli co-exist and must be handled in a flexible yet coherent manner. Although animations tend to provide far more information than corresponding static pictures, the process of learning from animation is not therefore necessarily more demanding than the process of learning from static pictures. The level of processing capacity that is required ultimately depends on the extent to which a learner is equipped with task-appropriate perceptual and cognitive schemas. This, rather than whether the depiction is static or animated, is the key issue that should be taken into account when considering likely consequences for learning.

In current educational design practice, it is often the case that decisions about whether a static picture or an animation should be used in a learning resource are based primarily on the nature of the to-be-learned subject matter. On this basis, static graphics are considered appropriate for the presentation of non-dynamic content that requires the construction of static mental models but animations are preferred for dynamic content that requires the construction of dynamic mental models. However, our analysis has shown that it is not necessary for the dynamic character of the depiction to match the dynamic nature of the subject matter it represents. In fact, it is quite common to construct dynamic mental models from static pictures because we often cannot help making dynamic inferences on the basis of a static picture.

Conversely, animations can support the construction of static mental models as occurs when they are used to show either the decomposition of a complex object into its parts and sub-parts or the reverse process of composition. Generally speaking, there is no strict one-to-one relationship between the static or dynamic characteristics of the learning content and the use of static or animated pictures.

The characterization of animations and static pictures as two separate and inherently different classes of depiction is also unhelpful in terms of improving picture-based learning. Designers of learning environments should be less preoccupied with simplistic questions about whether to use animations or static pictures. Rather, they should focus their efforts on the fundamental educational design quality of pictures irrespective of whether they are dynamic or not. Because animations and static pictures have far more in common than is generally acknowledged, the generation of educationally effective animations does not require totally different design principles. The educational effectiveness of an animation depends on the same fundamental set of human information processing capacities that applies in the case of static pictures. Accordingly, the most crucial determinants of effectiveness for both animated and static graphics are specific details of the way a depiction is designed and used.

Making decisions about the design and use of visualizations can be a complex process in which a number of quite subtle factors need to be considered. For example, a series of static pictures may be a more suitable choice for supporting the construction of a dynamic mental model, provided that the learner can readily infer the states between the displayed key-frames. On the one hand, the simultaneous presentation of static key-frames has the advantage over animation of allowing direct comparisons between specific states. An animation does not permit such comparisons to be made directly so the task of relating temporally separated states implies a high cognitive load on working memory. The learner would have to hold a previous state in working memory or to retrieve it from long-term memory in order to make a comparison with the present state. On the other hand however, the simultaneous presentation of multiple key-frames could interfere with the representational function of the display because it has the consequence of showing the dynamic information in a distorted manner. If detailed comparisons of different states within a process are less important because the main emphasis is on the overall dynamic character of the information, the use of an animation can be more advantageous than a series of static pictures. However, in this case further constraints may come into play and these arise from the temporal nature of animated displays. Dynamic systems typically contain different levels of event structure that together constitute hierarchies of temporal patterns. These range from temporal micro-structures to temporal macro-structures, and depending on the speed of the display, different levels of the system's dynamics are emphasized. Animations need to be designed to align the perceptual and cognitive aspects of processing as closely as possible so that the most readily perceptible features of the display are also those of most relevance to building the required mental model. Further, due to the fluent nature of animation, learners must direct their visual attention to the right place at the right time to ensure that high relevance information is noticed and extracted from the display. This requires not only that the attentional cues given by an animation are properly aligned with what is thematically relevant, but also that additional (e.g., verbal) support is provided to guide perceptual and cognitive processing. Because the information animations present is transitory, perceptual and cognitive processing costs are imposed on the learner. As we have seen, there are also processing costs associated with the use of static pictures. Media designers therefore need to make decisions based on principled trade-offs of the relative costs and benefits of using these visualization possibilities.

Because animations and static pictures have far more in common than is generally supposed, we can suggest that instructional design principles found to be successful with static pictures could also be applied to animations. For example, analogies can be made between the types of *visuospatial manipulations* that are used in static pictures to emphasize details of objects by magnification or visual cueing, and *temporal manipulations* of animations that could be used to emphasize details of events by changing the presentation speed, direction, and continuity. In both cases, the principle involved is to align display of information more closely with the capacities of the learner's perceptual and cognitive system. Well-designed static pictures display information in ways that ensure the perceptual gestalts are closely aligned with the conceptual structures required to build an adequate mental model. If the perceptual gestalts and the conceptual structures correspond, comprehension is facilitated because there is a good fit between the perceptually driven bottom-up processing and the concept-driven top-down processing. With static pictures, the graphic manipulations used are directed at visuospatial characteristics of the display but the same basic principle can also be extended to the depiction of change in animations. In this case, the design should take account of not only visuospatial characteristics of the display, but also its temporal characteristics in order to align perceptual and conceptual processing. Generally speaking, our integrated approach suggests that fundamental principles for designing educational animations should have much in common with principles for designing static educational pictures. These latter principles have emerged from informal practitioner experimentation and accumulated experience with static graphics and have been used successfully for hundreds of years because they obviously fit well with the capacities of human information processing. In order to enhance knowledge acquisition from animations, we should learn from this legacy and find ways to apply and adapt the design principles that evolved with static graphics to the dynamic context of animated presentations.

In designing static educational pictures, the economy with which the subject matter is presented to learners can be a key contributor to instructional effectiveness (Dwyer, 1978). One approach for helping learners to concentrate on the features of most relevance to a particular learning task is to omit everything else. This can be regarded as a form of visuospatial minimalism in the design of static graphics, perhaps somewhat akin to Tufte's (1983) suggestion about maximizing the data-ink ratio. The basic principle of minimalism can also be applied to the design of animations in terms of their temporal characteristics. For example, animations do not have to be made as realistic as possible by including all details of the subject matter's dynamics. Rather, an animation could be selective and omit temporal details that are not strictly necessary for building the requisite mental model. A general rule might be that nothing in the display should change over time that does not have a relevant representational and attention-directing function. However, because we consider animations and static pictures as not fundamentally different in processing terms, this principle could be restated as follows: The display of an instructional animation should include as little dynamic contrast as possible and only as much dynamic contrast as necessary. We can see this as paralleling the established principle in static graphics of minimizing visuospatial contrast when it serves no supportive function, but using such contrast strategically when it serves to cue thematically relevant information.

Too many designers of educational materials are also easily seduced by the glamour of the latest cutting-edge developments in information and communications technology. Given the rapid advances in hardware and software for producing animations, it is perhaps not surprising that current approaches to developing educational animations rely mainly on the intuition of designers rather than on research-based principles derived from empirical investigations of how people actually learn with animations. One possibility for taking a more principled approach to the design process would be to require rigorous specification of proposed educational visualizations before any work starts on production. Such a specification should be based on a thorough analysis of the subject matter, careful identification of key states that could be central components of the learners' developing mental models, and informed consideration of possible perceptual and cognitive processing consequences of alternative design options. The more rigorously such analysis, identification, and consideration are undertaken, the more constraints are likely to be available to guide effective visualization (cf. Kosslyn, 1989).

One of the more recent developments in multimedia learning environments is the inclusion of user-controllable animation. Compared with a system-controlled animation that presents a dynamic sequence just once with a fixed presentation regime, a user controllable animation offers great presentational flexibility. User control allows learners to manipulate parameters such as an animation's display rate in order to match the presentations regime to their own individual processing capacities. However, for such a facility to benefit mental model construction, learners must be able to exploit these possibilities properly by exercising the available control in a strategic manner. This need for strategic interrogation of the animation means that user control makes its own demands on the learner's processing capacity. It is unlikely that domain novices would be able to exercise appropriate exploration strategies when provided with user-controllable animation unless they are give appropriate support. The notion that giving learners complete control of an instructional animation will be beneficial for learning, especially if it deals with complex and unfamiliar subject matter, therefore seems seriously misguided. An alternative would be to implement a constrained form of user control that is carefully tailored to the learner's prior knowledge and information processing capacities. The constraints could include design features such as allowing only a limited range of options with respect to the animation's display speed rather than allowing continuously variable control over this aspect. For example, different set speeds could be made available at different times to enable learners to extract different levels of dynamic information from the subject matter at different stages of the learning process. Constraints could also be placed on the temporal segmentation of the subject matter by limiting the number and nature of sub-sequences from the animation that can be played. For example, fostering strategic exploration by the learner may require an animation to stop automatically at particular key frames, or to single out key events that need to be interrogated more intensively because they are especially informative. Design of user controllable animations needs to balance the possibilities of free exploration with the constraints on the learner's prior knowledge and processing capacities by putting appropriate restrictions on the control as well as providing strategic guidance for its effective use.

Learning from animation is a two-edged sword that can have either positive or negative effects on learning. It is neither inherently superior to learning from other kinds of depiction nor does it generally impair learning. Whether or not animation can be beneficial for learning depends on multiple subtle constraints that are related to the functioning of the perceptual and cognitive system, the expertise of the learner, and the desired educational outcomes. Effective design and use of animations for learning cannot therefore be based on intuition or simple rules-of-thumb. Rather, it requires a deeper understanding of how visual displays interact with the perceptual and cognitive system and how dynamic information can be most closely aligned with the requirements of the human information processing system. It will be crucial for the success of research on learning from animation to ask the right questions within an adequate conceptual framework for visual communication of knowledge.

References

Baddeley, A. (1992). Working memory. *Science, 255*, 556–559.

Baek, Y. K. & Layne, B. H. (1988). Color, graphics, and animation in a computer-assisted learning tutorial lesson. *Journal of Computer-based Instruction, 15*, 131–135.

Bétrancourt, M. & Tversky, B. (2000). Effects of computer animation on users' performance: A review. *Le Travail Humain, 63*, 311–330.

Bodemer, D., Ploetzner, R., Feuerlein, I., & Spada, H. The active integration of information during learning with dynamic and interactive visualizations. *Learning and Instruction, 14*, 325–341.

Brewer, W. F. & Nakamura, G. V. (1984). The nature and functions of schemas. In R. S. Wyer & T. K. Srull (Eds.), *Handbook of social cognition, Vol. 1* (pp. 119–160). Hillsdale, N.J.: Lawrence Erlbaum Associates.

Carpenter, P. A. & Just, M. A. (1981). Cognitive processes in reading: Models based on readers' eye fixations. In A. M. Lesgold & C. A. Perfetti (Eds.), *Interactive processes in reading* (pp. 177–213). Hillsdale, N.J.: Lawrence Erlbaum Associates.

Dwyer, F. M. (1978). *Strategies for improving visual learning*. Pennsylvania: Learning Services.

Gentner, D. (1983). Structure-mapping: A theoretical framework for analogy. *Cognitive Science, 7*, 155–170.

Graesser, A. C. (1978). How to catch a fish: The memory and representation of common procedures. *Discourse Processes, 1*, 72–89.

Hacker, W. (1986). *Arbeitspsychologie. Psychische Regulation von Arbeitstätigkeiten*. Berlin: VEB Deutscher Verlag der Wissenschaften.

Haviland, S. E. & Clark, H. H. (1974). What's new? Acquiring new information as a process in comprehension. *Journal of Verbal Learning and Verbal Behavior, 13*, 512–521.

Hegarty, M. (1992). Mental animation: Inferring motion from static diagrams of mechanical systems. *Journal of Experimental Psychology: Learning, Memory and Cognition, 18*, 1084–1102.

Hegarty, M., Narayanan, N. H., & Freitas, P. (2002). Understanding machines from multimedia and hypermedia presentations. In J. Otero, J. A. Leon, & A. Graesser (Eds.),

The psychology of science text comprehension (pp. 357–384). Hillsdale, NJ: Lawrence Erlbaum Associates.

Kintsch, W. (1998). *Comprehension. A paradigm for cognition.* Cambridge: Cambridge University Press.

Kosslyn, S. (1989). Understanding charts and graphs. *Applied Cognitive Psychology, 3,* 185–226.

Kosslyn, S. M. (1994). *Image and brain.* Cambridge, MA: MIT Press.

Lowe, R. K. (1993). Constructing a mental representation from an abstract technical diagram. *Learning and Instruction, 3,* 157–179.

Lowe, R. K. (1994). Selectivity in diagrams: reading beyond the lines. *Educational Psychology, 14,* 467–491.

Lowe, R. K. (1996). Background knowledge and the construction of a situational representation from a diagram. *European Journal of Psychology of Education, 11,* 377–397.

Lowe, R. K. (1999a). Extracting information from an animation during complex visual learning. *European Journal of Psychology of Education, 14,* 225–244.

Lowe, R. K. (1999b). Domain-specific constraints on conceptual change in knowledge acquisition from diagrams. In W. Schnotz, S. Vosniadou & M. Carretero (Eds.), *New perspectives on conceptual change* (pp. 223–245). Amsterdam: Elsevier.

Lowe, R. K. (2001). Understanding information presented by complex animated diagrams. In J-F. Rouet, J. J. Levonen, & A. Biardeau (Eds.), *Multimedia learning: Cognitive and instructional issues* (pp. 65–74). London: Pergamon.

Lowe, R. K. (2003). Animation and learning: Selective processing of information in dynamic graphics. *Learning and Instruction, 13,* 157–176.

Lowe, R. K. (2004). Interrogation of a dynamic visualization during learning. *Learning and Instruction, 14,* 257–274.

Lowe, R. K. (2005). Multimedia learning of meteorology. In R. E. Mayer (Ed.), *The Cambridge handbook of multimedia learning* (pp. 429–446). New York: Cambridge University Press.

Lowe, R. K. (2006). Changing perceptions of animated diagrams. In D. Barker-Plummer, R. Cox, & N. Swoboda (Eds.), *Diagrammatic representations and inference* (pp. 168–172). Berlin: Springer.

Lowe, R. K. & Pramono, H. (2006). Using graphics to support comprehension of dynamic information in texts. *Information Design Journal, 14,* 22–34.

Marey, E. J. (1874). *Animal mechanism: A treatise on terrestrial and aerial locomotion.* New York: Appleton and Co.

Mayer, R. E. (2001). *Multimedia learning.* New York: Cambridge University Press.

Mayer, R. E. (Ed.) (2005). *Cambridge Handbook of Multimedia Learning.* Cambridge: Cambridge University Press.

Mayer, R. E. & Chandler, P. (2001). When learning is just a click away. *Journal of Educational Psychology, 93,* 390–397.

Mayer, R. E. & Moreno, R. (1998). A split-attention effect in multimedia learning: evidence for dual processing systems in working memory. *Journal of Educational Psychology, 90,* 312–320.

Mayer, R. E. & Moreno, R. (2002). Animation as an aid to multimedia learning. *Educational Psychology Review, 14,* 87–99.

McCloud, S. (1994). *Understanding comics: The invisible art.* New York: Harper Perennial.

McNamara, T., Hardy, J., & Hirtle, S. (1989). Subjective hierarchies in spatial memory. *Journal of Experimental Psychology: Learning, Memory and Cognition, 15*, 211–227.

Moreno, R. & Mayer, R. E. (2002). Verbal redundancy in multimedia learning: When reading helps listening. *Journal of Educational Psychology, 94*, 156–163.

Narayanan, N. H. & Hegarty, M. (1998). On designing comprehensible interactive hypermedia manuals. *International Journal of Human-Computer Studies, 48*, 267–301.

Narayanan, N. H. & Hegarty, M. (2002). Multimedia design for communication of dynamic information. *International Journal of Human-Computer Studies, 57*, 279–315.

Neisser, U. (1976). *Cognition and reality.* San Francisco: Freeman.

Ohlsson, S. (1984a). Restructuring revisited. I. Summary and critique of the Gestalt theory of problem solving. *Scandinavian Journal of Psychology, 25*, 65–78.

Ohlsson, S. (1984b). Restructuring revisited. II. An information processing theory of restructuring and insight. *Scandinavian Journal of Psychology, 25*, 117–129.

Radach, R. & Kennedy, A. (2004). Theoretical perspectives on eye movements in reading: Past controversies, current issues, and an agenda for future research. *European Journal of Cognitive Psychology, 16*, 3–26.

Rosch, E. (1978). Principles of categorization. In E. Rosch & B. B. Lloyd (Eds.), *Cognition and categorization* (pp. 27–48). Hillsdale, N.J.: Lawrence Erlbaum Associates.

Salomon, G. (1994). *Interaction of media, cognition, and learning.* Hillsdale, NJ: Erlbaum.

Schank, R. C. & Abelson, R. P. (1977). *Scripts, plans, goals and understanding. An inquiry into human knowledge structures.* Hillsdale, N.J.: Erlbaum.

Schnotz, W. (1993). On the relation between dual coding and mental models in graphics comprehension. *Learning and Instruction, 3*, 247–249.

Schnotz, W. (2001). Sign systems, technologies, and the acquisition of knowledge. In J. F. Rouet, J. Levonen & A. Biardeau (Eds.), *Multimedia learning: Cognitive and instructional issues* (pp. 9–29). Amsterdam: Elsevier.

Schwan, S. & Riempp, R. (2004). The cognitive benefits of interactive videos: learning to tie nautical knots. *Learning and Instruction, 14*, 293–305.

Sekuler, R. & Blake, R. (1994). *Perception.* New York: McGraw-Hill.

Sims, V. K. & Hegarty, M. (1997). Mental animation in the visuospatial sketchpad: Evidence from dual-tasks studies. *Memory & Cognition, 25*, 321–332.

Sweller, J. (1999). *Instructional design in technical areas.* Camberwell, Australia: ACER Press.

Sweller, J. & Chandler, P. (1994). Why some material is difficult to learn. *Cognition and Instruction, 12*, 185–223.

Sweller, J., van Merriënboer, J. G., & Paas, F. G. W. C. (1998). Cognitive architecture and instructional design. *Educational Psychological Review, 10*, 251–296.

Taylor, H. A. & Tversky, B. (1992). Spatial mental models derived from survey and route descriptions. *Journal of Memory and Language, 31*, 261–292.

Tufte, E. R. (1983). *The visual display of quantitative information.* Cheshire, CT: Graphics Press.

Tversky, B., Morrison, J. B., & Bétrancourt, M. (2002). *Animation: Does it facilitate? International Journal of Human-Computer Studies, 57*, 247–262.

Ullman, S. (1984). Visual routines. *Cognition, 18*, 97–159.

Wertheimer, M. (1938). *Laws of organization in perceptual forms in a source book for Gestalt Psychology.* London: Routledge & Kegan Paul.

White, B. Y. & Horwitz, P. (1987). Thinkers Tools: Enabling children to understand physical laws. Report 6470. Bolt, Beranek & Newman Laboratories. Cambridge, MA.

Wright, P., Milroy, R., & Lickorish, A. (1999). Static and animated graphics in learning from interactive texts. *European Journal of Psychology of Education, 14*, 203–224.

Zacks, J. M. & Tversky, B. (2001). Event structure in perception and conception. *Psychological Bulletin, 127*, 3–21.

15

Animating the Issues for Research on Animation

Commentary on Sections Three and Four

Susan R. Goldman

Researchers of learning and designers of learning materials currently confront the reality of a public that is increasingly able to access information in multiple forms of media any time and almost any place. Trends in the availability of technology suggest that such widespread, nearly effortless information access will only continue, probably at accelerated rates (Alexander & Fox, 2004; Grabinger, Dunlap, & Duffield, 1997; Jones, 2002). Researchers of learning who take a cognitive perspective are exploring a variety of issues that focus on the processing, representation, understanding, and use of different forms and types of information by individuals who are at different developmental levels and who may differ with respect to various kinds of processing skill (e.g., spatial and verbal), capacity (e.g., attention, working memory), or knowledge. Designers of learning materials and environments in which they are embedded are concerned with the "wise" design and deployment of different forms of information resources. When should information be presented in print? With pictures? With dynamic displays such as videos or simulations? Of course, these are questions that researchers of learning and designers have been concerned with for a long time. The newest twist on these questions arises from the ubiquity of the World Wide Web and the increasing adoption of hand-held devices (e.g., iPods), making animations accessible virtually anytime and anyplace. Thus, a volume on animations is quite timely for purposes of taking stock of what we know about animations, learning that involves them, and the design of animations that support and assist learners in their efforts to make sense of information.

This particular volume on animations is a natural continuation of efforts by Lowe and Schnotz to understand representations of complex phenomena and how people use them in learning situations. The chapters as a whole provide a detailed look at animation from the perspective of its potential affordances for learning, what it takes to realize these affordances in designed animations, and what it takes for learners to capitalize on the affordances. The issues surrounding learning from animations and the design of animations that support learning have considerable overlap with those relevant to learning from other visual representation forms (e.g., static diagrams, pictures, tables). But there also appear to be unique aspects to animated representations that may present new issues for learning from them as well as design challenges that are relevant solely to animations. The body of work collected in this volume draws on the similarities to other forms of representation while concentrating on examining those things that might be specific to animations. The contributions in sections 1 and 2 examine processes and strategies for working with animations that have been observed in individuals of different ages and who have different levels of knowledge and skill relevant to the topic about which they are learning. Kirby (this volume) has provided discussion and commentary on these. This chapter focuses on the contributions in sections 3 and 4.

The chapters in sections 3, Interactivity in Learning, and 4, Instructional Issues, build on the rich theoretical perspectives and empirical data of the first two sections to consider some of the mechanisms that underlie effectiveness of animations in the context of the broader learning environments in which they are embedded. The contributions in sections 3 and 4 take on the challenge of understanding what kinds of animations, interactions, and guided learning experiences contribute to effective contexts for learning, individually and in combination. What becomes evident in reading the accumulated body of work is that there are more similarities between animations and other forms of visual representations than there are differences. Many of the same general principles for effective learning with animations and the design of animations that support effective learning are similar in broad strokes to those that hold for static representations. However, the way in which instruction and designed learning environments enact these principles is somewhat different for static as compared to dynamic visual animations.

A major goal of this commentary is to highlight the challenges for learning with dynamic visuals and for designing animations in ways that optimize their effectiveness. First, however, it is important to draw a conceptual distinction between two senses of animation because the research and design issues associated with each are quite different. The remainder of the commentary then focuses on what we know about learners' interactions with animations, the challenges we need to consider based on this research, and the lessons we have learned in our efforts to respond to the challenges. These lessons have important implications for theories of learning, multimedia learning, and the design of environments that support learning.

TWO SENSES OF ANIMATION

It is important to distinguish between two different senses of animation reflected in the set of chapters in sections 3 and 4: animations as embodied agents and animations as representations of content. Animated agents are pedagogical adjuncts to the content and are intended to support and guide the learner through the content. They are not themselves the content that is to be learned. Although only the chapter by Moreno focuses on this sense of animation, work on animated agents has important implications for the design of learning environments. Animations as content or representations of content is the dominant view on animations adopted by the remainder of the chapters in sections 3 and 4. I focus first on animated agents.

Animated Agents

Moreno discusses embodied pedagogical agents who are "live" in computer-based learning environments. These animated agents have a visible, physical presence in the environment. They provide input of various forms to learners, in some cases adapting that input to learners' responses. Some of the more well-known animated agents are *Autotutor* (Graesser, Wiemer-Hastings, Wiemer-Hastings, & Kreuz, 1999), *Steve* (Johnson, Rickel, & Lester, 2000), and *Herman* (Lester, Stone, & Stelling, 1999), the specific focus of the research reported in Moreno's chapter. Moreno's work reflects a highly systematic approach to understanding what elements of animations seem to be important for learners' engagement and improvements in learning. Across the environments she has investigated, Moreno has amassed compelling evidence regarding the importance of the voice of the agent but not the visual image of it, a finding echoed by other researchers (e.g., Baylor & Ryu, 2003). However, other research suggests that the interactivity of the agent and the coordination of eye gaze, voice, and gesture are critical issues in the effectiveness of embodied agents for engagement and learning (e.g., Cassell 2004; MacLeod, O'Day, Kehoe, Allende-Pellot, & Goldman, 2006; Ryokai, Vaucelle, & Cassell, 2003). Although Moreno's work could be interpreted as indicating that designers can reduce production costs of embedded agent environments and just use voice, this conclusion seems premature. Decisions about the value of visual embodiment must await more extensive testing in a wider set of learning environments and populations, specifically with respect to the kinds of processing embodied agent systems encourage on the part of learners. What Moreno's work does indicate is that animated agents have substantial value for engaging and guiding learners. To realize this potential across a broader range of learning environments and learners, collaborations between learning researchers and designers are needed.

Animations as Representations of Content

The second sense of animation is the concern of the bulk of the chapters in sections 3 and 4 and the focus of the remainder of my commentary: Animations as dynamic visuals that convey content information. Visuals are the essence of this kind of animation. Dynamic visuals are a means of portraying the phenomena that are the objects of study, learning, and understanding. They portray the content that learners are trying to make sense of by using dynamic visuals. These dynamic or "fluid visuals" and are often accompanied by verbal narratives (Hubscher-Younger & Narayanan, this volume). Schnotz and Lowe's brief historical overview of dynamic visuals reminds us that there are many forms of dynamic visualizations and that these have been "around" for a long time (this volume). Although it may first appear that there is a sharp, clean line between static and dynamic visualizations, the two are often different versions of one another. For example, in some learning environments, "animations" initially appear as static pictures until they are "put into motion" either automatically by the system in which they are embedded or under the control of the learner. Animations are simply a branch of the broader family of external graphic representations and take their place alongside static pictures, diagrams, graphs, and maps. Whether learners understand any of these representations and the content they depict depends on whether the learner has the knowledge and skills to "read" the representation; and if the representation can be read, whether the information supports task performance (Goldman, 2003). There may be differences between how the designers of animations conceive of them supporting task performance and the way learners actually "read" and interact with these animations. It only takes a few moments of reflection on how well – or poorly – the general public "reads" those wonderfully animated maps of weather systems that seem ubiquitous in television weather reporting to see the gap between how an animation is supposed to be read and how it is read.

In other words, concerns about the usefulness of animations overlap with concerns about graphic representations more generally, including issues of design, relationships to text, and differences in interpretation related to prior knowledge in the domain and to more general characteristics such as spatial ability. Indeed, Schnotz and Lowe (this volume) provide a compelling argument for a unified approach to static and dynamic visualizations. A key piece of their argument lies in the characteristics of the human perceptual and cognitive processing systems. Essentially, humans can mentally "animate" static pictures and they can focus in on, or isolate, "slices" of an ongoing dynamic visualization. The importance of a unified approach is that it moves the discourse about research and design – and the hypotheses and designs themselves – in a refreshing direction. In fact, what is refreshing about each of the chapters in sections 3 and 4 is the evident and thoughtful engagement with the complexity of understanding when, why, for whom, and under what conditions animations appear to facilitate learning. This is in contrast to the simplistic but often-made assumption that such media will be beneficial because they are more veridical to the actual phenomena to be understood and learned.

BEYOND SIMPLE QUESTIONS AND ANSWERS

By embracing the complexity of animations and attempting to understand their use and role in learning, the work in these chapters moves us away from "magic bullet" answers to questions about how we can improve learning. This is a good thing. Too often simple answers have created inappropriate expectations regarding the benefits of new technologies and materials for learning outcomes. The answers to such questions – and there is not just one answer – have to come from more sophisticated understanding of characteristics of effective learning *environments* not just of the particular kind of material in the learning environment. It isn't that text with animations is better – or worse – than text without animations; or that animations are better – or worse – than static pictures. The questions must focus on how the learner interacts with the material and whether that interaction achieves processes and outcomes that are meaningful to the learner and have the potential to advance the learner's understanding of the topic.

In many ways, the idea that the key to animation effectiveness is whether learners interact meaningfully and productively with them is another instantiation of the "active learner" principle that permeates contemporary instructional theory. Ever since the cognitive revolution in the early 1960s we have been aware of the need for learners to actively engage with the material they are trying to learn. It is not difficult to make this assertion. It is difficult to determine what *kinds* of interactions for what kinds of learners produce meaningful content understanding. Animations somehow seem to seduce us into believing that they inherently create an interactivity that is productive for the learner and allows the learner to actively build the intended or desired explanatory models of the content to be learned. Yet the research base informs us that few, if any, dynamic visuals create transparent explanations of system functioning. In fact, a dynamic visual may make it more difficult to understand the explanatory principles of a system. Tversky (this volume), Rogers (this volume), and Schnotz and Lowe (this volume) remind us of the inappropriateness of equating dynamism in a visual with a dynamic visualization and the presence of a dynamic representation with dynamic processing of it on the part of learners. Learners can passively watch animations just as they can passively listen to lectures, read text, and look at diagrams. And even if they actively engage with a dynamic visual, the underlying explanatory mechanisms may not be emergent for the learners.

At issue then is what meaningful and productive interactions might be. The chapters in sections 3 and 4 deeply engage this question. They probe what it means for learners to interact productively with dynamic representations and how productive interactions can be facilitated by the design of the representations (and of the animated agents), and the guidance provided by the system in which the animations are embedded. For example, Tversky and colleagues (this volume) review an impressive set of results from their work on both static and dynamic representations. They argue compellingly that although dynamic representations show "systems in action" there is little reason to believe that watching the system in action will enable understanding of how it functions. Indeed, if learners engage in something more than passive watching, they may not focus on the most informative elements of the animation or the animation may move too quickly for the learner to achieve understanding. They suggest that just as with static representations, animations may need to be "parsed," or spotlighted, for learners. This might be done by animated agents or by augmenting dynamic visuals with attention-directing mechanisms such as arrows or highlights. In the case of maps, Tversky and colleagues have shown the value of using map insets and other forms of distortions in size to focus attention on critical elements of static representations.

Based on research in a number of domains and across a number of kinds of text and diagrammatic materials (Chi, de Leeuw, Chiu, & LaVancher, 1994; Coté & Goldman, 1999; Coté, Goldman, & Saul, 1998; McNamara, Kintsch, Songer, & Kintsch, 1996), we can expect that active processing of animations in which learners explain or self-explain the causal and functional mechanisms of the phenomena will lead to better learning. However, despite the inclusion of adjuncts such as "pointers" or highlighters, or animated agents that mediate pointing and highlighting, there are a number of challenges that learners face in processing animations meaningfully.

CHALLENGES TO LEARNING WITH ANIMATIONS

Dynamic visual representations present several challenges that are not present in static representations. Some of these challenges are constraints set by the human cognitive architecture. In particular, attentional resources are limited and complex representations – dynamic or static – require that there be selective and directed attentional allocation. For example, in dynamic representations of complex systems there are frequently many dimensions of the representation that change simultaneously (Boucheix, this volume; Rogers, this volume; Schnotz & Lowe, this volume; Tversky et al., this volume). Learners must figure out what to watch, which changes are meaningful and important to system functioning, and how changes in one part of the system are – or are not – temporally or causally related to changes in other parts of the system. Attention must be allocated to appropriately address each of these facets of animations. Tversky summarizes these challenges with three "aphorisms for animations": Seeing isn't perceiving; Perceiving isn't understanding; and Showing isn't explaining (Tversky et al., this volume). Being presented with an animation does not mean that appropriate and relevant aspects of the animation will be the ones noticed. Even if the appropriate and relevant aspects are noticed they may not be understood. Even if they are understood – in isolation or in relation to one another, understanding how the perceptually available parts of a phenomenon are related does not explain why they are related in that way. Often the *why* simply cannot be shown and is only available through verbally mediated or transmitted information regarding forces not visible in a representation. For example, in data we have collected on understanding causal models of plate tectonics, we find that learners can watch an animation in which one plate moves under another to create a subduction zone but they are not able to explain why it happens (Goldman et al., 2004; Singer, Radinsky, & Goldman, in press). This occurs among students whose gestures indicate that they are actively processing the movement when they see the animation and can re-enact it days after they watch it. But their explanations for the causal mechanisms reflect partial, faulty, or no understanding of the causal mechanisms of subduction. This is because what sets plates in motion lies outside the dynamic visual that illustrates subduction, namely heat currents in the mantle of the Earth's core. Thus subduction can be "shown" in a dynamic visual but its explanation is not emergent merely from seeing the two plates collide and subduct.

Boucheix (this volume) extends the landscape of challenges related to attentional limitations by examining prior knowledge and ability requirements. He refers to a general "mismatch" challenge. The mismatch refers to the gap or distance between what is required to understand the animation as designed and intended and learners characteristics in three areas. Do the ways in which learners perceive and attend to the animation match what is needed? Do learners bring the requisite knowledge to their processing of animations? Do learners have spatial ability sufficient for them to follow the animation? If there is a mismatch between processing requirements of animations and learners' capacities, animations will not be helpful. Boucheix appeals to four areas of mismatch, two related to architectural constraints, perceptual and attentional; one related to prior knowledge, conceptual; and one to the ability to follow the animation, spatial ability. In investigating these potential sources of mismatch he examines learning situations in which learners have more control over how they view animations as compared to less or no control. Boucheix manipulates control over the animation by providing learners with options for regulating the running of the animation, that is, stop action, replaying, and so on. Interestingly, he found that learners' success at using these animation regulators was itself limited by prior knowledge in the domain. For low domain knowledge individuals, learning while controlling the animation was not as good as when it was played for them. Low knowledge learners were also helped by cues that pointed them to what to attend to in the animation. However, for high domain knowledge learners, cues and external control led to the poorest learning.

The interaction between conditions that lead to better learning for high versus low knowledge individuals parallels the work in text comprehension (McNamara et al., 1996). In that work, the surprising finding was that readers who were high knowledge in the domain learned more deeply when they had to fill in gaps in the text information by making inferences. In contrast, readers who possessed relatively little domain knowledge learned more with texts in which they did not have to fill in gaps. A general principle emerging from the high/low knowledge patterns is that it is better to do the inference work that is needed to construct a meaningful and coherent representation than it is to have it done for you *provided you have the knowledge to construct the coherence.* If you do not have the requisite knowledge, as is the case with most low domain knowledge learners, external help is needed. The "external" help can be "in" the content and structure of the materials, in cues or prompts that guide the construction of coherence, or in agents, animated or otherwise, who interact with and scaffold learners as they attempt to make sense of the information. The underlying principle regarding knowledge and knowledge acquisition is fundamentally an issue of the sense-making you are able to do based on what you know at the time you are interacting with whatever is to be learned. If learners have the knowledge needed to create the understanding themselves, they learn better by performing this creation than if they are "given" or told what to understand. However, if learners lack the knowledge they are severely hampered in understanding unless some kind of external source mediates the learning process.

OVERCOMING CHALLENGES FOR LEARNING WITH ANIMATIONS

In addition to making us aware of the challenges for understanding posed by animations, all of these chapters attempt to address these challenges and ask how animations can improve or impact learning, despite limitations that may exist in learners' capacities, knowledge, and abilities. Some of chapters discuss ways in which animations can be presented to increase the likelihood that learners will notice or process the key functional principles. For example, Tversky et al. (this volume) suggest that "stepping through" the operation of a dynamic system can be quite helpful to learners, much as directional arrows and picture sequences are helpful when static picture sequences are used to capture dynamic processes. In this regard, Rogers (this volume) suggests that animation designers employ a componential approach to dynamic representations to mitigate the high cognitive processing demands. She advocates the use of simple animations of specific processes or features of a system over depicting "all the interdependent processes of a system at the same time." She makes the further interesting but speculative claim that "It can make it easier for the learners to focus their attention on the different aspects of a system and to gradually build up their knowledge of the system by integrating over time how the different components relate to one another." Although this seems intuitively plausible, it remains to be seen how well learners actually integrate information over time. It could turn out that integrating the operations of system components is quite a difficult process, much like blending individual phonemes to produce a word is difficult for young children learning to read. Indeed, Hubscher-Young and Narayanan (this volume) found that integrating across multiple static representations was difficult for students learning computer algorithms.

Rather than, or in addition to, more easily and effectively processed designs for animations, Moreno examined whether reducing demands on visual load through the use of visual and auditory input assists learners in processing animations. In several studies, she and colleagues found that learning was better when animations were seen and learners heard oral narrations of them as compared to animations accompanied by text containing the narration and which learners had to read. Listening while looking reduces the visual processing load and allows the learner to attend to two sources of complementary input at the same time. The parallel nature of the two inputs may make it easier for the two to be integrated. Moreno's work is also important in showing that guidance in the form of explanatory feedback facilitates learning. This finding, too, makes contact with a large body of work on the importance of explanation in understanding and learning (e.g., Bransford, Brown, & Cocking, 1999; Chi et al., 1994; Coté & Goldman, 1999; Coté et al., 1998; Graesser & Bertus, 1998).

At a more general level, these efforts to meet some of the challenges associated with learning from animations can be summarized in terms of whether they enable or facilitate learners' being able to capitalize on the enabling or facilitating affordances of animations, two functions detailed by Schnotz and Lowe (this volume). In other words, the kinds of manipulations featured in the research discussed in sections 3 and 4 enlighten us about the outcomes of various ways in which dynamic visuals can be presented, unpacked, or scaffolded. And the principles of effective learning environments that emerge from this research are strikingly similar to those that have emerged from work on other forms of visual representations (see Schnotz & Lowe, this volume). The perspectives adopted in these studies are those of researcher and designer rather than learner. But there are some interesting insights to be gained from adopting the perspective of learners on the visuals that appear in their learning materials and on those visuals that learners think would be helpful in learning.

LOOKING AT LEARNERS' VISUALS: SOME IMPORTANT INSIGHTS AND REMINDERS

One way to examine learners' perspectives on visuals is to look at the visuals and representations that they themselves produce. The assumption of this line of research appears to be that representations will be more meaningful and effective in promoting learning to the degree that they resemble the representations that learners create for themselves. As the research reported in this volume suggests, this is probably far too simple an assumption and the data arising from studies based on this assumption are difficult to apply to the improvement of learning environments. For example, Hübscher-Younger and Narayanan (this volume) examined the representations that learners created for algorithms that the authors claimed are amenable to animation. Although learners did create their own representations, they seemed to be guided by their ideas of conventional forms for representing the particular algorithm and they rarely included animations in their representations.

The lack of inclusion of animations in learners' generated representations can be explained in a variety of ways. First there is the possibility of a "generational" effect insofar as the participants in this research are less familiar with information displays that include lots of animation or dynamic visualizations. The representations they produced reflect the kinds of graphics they are used to seeing in instructional situations. A second possibility relates to the demand characteristics of tasks and the utility of animations for accomplishing them. For example, Tversky, Schnotz, Lowe, and others in this volume point out that a dynamic visualization may not be needed to understand a dynamic process. Learners may be able to animate a static representation mentally. When asked to produce a visual they produce a static representation.

There are also two other explanations for visuals that learners produce being less informative to the design of animations for learning than might be expected initially. The first takes us back to the issue of knowledge. If the learners are novices and beginners with little domain knowledge, dynamic visualizations may not be helpful in supporting learning. Simply put, learners may not have sufficient knowledge in the domain to capitalize on the affordances of dynamic visuals. Thus when presented they do not find them helpful. When asked to produce visuals for learning they do not produce them. The impact of domain knowledge on choice of helpful scaffolds resonates with a point made by Spiro in discussing cognitive flexibility theory: "Criss-crossing the landscape" of the domain is a useful learning strategy for those who have at least an intermediate amount of knowledge on the topic. However, novices and beginners need a clear path through the landscape – one that supports learners in creating a representation that can subsequently be embellished, modified, and expanded (Spiro, Feltovich, Jacobson, & Coulson, 1991).

Second, we need to distinguish between visuals that learners create to show what they have learned and those that they think are helpful to the learning process per se. In other words, there is an important difference between learners generating representations once they have understood the content and learners generating representations that help them *in the process* of understanding. The former make the end product of understanding visible but do not necessarily reflect how the end product was arrived at. Visuals that reflect the process of sense-making should inform us about supports learners' find helpful in identifying important elements in a system, their interrelationships, and why those interrelationships are important. Once a system is understood visuals are likely to reflect where learners ended up in their understanding and show what they "in the end" understand about the elements of the system and their relationships. For example, the "map" I might draw enroute to a particular location shows my way-finding process, including wrong turns, mid-course corrections, serendipitous navigation decisions. Having arrived, I can represent a more optimal path to the location because, in part, the knowledge I acquired in navigating to the location informs my understanding of the larger geographical space in which my start and destination locations exist. The "map" I draw does not have to represent the process by which I got there but I am likely to want to share my understanding of how to more optimally get there – a product of having learned the route. Thus, depending on the assumptions that learners make when they are asked to generate representations of what they are learning, the visualizations they generate might or might not be ones that help them learn and understand what they are learning. They may be better assessments of learning outcomes than windows into effective supports for learning processes.

CONCLUDING COMMENTS

It is fitting that the last chapter in section 4 presents an impressive argument for a unified approach to animations as one type of visual representation (Schnotz & Lowe, this volume). Clearly many of the principles of learning and the design of learning environments that are emerging for learning with animations are strikingly similar to the principles that apply to other visual forms. Likewise, the supports that appear to facilitate or enable learning with other visual forms show promise for improving the design effectiveness for animations and therefore improving the likelihood of successful learning with animations. Of course, there are some unique and exciting areas of research that have been stimulated by dynamic visuals, including information integration over time, space, and modalities.

The contributors to this volume also demonstrate a necessary trend in the field of learning research. This trend moves beyond questions of whether this particular kind of stimulus or that kind of stimulus will help learners. It is a trend that recognizes the need to think more complexly about learning *tasks* as well as the materials available in the task environment. It is a trend that recognizes that we need to engage learners in meaningful processing of information. Key to truly making advances in the research and development of learning environments that are responsive to learning needs of diverse learners is a specific way in which we need to alter our thinking about learning tasks: We need to recognize that the learning task is simply not the same for individuals who have high as compared to low domain knowledge, or more versus less attentional capacity or spatial ability. We need to better understand what and how people perceive and interpret animations, as well as other forms of knowledge representations, when they are at different levels of competence in a domain (e.g., novice as compared to intermediate as compared to advanced or expert). Although we often acknowledge the diversity among learners, we tend to design learning environments, both the informational materials and the supports for learning with them, from the experts' vantage point and as if the same learning materials and supports are appropriate for all. The Vygotskyan construct "zone of proximal development" (Vygotsky, 1978) has impacted developmental research substantially; it needs to impact research on learning far more substantially than it has thus far. We spend too little time asking what makes sense and would be helpful from the viewpoint of learners at different developmental levels in the target domains. We need to ask these questions far more often and more deeply if we are to be effective in engaging learners in meaningful processing of information, animated or otherwise.

References

Alexander, P. A. & Fox, E. (2004). Historical perspective on reading research and practice. In R. B. Ruddell & N. Unrau (Eds.), *Theoretical models and processes of reading* (5th ed., pp. 33–68). Newark, DE: International Reading Association.

Baylor, A. L. & Ryu, J. (2003). Does the presence of image and animation enhance pedagogical agent persona? *Journal of Educational Computing Research, 28*(4), 373–395.

Bransford, J. D., Brown, A. L., & Cocking, R. R. (1999). *How people learn: Brain, mind, experience, and school.* Washington, DC: National Academy Press.

Cassell, J. (2004). Towards a Model of Technology and Literacy Development: Story Listening Systems. *Journal of Applied Developmental Psychology, 25*(1), 75–105.

Chi, M., de Leeuw, N., Chiu, M., & LaVancher, C. (1994). Eliciting self-explanations improves understanding. *Cognitive Science, 18*, 439–477.

Coté, N. & Goldman, S. R. (1999). Building representations of informational text: Evidence from children's think-aloud protocols. In H. V. Oostendorp & S. R. Goldman (Eds.), *The construction of mental representations during reading* (pp. 169–193). Mahwah, NJ: Lawrence Erlbaum Associates.

Coté, N., Goldman, S. R., & Saul, E. U. (1998). Students making sense of informational text: Relations between processing and representation. *Discourse Processes, 25*, 1–53.

Goldman, S. R. (1999). Issues for deeper understanding of visual learning processes and representations. *European Journal of Psychology of Education, XIV*(2), 295–300.

Goldman, S. R. (2003). Learning in complex domains: When and why do multiple representations help? *Learning and Instruction, 13*(2), 239–244.

Goldman, S. R., Braasch, J. L., Gepstein, R., Brodowinski, K., Wiley, J., & Graesser, A. C. (2004, August). *Doing research on the web: Comprehending complex science information.* Paper presented at the Annual meeting of the Society for Text and Discourse, Chicago, IL.

Grabinger, S. R., Dunlap, J. C., & Duffield, J. A. (1997). Rich environments for active learning in action: problem-based learning. *Journal of the Association for Learning Technology, 5*(2), 5–17.

Graesser, A. C., & Bertus, E. L. (1998). The construction of causal inferences while reading expository texts on science and technology. *Scientific Studies of Reading, 2*, 247–269.

Graesser, A. C., Wiemer-Hastings, K., Wiemer-Hastings, P., & Kreuz, R. (1999). AutoTutor: A simulation of a human tutor. *Journal of Cognitive Systems Research, 1*, 35–51.

Johnson, W. L., Rickel, J. W., & Lester, J. C. (2000). Animated pedagogical agents: Face-to-face interaction in interactive learning environments. *International Journal of Artificial Intelligence in Education, 11*, 47–78.

Jones, S. (2002). The Internet goes to college: How students are living in the future with today's technology. *Pew Internet & American Life Project Report.* http://www. pewinternet.org/pdfs/PIP_College_Report.pdf

Lester, J. C., Stone, B., & Stelling, G. (1999). Lifelike pedagogical agents for mixed-initiative problem solving in constructivist learning environments. *User Modeling and*

MacLeod, S., O'Day, T., Kehoe, C., Allende-Pellot, F., & Goldman, S. R. (2006, April). *Sustaining Children's Interest in a Virtual Peer Storytelling Context.* Paper presented at annual meeting of American Educational Research Association, San Francisco, CA.

McNamara, D., Kintsch, E., Songer, N., & Kintsch, W. (1996). Are good texts always better? Interactions of text coherence, background knowledge, and levels of understanding in learning from text. *Cognition and Instruction, 14(1)*, 1–43.

Ryokai, K., Vaucelle, C., & Cassell, J. (2003). "Virtual Peers as Partners in Storytelling and Literacy Learning". *Journal of Computer Assisted Learning, 19(2)*: 195–208.

Singer, M., Radinsky, J., & Goldman, S. R. (in press). The Role of Gesture in Meaning Construction. *Discourse Processes.*

Spiro, R. J., Feltovich, P. J., Jacobson, M. J., & Coulson, R. L. (1991). Cognitive flexibility, constructivism, and hypertext. *Educational Technology, 31(5)*, 24–33.

Vygotsky, L. S. (1978). *Mind in society: The development of the higher psychological processes* (A. Kozulin, Trans.). Cambridge, MA: Harvard University Press.

Author Index

Subject Index